Democracy and the Left

Democracy and the Left

*Social Policy and Inequality
in Latin America*

EVELYNE HUBER AND
JOHN D. STEPHENS

THE UNIVERSITY OF CHICAGO PRESS   CHICAGO AND LONDON

EVELYNE HUBER is the Morehead Alumni Distinguished Professor of Political Science at the University of North Carolina, Chapel Hill. JOHN D. STEPHENS is the Gerhard E. Lenski, Jr. Distinguished Professor of Political Science and Sociology at the University of North Carolina, Chapel Hill. Together, they are the coauthors, most recently, of *Development and Crisis of the Welfare State.*

The University of Chicago Press, Chicago 60637
The University of Chicago Press, Ltd., London
© 2012 by The University of Chicago
All rights reserved. Published 2012.
Printed in the United States of America
21 20 19 18 17 16 15 14 13 12   1 2 3 4 5

ISBN-13: 978-0-226-35652-5 (cloth)
ISBN-13: 978-0-226-35653-2 (paper)
ISBN-13: 978-0-226-35655-6 (e-book)
ISBN-10: 0-226-35652-3 (cloth)
ISBN-10: 0-226-35653-1 (paper)
ISBN-10: 0-226-35655-8 (e-book)

Library of Congress Cataloging-in-Publication Data

Huber, Evelyne, 1950–
    Democracy and the left : social policy and inequality in Latin America / Evelyne Huber and John D. Stephens.
        pages ; cm
    Includes bibliographical references and index.
    ISBN-13: 978-0-226-35652-5 (cloth : alkaline paper)
    ISBN-10: 0-226-35652-3 (cloth : alkaline paper)
    ISBN-13: 978-0-226-35653-2 (paperback : alkaline paper)
    ISBN-10: 0-226-35653-1 (paperback : alkaline paper)
    [etc.]
    1. Latin America—Social policy. 2. Equality—Latin America. 3. Welfare state—Latin America. 4. Income distribution—Latin America. 5. Latin America—Social conditions—20th century. 6. Latin America—Economic conditions—20th century.
    I. Stephens, John D., 1947– II. Title.
    HN110.5.A8H83 2012
    303.3—dc23

2011050824

FOR KLARA AND SEPP

Contents

Figures

Tables

Acronyms

AD	Acción Democrática (Democratic Action, Venezuela)
AFPs	Administradoras de Fondos de Pensiones (Pension Fund Administrators, Chile)
APRA	Alianza Popular Revolucionaria Americana (American Popular Revolutionary Alliance, Perú)
ARENA	Aliança Renovadora Nacional (Brazil)
AUGE	Acceso Universal de Garantías Explícitas (Regime of Explicit Health Guarantees, Chile)
BPC	Benefício de Prestação Continuada (Continuous Cash Benefit, Brazil)
CCOO	Confederación Sindical de Comisiones Obreras (Communist Workers' Commissions, Spain)
CCSS	Caja Costarricense del Seguro Social (Costa Rican Social Security Institution, Costa Rica)
CCT	Conditional cash transfer
CEPAL (ECLAC)	Comisión Económica para América Latina y el Caribe (Economic Commission for Latin America and the Caribbean)
CGTP	Confederação Geral dos Trabalhadores Portugueses (General Confederation of Portuguese Workers, Portugal)
CPCS	Conselho Permanente de Concertação Social (Permanent Council for Social Dialogue, Portugal)
ECLAC	Economic Commission for Latin America and the Caribbean
EMU	Economic and Monetary Union
EU	European Union

FA   Frente Amplio (Broad Front, Uruguay)
FDI   Foreign direct investment
FODESAF   Fondo de Desarrollo Social y Asignaciones Familiares
              (Social Development and Family Allowance Fund,
              Costa Rica)
FONASA   Fondo Nacional de Salud (National Health Fund, Chile)
FUNDEF   Fundo de Manutenção e Desenvolvimento do
              Ensino Fundamental e de Valorização do Magistério
              (Elementary Education and Teacher Valorization Fund,
              Brazil)
FUNRURAL   Fundo de Assistência ao Trabalhador Rural (Rural
              Workers' Assistance Fund, Brazil)
GDP   Gross national product
IALS   International Adult Literacy Survey
IAMC   Instituto de Asistencia Médica Colectiva (Collective
              Mutual Care Institution, Uruguay)
IDB   Inter-American Development Bank
IFIs   International financial institutions
ILO   International Labour Organization
IMF   International Monetary Fund
INPS   Instituto Nacional de Previdência Social (National Social
              Insurance Institute, Brazil)
ISAPRES   Instituciones de Salud Previsional (Health Provider
              Institutions, Chile)
ISI   Import substitution industrialization
IU   Izquierda Unida (United Left, Peru)
LIS   Luxembourg Income Study
MNR   Movimiento Nacionalista Revolucionario (Revolutionary
              Nationalist Movement, Bolivia)
NDC   Notional defined contribution
NDP   New Democratic Party (Canada)
NHS   National health service
OECD   Organization for Economic Co-operation and
              Development
OLS   Ordinary least squares (regression)
PAMI   Programa de Atención Médica Integral, Instituto
              Nacional de Servicios Sociales para Jubilados y Pen-
              sionados (Comprehensive Medical Attention Program,
              Argentina)

PC	Partido Comunista de Chile (Communist Party, Chile)
PCC	Partido Conservador Colombiano (Conservative Party, Colombia)
PCP	Partido Comunista Português (Portuguese Communist Party, Portugal)
PDC	Partido Demócrata Cristiano (Christian Democratic Party, Chile)
PFL	Partido da Frente Liberal (Liberal Front Party, Brazil)
PJ	Partido Justicialista / Partido Peronista (Peronist Party, Argentina)
PJJHD	Plan Jefes y Jefas de Hogar Desocupados (Program for Unemployed Male and Female Heads of Households, Argentina)
PLN	Partido Liberación Nacional (National Liberation Party, Costa Rica)
PMDB	Partido do Movimiento Democrático Brazileiro (Brazilian Democratic Movement)
PP	Partido Popular (People's Party, Spain)
PPD	Partido por la Democracia (Party for Democracy, Chile)
PPPs	Purchasing power parities
PRI	Partido Revolucionario Institucional (Institutional Revolutionary Party, Mexico)
PS	Partido Socialista de Chile (Socialist Party, Chile)
PS	Partido Socialista (Socialist Party, Portugal)
PSD	Partido Social Democrata (Social Democratic Party, Portugal)
PSDB	Partido da Social Democracia Brasileira (Brazilian Social Democratic Party, Brazil)
PSF	Programa Saúde da Família (Family Health Program, Brazil)
PSOE	Partido Socialista Obrero Español (Spanish Socialist Workers' Party, Spain)
PT	Partido dos Trabalhadores (Workers' Party, Brazil)
PTB	Partido Trabalhista Brasileiro (Brazilian Labor Party, Brazil)
PUSC	Partido Unidad Social Cristiana (Social Christian Unity Party, Costa Rica)
RN	Renovación Nacional (National Renewal, Chile)

SEDLAC	Socio-Economic Database for Latin America and the Caribbean
SNS	Servicio Nacional de Salud (National Health Service, Chile)
UCR	Unión Cívica Radical (Radical Civic Union, Argentina)
UDI	Unión Demócrata Independiente (Independent Democrat Union, Chile)
UGT	Unión General de Trabajadores (General Union of Workers, Uruguay)
UGT	Unión General de Trabajadores (General Union of Workers, Spain)
UNCTAD	United Nations Conference on Trade and Development
UNDP	United Nations Development Programme
UNU-WIDER WIID	United Nations University World Institute for Development Economics Research World Income Inequality Database
UP	Unidad Popular (Popular Unity, Chile)
USAID	United States Agency for International Development
VAT	Value-added tax
WB	World Bank

COUNTRY ACRONYMS USED IN FIGURES

ARG	Argentina
AUL	Australia
BEL	Belgium
BOL	Bolivia
BRA	Brazil
CAN	Canada
CHL	Chile
COL	Colombia
CRI	Costa Rica
CZR	Czech Republic
DEN	Denmark
DOM	Dominican Republic
ECU	Ecuador
ELV	El Salvador
FIN	Finland
FRG	Germany
GTM	Guatemala

HON	Honduras
HUN	Hungary
IRE	Ireland
ITA	Italy
MEX	Mexico
NET	Netherlands
NIC	Nicaragua
NOR	Norway
NZL	New Zealand
PAN	Panama
PER	Peru
POL	Poland
PRT	Portugal
PRY	Paraguay
SLO	Slovenia
SWE	Sweden
SWZ	Switzerland
UKM	United Kingdom
URY	Uruguay
USA	United States
VEN	Venezuela

Preface and Acknowledgments

This book has a long personal intellectual history. In the late 1970s, we began our first collaborative work. Our focus then was at the intersection of our previous work, European social democracy and reformist redistributive or egalitarian political change in Latin America. At the time, the Latin American region was covered by dictatorships, but there was some movement toward transition, and we anticipated that the return to democracy would make reformist redistributive politics relevant once more. One of the only extant experiments at that time was the Manley government in Jamaica (1972–80). By the time we got into the field in 1981–82, Manley had been voted out of office, but precisely because the government had many failures as well as successes, we thought that an analysis of these successes and failures would be instructive for other left governments in other countries in Latin America. By the time the book was published in 1986, the region was already on its way (back) to democracy.

Unfortunately for the relevance of the book on Jamaica, the debt crisis and exhaustion of import substitution industrialization (ISI) had already made one element of the left models of the 1970s irrelevant. The project of the Manley government married redistributive social reform with dependency theory–based economic strategy that called for state-led development and deepening (if highly selective) of ISI. The left governments of the 1970s envisioned deep-going social and economic transformation—more radical in the case of the Allende government, more modest in the case of the Manley government, to take two examples. This kind of economic model was off the agenda in the region by the mid-1980s, in part because ISI was not a viable way forward, but equally importantly because it conflicted with the neoliberal Washington Consensus, which the international financial institutions (IFIs) were able to impose on countries in the region as a result of the debt crisis. The non-viability of an import substitution industrialization economic model might have left the project of redistributive reform through social policy on the table, but this project too conflicted with the Washington Consensus.

We then turned our attention to the conditions that make democracy possible and sustainable, and, in collaboration with our colleague and friend Dietrich Rueschemeyer, engaged in a broad comparison of the historical development of democracy in Western Europe, North, Central, and South America and the Caribbean, and the Antipodes. What followed was a study of the development of social policy in the twentieth century in advanced capitalist democracies. In the course of these studies, we developed a unified theoretical framework to explain the development of democracy and egalitarian social policy. We further extend this theoretical framework in the present book.

When we began to focus again on Latin America around the turn of the century, prospects for egalitarian social policy seemed dim. The hegemony of the Washington Consensus was beginning to erode, though, and after a couple of years the turn to the left ushered in a period of new policy departures that allowed room for hope that the seemingly deeply entrenched structures of inequality might begin to come under attack. The research for this book, which includes the first decade of the twenty-first century, has given us reason for cautious optimism regarding the potential long-term effects of democracy on social policy and poverty and inequality in the region.

While working on this book, we have been fortunate to receive help from many generous scholars and institutions. For financial support we thank the National Science Foundation grant SES 0241389; the Hanse-Wissenschaftskolleg in Delmenhorst, Germany; the Collegio Carlo Alberto in Moncalieri, Italy; the Kellogg Institute for International Studies at the University of Notre Dame; the John Simon Guggenheim Memorial Foundation; and the Morehead Alumni Distinguished Professorship and the Margaret and Paul A. Johnston Professorships (funding the Gerhard E. Lenski, Jr., Distinguished Professorship) in the College of Arts and Sciences at the University of North Carolina at Chapel Hill. For leaves from our teaching and administrative responsibilities we thank the College of Arts and Sciences at the University of North Carolina at Chapel Hill.

We are grateful for invitations to present parts of this work and for

the feedback we received from the participants at the following institutions: Brown University, the Collegio Carlo Alberto, the Comparative Working Group of the Department of Political Science at UNC,
Columbia University, the Graduate School of Social and Political Sciences at the University of Milan, the Hanse-Wissenschaftskolleg, Hum-
boldt Universität in Berlin, the Kellogg Institute for International Stud-
ies at the University of Notre Dame, Pontificia Universidad Católica de
Chile, Princeton University, Universidad Diego Portales in Santiago,
Chile, Universitat Pompeu Fabra, and the University of Texas at Austin.
We also benefited greatly from participating in the conferences where
the contributions to the following volumes were presented: *Democratic
Governance in Latin America* (Mainwaring and Scully 2010a), *Leftist
Governments in Latin America: Successes and Shortcomings* (Weyland,
Madrid, and Hunter 2010), and *The Resurgence of the Latin American
Left* (Levitsky and Roberts 2011). We particularly thank the editors of
these volumes for comments on our contributions.

The following colleagues offered us valuable feedback or other kinds
of assistance, such as information, advice, or data, for this book: Rossana
Castiglioni, Mauricio Castro, Michael Coppedge, Christina Ewig, Tasha
Fairfield, Maurizio Ferrera, Fernando Filgueira, Jonathan Hartlyn, Alexander Hicks, Wendy Hunter, Robert Kaufman, Juan Pablo Luna, Raúl
Madrid, Scott Mainwaring, James McGuire, Alberto Mora Román, Vic-
toria Murillo, François Nielsen, Kenneth Roberts, Timothy Scully, Ot-
tón Solís, María Elena Valenzuela, Jorge Vargas Cullell, Cristiani Vieira
Machado, and Kurt Weyland. We are particularly grateful to the follow-
ing scholars for reading major portions or all of the manuscript and giv-
ing us detailed feedback: Santiago Anria, Russell Bither-Terry, Merike
Blofield, David Brady, Tiago Fernandes, Robert Fishman, Barrington
Hill, Fabrice Lehoucq, Juliana Martínez Franzoni, Sara Niedzwiecki,
Sandra Chapman Osterkatz, Jennifer Pribble, Dietrich Rueschemeyer,
Lars Schoultz, Milada Vachudova, and two anonymous readers for the
University of Chicago Press.

This is the third book for which John Tryneski has been our editor. It
has been great to work with him, and we thank him for his support of our
scholarship. Last but not least, we express our profound gratitude to our
former and present research assistants who have worked with us over the
years on this project: Santiago Anria, Juan Bogliaccini, Kirk Bowman,
Michelle Dion, Juan Pablo Luna, Thomas Mustillo, Sara Niedzwiecki,
Indira Palacios, Jennifer Pribble, and Frederick Solt. We are happy to

see their careers flourish, and we know that we could not have written this book without them.

We dedicate this book to our children, Klara and Sepp. It has been a joy to see them develop from the state of "no political science at the dinner table!" to the present, where they engage us in animated conversations about their views of the world.

CHAPTER ONE

Introduction

This book argues that political forces can bring about peaceful redistributive change in Latin America. Scholars have long agreed that Latin America has an extremely unequal income distribution. Most would also agree that it has the worst income distribution of any region in the world (Frankema 2009). Traditionally, Latin American governments and international organizations dealing with the region focused on economic growth and poverty reduction rather than on inequality. By the turn of the century, however, a number of factors had come together to bring the problem of inequality into the limelight. First, econometric studies had shown that inequality can be an obstacle to economic growth (e.g., Alesina and Rodrik 1994). Second, public opinion in Latin America had become increasingly critical of the austerity and structural adjustment policies championed by the international financial institutions (IFIs) because of the failure of economic benefits from the reforms to trickle down.

Toward the end of the decade, the Inter-American Development Bank produced a major study of inequality (IDB 1998), followed in 2004 by the World Bank (Ferranti et al. 2004). The World Bank study was remarkably critical in that it pointed to negative consequences of inequality not only for poverty rates but also for economic growth and democracy. The United Nations Economic Commission on Latin America and the Caribbean (ECLAC 2002) warned that the millennium goals of cutting poverty and extreme poverty in half by 2015 would not be achieved without a change in distribution. Other studies confirmed that high degrees of inequality reduced the effect of growth on poverty reduction (Bourguignon 2002). The United Nations Development Programme (UNDP 2004) report on the state of democracy in Latin America argued strongly that the degree of inequality prevalent in most Latin American countries obstructed the construction of a democracy of full citizenship.

Economists have explained the high degree of inequality in Latin America by the unequal distribution of productive assets—land, skilled labor, and capital—(Morley 2001, 51), and in addition by the frequency of macroeconomic crises (Ferranti et al. 2004, 157, 227–34), and by geography and resource endowments (IDB 1998, 97–100). The World Bank team further traced the historical origins of inequality to the concentration of wealth and power by the colonizers, the exploitation of indigenous and imported slave labor, and the survival into the independence period of the concentration of wealth and the political exclusion of the majority. These conditions gave rise to clientelistic politics and states with low capacity to ensure macroeconomic stability, property rights, and basic services in the twentieth century. Specifically, they entailed a neglect of the expansion of public education. The ensuing struggles over economic and political inclusion caused political instability and erratic economic policies and growth. Social policies on average did little to mitigate inequalities because tax burdens and social expenditures were comparatively low and most social spending was regressive (Ferranti et al. 2004, 109–47, 247–72).

We certainly agree with the general contours of this analysis. The debt crisis of the 1980s and the ensuing abandonment of the import substitution industrialization (ISI) model were but the latest manifestations of radical changes in economic policies, which had the result of increasing economic inequality. The reduction of social expenditures as part of austerity packages allowed the quality of public social services to deteriorate even further. Thus, by the end of the century, inequality and poverty in Latin America appeared close to intractable, largely immune to political intervention. Indeed, popular commentators contended that the deepening process of globalization tied the hands of governments in the region more than ever.

Political scientists have attributed the absence of significant redistributive reforms under the newly democratic regimes to the dysfunctional nature of political institutions. In the important case of Brazil, for instance, they emphasized fragmentation of the state, political parties, and civil society (Weyland 1996), and candidate-centered electoral systems that promote clientelism and weakness of party discipline (Ames 2001). Other social scientists underlined the staying power of racial, ethnic, and gender hierarchies (Gurr 2000; Gootenberg 2010; Ewig 2010), and still others invoked the enduring power of hierarchical cultural traits (Wiarda 1982).

Yet, in the ensuing decade, the region began to turn the corner as new emphasis on redistributive social policy spread. For the first time since reliable data became available, inequality declined in most countries in the region (López-Calva and Lustig 2010). This historic turn, the earlier decline in poverty in some countries, as well as the large differences in redistributive social policy across Latin America, suggest that inequality and poverty may not be so intractable after all.

In this book, we explain the differences in redistributive social policy and inequality between countries and over time. We base our account on quantitative analyses and comparative historical case analysis of the development of social policy over seven decades in five Latin American countries and further comparisons to developments in the two Iberian countries.[1] We find that democracy is one of the most important determinants of redistributive social policy. One mechanism by which democracy promotes egalitarian social policy is that it is a precondition for the development of left parties and their access to governmental power, but our evidence indicates that it has additional effects, such as political competition of nonleft parties with left parties. We also show that international structures of power affect the fate of egalitarian social policy. This impact appeared in the differences within Latin America between the 1980s and 1990s on the one hand, when the debt burden and Washington Consensus greatly constrained Latin American social policy, and the 2000s on the other hand, when many countries in the region freed themselves from the IFIs and there was no longer a consensus in the U.S. capital about desirable social policy, certainly not a neoliberal one. It appeared yet more strongly in our comparison of Latin America and Iberia, where the Europe-oriented Iberian countries never even considered neoliberal social policies such as pension privatization.

With regard to social policy and inequality, our quantitative analysis and case studies highlight the centrality of investment in human capital. On the basis of studies of microdata on household income distribution, by ECLAC (see chap. 3) and UNDP (see chap. 6) and our own quantitative analysis, we demonstrate that social insurance is not very redistributive and sometimes even perversely redistributive in Latin America, whereas health and education spending and targeted social transfers are quite redistributive. Moreover, education spending, to the extent that it is aimed at expanding the educational level of the mass citizenry, reduces inequality by reducing the skill income premium. Investment in human capital, however, cannot be pursued in isolation; it must be pursued in conjunction with reductions in poverty. The correlation between national-level poverty and average cognitive skill is very high (−.84; see chap. 5), and the causal relationship is almost certainly reciprocal. The beauty of the conditional cash transfer programs (see chap. 6) is the explicit recognition of the link between poverty and investment in human capital. Finally, upgrading of human capital is essential in setting Latin American countries on a new development path in which the region no longer competes in export markets solely on the basis of export of raw materials and low-wage, low-skill manufactured goods.

Outline of the Argument

In chapter 2, we outline our theoretical and methodological approach. We build on power constellations theory presented in Rueschemeyer, Stephens, and Stephens (1992) and further developed in Huber and Stephens (2001a). The first cluster of power is the balance of domestic class power and party political power, which is the core explanatory factor in the power resources theory of welfare state variations in advanced capitalist democracies. The second cluster of power is the structure of the state and state–society relations. The third is transnational structures of power, the complex of relations in the international economy and systems of states. Our adaptation of the theory as we applied it to welfare state development in advanced capitalist democracies (Huber and Stephens 2001a) follows the differences in our explanations of the development of democracies in those countries and Latin America and the Caribbean (Rueschemeyer, Stephens, and Stephens, 1992, cf. chap. 4 and chaps. 5 and 6).

Of great importance for the first cluster of power, Latin American economic development was historically late and dependent on development in core capitalist countries and thus differed sharply from the historic development of Europe. For these reasons and because of a historical inheritance of highly unequal distributions of land, the class structure developed differently, consisting of a significant class of large landlords, a larger class of poor peasants and rural workers, a smaller urban working class, and a larger class of informal workers. We argued in *Capitalist Development and Democracy* that this class structure was not favorable to democracy. Thus, as compared to Huber and Stephens (2001a), in which we focused on the post–World War II period in advanced capitalist democracies, in this analysis democracy is a variable, not a constant, and we hypothesize that political regime appears as a major determinant of egalitarian social policy. These same features of the class structure weaken the political left, which, following the power resources theory hypothesis, should also be a major determinant of egalitarian social policy.

In the second cluster of power, state–society relations appear as more important in the analysis of social policy development in Latin America. In periods of authoritarian rule, the state was arguably more autonomous from civil societies and, once the urban working class became a significant social force, the authoritarian state was faced with the need to co-opt it, if the state was not willing to resort to outright repression. State capacity, which was not an issue for the post–World War II advanced industrial societies, is a problem for many Latin American countries, particularly at the beginning of the period under investigation. Constitutional structure veto points, which loomed large in our explanation of social policy variations, play a smaller role in Latin American social policy developments, presumably because they were only relevant under democratic regimes.

We hypothesize that our third cluster of power, transnational structures of power, would be much more important in Latin America. During the debt crisis period of the 1980s and afterward in the 1990s, the heyday of the Washington Consensus, the International Monetary Fund and the World Bank pressed for the neoliberal agenda and had powerful negative (conditionality) and positive (loans) inducements at their disposal to push the agenda of neoliberal reform, including social policy reform, on Latin American countries.

In chapter 3, we outline a strategy for redistribution for Latin American countries. We begin with an exposition of the simple arithmetic of redistribution because there are so many misunderstandings about this even among some scholars of comparative social policy. The basic point we make here is that proportional taxation combined with flat rate benefits (e.g., each decile receives 10 percent of the benefits) is very redistributive. It is an easy step from here to the seemingly counterintuitive observation that slightly regressive taxes and a transfer system that is mildly earnings related (i.e., the upper deciles get slightly more that 10 percent of the benefits) can be redistributive.

We then explore the possible coalitions for redistributive social policy by examining data on income distribution and class structure in Latin America. We conclude that two-thirds of Latin American households, whether seen from the point of view of class position or position in the income distribution, have an interest in egalitarian social reforms. On the basis of the discussion of domestic class relations in the previous chapter, we proceed to explain why this seemingly favorable terrain has produced so little redistributive reform in Latin America, even during democratic periods. Consistent with power resources theory but directly contrary to the Meltzer-Richard theory of redistribution (Meltzer and Richard 1981), we argue that the reason for this lack of reform is that inequality in material resources is accompanied by inequality in political resources and thus less, not more, redistribution transpires.

In chapter 3, we also flesh out what a solid and effective redistributive social policy regime in Latin America might look like. We build on the concept of basic universalism, as developed by Filgueira et al. in Molina (2006). In the areas of health and education, the essence is guaranteed universal access to free or subsidized (according to household income) quality services. In the area of transfers, basic subsistence should be guaranteed by a combination of social insurance and social assistance. Social assistance is crucial in the context of high informality, where social insurance leaves about half of the labor force uncovered. Means testing is compatible with basic universalism as long as the transfers are broadly targeted and seen as a citizenship right, not as charity.

Chapter 4 covers the development of social policy up to the end of the import substitution industrialization (ISI) period, circa 1980. The chapter opens with a cross-national analysis of social policy development in this period. We show that the size of the urban working class and democratic history (measured by cumulative years of democracy after 1945) appear as the strongest determinants of social welfare effort as of 1980. The social welfare effort measure, a combination of social spending and coverage, also allows us to identify five welfare state leaders—Argentina, Brazil, Chile, Costa Rica, and Uruguay. These high social effort countries are selected for in-depth comparative historical analysis in the remainder of this chapter and in chapters 6 and 7.[2] A scatter plot of social welfare effort by democratic history suggests that there were two paths to early welfare state leadership—a democratic/left political strength path, represented by Chile, Costa Rica, and Uruguay, and a path characterized by authoritarian elite co-optation of a large urban working class, represented by Argentina and Brazil. The comparative historical analysis in the rest of the chapter confirms the existence of two paths and fleshes out the process of early welfare state formation.

Chapter 5 presents a pooled time series analysis of the determinants of social spending, inequality, and poverty in the period 1970 to 2005. Democracy emerged as the most important variable in this analysis, in part because of its direct effects, but more importantly because it was at the beginning of a causal chain that influenced all of the dependent variables in our analysis: social spending, inequality, and poverty. Democracy had a strong direct influence on all three spending variables (health, education, and social security and welfare), on poverty, and on inequality. The polar opposite of democracy, repressive authoritarianism, had negative effects on education spending. Democracy made left political mobilization possible, and left political strength had important effects on inequality and poverty. Democracy pushed up spending on education, which had a strong direct effect on poverty and strong indirect effects on inequality and poverty through its effect on the average educational level of the population. Finally, social security and welfare spending had a negative effect on inequality but only if it developed in a democratic context. We also found support for Muller's (1989) argument that the effect of democracy on inequality appears only after some twenty years of democracy. We found a similar relationship with poverty.

In sharp contrast to our findings for developed democracies (Bradley et al. 2003), we found that social spending did not have unambiguous negative effects on inequality in Latin America. Given this outcome, it is not surprising that we did not find much evidence of left political effects on the level of social spending, again in sharp contrast to our finding for developed democracies (Huber and Stephens 2001a). Since left strength affected inequality, we surmised that left political strength affected the composition and allocation of expenditures. We found strong evidence of this in the comparative historical analysis. Finally, it is worth underlining the importance of investment in human capital for lowering poverty and inequality in Latin America. Our analysis shows strong statistically negative relationships between average years of education and both poverty and inequality as well as a strong negative relationship between health spending and poverty.

Chapter 6 examines the development of social policy, poverty, and inequality in our five focus cases since 1980. The period can be broken into two distinct subperiods: neoliberal reform from 1980 to 2000 and the left turn after 2000. Allowing for some variations in timing between the countries, we see that the first period was characterized economically by the debt crisis, GDP stagnation or decline, and economic instability until the early 1990s, then economic stabilization and renewed growth, though punctuated by financial crises. The whole period witnessed not only the transition from ISI but also economic liberalization in areas other than trade (e.g., privatization, liberalization of external capital controls, liberalization of domestic financial systems). Politically, all of our focus cases and most other countries in the region transited to democracy by 1990. This was the Washington Consensus period, and the IFIs pushed neoliberal reforms in economic and social policy in the region. In only one area, educational policy, did we find a significant push in social policy in a progressive direction during this period. Argentina and Brazil passed significant educational reforms in the 1990s, and most countries in the region significantly expanded primary and secondary school enrollment. In Brazil and Argentina, it is clear that the return of democratic political competition was responsible for the reforms, and we surmise that this was probably part of the story elsewhere.

Inequality rose in this period, and on the basis of our data analysis, pooled time series analysis by Morley (2001), and analysis of microdata on household income distribution by the contributions to López-Calva and Lustig (2010), we can pinpoint fairly precisely why this rise happened. The transition from ISI to open economies led to deindustrialization, which increased inequality. Part of the mechanism here was the shedding of low-skill industry and deployment of investment to higher-skill activities, which led to skill-biased technological change and thus an increase in the skill/education income premium. The development of poverty rates varied across Latin America in this period. The transition from ISI increased informalization and led to upward pressure on poverty levels across the region. Poverty, however, declined in some countries after 1990 as a result of the return of growth or the adoption of compensating social policy. Among our focus cases, this decline happened in Brazil, Chile, and Costa Rica.

The turn of the century was also an important turn for politics, social policy, and inequality in Latin America. Domestic power relations changed as roughly two-thirds of the population of the region was governed by left executives by mid-decade. The international structures of power became more benign as Latin American countries freed themselves from debt and thus IFI conditionality, and as particularly the World Bank turned from neoliberalism in social policy toward advocacy of social investment policy. Left governments in the region passed new progressive social policies (see the contributions to Weyland, Madrid, and Hunter 2010, and to Levitsky and Roberts 2011). In our focus cases, the Lula government in Brazil substantially increased the conditional cash transfer programs initiated by Cardoso and greatly increased the value of the minimum wage, which also increased the value of government transfers tied to the minimum wage; the Lagos and Bachelet governments in Chile passed basic universalistic health care and pension reforms; the Kirchner governments in Argentina expanded conditional cash transfers and access to basic medicines and reformed labor legislation, which strengthened unions and their hand in bargaining; and the Vázquez government in Uruguay reformed the tax system, unified the health care system, increased family allowances, and revived the wage councils.

Inequality fell in Latin America after 2000, and our data analysis and the contributions to López-Calva and Lustig (2010) again allow us to pinpoint why. By 2000, the transition from ISI to open economies had run its course, and with it skill-biased technological change petered out. As the education expansions of the 1990s began to change the education and skill composition of the workforce, the skill premium actually fell, which contributed to a decline in inequality in labor incomes. In addition, in some countries, labor legislation reforms and increased minimum wages also contributed to lower labor income inequality. The decline in inequality of disposable income was furthered by increases in targeted transfers, most notably conditional cash transfers, by increases in the minimum wage that pushed up transfers that were linked to the minimum wage, and by increased progressiveness of other transfers.

In chapter 7, we compare the development of our four South American cases with Portugal and Spain in the period after 1970. The similarities between these countries in social, political, and economic terms in 1970 are striking. Both groups of countries were characterized by high levels of land inequality, high levels of inequality in the distribution of education, similar average educational levels, similar levels of GDP per capita, similar social protection systems both in terms of the level of effort and the structure of the system (Bismarckian contributory social insurance), similar ISI economies, and by authoritarian political systems, at that point or in the near future. By 2000, the Iberian countries were very different from Latin America in that they had levels of social welfare effort close to European averages, GDP per capita levels significantly higher than those in our four South American countries, and levels of inequality much lower than those in the Latin American countries. In this chapter, we account for the differences in social policy and its outcomes.

Part of our explanation mirrors our explanation of variations within Latin America through time and across cases: the Iberian countries democratized a decade earlier and had much longer experiences with left government. Indeed, left executives were nonexistent in postredemocratization Argentina, Brazil, Chile, and Uruguay until after 2000. The other part of our explanation concerns the different effect of transnational structures of power. Our historical analysis indicated that the Washington Consensus neoliberal formula had important impacts on social policy reform in Latin America. The different position of Iberia in transnational structures of power, next to and increasingly integrated into Social Europe, demonstrated just how important this factor was for social policy. Nowhere was this clearer than in the case of pension reform. Both groups of countries had contributory-defined benefit pension systems that were in deep trouble in this period. In all of the Latin American countries, pension privatization along the lines of the Chilean system, recommended, and indeed financed, by the World Bank, was on the agenda, and most countries adopted some system of at least partial privatization. In Iberia, however, privatization was not on the agenda, and both countries adopted parametric reforms of the existing system.

Theoretical Contributions

Our main theoretical contribution is to demonstrate the explanatory power of power constellations theory for the development of welfare states or—more modestly—social policy regimes and their redistributive effects in Latin America. Politics matter fundamentally and have the potential of modifying the seemingly immutable structures of inequality in Latin America. We also want to demonstrate that power constellations theory is much more powerful than the widely used Meltzer-Richard median voter model in explaining redistribution. Indeed, we argue that the assertion of Meltzer-Richard is plain wrong. The model postulates that greater distances between the median and the mean income generate greater demands for redistribution that are met by government policy. One can certainly agree that a greater distance between the median and the mean income generates a greater need for redistribution, but this need does not necessarily translate into political demands, and political demands do not necessarily translate into policy. Political socialization shapes perceptions and thus the probability that demands are formulated. The distribution of material resources and of organizational networks shapes political power distribution and thus the probability that demands are met.

A greater distance between the median and the mean income tends to be accompanied by a more skewed distribution of political power and thus lower responsiveness to demands for redistribution. And highly skewed distributions of political power shape political socialization so as to restrict the range of perceived policy options and thus demands for redistributive policy. Democracy and the rise of left parties reduce the degree to which political power distributions are skewed and thus open the possibility for a greater range of policy options to be perceived, for demands for new policies to be articulated, and for those demands to be met. Again, there is nothing automatic or necessary or functionalist about these processes. Redistributive policies are a result of political action, but democracy makes the rise of actors committed to redistribution and the pursuit of actions aimed at redistribution possible.

Another theoretical contribution is to demonstrate that democracy in the longer run makes a difference for poverty and inequality—at least in Latin America—and to explain why this is so. Ross (2006) found no difference between authoritarian and democratic regimes in poverty, taking into account nonincome poverty and corrections for missing data from authoritarian governments. Certainly, if one were to focus on Eastern Europe and the former Soviet Union, one could show that the transition to democracy has been followed by increasing poverty and inequality. This was the result of the transition from socialist to capitalist economies that accompanied the democratic transition, and the tremendous economic and social dislocations generated by this transition. In Latin America, however, the alternative to democracy has with few exceptions been right-wing authoritarianism, and these regimes lacked any commitment to egalitarianism and solidarity. On the contrary, they repressed autonomous organization and mobilization from below and thus kept those forces weak that might pressure for redistribution. Democracy made it possible for social movements, civil society organizations, and parties of the left to form, grow, and slowly gain influence on policy to shape it in a more egalitarian direction. Democracy does not guarantee uniform movement toward lower poverty and inequality, but it makes gradual movement in this direction possible.

CHAPTER TWO

Theoretical Framework and Methodological Approach

In this chapter, we briefly present the main theoretical approaches to the explanation of welfare state development in advanced capitalist democracies and then elaborate our own theory of social policy development in Latin America, based on our previous works on the development of democracy and on social reform and distributive outcomes in developed capitalist democracies and the developing countries of Latin America and the Caribbean (J. Stephens 1979; E. Stephens 1980; Stephens and Stephens 1982, 1986; Rueschemeyer, Stephens, and Stephens 1992; Huber, Ragin, and Stephens 1993; Huber, Rueschemeyer, and Stephens 1997; Huber and Stephens 2001a; Bradley et al. 2003; Moller et al. 2003). We elaborate how the analytical framework we developed for the patterns of social policy change in advanced industrial democracies (Huber and Stephens 2001a) must be adapted to make it travel to Southern Europe and Latin America. We conclude with a discussion of the methodological strategy of the research. As in our work on advanced industrial democracies, we set as our theoretical task the goal of explaining long-term change within countries and the patterns of outcomes across countries. Thus, concretely, to meet our criterion of theoretical adequacy, a theory must provide clear hypotheses about the direction of change and the patterns across countries. To meet our criteria of empirical adequacy, a theory must be empirically corroborated by the quantitative or comparative historical evidence, and it cannot be contradicted by either one.

Theoretical Framework

Review of Main Theories

ADVANCED CAPITALIST DEMOCRACIES. The debate of the past quarter century about determinants of welfare state development in advanced capitalist democracies has been carried out among proponents of three different theoretical approaches—the logic of industrialism, a state-centric approach, and political class struggle or power resources approaches. More recently, feminist scholars have made important contributions to the debate, moving from early critiques of the welfare state as reinforcing patriarchy to more nuanced assessments of the differential effects of different welfare state regimes on the status of women and of the role of women as actors in welfare state development. We begin with a brief exposition of these three theoretical schools.

According to the logic of industrialism, both the growth of the welfare state and cross-national differences in "welfare state effort" are by-products of economic development and its demographic and social organizational consequences (Wilensky 1975; Pampel and Williamson 1989). Those insisting on a state-centric approach have focused on the policy-making role of bureaucrats, who are assumed to be relatively autonomous from social forces, on the capacity of the state apparatus to implement welfare state programs, on the effects of state structure (e.g., federalism), and on the influence of past policy on new social policy initiatives (Heclo 1974; Orloff 1993; Weir, Orloff, and Skocpol 1988; Skocpol 1988). Finally, the proponents of power resources theory identify the distribution of power based on organization or property between labor organizations and left parties on the one hand and center and right-wing political forces on the other hand as primary determinants of differences in the size and distributive impact of the welfare state across countries and over time (Stephens 1979; Korpi 1983).[1]

Another important argument, that the strength of political Catholicism led to the development of generous welfare states, fits uneasily, if at all, into any of these three theoretical approaches. Stephens (1979, 100, 123–24) argues that political Catholicism leads to welfare states almost as generous in expenditure but less redistributive in structure than those developed under social democratic auspices. Wilensky (1981) presents cross-national data showing that Christian democratic cabinet share is the most important determinant of his measure of social spending.

On the basis of a variety of indicators of welfare state patterns, Esping-Andersen (1990) argues for the existence of a distinctive type of "conservative" though generous welfare state regime created largely by European continental Christian democratic parties. Kersbergen (1995) finally squared the circle by providing a power resources interpretation for the development of the Christian democratic welfare state and supporting it with quantitative and an in-depth case study analyses.

LATIN AMERICA.   The theoretical literature on the causes of the formation of Latin American welfare states or—more modestly—social policy regimes, is not nearly as abundant as that on advanced industrial democracies, but it is growing rapidly. The pioneering works of Mesa-Lago (1978) and Malloy (1979) emphasized elite responses to pressures from politically influential or militant groups, resulting in a gradual extension of social protection. Where democracy could take hold, the dynamics included electoral competition. In authoritarian systems, social security schemes reflected elite attempts to co-opt and incorporate important groups. Responses to labor militancy were frequently influenced by the European example, and thus the emerging welfare states took a Bismarckian form, similar to the continental European welfare states. The hallmarks of Bismarckian welfare state regimes are employment-based social insurance and stratification of welfare state programs, with different occupational categories having different social security schemes that grant access to cash benefits and health services of widely varying generosity and quality.

Subsequent works linked the origins and particular forms of social policy regimes in Latin America to processes of state building and late and dependent development and its impact on the occupational and class structure. Writing on the case of Uruguay, Filgueira (1995) emphasized the role of social policy, particularly education policy, in Batlle's project of nation-state building and modernization. In the context of a heavily rural society based on cattle and sheep ranching, Batlle and his allies began to create a state-led model of an industrializing and increasingly urban society with an expanding middle class and a working class with labor rights. In most other Latin American countries, the export-import model solidified historically extreme inequality in landholding patterns, which kept the rural population excluded and prevented the emergence of peasant-worker alliances in support of broad-based social policy. The rise of import substitution industrialization (ISI) with high economic protection made it possible for employers to simply pass on high pay-roll taxes to the consumers, which in turn made it politically easier for governments to expand coverage and increase the value of benefits of social protection for the urban population. This scenario happened in two different contexts—long periods of democracy or authoritarian re-gimes making strong incorporation attempts toward the emerging ur-ban sectors (Huber 1996). The decline of ISI and opening of the Latin American economies led to the eruption of sharp conflicts over payroll taxes, at a point in time when demographic, administrative, and macro-economic problems threatened to bankrupt existing social security sys-tems (Mesa-Lago 1989).

More recent contributions have proposed a typology of Latin Amer-ican welfare states with distinctive origins, and they have extended the analytical frame from the origins to the period of reform. Filgueira and Filgueira (2002) distinguish between welfare states characterized by stratified universalism (Uruguay, Argentina, Chile), dualism (Bra-zil, Mexico), and exclusionary regimes (Guatemala, Honduras, El Salva-dor, Nicaragua, Bolivia). They see stratified universalism as the product of contending elites seeking popular support, dualism as the product of elite statecraft and co-optation accompanied by repression of the popu-lar sectors, and exclusionary regimes the product of predatory elites.

Segura-Ubiergo (2007) examines variations in the comprehensive-ness of systems of social protection and proposes an explanation for these variations in Latin American countries as of 1979, based on eco-nomic conditions, democracy, and left-labor power. Where the level of economic development and protection from international market com-petition were comparatively high, either democracy or high levels of left-labor power were sufficient to produce comprehensive systems of social protection (Argentina, Brazil, Chile, and Uruguay). Where the level of economic development and protection from international market com-petition were comparatively low, both democracy and left-labor power were necessary to develop a comprehensive system of social protection (Costa Rica).

Haggard and Kaufman (2008), in their pathbreaking examination of the construction and reform of social policy regimes in Latin Amer-ica, East Asia, and Eastern Europe, provide an explanation of the con-struction of the welfare state during the transition from the old export-import model to ISI that is based on the rise of new ruling coalitions and their approach to inclusion or exclusion of the expanding urban working class and the peasantry. The collapse of ISI then forced a renegotiation of the social contract in the context of democratization and policy legacies from the previous period. They argue that economic performance and fiscal constraints were pivotal but that regime form did make a difference, as political competition under democratic regimes tended to expand social expenditures.

McGuire (2010) focuses on health policy, not on social policy regimes more broadly, but his theoretical explanation and his empirical findings are highly relevant. He treats decline of premature mortality as an indicator of improvement in human welfare and demonstrates that the provision of basic health services is crucial to bring it about. He combines statistical analysis of a worldwide set of countries with a comparative analysis of four middle-income countries in Latin America and four in East Asia and finds that the expansion of access of poor people to comparatively low-cost quality basic health services is more important than economic growth for the decline of premature mortality. He further argues that democracy promotes the provision and utilization of these services, and presents compelling evidence in support of this contention. The mechanisms through which he argues that democracy favors expansion of basic health services is not just electoral competition but includes organization of advocacy groups, a free press, and the spread of expectations among the poor that such services be provided.

In some explanations of welfare state reform trajectories in the post-ISI economic adjustment period, the influence of international economic and political structures of power looms large; in others it is downplayed. The international financial institutions (IFIs), particularly the IMF and the World Bank, as well as the U.S. Agency for International Development (USAID), for over a decade consistently pushed a neoliberal residual model of welfare state reform, aimed at reducing state commitments, increasing the role of the private sector in financing and delivering social insurance and social services, including health and education, and narrowly focusing policies on the poorest groups. The outcomes of these pressures differed greatly, shaped by different constellations of domestic forces, but the same basic model was put on the agenda everywhere (Huber 1996).

Madrid (2003) conceptualizes the influence of international financial markets as incentives for pension reform in the face of domestic capital shortages, and he also acknowledges the influence of the World Bank and the regional diffusion of the Chilean model, to which he adds the control of executives, as would-be reformers, over the legislatures and the rise of neoliberal economists to leading policy-making positions. Weyland (2004), in contrast, conceptualizes international influences as processes of diffusion and focuses on cognitive processes of decisions makers who learn from foreign models through cognitive shortcuts. In his earlier work, the emphasis was on obstacles to redistributive reform in the form of fragmentation of political institutions and of social and political actors (Weyland 1996).

The influence of the World Bank and the neoliberal model was most pronounced in pension reform. As Kaufman and Nelson (2004b, 12) point out, in the health and education sectors there were no widely accepted international policy templates. Chilean-style privatization of significant parts of health and education was hardly imitated elsewhere. Nevertheless, decentralization, competition, and user choice in health services and education were widely followed principles. We would add to this an emphasis on very narrow targeting of free services on the poorest groups and increased user fees for everyone else. Moreover, prolonged neglect of the quality of public services had the effect of encouraging exit among those who could afford it and thus, by default, a growing reliance on private health and education services.

Our Analytical Framework

In *Capitalist Development and Democracy*, we developed a theoretical framework that explained the development of democracy in Europe, the English settler colonies, Latin America, and the Caribbean with the development of shifting power relations in three clusters of power: domestic class power, the power balance between state and society, and international structures of power. In *Development and Crisis of the Welfare State*, we applied and adapted this theory to the explanation of the development of the welfare state in advanced capitalist democracies. In that work, we labeled the theory as "power constellations theory" to differentiate it from power resources theory, which is restricted to the domestic cluster of power.

In the 2001 work, we argued that the domestic structure of power was most decisive for welfare state development in advanced capitalist democracies and that the proximate driving force was partisan government (Huber and Stephens 2001a). In our view, Esping-Andersen's "three worlds of welfare capitalism" were the product of long-term government by social democratic parties, Christian democratic parties, or center and right secular parties. Both social democratic governance and Christian democratic governance resulted in generous, but different kinds, of welfare states: the former more universalistic and egalitarian in both gender and class terms, and the latter with occupation-based entitlements and less egalitarian in class and, especially, gender terms. The strength of these three party groupings can be explained in turn by the historic religious cleavage that created Catholic majorities or minorities, and therefore moderate to strong Christian democratic parties in almost all continental European countries, and the strength of organized labor and alliance possibilities with centrist parties, which distinguishes the Nordic countries from the liberal countries.

In the Nordic countries, powerful social democratic parties first formed alliances with farmers' parties to pass basic citizenship-based welfare state programs and later supplemented them with earnings-related transfer programs. They also developed a wide array of free or subsidized social services, which became increasingly important in facilitating women's entry into the labor market and the reconciliation of work and family. As just noted, Christian democratic parties were particularly influential in continental Europe, and there we find welfare states built on the Bismarckian model, with access to welfare state programs based on employment, different programs for different occupational groups, and a heavy emphasis on the male breadwinner as provider of insurance to his dependents. In accordance with the subsidiarity principle (Kersbergen 1995), Christian democratic parties developed social services to a much smaller extent than the social democratic parties, and to the extent that they did finance social services, they relied preferentially on private providers. This is precisely the model that was followed by the leading Latin American countries in the construction of their welfare states.

Long-term governance by secular right and center parties in the Anglo-American countries resulted in liberal or residual welfare states. Benefits are poor, so that those who can afford it rely on supplementary private insurance. Public financing for services is low, and providers are mostly private.[2] Many of the programs are targeted at the poor only, with the result that they are susceptible to cuts in economically difficult times. This model of social policy was the one advocated by the IFIs in the aftermath of the debt crisis in Latin America.

For all of these countries, democracy is a constant by fiat of research design. Like most studies of welfare states in advanced capitalist countries—and virtually all of the quantitative studies—our 2001 study was limited to the eighteen industrial countries with populations of over one million which had continuous histories of democracy since World War II. Second, again by fiat of research design, these countries were all considered "industrialized"—and thus rich. While there is, or rather was in 1950, variation between these countries in level of economic development, by the 1990s the laggards, for example, Japan, Italy, and Ireland, had caught up to the rich countries.[3] As a result of roughly similar levels of development, the class structures of these countries were similar. On the basis of the conceptualization of class that we outline below, we distinguished the following classes in advanced industrial societies in the second half of the twentieth century: the bourgeoisie proper (owners of capital who employ large numbers of workers), the petty bourgeoisie (owners of small and medium enterprises), the upper middle class of professionals and managerial employees, the lower middle class of nonmanual employees, the working class of manual employees, and the farmers (Huber and Stephens 2001a, 18). In all of these countries, the manual working class was the largest of these classes, but, except in the United Kingdom, never a majority by itself, until the peak of industrial employment in the 1960s or 1970s (see below), at which point it began to decline relative to the two middle classes.

Our conceptualization of the impact of the state on welfare state formation focused on the concentration versus dispersion of political power. State capacity was not an issue, as all of the advanced industrial states had sufficient capacity to build and operate income transfer programs and social services. Inspired by Immergut's work (1992), however, we analyzed constitutional dispersion of political power and captured it with the concept of veto points. The presence of veto points offered opportunities for opponents of generous welfare state reforms to block these reforms, and it encouraged them to try to do so. By the same token, veto points could and did slow down welfare state retrenchment from the 1980s onward.

The role of international constellations of power on welfare state formation in advanced industrial societies in the post–World War II period did not assume a high profile in our analysis. These countries were not subject to pressure from more powerful states or economic institutions. Economic internationalization, specifically the liberalization of capital markets, presented a challenge for macroeconomic management and thus indirectly for the welfare state through a decreased ability of governments to promote full employment. Another source of international influence on the domestic social policy of many European countries was just emerging—the European Union as promoter of the European Social Model. EU efforts to influence social policy started in the 1980s, but they did not become strong until the Open Method of Coordination was adopted in 1997, which required governments to develop national action plans. Moreover, EU influence remained much less important in the leading countries with the most developed welfare states than in the new member states, as we shall see in chapter 7.

Does our explanation of social policy, particularly redistributive social policy, travel to Latin America and Southern Europe? The most obvious limitation is that it assumes democracy, and with the exception of Italy in Southern Europe and Costa Rica in Latin America, none of these countries have a record of continuous democratic government dating back to the early postwar period (see table 2.1). Not only is democracy the prerequisite for party government, the driving force in our explanation of social development in industrial democracies, but our theoretical framework also postulates that formal democracy should make a difference for social policy because it at least opens the possibility of government responsiveness to citizen pressures or of party competition on the basis of promises to improve social policy.

In addition, because of their lower level of development, late development, position in the world economy, and legacies of large landholding, the Latin American countries have very different class structures from those in the advanced capitalist democracies. This difference not only affects the prospects of parties of various political colorings, but it affects the very operation of parties. Thus, with some reason, knowledgeable skeptics might contend that the prospects of social policy development driven by party government are not good in a region where party systems are seen as inchoate and the very meaning of left and right is open to question. Nevertheless, we find that the strength of left parties has shaped social policy and inequality in Latin America.

Southern Europe (less so Italy) lies somewhere in between Latin America and the rest of Western Europe in terms of democracy, class structures, and party structure. What is interesting for our comparative analysis is that Iberia was closer to Latin America in 1960 but by 2000 was closer to Western Europe. As we shall see in chapter 7, in 1960, both Iberian countries were authoritarian, their levels of development not above those of the advanced Latin American countries, their class structures similar to those countries, and their social policy regimes also similar. By 2000, they were closer to other Western European countries on all of these dimensions but nonetheless still shared some characteristics—and characteristic social policy problems—with the advanced regimes of Latin America.

CLASS AND SOCIAL POLICY REGIMES: CLASS STRUCTURES, CLASS ORGANIZATION, AND POLITICAL PARTIES. In *Capitalist Development and Democracy* (Rueschemeyer, Stephens, and Stephens 1992, 51–53), we define a class as a group of people who by virtue of their assets are compelled to engage in similar activities in the productive process if they want to make the best use of these assets. Assets include tangible property, intangible skills, and more subtle cultural traits. Though our definition of class combines Marxist (production relations) and Weberian (market situation) elements, it shares with the Weberian view the problem that it identifies no clear boundaries between classes. Giddens (1973) observes that the Weberian view leads to the identification of an almost infinite number of theoretically different class situations. Weber's solution (1968, 302) was to distinguish a "social class" as "the totality of class situations within which individual and generational mobility is easy and typical." Giddens adopts this definition and adds that a number of features of advanced capitalist society (e.g., class residential segregation) reinforce these class boundaries. In our view (Stephens 1979), the commonality of these features is that they create interactional closure, the tendency to interact on a day-to-day basis with others of the same social class.

Using these criteria for identifying classes, on the basis of data presented in Portes and Hoffman (2003), we identify the following classes in modern Latin America: the informal working class, the formal working class, nonmanual employees, the petty bourgeoisie, and the dominant classes (professionals, and executives and capitalists). Portes and Hoffman (2003, 46–49) estimate that, on average, 45.9 percent of the region's workers operate in the informal sector and are part of the informal working class. The more traditional categories of manual labor or nonmanual white-collar workers make up a small share of the occupational structure—just 23.4 percent and 12.4 percent, respectively. A similar conclusion regarding the size of the lowest categories emerges from the Economic Commission for Latin America and the Caribbean's comparative analysis (ECLAC 1999) of seven countries: Brazil, Colombia, Costa Rica, El Salvador, Mexico, Panama, and Venezuela. The study finds that occupational categories in the region can be divided, based on the income they generate, into three fairly homogenous groups: lower, intermediate, and higher, with the "higher" category covering just 9 percent of the population. The intermediate sector, meanwhile, groups an additional 14 percent of the population, while 75 percent of working-age individuals fall into "lower"-income occupational categories (ECLAC 1999, 61).

The one lacuna in the Portes and Hoffman classification is that they do not separate out the rural classes, landlords and peasants. For all eighteen of the Latin American countries included in our statistical analysis, 43 percent of the labor force was engaged in agriculture in the 1960s. Even in the three advanced Southern Cone countries, an average of over one-fifth of the labor force was working in this sector. During this period, Iberia was more agricultural than the Southern Cone countries (see chap. 7). Thus, in all of these countries in this period, the rural classes were still important political actors. By the contemporary period, agricultural employment has declined sufficiently in Iberia and the Southern Cone that these classes are not central to political developments. In many other Latin American countries, however, these classes retain a central role as indicated by the fact that in seven of our eighteen countries, agricultural employment is greater than one-quarter of the labor force. Although the presence of a significant class of landlords did not rule out any social policy innovation, it did rule out universalistic transfers and limited transfers to Bismarckian contributory insurance targeted at select urban occupational groups (see chap. 4).

Class structure differences between Latin America and Iberia on the one hand and the rest of Western Europe on the other are not just a product of lower levels of economic development. In analyzing the development of the welfare states of Southern Europe, Ferrera (2005) observes that these countries' transition to Fordism was incomplete. That is, because of their position in the European/world economy and late development, these countries' industrial employment peaked at a lower level than occurred in the rest of Western Europe, as one can see from table 2.1. The table underestimates the differences between Mediterranean Europe and the rest of Western Europe as it does not include some sectors that, though not part of industry, are part of the core of some of these countries' competitive niche in the world economy. Wood and wood products (part of the primary sector) were a key part of the economic niche of Sweden, Norway, and Finland, while processed agricultural products played the same role in Denmark. For Belgium, Netherlands, and Norway, shipping and trans-shipment, part of the tertiary sector, played a similar role in their historic economic development. Were one to add employment in theses subsectors to the industrial employment figures in table 2.1, the gap between Southern Europe and the rest of Western Europe would be even larger. Extending the comparison to Latin America, we see that in the Southern Cone countries, industrial employment peaked at an even lower level than in Mediterranean Europe. In other words, in the Southern Cone, transition to Fordism was arrested at an even lower stage.

We can extend Ferrera's observation about the incomplete Fordism and its effect on systems of social protection in Southern Europe to Latin America. His point is that at the peak of Fordist industrialism in northwestern Europe, the vast majority of heads of households were in "standard employment relations," that is, lifelong, full-time work in the formal sector. Palier (2010) points out that, under these conditions, the continental European countries could reach Beveridgean (i.e., universalistic) goals through Bismarckian (i.e., employment-based) means. That is, by progressively extending Bismarckian contributory social insurance to all occupational groups and by reducing the difference in entitlements between the groups, virtually every wage and salary earner, and by extension all members of their families, would have access to generous welfare state benefits. By contrast, in the Southern Cone even during the heyday of ISI in the 1970s, roughly one-quarter to one-third of the work force was employed in the informal sector, and many more spent at least part of their work career in nonstandard employment. Thus, their Bismarckian systems fell far short of providing universal coverage even to the urban population.

Moreover, the class structure of Latin America is inhospitable to class organization and class political mobilization compared to that of Western Europe. Because of the large size of the informal sector and agricultural sector, and the limited size of the industrial sector, the scope for union organization is much more limited in Latin America. These same features of class structure have not been favorable to democracy, and authoritarian regimes have repressed unions and installed labor codes that make organization difficult even in subsequent democratic periods, if they are not repealed, which is often the case.

These features of class structure, along with the very high degrees of inequality characteristic of Latin America, also weaken the density of

TABLE 2.1. **Transition to democracy and peak industrial employment, Europe and Latin America**

Europe

	Year of transition to full democracy	Peak industrial employment	
		Year	Peak (%)
Social democratic welfare states			
Denmark	1915	1965	37.4
Finland	1945	1974	36.1
Norway	1898	1970	37.2
Sweden	1918	1965	42.8
Christian democratic welfare states			
Austria	1945	1973	44.9
Belgium	1918	1964	47.2
France	1877	1964	39.2
Germany	1949	1970	49.6
Netherlands	1917	1965	40.9
Switzerland	1848	1963	48.8
Liberal welfare states			
Ireland	1922	1974	32.6
UK	1918	1911	51.6
Mediterranean welfare states			
Greece	1974	1980	30.2
Italy	1945	1971	39.7
Portugal	1976	1981	37.0
Spain	1977	1971	37.3

Latin America

	Year of transition to democracy		Peak industrial employment	
	Restricted	Full	Year	Peak (%)
Argentina	–	1983	1970	34.3
Chile	1990	2005[b]	1960	30.4
Costa Rica	1949	1955	1990	26.8
Uruguay	–	1985	1970	29.1
Brazil	1985	1990	1993	25.3
Mexico	1995[b]	2000	1980	25.3
Panama	1990	1994	1994	29.1
Venezuela[a]	1958	1969[b]	1990	27.8
Bolivia	1983	1993	1960	23.8
Colombia	1958	–[b]	1990	22.9
Dominican Republic	–	1978[c]	1990	24.4
Ecuador	–	1979	1980	18.3
El Salvador	1984	1997[b]	2000	23.2
Guatemala	1986	2000	1998	22.4
Honduras	1982[b]	–	2004	–
Nicaragua	1985	–	2003	18.4
Peru	1995	2002	1980	28.3
Paraguay	1990	2000	1990	–

[a] Venezuela was downgraded to a restricted democracy in 2003.
[b] Mainwaring, Brinks, and Pérez-Liñán (2001) date full democracy in Chile as 1990, in El Salvador as 1992, and in Honduras as 1994, restricted democracy in Mexico as 1988, and Colombia as fully democratic in 1974–89.
[c] This date ignores the semidemocratic interlude in the early 1990s.

civil society and thus the potential for autonomous (i.e., nonclientelistic) political mobilization of lower-class groups. We define civil society as the totality of "horizontal" relationships, institutions, and associations, both informal and formal, that are not strictly production related nor government or familial in character.[4] Thus, civil society includes everything from informal card-playing groups to parent-teacher associations, from the local pub to trade unions, from choral societies to church groups. We specifically exclude the vertical relationships and social ties characteristic of clientelism from our concept of civil society. It is an established regularity in the literature on clientelism that high degrees of inequality are fertile grounds for the development of clientelistic relationships (Kitschelt and Wilkinson 2007).

Of course class interests are not the only interests that can be the basis for collective action and political mobilization. Religious and ethnic divisions are relevant in so far as they form the basis for organizations that may reinforce but more typically divide the constituency of class-based organizations. Unions in ethnically divided societies tend to be weaker and more fragmented than in homogeneous societies. The same is true for working-class parties. Religious appeals have frequently been instrumental for conservative parties to attract the female lower-class vote as well.

Adopting a class analytic frame as a core feature of our explanatory theory does not mean that we claim to be able to read off individuals' or classes' political behavior from their class (or gender) position. As we argued in *Capitalist Development and Democracy* (Rueschemeyer, Stephens, and Stephens 1992, 53), "classes may indeed have *objective* interests, but in historical reality class interests are inevitably subject to *social construction*." The expression of collective interests may take different forms for groups in similar locations as a result of particular historical constellations. For instance, different segments of the working class may find their interests articulated at different points in time and in different countries through social democratic, anarchist, communist, Christian democratic, personalistic populist, or even conservative parties, depending on the cleavage structure of the society and the pattern of political mobilization.[5]

Political parties are among the main actors responsible for the social construction of class interests and for the defense of these interests in the political arena. Compared to parties in advanced industrial democracies, Latin American parties on average are newer and weaker as organizations. This feature is mainly a result of the weaker record of democracy. Parties cannot take root in society and develop functioning structures if they do not have room to participate in elections and the exercise of power. In particular, in the absence of democratic procedures, it is difficult for parties to build programmatic profiles in the minds of the electorate. There is, however, important variation among individual parties and among party systems in different countries in the extent to which they are consolidated and structured along programmatic lines. Some are well consolidated and have roots in civil society, others are less well rooted and in transition, and still others are inchoate (Mainwaring and Scully 1995a, 1995b). With regard to programmatic commitments, there certainly are parties with a clear history of an identifiable commitment to the interests of the underprivileged (PC and PS in Chile, PLN in Costa Rica, PT in Brazil) or the interests of economic elites (UDI and RN in Chile, ARENA in El Salvador, Conservative Party in Colombia), and parties with a clear secular (Radicales in Argentina) or a clear Christian agenda (Christian Democrats in Chile).

The original formulation of power resources theory emphasized the power of labor, organized in unions and political parties. Our modification of this original formulation in the domestic cluster of power in our power constellation framework introduced mobilization on the basis of gender and emphasized the leading role of parties with different ideologies, social democratic and Christian democratic, in mobilizing voters and shaping social policy. When thinking about power resources, we see organization as pivotal for their actualization. Control over labor power is one power resource that allows for disruption of production and public life and thus bestows bargaining leverage. The capacity to mobilize people to demonstrate and block roads is another such resource; it also allows for disruption of public life. Finally, in democracies, control over votes is an important power resource. The classical European model of left-labor power, with a crucial role for the formal alliance between organized labor and left parties as more or less equal partners, is not applicable to Latin America because of the differences in economic development and class structure outlined earlier. Industrialization came later and remained below European levels, which kept the working class smaller and organized labor weaker. In all European countries, labor movements and socialist parties emerged in the late nineteenth century and became important actors by World War I (Rueschemeyer, Stephens, and Stephens 1992, chap. 4). As Bartolini (2000, 10) points out, "the class conflict is mostly responsible for the similarity of 'party land-scapes' across Europe. It was the only social conflict to be politically mo-bilized in every European country, contributing to the standardization of party systems." In some cases, unions initially depended on the party (e.g., Germany and Finland), and in others the party depended on union personnel and guidance (e.g., Great Britain and Ireland); in still others, the relationship was so close that the party operated as the coordinat-ing body of the unions (e.g., Sweden and Norway). Over time, unions and left parties in all countries developed overlapping ancillary organi-zations, leadership, and activities (Bartolini 2000, 256).

In contrast, in Latin America, the leading role in forging progressive alliances has clearly fallen to parties, and relationships to unions have been more varied and generally weaker. Depending on the class struc-ture and historical conjuncture, left-of-center parties sought alliances with organized labor, social movements, and civil society organizations, or they simply appealed to their members as voters. What makes par-ties left or center-left in our assessment and in the assessment of experts is their ideological commitment to the values of egalitarianism and soli-darity and their class appeals to subordinate classes.[6]

Left-of-center parties, committed to redistribution and appealing to and representing (at least at the point of their emergence) the interests of subordinate classes, have emerged and grown in four different Latin American historical contexts. The first context was mineral export econ-omies during the period of export expansion, which gave rise to par-ties attempting to mobilize the workforce connected to the export sec-tor into a reformist or revolutionary alliance with urban workers and sectors of the middle classes. Examples are Acción Democrática (AD) in Venezuela, APRA in Peru,[7] the Socialist and Communist parties in Chile, and the Movimiento Nacionalista Revolucionario (MNR) in Bo-livia. The second context was the expansion of the industrial sector un-der ISI, which facilitated efforts of populist leaders to forge an alliance of parties with organized labor (therefore these parties are often re-ferred to as labor-based parties). This is the case, for instance, of the Peronist Party in Argentina, the Partido Trabalhista Brasileiro (PTB) in Brazil, and the Partido Revolucionario Institucional (PRI) in Mexico. The third context was the 1960s and 1970s, when new parties emerged in the struggle against authoritarian regimes, such as the Partido dos Tra-balhadores (PT) in Brazil and the Izquierda Unida (IU) in Peru, or in opposition to long-ruling traditional parties, such as the Frente Amplio (FA) in Uruguay.

The parties formed by populist leaders never had clear ideological profiles; they were anti-oligarchic and anti-imperialist and for the people, but in terms of general reform commitments they followed their leaders. This state of affairs is clear in the case of the Peronist Party; Perón never wanted to build a strong party apparatus (Collier and Collier 1991, 344), and flexibility and responsiveness to the leadership have remained characteristic of the party to the present (Levitsky 2003). In fact, experts asked to classify the party disagreed to such an extent that Coppedge classified it as "other." APRA formed under different historical circumstances and had a stronger organizational apparatus, particularly in the north, but it also changed ideologically with its leader. Under the repeated experience of being banned from political activity, Haya de la Torre moved to the right, finally making common cause with the conservative opposition against the reformist Belaúnde government of the 1960s. The PRI became the instrument of presidents at the national level and governors at the state level, retaining the revolutionary cloak but in practice supporting the pro-growth, pro-business policies of a long string of presidents. The PTB was only one of two parties created from above by Vargas, and he did not use it to mobilize working-class support. It remained centered on bureaucrats in the Labor Ministry and was unable to establish strong organizational roots among the rank and file (Collier and Collier 1991, 548). Nevertheless, its move to the left in the 1960s made it a target for repression by the military regime after 1964 as well. In all these cases, the leading role in social policy formation was played by the populist leaders (to the extent that they achieved executive office), not by the parties formed by them. As leaders changed, so did these parties. To the extent these parties were relevant for social policy, they became the defenders of programs implemented on the initiative of their leaders against attempts by other governments to cut them.

Repression by authoritarian regimes was a powerful factor weakening left parties. It not only took its toll on APRA but also on AD in Venezuela after the 1945–48 period. The party moved toward the center to engineer the Pact of Punto Fijo, and that pact took any serious redistributive reforms off the table in the interest of stabilizing the democratic regime. The Communist and Socialist parties of Chile also experienced severe repression under Pinochet, but they had been able to operate as legal po-

litical parties longer than AD and thus had a broader base of ideologically committed leaders and followers. The Socialists also moderated
their positions in exile, and for the first decade after redemocratization
prioritized consolidation of democracy. As a result of retrospective analysis of the intensity of popular pressures on the Allende government,
they severed their previously close relationships to the labor movement
and kept their distance from social movements more generally. Nevertheless, a strong nucleus of leaders managed to reconstitute a party with
a continuing commitment to the principles of solidarity and redistribution. Socialist presidents Lagos and Bachelet then implemented important egalitarian social policy reforms after 2000.

Socialist and communist parties of course existed in many other
countries, but they grew nowhere as electorally strong and politically influential as in Chile. The latest generation of left parties that emerged in
the 1960s and 1970s has cultivated close ties to the labor movement and
other social movements and civil society organizations. This arrangement has given them considerable mobilization capacity and support for
moving in a universalistic direction with social policy. It has also presented them with the problem of having to confront occasional opposition from parts of their social base against their social policy reforms.
This has been the case, for instance, with efforts to curtail privileges in
special pension systems and to reform the educational system, as we discuss in chapter 6.

There is yet a fourth context that gave rise to center-left parties with
a cross-class appeal to middle and lower classes and a strong commitment to investment in human capital and poverty reduction. The cases in
point are the Colorados in Uruguay and the Partido Liberación Nacional (PLN) in Costa Rica. Both of these parties emerged victorious out
of armed conflicts and championed social policy that was advanced for
their time and level of economic development. Arguably, these initiatives
were part of their efforts to unify their countries and establish their legitimacy as governing parties, but the commitment to expansion of public
education, health care, and a social safety net became a defining feature
of these parties' appeals. In Uruguay, the Colorado governments under
Batlle (1903–7 and 1911–15) recognized the right to strike and passed a
variety of labor laws that strengthened the labor movement, although the
Colorados did not form organizational relations to labor, nor did they
try to establish state controls over labor organization (Finch 1981). Nevertheless, urban labor became an important electoral constituency for

the progressive factions of the Colorados, and the party used its long-term incumbency to expand social protection and public education significantly until the 1950s. In Costa Rica, Figueres, the winner of the civil war in 1948 and leader of the reformist junta that abolished the military and nationalized the banks, was outright hostile toward organized labor because the labor movement was dominated by the communist party, which had been allied with the losing side in the civil war. He founded the PLN in 1951 and was president during 1953–57 and 1970–74, and the PLN became the electorally strongest party. It appealed to a cross-section of rural and urban middle and lower classes and consistently promoted expansion of the universalistic national health care system, public education, and a comparatively unified social safety net.

Not only are there Latin American parties with ideological identities and distinctive class appeals, but citizens in Latin America also find the left–right dimension meaningful for structuring politics. Colomer and Escatel (2004) demonstrate, on the basis of data from Latinobarometer surveys from 1995 to 2002, for seventeen Latin American countries, that an average of 78 percent of citizens are able to place themselves on a left–right scale. They further show that political party positions, as measured by the average self-placement of their supporters, are highly consistent with the left–right dimensionality. Luna and Zechmeister (2005) demonstrate on the basis of elite and mass survey evidence the presence of what they call strong representation, that is, clear, significant divides among elite and mass positions *and* a strong, positive correlation between the elite and mass mean positions, in Chile and Uruguay, followed by Argentina and Colombia, with weak representation in Ecuador, Mexico, and Bolivia, with Brazil and Costa Rica in between.

Finally, scholars have demonstrated the impact of partisan preferences on policy formation in Latin America. Gibson (1997) traces the connection between policy and electoral coalitions in the shaping of market reforms. Murillo (2001) discusses the behavior of labor unions and partisan coalitions in market reforms. Moreover, Murillo (2002) demonstrates how partisan beliefs and partisan constituencies shaped the choice of regulatory institutions and selling conditions in the privatization of state enterprises in Chile, Argentina, and Mexico.

The evidence presented by Luna and Zechmeister (2005) and by Colomer and Escatel (2004) is relatively recent, and one might ask whether parties have become more programmatic during this third wave of democratization. On the one hand, several factors might account for a shift

to more programmatic competition and representation. State retrenchment has certainly decreased the opportunity for parties to dispense patronage from state resources and has thus created incentives to look for
other, more programmatic appeals. At the same time, neoliberal reforms
have been highly controversial in some countries and thus have opened a
new issue area for programmatic competition, including in Brazil (Hagopian 2004).

The PT in Brazil has been a programmatic party from its inception
(Keck 1992; Hunter 2007), and its growing electoral success may well
have unleashed "contagion from the left," a phenomenon that observers
of European party systems noted in the emergence of mass politics there
(Duverger 1954). While left opposition parties consolidated as organizations and demonstrated strong programmatic commitments, center
and right parties were forced to follow suit to some extent in strengthening their organizations and programmatic profiles. This argument might
also be applicable to the rise of the left in Uruguay.

On the other hand, issue representation was found to be strongest in
Chile and Uruguay (Luna and Zechmeister 2005), and the group of ideological voters largest in Uruguay and Costa Rica (Colomer and Escatel
2004), the three countries with the longest democratic traditions in Latin
America. This finding confirms that length of the democratic record is a
crucial variable in so far as longer periods of democracy allow parties to
assume a stronger programmatic profile. Programmatic representation,
then, is not a variable that suddenly appears in the 1990s but can already
be used as an explanatory tool for the 1960s.

Contrary to the contentions of some scholars writing about parties in
Latin America, we argue that expectations regarding policy preferences
of left parties derived from the work on social policy in Europe travel
relatively well to Latin America. Generally, these parties favor social
programs that are redistributive and benefit the large majority of underprivileged citizens. Critics of the left have argued that these parties were
or are too closely tied to organized labor and thus really defended the interests of the "labor aristocracy," because organized labor has generally
constituted a comparatively small percentage of the labor force that in
many countries belonged to the upper third of income earners. This contention is at best partially true for the period before the 1980s, and it is
by and large incorrect for the last quarter century. It is true that the democratic left before the 1980s was heavily oriented toward the urban pop-

ulation, and for good reasons. Most countries had literacy restrictions on the franchise, which heavily depressed voter participation in rural areas. Moreover, where the rural population was allowed to vote, the voting process tended to be heavily controlled by local notables who represented landlord interests.

Orientation toward the urban population, however, did not mean an exclusive focus on organized labor. Some left parties also organized and campaigned in urban poor neighborhoods where large numbers worked in the informal sector (e.g., the member parties of the Unidad Popular in Chile up to 1973). With the decline of the formal sector and organized labor in the wake of the debt crisis and structural adjustment programs, this orientation has become more pronounced. In terms of policy preferences, this means that historically left parties have supported social security schemes, but that they have also promoted the inclusion of self-employed and domestic workers into those schemes. More recently many of them have begun to promote basic income support programs for poor families. In addition, they have supported public education and health services, including nutritional programs for the poor, as well as subsidies of basic foodstuffs and transport, all programs that benefit low-income earners in general, not just organized labor.

Center parties in Latin America have mostly emphasized a commitment to democracy, honest government, and modernization, rather than a redistributive agenda. Education has played a major role in modernization projects of centrist Latin American political forces. Christian democratic parties have been electorally successful only in a few countries in Latin America, and their policy preferences have been more heterogeneous than those of European Christian democratic parties (Mainwaring and Scully 2003, 49ff.). Therefore we would not expect to see any identifiable general influence of Christian democratic party strength on social policy. Much depends on alliance possibilities and thus the distribution of power in the party system in question. Where centrist and Christian democratic parties formed alliances with the center-left, they tended to espouse social policy schemes aimed at alleviating poverty and promoting health and education for the lower income groups.

Right parties have held somewhat different policy preferences from those of secular right parties in advanced industrial societies, as shaped by differences in the social and economic context. On the one hand, they too have favored low taxes. On the other hand, before the 1990s there was hardly a private social insurance market, particularly for pensions, so even the middle- and higher-income-earning constituencies of these parties looked to the state for social protection. Accordingly, right parties tended to support occupationally based social security programs for white-collar employees and civil servants. One should keep in mind here that advocacy of social security schemes financed by employee and employer contributions did not necessarily entail a conflict with employers' interests before the 1980s. As noted earlier, in the highly protected markets of the ISI period, employers could simply pass on the costs of social security contributions to consumers. In liberalized markets, this state of affairs has changed, and right-wing parties have become divided between those reluctant to endorse social security reforms designed to cut expensive benefits for privileged groups and those suggesting radical neoliberal reforms.

When conceptualizing the impact of class and party effects, it is important to keep in mind that shifting power distributions resulting from economic and organizational changes can affect social policy through several different mechanisms. The first and most obvious mechanism is an increase in the organizational strength of unions and left parties that become the agents of policy change by promoting a specific social policy in the legislative process, broadly understood to include mobilization and agitation on the issue, and the policy position of the unions or left parties prevails in the legislative process. Generally, this only occurs when left parties form the government alone or in coalition with other parties. It can occur, however, when other parties, usually centrist parties, adopt the position that had previously been promoted by the left, as in the case of the Canadian Liberals and the passage of national health insurance in the 1960s, a policy that had been implemented by forerunners to the social democratic New Democratic Party at the provincial level and promoted by the NDP at the national level (Maioni 1998).

A second and indirect mechanism is exemplified by instances in which civil society organizations and left parties put a policy on the agenda and governing parties respond by passing alternative policies that are less to the liking of left forces but acceptable to them. A third also indirect mechanism is instances of social legislation passed by incumbent political elites as a response to increasing working-class mobilization, often in an effort (successful or not) to dampen such mobilization or co-opt the working-class movement, as in the case of Bismarck's social legislation. In this case, working-class leaders may even oppose the legislation.[8]

EXCURSUS: POWER RESOURCES THEORY AND RATIONAL CHOICE POLITI-
CAL ECONOMY ON INEQUALITY AND REDISTRIBUTION. A number of recent contributions to the literature on redistribution based on the rational choice approach to comparative political economy have taken
the Meltzer-Richard model as their point of departure (e.g., see Boix
2003; Acemoglu and Robinson 2006). Interestingly, the Meltzer-Richard
model and power resources theory make exactly the opposite predictions about the relations between inequality and redistribution.[9] The
Meltzer-Richard model starts with the reasonable assumption that income distribution is skewed toward the top and thus the mean income
household is above the median income household. Consequently, the
median voter has an interest in redistribution. The greater inequality is,
the greater the distance between the median and mean is, and therefore
the greater the redistribution favored by the median voter. Thus, the theory predicts that in democracies, inequality will be positively related to
redistribution.

For advanced capitalist democracies, power resources theory makes
the exact opposite prediction (Stephens 1979, 55; Korpi 1983). According
to the theory, both bargaining outcomes and state policy reflect the balance of class power in society. Thus, strong unions will result in low levels of wage and salary dispersion and thus lower levels of market (pre-
tax and transfer) household income. Strong unions are associated with
strong social democratic parties (here the causality clearly goes both
ways) and thus with more frequent left government and consequently
more redistributive tax systems and social policy configuration.

One can easily put one's finger on the reasons for the radical differences in the predictions of the two theories. First, the Meltzer-Richard
model assumes that, in democracies, all citizens have equal amounts of
power. By contrast, power resources theory assumes that property and
organization are political power resources and that, in the absence of organization, political power resources will be highly asymmetrically distributed and political decisions will reflect the interests of property holders. The importance of this basic assumption can be seen in the fact that,
when Acemoglu and Robinson (2008) and Robinson (2010) move away
from the assumption that all voters are equally influential, and when
they allow for political power asymmetries between voters of different
income levels, they come much closer to the power resources model. In
fact, Robinson (2010) makes little reference to the degree of inequality
as an important determinant of redistribution and instead highlights de-

mocracy and left government, the same factors that we showed as being the most important determinants of poverty and inequality in our earlier quantitative articles on Latin America (Huber et al. 2006; Pribble, Huber, and Stephens 2009) and that we show in the quantitative and comparative historical analyses in this book.

Second, in our version of power resources theory (Stephens 1979; Rueschemeyer, Stephens, and Stephens 1992; Huber and Stephens 2001a), we insist that class interests are socially constructed while rational choice political economy makes the simplifying assumption that interests can be derived from positions in the income distribution.[10] Unions and social democratic parties do not simply mobilize voters; they also shape their opinions and thus shape the distribution of preferences in society. Both consensus and class analytic theories in sociology agree on the centrality of socialization to the formation of preferences; they disagree on the class content. Class analytic theory insists that upper classes throughout history have attempted to legitimate their rule, usually successfully, through influencing the norms, values, and preferences of subordinate classes.[11] What is distinctive about the industrial era is that industrialization created the conditions—concentrations of workers in urban areas and factories—that allowed the subordinate classes to organize themselves and partially escape upper-class ideological hegemony. As we show in *Capitalist Development and Democracy*, the takeoff of industrialization in Western Europe after the mid-nineteenth century explains why unions and socialist parties were weak or nonexistent in 1870 and important actors in almost every country by the eve of World War I. In the asociological Meltzer-Richard conception of stratification, it is impossible to get a theoretical handle on these developments: urban industrial workers are no different from any other low-income group, such as peasants, farm workers, or pre-industrial cottage industry workers.

For contemporary advanced capitalist democracies, the empirical evidence in support of power resources theory and against Meltzer-Richard is strong and the relationship robust. To cite just a few representative studies, Wallerstein (1999) shows that union density and union centralization are strongly related to wage and salary dispersion; Pontusson, Rueda, and Way (2002) add that left government is as well. In our analysis of pre-tax and transfer household income distribution and redistribution, we show that union density is one of the main determinants of household market income distribution and that left government is by far the most important determinant of the redistribution effected by the tax and transfer system (Bradley et al. 2003).

With only a little reflection, one can see that the basic premise of Meltzer-Richard is implausible. It asserts that a major feature of social structure, the very system of stratification of society, is self-negating. The usual assumption in sociology, political science, and anthropology is that social structures reproduce themselves—from day to day, from year to year, from generation to generation. The socialization process is a central feature of this process of societal reproduction. In a series of quantitative studies of the relationship between inequality and public opinion, Solt (2008, 2010, 2011; Solt, Habel, and Grant 2011) shows that greater inequality is associated with attitudes (greater nationalism and religiosity) and behaviors (less participation and political engagement) that serve to reduce the pressure for redistribution in mass publics. Of course, rational choice political economists know socialization shapes preferences, but they justify their simplifying assumption as a necessary step in proceeding to the formal modeling stage of their theory-building process. The fact that the empirical evidence is so overwhelming against the theory's predictions shows that scholars make such simplifying assumptions at their own peril.

CLASS AND SOCIAL POLICY REGIMES (RESUMED).   To make power resources theory travel to Latin America, we begin by recognizing that its theory of market income distribution is far too simple. If we examine the determinants of market income among individuals and thus leave demographic factors and household composition aside for the moment, distribution is determined not only by union organization but also by the distribution of marketable assets: land, physical capital, financial capital, human capital, social capital, cultural capital, and labor.[12] For instance, Nickell (2004) shows that the distribution of skills as measured by the dispersion of scores on the International Adult Literacy Survey explains variation in wage and salary dispersion when controlling for the variables in Wallerstein's study, union density and union centralization.[13] Parallel to union organization, owners of other similar assets can organize to increase the market value of their asset by limiting supply or increasing demand, as in the case of many professions. While market income is pretax and transfer, it is not pre-government as governments set the rules for the operation of the market (labor laws, minimum wages, laws governing professions, etc.), which can alter the market value of various assets. The education systems of countries obviously affect the supply of people with various amounts of human capital. For example, Mosher (2011) argues that the increase in inequality in the United States in the last four decades would have been much greater were it not for the expansion of secondary and tertiary education, which acted to dampen the increase in returns to education. The structure of the economy also affects market distribution. For instance, the transition to a service economy has increased market income inequality in most postindustrial countries.

Moreover, the effect of the distribution of market assets and organization of similarly situated asset holders is not limited to union organization, as it might appear in power resources theory, at least in the attempts to test the theory empirically. Organizations of professionals, farmers, employers, and various sorts of sectoral interests also influence the political process. The greater the inequality of these marketable assets and the greater the asymmetry of organization of assets holders, the greater is the asymmetry of inputs into the political process. This condition operates in part through lobbying activity but also through attempts to shape public opinion. All of these factors are additional reasons why power resources theory predicts that unequal societies will be associated with less redistribution, not more.

That the distribution of market income has a large effect on the financing of political activity is so obvious that it hardly needs mentioning. The strength of this effect, however, depends on the quality of the political parties in the country. The presence of strong parties, with consolidated organizations, deep roots in society, ideological cohesion, and party discipline in parliament can to some extent counterbalance the impact of money on political outcomes. Strong parties that can mobilize activists can provide a counterweight to well-financed media campaigns, and legislators from disciplined parties are more difficult for lobbyists to sway.

Since the Meltzer-Richard thesis only applies to democracies, we confine our discussion to the relationship of inequality to redistribution in democratic periods. We have already discussed the differences in class structure between Western Europe and Latin America: greater inequality in land distribution, much larger informal sector, a smaller urban working class, and a larger peasantry. All of these features are associated with greater inequality of market income distribution. In chapters 5 and 7, we document that the average level of education is lower in Latin

America and that the inequality in the distribution of education is higher than in Western Europe, which further contributes to greater income inequality in Latin America. As we mentioned, these differences in class structure result in lower levels of union organization, which also increases income inequality.

As we pointed out earlier in this chapter, these differences in class structure and market income inequality also translate into greater inequality in input into the political process in Latin America and thus into less egalitarian policy output. Weaker union organization, weaker civil society, high levels of clientelism, weaker social capital, greater concentration of financial resources at the top, lower levels of literacy, greater inequality in education: all of these features contribute to greater class asymmetries in political influence. They all weaken the counter-hegemonic position of progressive forces and thus translate into a less hospitable climate of public opinion for left political parties. Moreover, the different history of emergence of political parties and the generally lower degrees of organizational consolidation of left parties have kept left parties, the crucial driver of redistributive policy, in a weaker position than in most advanced industrial countries. As a result, power resources theory predicts that the outcome in terms of policy will be less redistributive in Latin America than in Western Europe, and Hill (2009, 2; following Schneider and Soskice 2009) shows that this prediction is correct.

State Structure and Social Policy.   In our study of social policy development in advanced capitalist democracies, state structure—in particular, constitutional structure "veto points"—and policy legacies figured strongly in our explanatory apparatus, and we have similar expectations for social policy development in Latin America. Two other arguments from the state-centric literature that appeared to us not to carry much explanatory power were state autonomy, that is, the autonomous role of the state in social policy making, and state capacity. In the case of Latin America, both of these factors could be of much greater importance for the development of social policy.

In our work on industrial democracies, we found strong support in both our quantitative analysis and our case studies for Immergut's (1992) argument that "veto points" in the policy process (e.g., second chambers, presidency, etc.) slowed social policy expansion. By the same token, they also hindered attempts to cut entitlements (Huber, Ragin, and Stephens 1993; Huber and Stephens 2000a, 2001a; Huber et al. 2006). We expect the same dynamics to be at play in Latin American countries during democratic periods.

We also found support for the argument that policy legacies had a significant impact on subsequent social policy development. We found abundant evidence for Pierson's (1996) contention that policies create political constituencies for their defense, the beneficiaries of the policies, and thus we should expect resistance to cutbacks. For the politics of retrenchment this was an important and powerful explanatory factor. For the period of expansion the policy legacies approach implies that the organizational forms of welfare states have a certain inertia. For instance, after World War II the groups that had held privileged positions in the previously existing fragmented pension and health programs pushed for a reestablishment of these programs and opposed the plans for unified social insurance in Germany and the Netherlands. We expect a similar dynamic to hold for Latin American countries that adopted Bismarckian contributory pensions systems with special privileges for certain groups such as the military and high-level civil servants. Specifically, we expect movement toward more universalistic social policy to be hampered to the extent that existing privileged schemes are threatened.

As for the autonomous role of the state in shaping social policy, it is clear that during authoritarian periods, Latin American states enjoyed policy autonomy from domestic social forces. The military regime under Velasco in Peru (1968–75) pursued policies that were strongly opposed by powerful domestic groups and foreign interests and that benefited the poor and the working class. In the 1970s the bureaucratic authoritarian regime in Chile carried through radical neoliberal social policy prescriptions to such an extreme degree that they hurt the vast majority of the population.

In our study of advanced welfare states, we did not find support for the variant of the state-centric theoretical framework in comparative welfare state studies that postulates a strong role for state bureaucrats in social policy innovation, ascribing to them responsibility for the design of major programs and for getting these designs accepted by governments (e.g., see Heclo 1974). There is no question that the actual text of much social policy legislation was written by bureaucrats, but the approach did not provide an adequate explanation for long-term change within countries and the patterning of policy across countries for several reasons. Social policy bureaucrats simply had too little space for maneuver given the strength of parties and interest groups in these societies.

Precisely because parties and interest groups are weaker and because civil society is less dense, it is plausible that public policy bureaucrats and leading government officials (e.g., the finance minister) enjoy more policy autonomy in Latin America during democratic periods than they do in advanced capitalist democracies. Nevertheless, their latitude of action is also circumscribed by the realities of the political power distributions in their societies, or by structural limitations (see below).

We did not find strong support for the view that state capacity was an important constraint on policy making in advanced capitalist democracies, but again this argument might be more plausible for Latin America. It is often observed that Latin American countries are undertaxed, that is, that the tax burden is much lower than one would expect given their level of development. The implication is that the state lacks the capacity to levy taxes effectively. That is a possible interpretation, but it might also (or instead) be the case that powerful social groups in these countries successfully oppose increases in the tax burden. The Chilean example is a case in point. The Chilean state is generally regarded as the most efficient and least corrupt in Latin America, yet its tax burden is lower than that of several other Latin American countries at the same level of economic development because of the power of business and the right (Fairfield 2010a).

Transnational Structures of Power and Social Policy.   The era of rapid welfare state expansion in OECD countries came to a close in the mid-1980s, and many of these countries began to make cuts, albeit modest ones, in some of their entitlement programs. The commonplace explanation for this welfare state retrenchment was globalization, that is, the increased competitiveness in international markets had made generous social policy a liability. By the turn of the century, most scholars working on social policy correctly rejected this argument, contending instead that changes in demography, family patterns, and expansion of the service sector were responsible for the welfare state adjustments that were under way (e.g., see the contributions to Pierson 2001). By contrast, there is no question that social policy developments in Latin America were affected by the changing international economy and by the actions of international financial institutions (IFIs), primarily the International Monetary Fund (IMF) and the World Bank. How strong these effects were remains a point of dispute. There is no doubt that the IFIs put neoliberal economic and social policies on the agenda everywhere. There is also no doubt that the resulting policy reforms were heavily shaped by the domestic constellation of forces. Arguably, the smaller the Latin American country, the more powerful were the pressures from the IFIs.

Long-Term Trajectories of Social Policy. As in *Development and Crisis of the Welfare State*, we are interested in the long-term trajectories of the development of social policy. In that work, we argued that social policy regimes are heavily path dependent, and we identified four mechanisms that account for the high degrees of path dependence: structural limitation, the policy ratchet effect or more simply the policy legacies effect, ideological hegemony, and regime legacies (Huber and Stephens 2001a, 28–31). By "structural limitation," we mean the policy options that are limited by the constellations of power in a country in a given time period. A whole range of policy alternatives is ruled out by power relations within the society. One of the most obvious manifestations of structural limitation in Latin America was the inability of governments, even left governments, to propose universalistic social policies or, in general, social policies that included rural workers during the ISI period. A second important manifestation of structural limitations is the constraints imposed by the international structures of power which greatly favor certain policy options over alternatives, such as neoliberal policies during the Washington Consensus era.

Here we use the more general term of "policy legacies," rather than the narrower one of "policy ratchet effect," to describe the second mechanism contributing to path dependence. In the earlier work, we were impressed with how hard it was for conservative governments to roll back entitlements introduced by left governments. With a few notable exceptions such as the Thatcher government in Britain, conservative governments generally accepted the reforms after they had been instituted, and these became the new floor or center of gravity in the system. The reason for the change in posture of the conservative parties was that the reforms were popular with the mass public, especially the broad-based policies in the areas of pensions, education, and health care, which constituted the overwhelming majority of social expenditure in the countries under study in that work.

We used the term "policy ratchet effect" to indicate the fact that the main effect of policy legacies in advanced capitalist democracies was to push policy in a more progressive direction in the long run by putting a floor on entitlements in the short run. In Latin America, the effect of policy legacies has been less benign. There are two particularly striking inegalitarian policy legacies in the region. First, the occupationally stratified character of contributory pension schemes in almost all Latin American countries has proven very difficult to change, despite the bankruptcy of the systems due to demographic change and political manipulation. Second, high levels of private spending on health and education in some countries, which for instance were greatly increased under the Pinochet government in Chile, have made upper-income groups very resistant to tax increases to improve the public system and to measures to incorporate their offspring in the public system.

The third mechanism producing path dependence, "production regime effects," refers to the complementarities between production regimes and the welfare state regimes.[14] In our analysis of advanced capitalist democracies, the term refers to the complementarities between the high-wage coordinated market economies and the generous social democratic and Christian democratic welfare states, on the one hand, and the low-wage liberal market economies and miserly liberal welfare states, on the other. In Latin America, we find complementarities between the ISI production regime and the stratified Bismarckian contributory social insurance systems with relatively good benefits for employees in the protected sector of the formal economy. The transition to the open economies in the 1980s and 1990s put pressure on these insurance systems.[15] Since then, both production regimes and social policy regimes have been in flux. As Sheahan (2002) argues, Latin American countries have never adhered to particular sets of policies long enough to establish stable and successful models of capitalism with complementarities between production regimes and social policy regimes.[16] For advanced capitalist countries, our fourth mechanism, "ideological hegemony," refers to how social and political movements, along with the three mechanisms set out, shape the policy preferences of both elites and mass publics. The construction of an ideological counterhegemony to dominant classes presupposes a dense civil society autonomous from the state and from economically dominant classes. In Latin America, civil society has been weaker and more often linked to dominant classes, particularly through the Catholic Church, than in Western Europe. Unions and left parties have not been strong enough for long enough to establish an ideological hegemony rooted in the values of equality and solidarity.

The international system entered our discussion in *Development and Crisis of the Welfare State* in an ad hoc fashion. For Latin America, one must be more systematic about international effects, especially at the elite level. A case in point is the international hegemony of neoliberal economic thinking in the 1980s and 1990s. Certainly, a large part of the effect of neoliberal prescriptions on Latin American social policy was in response to conditionality imposed by the IFIs, but this is hardly the whole story. After the exhaustion of ISI, the progressive forces in Latin America lacked an alternative set of policy prescriptions to counter those coming from Washington. Their agenda was mainly negative; they knew what they did not want but did not have a clear viable alternative.

INEQUALITY, SOCIAL POLICY, AND ECONOMIC DEVELOPMENT MODELS.   In our quantitative analysis of the determinants of social policy in Latin America, we are less concerned with the level of spending per se than we were in our work on advanced capitalist democracy. Instead, we focus on the outcomes, poverty and inequality. The reason for this shift in focus is that social spending in the advanced welfare states is a strong predictor of poverty and inequality (Bradley et al. 2003; Moller et al. 2003; Brady 2009), whereas in Latin America it is not (see chaps. 3 and 5). Poverty and inequality are affected by factors other than social policy, of course, so it is necessary briefly to explore these other factors in order to set up the hypotheses we develop and test in the quantitative analysis in chapter 5. As it turns out, this discussion of the (nonsocial policy) causes of inequality and poverty is not tangential to our main theme of social policy development. Rather we argue that a viable economic development model in the post-ISI era requires complementary social policy and reductions in poverty and inequality.

Market income distribution is determined by the supply of marketable assets, as we outlined in our discussion of class earlier in the chapter, by unions or cartels among holders of similar assets, and by the demand for these assets. Thus, one might hypothesize that concentration or dispersion of these assets would be a strong determinant of market income distribution. The high degree of income inequality in Latin America has often been attributed to the high degrees of concentration of land and education (e.g., see Morley 2001; Frankema 2009). The structure of the economy is the main factor on the demand side, and, as we saw in the discussion of class formation, the size of the industrial sector was limited in Latin America as a result of ISI and late development; thus the demand for skilled and semi-skilled manual and nonmanual formal industrial work was limited. The flip side of this was the development of a large very-low-wage informal sector. The movement from ISI to open economies which occurred in Latin America in the 1980s and 1990s further exacerbated this situation, because it resulted in deindustrialization and increased informalization. The same processes further weakened unions, which were already weak by European standards.

As pointed out previously, pre-tax and transfer income distribution, that is, "market income distribution," is not "pre-government." The distribution of assets itself is the result of governmental decisions or non-decisions. Perhaps the most striking example is the land reforms and educational expansion carried out by the authoritarian governments of Taiwan and South Korea, which resulted in these two countries having very equal income distributions compared to other capitalist countries at a similar level of development (Haggard and Kaufman 2008). Given the very low social transfer spending, this outcome could not be attributed to government social transfers. Latin America represents the opposite case, with few governments willing to undertake land reform and with education systems that are highly biased toward upper-income groups. In addition, governments set the rules for industrial relations and for the operation of labor markets, which has evident effects on income distribution. In advanced industrial countries, left governments have shaped labor market rules to strengthen the position of labor. In Latin America, we can see the same tendency. The center-left Concertación in Chile repeatedly sought to reform the restrictive labor code left by the Pinochet dictatorship, and the Frente Amplio government in Uruguay reinstated the wage councils and expanded their coverage.

For advanced industrial countries, we have argued that there are strong complementarities between the production regime and the welfare state (Huber and Stephens 2001a, chap. 4; also see Estevez-Abe, Iversen, and Soskice 2001). It is no accident that the generous welfare states of northern continental European and Nordic countries are coordinated market economies that specialize in export production in market niches that demand high levels of skills and education. There are also complementarities between the production regime and social policy in Latin America. We have already pointed to the link between ISI and Bismarckian contributory social insurance, which covers only formal sector workers and even among those covered does so in a highly stratified fashion.

Since the end of ISI and the advent of open trade economies, no Latin American country, not even the more developed countries with advanced social policy regimes, has found a clear export niche outside of raw materials. Rather, the commodity boom has deepened Latin America's traditional dependence on primary exports and low wages (Martínez Franzoni, Molyneux, and Sánchez-Ancochea 2009). It is clear, however, what that niche must involve if the new production regime is going to result in economic *and* social development. Trying to compete on low-cost production is impossible because China and Southeast Asian countries can undercut Latin American labor costs. Moreover, such a strategy does not result in *development* because it does not raise the living standards of the mass of the population, at least not in the long run. Latin American countries must take the path followed by the backward economies of early twentieth-century Europe, like that of Finland, and then replicated by those of the East Asian newly industrialized countries (Vartiainen 1999). This route involves moving up the product cycle through industrial upgrading. The East Asian countries began with labor-intensive products such as textiles and apparel and then moved up the product cycle, taking over export production in industries such as ship building, which the Nordic countries no longer do competitively, and then moving on to automobiles and electronics. To do this, these countries needed a highly skilled work force, and thus this path required government investment in mass education.

That investment in human capital is essential for a viable development path in Latin America is already widely recognized (Perry et al. 2006). Just how central it is, and how close its links are to other social policy areas, such as poverty reduction, is perhaps not so widely realized. The importance of human capital investment for economic growth was a central insight of endogenous growth theory (Romer 1986, 1990, 1994) and has been supported by many quantitative analyses of the determinants of economic growth since (e.g., see Barro 1991, 1997). These insights have also stimulated Evans (2008) to reconceptualize the developmental state for the twenty-first century. He argues that the primary function of the successful developmental state has become the generation of intangible assets—ideas, skills, and networks—which makes investment in human capabilities critical.

In quantitative studies of the impact of human capital on economic growth, the stock of human capital is usually measured by average years of education of the adult population. In a recent review and reanalysis of quantitative work on the determinants of economic growth, Hanushek and Woessmann (2008) have shown that previous estimates of the effect of human capital on economic growth grossly underestimated the effects of the level of human capital because of error in the measure of human capital, using average years of education, rather than actual cognitive skills as measured by test scores on cognitive skills tests. In their reanalysis of economic growth in Latin America, Hanushek and Woessmann (2009, 14–15) show that "test scores that are larger by one standard deviation are associated with an average annual growth rate in GDP per capita that is 2.6–2.9 percentage points higher over the whole 40-year period" covered in their analysis. Average years of education is not significant when test scores are in the equation.

With regard to linkages to other social policy areas, we cite evidence that the existence of high levels of inequality and poverty undermine efforts to raise the skills of the working population through investment in education and health alone (chap. 5). On the basis of the evidence we present in this book, we argue that economic growth models for Latin America *must* aim at simultaneously raising the level of human capital and reducing the levels of inequality and poverty in the region.

Methodological Approach

As in our previous book, we test and substantiate our arguments through both cross-national quantitative and comparative-historical analyses, engaging the two methods in a dialogue. The combination of these two methods allows us to achieve generalizability and to establish causality through tracing links between events and actors' behavior in the historical narrative. The quantitative analysis includes all of the countries in Latin America. Our initial analysis of the data on inequality and social spending included the Caribbean countries, but we did not include them in the analysis of poverty because of missing data on the dependent variable (Huber, Mustillo, and Stephens 2004; Huber et al. 2006). We found that the determinants of social spending were significantly different in the English-speaking Caribbean, so we excluded them from subsequent analyses (Huber, Mustillo, and Stephens 2008).[17] The results for inequality were very similar with and without use of data from the English-speaking Caribbean; we exclude those countries from the analysis in this book so that our analyses of poverty, inequality, and social spending are on the same eighteen countries as previously.

Our annual data begin in 1970, which means that there are too few data points for the initial period of social policy formation during the ISI phase to conduct a pooled time series analysis. For this period, we test our theory and competing theories with cross-sectional data. We then compare historical sequences in the five cases identified in the quantitative analysis as social policy leaders: Argentina, Brazil, Chile, Costa Rica, and Uruguay. In chapter 4 and in chapter 6 on the contemporary period, we trace historical processes to establish the causal relationships among the variables examined in the statistical analyses and among other causal factors that were difficult or impossible to measure in the statistical analyses and with special focus on relations that are difficult to uncover in statistical analyses, such as conjunctural causation and multiple paths to the same outcome.

Critics of comparative historical analysis have considered selecting cases that all have high values on the dependent variable to be the cardinal sin of much qualitative research (e.g., see Geddes 1991). King, Keohane, and Verba (1994, 130) are uncompromising on the issue: "the cases of extreme selection bias—where there is by design no variation on the dependent variable are easy to deal with: avoid them! We will not learn about causal effects from them." Collier, Mahoney, and Seawright (2004, 94–98) correctly argue that this view fails to distinguish cross-case analysis and within-case analysis (process tracing). Collier, Brady, and Seawright (2004, 252–64) make the distinction between data-set observations, that is, observations in quantitative data sets, and causal-process observations, that is, data that result from examining the historical narrative within the cases. It is the latter, they argue (and we concur), that provide the "smoking gun" in establishing a causal link between a proposed explanatory variable and the outcome (Collier, Brady, and Seawright 2004, 252; also see Rueschemeyer and Stephens 1997).

In cross-case analysis, selection bias is an issue. Our main method of cross-case analysis consists of our statistical analyses, and there is no selection bias in those analyses because we include the universe of cases. In our qualitative comparisons, we conduct two different types of cross-case analysis. In our comparison of Iberia and the advanced Latin American countries (chap. 7), we employ a most-similar-cases design in which there is a difference in the outcome (the dependent variable) in that the countries start at similar points and end up varying greatly in their welfare-state redistributive efforts at the end point. In our comparison among the Latin American cases, we use cross-case comparison to identify different paths to similar outcomes (chap. 4).

The within-case analysis in this book is a comparative historical analysis in which we attempt to identify cause by tracing historical sequences. For example, our quantitative analysis shows that there is a robust relationship among democracy, social spending, poverty, and inequality. In our comparative analysis, we examine whether the historical sequence indicates that this relationship is causal by examining the exact mechanisms that link democracy to redistributive social policy. In the two comparative historical chapters on Latin America, we analyze developments over a long period of time, and all five countries vary greatly on the dependent and independent variables over this period of time. In fact, selecting some cases that were low on our dependent variables would not be very enlightening precisely because they do not vary through time; these cases are also low on all of our independent variables (democracy, left party strength, etc.; e.g., Guatemala).

It is useful to situate our case selection strategy in the recent debate about case selection in mixed methods research in which quantitative analysis of a large number of cases is combined with qualitative analysis of a smaller number of cases (Lieberman 2005; Fearon and Laitin 2008; Seawright and Gerring 2008; Goertz 2008). Similar to our approach, Lieberman's and Fearon and Laitin's strategy is to first carry out a large N quantitative analysis to establish robust relations among the independent variables and then to process trace in the small N analysis to verify that the linkages among the variables are causal (and not spurious) and to flesh out the mechanisms that link the causal and outcome variables. Fearon and Laitin recommend random selection of the cases for the qualitative analysis, whereas Lieberman, Seawright and Gerring, and Goertz recommend purposive selection.

In our view, random selection is far too costly. In-depth qualitative analysis is very time consuming, which of course is the reason for choosing only a few cases. In this study, a random selection strategy would have resulted in selecting two or three countries that are low on our independent and dependent variables, as in the case of Guatemala mentioned previously. As Goertz (2008, 12) points out, one cannot learn much from these cases. Since they have low values on both independent and dependent variables, one can learn nothing about the causal relationship between these two sets of variables that one did not already know from the quantitative analysis.[18]

Of the various purposive strategies, we follow Ragin's (1987, 2000, 2008) advice to focus on the positive outcome cases, so we select all cases that had high values on the dependent variable as of 1980.[19] This fits Goertz's (2008, 11) admonition to choose diversely among positive outcome cases and Lieberman's (2005, 444) to select for wide variation in the explanatory variables among the cases that fit the theory according to the quantitative analysis. All of these discussions of case selection in qualitative analysis neglect the time frame of the analysis, and we think the long time frame is important because it allows both our independent and dependent variables to vary within the cases. The long time period over which we examine social policy developments in these five countries follows the methodological approach we adopted in our comparative historical analyses in *Capitalist Development and Democracy* and *Development and Crisis of the Welfare State* (see Rueschemeyer, Stephens, and Stephens 1992, 32ff.; Huber and Stephens 2001a, 35–36). To draw the sharpest contrast to our approach, we take the case of the analyst studying development in a single case over a short period of time.[20] In this type of research, the actions or intentions of various actors are examined in detail, and the outcome is attributed to the clashes and cooperation of these actors, thus privileging agency and process and ignoring the four mechanisms (structural determination, policy legacies, production regime legacies, and ideological hegemony) that produce long-term change discussed in the theory section of this chapter. Likewise, this type of historical case analysis will not detect the indirect effects of shifting class power discussed previously in this chapter.

The comparative method allows one to uncover those instances in which indirect causality is involved, that is, instances in which an agent (e.g., a working-class organization or international actor) does not directly press for a given policy outcome but in which the domestic or international power distribution constrains the policy outcome.[21] To examine the variables hypothesized by our theories and competing theories, we need to stretch the time period covered in each country to include periods when the left was in power and periods when it was not; democratic periods and authoritarian periods; periods in which the country was at a low level of economic development and more recent periods; periods of low industrialization and periods of higher industrialization; low levels of urban working-class strength and periods of higher levels of urban working-class strength; and so on. In each of the five countries, we begin our historical narrative well before World War II, back to the beginning of the twentieth century in some cases, and extend it to the present, which assures that we will have variation on all of these variables.[22]

In chapter 5, we analyze pooled time series data covering the period 1970 to 2006. The dependent variables are spending on education, health care, and social security and welfare; income inequality; and poverty. In discussions of the selection of statistical techniques in quantitative journal articles, the selection of the appropriate technique is often treated as an entirely technical problem that can be solved by reference to the latest technical innovation and without reference to the hypothesized theory or even the nature of variation in the data at hand. This is a huge mistake and can and often does lead to the selection of an inappropriate technique for testing the theory. In our case, much of the variation in our data is among countries, and we are as interested in explaining this variation as we are in explaining variation through time. Given the theoretical concerns and the nature of variation in the data, it is inappropriate to employ a fixed effects specification, that is, country unit dummies.[23]

By the same token, since a lot of the variation that we explain in the statistical analysis is among countries, we forego one advantage of the time structure of pooled time series data, that is, using the time sequence in the data to make claims about causality. As in our previous work (Huber and Stephens 2001a), however, we do not make claims about causality on the basis of the quantitative analysis. As we just noted, we make our claims to have uncovered causal relations through examining the historical sequence in the comparative historical analysis. The role of the quantitative analysis is to demonstrate that these relations hold over a large number of cases over long periods of time and to rule out alternative explanations. We agree with Hall (2003), who argues that causation in the real world is highly complex, as characterized by multiple paths to the same outcomes, complex interaction effects, path-dependent effects, reciprocal causality, and diffusion, and one is not likely to uncover these causal processes with techniques like multiple regression or any other statistical technique for that matter.

In chapter 7, we further subject our explanation to a test in a cross-regional comparison of our four South American cases with Portugal and Spain. These two countries were similar to the Latin American countries circa 1960 or 1970 in terms of high inequality of landholding, low levels of educational attainment, similar levels of GDP per capita, similar social policy patterns, authoritarian political regimes, and reliance on an import substitution economic model. By 2000, Spain and Portugal had substantially narrowed the gap between themselves and the rest of Western Europe both in per capita income and in social policy generosity, and by the same token distanced themselves from our Latin American cases. Two of the master variables in our quantitative analysis and comparative historical analysis of Latin America—democracy and left government— also explain a significant part of the differences between our focal Latin American countries and Iberia. The cross-regional comparison also enables us to explore the effects of transnational structures of power, which vary greatly between the two regions but little within them.

CHAPTER THREE

Strategy for Redistribution and Poverty Reduction

In this chapter, we examine the technical and political aspects of a strategy for redistribution and poverty reduction in contemporary Latin America on a conceptual plane.[1] We begin by discussing the simple arithmetic of redistribution: How do tax and transfer programs have to be structured to produce redistribution? Amazingly, this arithmetic is poorly understood even by many social policy scholars. We then go on to examine successful redistributive policies in advanced capitalist democracies. How were (are) they structured and do the structures of the policies account for their success in both technical and political terms? Then, building on our discussion in chapter 2, we examine the class structures of contemporary Latin American societies to identify potential support bases for redistributive social policy. We follow up this topic with a discussion of the challenges faced by left parties, the main agent of redistribution, in mobilizing political support on the social terrain. Finally, we examine what kinds of social policies are likely to be successful in political and technical terms in contemporary Latin America. In the chapter as a whole we build a case for "basic universalism," policies that guarantee a minimum income and provide basic free or subsidized health care and child care and labor market training, along with quality primary and secondary education.

Policies for Redistribution and Poverty Reduction

The Arithmetic of Income Redistribution

It is disturbingly frequent that scholars working on the topic of social policy and income distribution (not to speak of politicians legislating on

the topic or political journalists writing on it) misunderstand the fundamental arithmetic of governmental income redistribution. Therefore, it
is essential that we begin this chapter with an overview of the matter before moving on to the more complex topic of the politics of income redistribution in Latin America. One often hears from educated observers
that a social policy is not redistributive because a lower-income group received less than its "fair" (proportionate) share of the benefit or because
an upper-income group received more than its proportionate share. For
instance, this would be a common observation about spending on higher
education. This view completely ignores the source of the revenue for
spending and the shape of market income distribution.

Tables 3.1 and 3.2, on Brazil and Uruguay, respectively, countries that
represent the opposite poles in Latin America in terms of income distribution and the distributive effect of social expenditure, show how misleading a one-sided focus on the distribution of expenditure can be. As
one can see, only in the case of social assistance does the bottom quintile receive a share of total expenditure that is larger than its share of
total households in both countries. Social security spending appears to
be highly regressive in its impact in both countries. In Brazil, education
spending appears to be somewhat regressive, whereas health spending
appears to be distributively neutral. In Uruguay, both health and education spending appear to be mildly progressive. These observations are
valid in and of themselves. The problem is that they ignore the revenue
side of the equation. Compare the distribution of household income in
the first column of the tables with the distribution of the various categories of social expenditure. One can see that income is more unequally
distributed than any of the spending categories except social security
spending in Uruguay, and in that case the differences are small.

Thus, it becomes a question of how the spending is funded, and one
has to look at the revenue side. The main problem with Latin American
tax systems is that they generate a low tax take. The tax burden is on average 18 percent of GDP, half of the tax burden in thirty OECD countries. The biggest weakness is the small amount of taxes generated by
direct taxes, which is on average only 5.6 percent of GDP, compared to
15.3 percent in the OECD, and particularly from personal income taxes,
which in Latin America is 1.5 percent compared to more than 9 percent
in the OECD. The overwhelming share of direct taxes comes from corporate taxes, mostly raw material producers. Most of the personal in-

come taxes come from wage and salary earners, as the self-employed at all income levels have many opportunities to avoid taxes. Noncompliance with payment of income taxes is a staggering 40–65 percent, much higher than noncompliance with the value-added tax. Within the Latin American context, Brazil has the highest tax burden, followed by Argentina. Among our cases, Chile has the lowest tax burden (ECLAC 2010, 57–59).

There is considerable disagreement about the best method to estimate the incidence of taxes. Among direct taxes, personal income taxes are easy, but not corporate taxes. Among indirect taxes, the distributive impact of the VAT and special consumption taxes on alcohol, gasoline, and the like can be estimated relatively easily, but not the impact of tariffs. Moreover, in several countries subnational levels have taxing authority as well, which complicates the estimations. On average, there is consensus that little redistribution is effected by the tax system (Goñi, López, and Servén 2008). In a comparison of pre- and post-tax income distribution, Gómez-Sabaini (2006) finds that the Gini coefficient increases after taxes in seven of the nine countries analyzed. The other two cases (Brazil in 2000–2001, and Costa Rica in 2000) exhibit no effect (Gómez-Sabaini 2006, 32). In other words, Latin America's tax systems are proportional at best and probably in most cases somewhat regressive, but not massively so. Estimates show the Chilean system as essentially proportional (Jorratt 2010), the Brazilian slightly regressive (Salvadori Dedecca 2010), the Argentine slightly progressive, the Costa Rican very slightly progressive (Barreix, Bes, and Roca 2009), and the Uruguayan also very slightly progressive (Roca 2010). In all the countries we examine, the expenditure side is redistributive, for transfers and even more so for health and education services.

At first blush, however, and counterintuitively, combining a proportional or somewhat regressive tax system with social spending that has the distributive profile of the education, health, or social assistance shown for Brazil or Uruguay in tables 3.1 and 3.2 results in substantial redistribution. This outcome can easily be seen by assuming a regressive tax burden in which the first two quintiles pay 50 percent more than their proportionate share (proportionate to their share of *income*, not households). Even in the case of education spending in Brazil, these two deciles experience a large net gain: they pay 10.5 percent of the taxes, but they get 35 percent of the benefits.

TABLE 3.1. **Household income and government expenditure by income quintile, Brazil 1997**

	Income	Social security	Social assistance	Health	Education
Top quintile	66	51	8	19	27
Fourth quintile	17	19	16	23	19
Third quintile	10	15	22	22	18
Second quintile	5	8	25	20	18
Bottom quintile	2	7	29	16	17
Gini, quasi-Gini	56	40	−20	4	9

Source: ECLAC 2005, 144, 158.

TABLE 3.2. **Household income and government expenditure by income quintile, Uruguay 1998**

	Income	Social security	Social assistance	Health	Education
Top quintile	50	52	12	18	15
Fourth quintile	22	24	20	18	16
Third quintile	14	15	17	20	19
Second quintile	9	7	21	20	23
Bottom quintile	5	3	29	24	28
Gini, quasi-Gini	41	46	−14	−6	−13

Source: ECLAC 2005, 146, 158.

With these calculations as background, we can see why it is an unwarranted assumption that transfer systems that provide for earnings-related benefits are necessarily not redistributive. In their analysis of Luxembourg Income Study (LIS) data on public pensions, Kangas and Palme (1993) have shown that in the countries in their analysis with earnings-related contributory pensions (the Bismarckian system that is also common in Latin America)—Finland, Germany, Norway, Sweden, and the United States—the quasi-Gini index for public pensions was between 8 and 19, which is much, much lower than the Gini for market income distribution in all cases.[2] As we have pointed out on several occasions, one cannot expect such redistribution from contributory social insurance in Latin America, because these benefits only accrue to formal-sector workers with a long contribution record, and moreover the benefits are almost always stratified by occupation. In their analysis of microdata on household income, ECLAC (2005) found that in three of eleven countries studied (one of them Uruguay; see table 3.1), social security income was actually more unequally distributed than net household income. Without information on the financing of the system, however, even for these cases one cannot infer that the system necessarily redistributes income upward. By the very structure of the system, only formal-sector workers make contributions to the system, which appears to reduce the distributively perverse aspects of the system precisely because only the beneficiaries make contributions to it. One needs to keep in mind, however, that the system, and particularly the generous benefits of high occupational groups, is subsidized by the state and thus by general taxation, and therefore, to the extent that informal-sector workers pay indirect taxes, they subsidize the benefits paid to formal-sector workers. Thus, one is on safe grounds in saying that at best, contributory social insurance will effect little redistribution and, in any case, cannot be expected to affect the high levels of redistribution that these systems do in some of the advanced capitalist democracies, most notably the Nordic countries.

The Paradox of Redistribution

Korpi and Palme (1998) have identified what they term the "paradox of redistribution" among postindustrial welfare states, that is, the welfare states that most target social benefits at the poor redistribute income the least. All welfare states in advanced industrial democracies redistribute income, though they do so to greatly varying degrees. Table 3.3 presents our own calculations, based on LIS data, of income redistribution among the working-age population, in order to counter the criticism that welfare states only redistribute income across generations. The first three columns document reduction in inequality as a result of taxes and transfers; the next three columns do the same for poverty reduction. The Nordic countries, with social democratic welfare states, effect the most reduction in inequality and poverty and end up with the lowest levels of poverty and inequality. The Anglo-American countries, with liberal welfare states, are at the opposite end, and the continental European countries, with Christian democratic welfare states, are in the middle.

There are two mechanisms that explain the paradox of redistribution. The first works through the effect of the structure of programs on political support for the welfare state and the second works through what we refer to as the crowding-out factor. Welfare state benefits can be classified into three types: (1) means or income-tested, tax-financed benefits (e.g., social assistance), (2) flat-rate, tax-financed benefits going to everybody (e.g., citizenship pensions, many social services), and (3) con-

TABLE 3.3. **Inequality and poverty by welfare state regimes**

	Inequality among working-age population			Working-age population in poverty		
	(1)	(2)	(3)	(4)	(5)	(6)
	Pre-tax and transfer Gini	Post-tax and transfer Gini	Reduction in Gini due to taxes and transfers	Pre-tax and transfer	Post-tax and transfer	Reduction in poverty due to taxes and transfers
Social democratic welfare states						
Sweden, 1995	38	20	47	22	4	82
Norway, 1995	32	22	31	16	4	72
Denmark, 1992	34	21	38	19	4	77
Finland, 1995	36	20	44	18	4	80
Mean	35.0	20.8	40.0	18.8	4.0	77.8
Christian democratic welfare states						
Belgium, 1992	35	21	40	15	4	75
Netherlands, 1994	36	25	31	18	7	62
Germany, 1989[a]	32	25	22	8	5	38
France, 1994	39	28	28	24	8	67
Switzerland, 1992	33	30	9	13	11	16
Mean	35.0	25.8	26.0	15.6	7.0	51.6
Liberal welfare states						
Australia, 1994	40	29	28	19	9	51
Canada, 1994	38	28	26	19	11	42
Ireland, 1995	44	33	25			
UK, 1995	46	35	24	25	12	52
US, 1994	43	35	19	19	16	13
Mean	42.2	32.0	24.4	20.5	12.0	39.5
Grand mean	37.6	26.6	29.4	18.1	7.6	55.9

Sources: Bradley et al. 2003; Moller et al. 2003.

[a] The 1989 figures for Germany are used because the 1994 figures show large changes resulting from unification and are unrepresentative of the rest of the German data.

tributory, income-related benefits (Bismarckian social insurance). It is clear that per dollar spent, one gets less redistribution as one moves from type 1 to type 2 to type 3.

The Anglo-American countries rely more heavily on targeting than the other two types, but they spend much less and thus, as one can see from table 3.3, they achieve less in reduction of poverty and inequality (Huber and Stephens 2001a). The targeting in and of itself is the reason why spending is low, because targeted programs benefit a comparatively small proportion of the population and thus have restricted political support. Thus, the political part of the solution to the paradox is that universalistic (whether flat rate or contributory) benefits generate much more political support and thus a much greater willingness of the households in the middle of the income distribution to accept high levels of taxation.

The crowding-out factor is best illustrated with the example of pensions, the largest public transfer program. With regard to pensions, the redistribution paradox is that the countries with the most unequal public transfers (Norway and Sweden) achieve the greatest amount of redistribution and the most equal post-tax and transfer income distribution among the elderly. The reasons are that all other sources of income are vastly more unequal than public transfers and that highly generous public transfers crowd out private pensions and capital income. To put it differently: in countries with comprehensive earnings related social transfer systems, social spending is much larger than in countries with residual welfare states that rely heavily on means testing, and the size factor overwhelms the distributive profile in determining redistribution.

Table 3.4 demonstrates this element of the paradox. The figures were calculated by Kangas and Palme (1993) on the basis of LIS data. The figures in columns 1–4 are quasi-Ginis (see n. 1). The quasi-Ginis show that Australia, Canada, and the UK have pension systems with benefits most clearly targeted to lower-income groups (col. 1), yet they end up with the most unequal income distributions behind the United States (col. 6).

TABLE 3.4. **Income inequality among the aged population**

	(1)	(2)	(3)	(4)	(5)	(6)	(7)
	Public transfers	Earnings	Private pensions	Capital income	Gross income	Net (after tax) income	% public
Australia	−7	74	61	63	34.1	28	59
Canada	−2	61	53	58	33.4	30	58
Germany	12	73	61	41	29	28	70
Netherlands	4	67	66	82	33	27	69
Norway	11	77	60	54	29.9	24	82
Sweden	15	78	49	44	23.8	14	86
UK	−1	73	53	61	30.9	26	67
US	8	63	52	60	37.8	34	60

Sources: Kangas and Palme 1993; Esping-Andersen 1990, 85; Palme, pers. corr.
Notes: All cell entries are Ginis or quasi-Ginis except those in col. 7.Col. 7 indicates public pensions as a percentage of total income.

The public pension systems in the Nordic countries have the most un-equal profile, but they account for over 80 percent of total income of the elderly (col. 7) and thus produce the most egalitarian final income distributions.

Latin American Class Structure Revisited

Tables 3.1 and 3.2 indicate that large majorities in the Latin American countries have an interest in redistribution. In fact, a breakdown by de-cile, rather than quintile as in the tables, shows that in every Latin Amer-ican country, the seventh decile receives less than 10 percent of national household income, and thus that over two-thirds of the population have an "objective" interest in redistribution (SEDLAC 2010). As we argued in chapter 2, however, reading off political preferences from income lev-els is a completely asociological and ahistorical way of thinking. To ar-rive at a judgment regarding possible political alliances, we need to move from income levels and examine the underlying class structure, and then, in the next section, the possibility and obstacles to left-party political mobilization on this class terrain.

The data in table 3.5 are derived from Portes and Hoffman's (2003) conceptual frame and analysis of household income surveys from eight Latin American countries which represent over three-fourths of the population of Latin America.[3] Portes and Hoffman's class categories are based on a combination of Weberian (marketable assets) and Marxist (production relations) criteria. The Marxist criteria are particularly im-portant in distinguishing between executives and professionals. In both cases, high levels of marketable skills (and probably cultural capital) are the main qualifications for employment in both classes, but the execu-tives are at the top of the chain of command in medium and large capi-talist enterprises and thus derive part of the income from the profitabil-ity of the firm and not just the scarcity of their skills. On the other end of the spectrum, the Marxist categories distinguish between formal and in-formal manual workers who are differentiated from one another by the fact that legal regulations modify the raw capitalist employment relation in the case of formal-sector workers.

As discussed in chapter 2, Weber identified a *social* class as a group of occupations within which intragenerational and intergenerational mo-bility was easy and typical. These social classes are identifiable social

TABLE 3.5. **Latin American class structure, 2000**

Class	Household survey occupations	Eight countries (%)	Brazil (%)	Chile (%)	Costa Rica (%)
Capitalists	Proprietors and managing partners of large/medium firms	1.8	2.0	1.5	1.7
Executives	Managers and administrators of large/medium firms and public institutions	1.6	1.8	1.1	2.4
Professionals	University-trained salaried professionals in public service and large/medium firms	2.8	1.4	6.9	3.2
Petty bourgeoisie	Own-account professionals and technicians, and micro-entrepreneurs with personally supervised staff	8.5	7.4	9.4	10.8
Nonmanual employees	Vocationally trained salaried technicians and white-collar employees	12.4	12.7	16.2	14.1
Manual formal working class	Skilled and unskilled wage workers with labor contracts	23.4	25.3	33.7	32.8
Informal working class	Noncontractual wage workers, casual vendors, and unpaid family workers	45.9	43.5	30.2	34.3
Unclassified		3.6	5.9	1.0	0.7
Total		100	100	100	100

Source: Portes and Hoffman 2003, 46–49, 52.

groups (and not just classifications created by social scientist) and arguably the basis for collective social action. It is possible to identify social classes empirically with social mobility data. On the basis of the data available, we cannot attempt to do that here, but we can identify several instances in which this might be important in moving from Portes and Hoffman's classification as shown in table 3.5 to identifiable social classes and thus to social groups that might be mobilized behind common political goals. Both involve the class categories mentioned in the last paragraph.

First, as we mentioned, both executives and professionals ("elite workers" in Portes and Hoffman's terminology) share a common occupational qualification, a high level of marketable skills. The intergenerational continuity of these groups depends on them being able to pass their qualifications on to the next generation and thus on the educational and cultural environment in the home and, especially important in Latin America, on the purchase of private education. Thus, it seems likely to us that these two groups form a common social class distinct from capitalists who can pass on their privileges through inheritance of productive property. For political action in Latin America, this distinction may not be so important: Portes and Hoffman combine all three groups in their designated "dominant classes," indicating an expectation of common political interests in defense of privilege on the part of these groups.

At the other end of the spectrum is the issue of whether informal and formal manual workers are a common social class based on similar inability to pass on any occupational qualifications to their offspring. This issue is important because many observers of Latin American politics and society underline the differences between the two groups in terms of material well-being. If, however, there is a lot of intergenerational and intragenerational movement between the two groups, and if indeed the same household often combines informal- and formal-sector workers, both of which seem likely, then we might expect few barriers to common political action.

Torche's (2005) study of social mobility in Chile throws some light on the question of mobility barriers in Latin American class structures. She uses a different class scheme than Portes and Hoffman which makes no distinction between informal- and formal-sector workers and which has the top strata accounting for 14 percent of the population, thus combining Portes and Hoffman's top three classes plus a lot more. Her findings show a high degree of closure at the top, indicating high social cohesion of the top three classes, and a lot of fluidity at the bottom (86 percent), indicating few social barriers to cross-class coalitions among the remainder of the population.

The identification of sociologically defined classes, then, reinforces the picture of the potential coalitional possibilities that emerged from our examination of income distribution: approximately two-thirds of Latin Americans are members of the bottom two classes. Thus, the numbers are there for parties interested in advancing an agenda to reduce poverty and redistribute income. That parties of the left have so infrequently reached governing positions, especially before the year 2000, is a very clear indicator of the difficulty of lower-class political mobilization in the region.

Building Effective Redistributive Coalitions in Latin America: Political Options and Challenges

If we lived in a Meltzer-Richard world, the politics of constructing coalitions for redistribution in Latin America would be simple and straightforward. Since two-thirds of households have a material interest in redistribution, party competition would normally produce redistributive governing coalitions. Because we do not live in such a world, the political challenges of translating common class position and interests in redistributive social policy into effective social policy regimes are daunting indeed. One needs to think about the many steps from objective interests to political articulation, agenda setting, legislation, and implementation. In other words, one needs to think about political organization, economic power, political institutions, and public administration.[4] Therefore, although our main concern in this book is with the analysis of the design of social policy effective in reducing poverty and inequality, and with the forces supporting such policies, it is also important briefly to take account of the institutional factors that favor or hinder the passing and implementation of social policy legislation. As we shall see, compared to most advanced industrial countries—with the notable exception of the United States—these institutional factors in Latin America are rather unfavorable for the passage of effective redistributive policies.

Political parties are the prime instruments for the articulation of political demands. By no means do all parties perform this function, however. Specifically, as Blofield and Luna (2011, 172) suggest, Latin American parties in the 1990s by and large failed to represent the socially polarized views on income inequality. A very large proportion of parties, particularly in Latin America, perform only the minimal function of providing labels for candidates for office. As a large literature has demonstrated, many of these candidates and parties seek office by creating clientelistic linkages to their supporters or by relying on charismatic appeals (Kitschelt and Wilkinson 2007; Ames 2001; Calvo and Murillo 2004). Even parties whose candidates run on the basis of broad promises to pursue policies that will improve the situation of particular social groups, such as the poor, the workers, the middle classes, may not have a clearly stated program nor the ability to ensure that their candidates, when elected, will reliably vote for the party's proposals. Again, a large literature has explored the impact of the electoral system on party discipline and shown that a closed list, proportional representation electoral system with possibilities for reelection is most conducive to party discipline, as opposed to a single-member district winner-take-all system and no reelection. The former type of system is by no means universal in Latin America.

Where the electoral system is favorable and programmatic, disciplined parties with a commitment to redistribution exist, they need to win elections to be able to shape social policy in a significant way. This means they need to be able to turn out their core supporters and gain the support of swing voters. Core supporters are voters with strong partisan identification that perhaps was formed in families, work environments, or residential communities with a politically dominant orientation, and who would not consider voting for any other party. As is obvious, only parties in existence for a considerable length of time—long enough to allow for political socialization in families and for the emergence of workplaces and neighborhoods with politically dominant leanings—can count on a sizable group of core voters. Turning out core supporters can largely be done through organizational channels directly, through party officials at various levels and party base organizations. Even Latin American parties with a considerable length of existence, however, do not necessarily have strong base organizations capable of mobilizing large numbers of members to help with election campaigns. In most Latin American countries, left parties in particular saw their organizations destroyed or greatly weakened by authoritarian periods.

Reaching large numbers of swing voters requires a major capacity for communication, and thus money. Mobilizing activists to put up posters and to organize rallies at which candidates speak is simply not enough. Even poster space in prominent places often needs to be rented, and rallies require sound systems and security. But the key to reaching large numbers of potential voters is the media, and media campaigns—if done professionally—are extremely expensive.

For instance, in the Chilean case estimates show that the cost of a campaign for the senate in 1997 and 2001 in districts with more than 500,000 voters, ranged from US$850,000 to US$5 million. For an average-sized district, the cost ranged from US$250,000 to US$3 million; the average cost of a campaign for the chamber of deputies ranged from

US$100,000 to US$340,000 (Fuentes 2004). It goes without saying that costly campaigns greatly disadvantage parties committed to redistribution, that is, parties of the left. Big business and wealthy individuals tend to fit the rational actor model and everywhere show a strong average preference for parties committed to low taxes. Where left parties are strong and have good chances of winning elections, big business may well make some contributions to them to ensure access to a potential left government, but the financial playing field for the left remains uneven.

In Latin America, hardly any countries provide public funding for parties or even regulate campaign contributions effectively. Chile is in the vanguard on that count, but still far from having evened the playing field. The right was able to block efforts to provide public financing to parties and regulate campaign expenditures for years. In 2003 the Congress finally passed a law that regulated the financing of campaigns (complemented in 2004 with a law that established sanctions for violations). The law was part of the Agenda for the Modernization of the State, which began to receive support in the midst of a number of corruption scandals (Garretón 2005). The law established caps on expenditures for each candidate, as well as limits on private donations from each individual, and it provided for state reimbursement of campaign expenditures. It did not, however, provide public funding to political parties for their ongoing activities, only for election campaigns, and it did not provide public funding for presidential elections. Moreover, the ceilings on expenditures and donations were set very high, thus perpetuating the advantage of the right. The enforcement capacity of the electoral administration has remained limited, and the right has continued to outspend the left greatly.

The influence of the media—mainly television—grows with the weakness of party identification and party organization. The political behavior literature has shown that selective perception is an important filter. In other words, persons with strong political identification select out and interpret messages that conform to their predispositions, which is another way of saying that they are not easily swayed by clever political advertising. Strong party organizations can reach more people face to face and thus counteract media messages. This situation can set in motion a vicious cycle wherein scarcity of strong political identification and party organization leave the great majority of voters susceptible to the most persuasive media images and sound bites, which in turn provides little incentive for ambitious politicians to invest in party building rather than in the search for wealthy donors and successful PR firms. Certainly, Latin American elections over the past three decades have been replete with successful candidates forming ephemeral electoral machines. The practice has given rise to the emergence of flash parties, that is, parties that win a good share of votes in one election and then decline rapidly to insignificance (Mustillo 2009).

What is needed is nothing less than repeated election of a party or coalition of parties with a strong commitment to the construction of a strong redistributive welfare state. We say repeated because it is impossible, even for a programmatic party with a clear majority in the legislature or control of the executive, to build such a welfare state in one term. The Frente Amplio in Uruguay was very active in legislating and implementing reforms in its first term, but the reach of the major reforms of the income distribution system remained at roughly one-third of the population—not sufficient to build a support base among beneficiaries who could constitute a solid political majority.

Policy Options for Income Redistribution

As the preceding discussion in this chapter makes clear, a successful policy package for a long-term strategy of redistribution and poverty reduction must both effectively redistribute income and generate support from a large majority of the electorate. Critically, the policy package needs to be able to generate support in the sixth- and seventh-income deciles and the corresponding class groups, better-off formal-sector workers and lower-income nonmanual employees. Thus, although policies targeted at the poor have a place in the overall package, they cannot be the centerpiece of the package because they do not tie the middle of the income and class distribution to the political coalition.

As tables 3.1 and 3.2 make clear, one cannot rely on contributory social insurance to redistribute income in Latin America. We saw in table 3.4 that contributory social insurance was (is) very important for producing income equality among the aged in advanced capitalist democracies. The data in that table are for the late 1980s and early 1990s and thus for an aged population whose working life largely coincided with the Golden Age of postwar capitalism (1945–75), when the typical family was headed by a male worker who worked his entire career in full-time formal-sector work. As Palier (2010) and Palier and Martin

(2008) point out, even in these countries, this is no longer the case, and thus Bismarckian contributory social insurance no longer achieves Beveridgean (universalistic) goals. The male breadwinner family is no longer the dominant family type, and many people experience career interruptions or work in temporary and part-time jobs, so the Bismarckian social insurance no longer delivers the near-universal social protection that it once did even in advanced capitalist democracies.

In Latin America, it was never the case that contributory social insurance reached near-universal coverage, and many of those covered did not work an entire career in a formal-sector job, so insurance never even delivered adequate social protection for all of those covered. Moreover, even in the advanced social policy regimes of Latin America where coverage was highest, the occupationally stratified structure of benefits meant that it resulted in little if any income redistribution, as one can see from tables 3.1 and 3.2. Although reducing the public pension privileges of upper-income groups belongs on the agenda of the left (see chap. 6), contributory social insurance will never be a source of significant redistribution in Latin America because of the size of the informal sector.

If one cannot expect that contributory benefits will result in much redistribution, and if targeted benefits will not generate broad support for the policy regime, one is left with tax-financed universalistic benefits or benefits that, though falling short of universal coverage, provide for very broad-based coverage. In advanced capitalist democracies, the usual structure of tax-financed transfers is flat rate, that is, all households or individuals receive the same benefit, though sometimes the benefits can be partly needs based, with, for example, larger child benefits for the third child or more children. In these countries, LIS studies have shown that, with few exceptions, little redistribution is achieved on the tax side, and it is transfers that account for the lion's share of redistribution (e.g., see Mahler and Jesuit 2005).

In fact, flat-rate benefits (transfers or services) financed by a proportional tax will be very redistributive. We illustrate this option using the examples of income distribution in Brazil in 1997 and Uruguay in 1998 (from tables 3.1 and 3.2) in tables 3.6 and 3.7. Panel A assumes that a proportional tax of 20 percent is levied to finance social spending, which is roughly the total social spending level of Brazil and Uruguay in 2000. Panel B redistributes this 20 percent in social benefits equally across the quintiles. As one can see, the bottom quintile is substantially materially better off in both cases. Our intention with these examples is to illustrate the redistributive impact of flat-rate benefits financed by a proportional tax, but we also think such a policy is a realistic goal for policy makers. As we noted earlier in this chapter, some Latin American countries already have essentially proportional taxes, so it is not an unrealistic goal for other countries, most of which have moderately regressive tax systems. As one can see from table 3.2, the incidence of health and education spending in Uruguay is more egalitarian than flat rate, and the social assistance spending is progressive. The table shows that the problem is social security spending. In this area, it is not realistic to aim at flat-rate benefits, but the example of the Nordic pension systems (table 3.4) shows that that is not necessary in order to achieve significant redistribution.

Basic universalism calls for policies that guarantee a minimum income and provide basic free or subsidized health care and child care and labor market training, along with quality primary and secondary education (Molina 2006). The limits with regard to flat-rate universalism in social transfers are that the benefits received by those in the top decile are "wasted" if the goals are poverty reduction and redistribution. One could preserve the principle of universalism and claw back a large part of benefits with high marginal taxes as the Nordic countries do, but the tax systems of Latin American countries are currently too ineffective to do this. Basic universalism solves the "waste" problem by targeting the top-income deciles out of the system, so that it retains the middle-class inclusion aspects of flat-rate universalism. Panel C in tables 3.6 and 3.7 illustrates the principle behind basic universalism. Cleanly targeting out the top two quintiles is not technically realistic and probably not desirable because of disincentive effects at the income threshold, so panel D is perhaps a more realistic illustration of how the systems would work.

The policy logic is different for the basic public services of health and education. Here, tax-financed, flat-rate universalism, that is, quality health and education as a right of citizenship, is necessary to prevent the upper middle classes from exiting the public system. The contrast between the Chilean educational system and health care system is indicative of the pitfalls of having the upper middle class outside of one of these essential public services (see chap. 6). With only 14 percent of the population in the private health care system, it was possible for the Lagos government to assemble broad support for the health care reform,

TABLE 3.6. **Illustration of flat-rate universalism and basic universalism using income distribution in Brazil, 1997**

A. Assume a proportional tax of 20 percent

Top quintile	66	−	(0.2 × 66)	=	13.2	
Fourth quintile	17	−	(0.2 × 17)	=	3.4	
Third quintile	10	−	(0.2 × 10)	=	2	
Second quintile	5	−	(0.2 × 5)	=	1	
Bottom quintile	2	−	(0.2 × 2)	=	0.4	

B. Add a flat-rate benefit to after-tax income (flat-rate universalism)

Top quintile	66	−	13.2	=	52.8	+	4	56.8
Fourth quintile	17	−	3.4	=	13.6	+	4	17.6
Third quintile	10	−	2	=	8	+	4	12
Second quintile	5	−	1	=	4	+	4	8
Bottom quintile	2	−	0.4	=	1.6	+	4	5.6

C. Assume that the bottom three quintiles receive all of the benefits (basic universalism)

Top quintile	66	−	13.2	=	52.8	+	0	52.8
Fourth quintile	17	−	3.4	=	13.6	+	0	13.6
Third quintile	10	−	2	=	8	+	6.7	14.7
Second quintile	5	−	1	=	4	+	6.7	10.7
Bottom quintile	2	−	0.4	=	1.6	+	6.7	8.3

D. Assume some leakage in the distribution of benefits

Top quintile	66	−	13.2	=	52.8	+	0	52.8
Fourth quintile	17	−	3.4	=	13.6	+	3	16.6
Third quintile	10	−	2	=	8	+	6	14
Second quintile	5	−	1	=	4	+	6	10
Bottom quintile	2	−	0.4	=	1.6	+	5	6.6

whereas with more than half of the student population in the private state-subsidized or full-private schools, education reform proved much more intractable.

To this point, we have focused on redistribution. Governments can also affect pre-tax and transfer distribution. By expanding enrollments in all levels of education and facilitating high completion rates, governments can increase the supply of workers with high education and thereby lower the income-skill premium. Governments can raise the minimum wage, which in many Latin American countries has a magnified effect because some government transfers, such as minimum pensions and disability payments, are indexed to the minimum wage. Finally, government can change labor market regulations to favor unions, which can increase unionization and increase the bargaining power of unions at the negotiating table. In fact, we know from the studies of income distribution in López-Calva and Lustig (2010) that all three of these fac-

TABLE 3.7. **Illustration of flat-rate universalism and basic universalism using income distribution in Uruguay, 1998**

A. Assume a proportional tax of 20 percent

Top quintile	50 −	(0.2 × 50)	=	10	
Fourth quintile	22 −	(0.2 × 22)	=	4.4	
Third quintile	14 −	(0.2 × 14)	=	2.8	
Second quintile	9 −	(0.2 × 9)	=	1.8	
Bottom quintile	5 −	(0.2 × 5)	=	1	

B. Add a flat-rate benefit to after-tax income (flat-rate universalism)

Top quintile	50 −	10	=	40	+	4	44
Fourth quintile	22 −	4.4	=	17.6	+	4	21.6
Third quintile	14 −	2.8	=	11.2	+	4	15.2
Second quintile	9 −	1.8	=	7.2	+	4	11.2
Bottom quintile	5 −	1	=	4	+	4	8

C. Assume that the bottom three quintiles receive all of the benefits (basic universalism)

Top quintile	50 −	10	=	40	+	0	40
Fourth quintile	22 −	4.4	=	17.6	+	0	17.6
Third quintile	14 −	2.8	=	11.2	+	6.7	17.9
Second quintile	9 −	1.8	=	7.2	+	6.7	13.9
Bottom quintile	5 −	1	=	4	+	6.7	10.7

D. Assume some leakage in the distribution of benefits

Top quintile	50 −	10	=	40	+	0	40
Fourth quintile	22 −	4.4	=	17.6	+	3	20.6
Third quintile	14 −	2.8	=	11.2	+	6	17.2
Second quintile	9 −	1.8	=	7.2	+	6	13.2
Bottom quintile	5 −	1	=	4	+	5	9

tors played a role in the decline of inequality that occurred in most Latin American countries after 2000 (see chap. 6).

The conditional cash transfer (CCT) programs that have been implemented in several Latin American countries in the past decade represent attempts to address both pre-tax and transfer income distribution by improving the human capital of future generations at the bottom and redistribution through transfers to alleviate poverty and inequality in the present generation. CCTs such as the Brazilian Bolsa Família, for instance, provide a small cash transfer to poor families as long as they keep their children in school and the children receive medical checkups. While it is not essential to link the goals of poverty reduction and investment in human capital in one policy, it is essential for the success of human capital investment policies that poverty reduction policies be pursued at the same time. The very strong link between poverty and cognitive skills shown at the end of chapter 5 is a testament to this strategy.

Conclusion

In the initial section of this chapter, we clarified some frequent misunderstandings about the relationship of the structure of social policies and redistribution. Welfare state benefits can be divided into three types: means or income-tested, tax-financed benefits; flat-rate, tax-financed benefits going to everyone; and contributory, income-related benefits. It is clear that per dollar spent, one gets less redistribution as one moves from the first type to the last. It is not true, however, that the other types of benefits are not redistributive. That depends on the structure of financing. In advanced capitalist countries, even contributory social insurance is generally quite redistributive. In Latin America, however, this is not the case because too few people work in formal-sector employment for their full working life, and thus contributory social insurance only adequately covers a minority of the population.

Thus, we argue that effective redistributive social policy in Latin America must focus on the other two types, means-tested benefits and flat-rate benefits, both of which are tax-financed. Even in advanced capitalist countries, most redistribution occurs on the benefits side rather than the tax side, and this is even truer in Latin America, where the tax systems are generally proportional or slightly regressive. From the data in tables 3.1 and 3.2, one can see that the main public services, health and education, roughly conform to a flat-rate benefit. In Uruguay, the benefits are somewhat more progressive than flat rate, and in Brazil somewhat less. Even in Brazil, however, social services are very redistributive as the Gini falls by 7 points once they are included along with taxes and contributory and noncontributory transfers (ECLAC 2005, 163). We argued that for an effective redistributive policy to be politically viable, it must include both types of benefits. Targeted benefits are most effective at reducing poverty, but alone they are not politically viable because they do not include the crucial middle sectors of the class and income distributions that are essential elements of a majority coalition for redistribution and poverty reduction.

The income distribution data showed that, in every Latin American country, the seventh decile got less than 10 percent of national income, so large majorities in all countries stand to benefit from redistribution. Our examination of data on class structures showed similarly

that class coalitions that include two-thirds of households could be as-
sembled without even including nonmanual employees, another 12 percent of households. Thus, the socioeconomic terrain is very favorable for
redistributive politics.

In the next section, we explored why sustained redistribution was so
rare in Latin America, even in democratic periods, despite the favorable terrain. Even in advanced industrial democracies, the barriers to
left party mobilization, left government, and effective policy making are
high. Class structures generate processes that reproduce themselves.
Material inequality begets political inequality, not just because of differences in income and wealth but also because of differences in literacy and education, cultural capital, and social networks. As Mann (1973)
points out, "socialism [or any counterhegemonic ideology] is learned."
The agents in this learning or socialization process are left parties and
social movements. In Latin America, the obstacles to left party and
movement mobilization are higher because of greater inequality, which
expresses itself through the multiple processes outlined in this chapter
and the previous one, such as weaker unions, greater clientelism, shorter
life spans of programmatic parties, greater asymmetry in media access,
greater differences in funding sources for parties of the left and right,
and so forth. In the final section, using data from Brazil and Uruguay,
we illustrated our argument that flat-rate benefits financed by a proportional tax would be very redistributive. We then argued for policies that
follow the principles of basic universalism: a guaranteed minimum income; basic free or subsidized health care and child care; and labor market training, and quality primary and secondary education. We ended by
illustrating the strong redistributive effects of basic universalism.

CHAPTER FOUR

The Development of Social Policy Regimes in the ISI Period

T he formation of welfare states or—more modestly—social policy regimes in Latin America has to be understood in the context of late
and dependent development. As laid out in chapter 2, this context con-
ditioned the weakness of democracy, labor, and the left, which in turn
gave rise to a sequencing of democratization, left incumbency in legislatures and executives, and welfare state construction that was different
from the sequencing in advanced industrial democracies. The first social
security programs in South America were generally established before
1940, but with the exception of Uruguay and to a lesser extent Chile, the
spread of democratization and significant left influence in legislatures or
executives did not emerge until the post–World War II period. Thus, left
parties and their leaders found fragmented and stratified social policy
configurations on which to build welfare states. The sequence was similar to the German one, where the Bismarckian legacy prevented a unification of the pension and health insurance systems after World War II
(Huber and Stephens 2001a). There are only two cases in Latin America in which center-left parties in democracies were able to shape the initial features of the welfare state and thus to leave their imprint: Uruguay
and Costa Rica. In Uruguay in the formative period it was less an ideologically left party that designed the initial programs of social protection
than a president, José Batlle y Ordóñez, with a strong commitment to
nation building, democratization, education, and social justice, emerging
victorious from putting down the last armed insurrection. Batlle, however, established control over the Colorado Party, and thanks to the persistence of democracy the party (or important factions in the party) was

able to consolidate and then came to play an important role in the further expansion of social protection.

A further important difference between the political economies of Europe and Latin America needs to be brought into relief: Latin American industrialization took off as a result of deliberate protectionist policies starting in the 1930s and were fully articulated and implemented as the strategy of import substitution industrialization (ISI) in the late 1940s (Prebisch 1950). In the post–World War II period, European countries pursued much more open trade strategies; in particular, they sought to be competitive in manufacturing exports, whereas Latin America continued to rely on raw material exports. The extremely high tariff protection enjoyed by the manufacturing sector in Latin America made it possible for governments to finance social security schemes with high payroll taxes, because employers could pass on those costs to the consumer. High import and export taxes also constituted an important source of revenue for the governments. Accordingly, governments could expand social security without taxing economically dominant and privileged groups directly and thus without strengthening tax systems, particularly income tax systems. The weakness of the tax systems was to become a major problem for the systems of social protection in the period of neoliberal reforms and thereafter.

Development of Social Policy Regimes

Throughout the first four decades of the twentieth century, coverage by pension and health insurance schemes in Latin America remained with few exceptions confined to the military, high-level civil servants, and a few additional strategically located groups of public- and private-sector employees. The thrust of efforts to expand coverage to most of the urban economically active population emerged during and particularly after World War II, along with the promotion of ISI.[1] The advance of ISI provided the growing constituencies for pensions and health care, the growing urban working and middle classes, and the fiscal bases for the insurance schemes. The large majority of financing came from a combination of employer and employee contributions, supplemented to varying degrees by the state. In cross-national perspective, the countries that advanced more with ISI were more likely to expand their social security systems.

The two early innovators in social policy were Uruguay and Chile.[2] Batlle in Uruguay was a pioneer in establishing broad-based social policy schemes; he was an innovator not only in Latin America but also internationally (Hicks 1999, 50–53; Social Security Administration 2010, 189–94).[3] By the early 1920s Uruguay had old-age pensions for civil servants and for employees in public and private providers of public services (railroads, telegraph, trams, telephone, gas, electricity), as well as noncontributory pensions for indigent disabled and elderly people, a maternal health care program, and an expanded system of public hospitals (Filgueira 1995; Papadópulos 1992). Chile established pension and health insurance schemes under the leadership of reformist president Alessandri in 1925, with the help of military pressure to break conservative resistance. The schemes covered miners and different groups of blue- and white-collar workers separately, thus initiating a pattern of extreme fragmentation and stratification that grew to some 150 different programs by the 1970s (Raczynski 1994).

In the 1930s, Brazil, Colombia, Peru, and Venezuela all passed some pension and/or health care legislation, but effective coverage remained highly restricted. The 1940s saw the establishment of major pension and health care funds in Argentina and Mexico, but coverage in Mexico reached less than 5 percent of the population by 1950 (Dion 2010, 154), whereas it came to include a much larger share of the population in Argentina. Perón rapidly expanded social security coverage to reach some 70 percent of the labor force (Mesa-Lago 1978). He also encouraged expansion of the mutual health insurance funds run by the unions, the *obras sociales*, and of public hospitals. The 1940s and 1950s was also a period of expansion of coverage and benefits in Uruguay. In 1943 family allowances were introduced for all employees in industry and commerce, and in 1958 they were extended to the unemployed. In 1943 rural workers were incorporated into the social security system (Filgueira 1995; Papadópulos 1992, 45). In Chile, the big expansions came between 1960 and 1973, at the same time that Costa Rica undertook a big push for expansion of social security. In 1961 an amendment to the Costa Rican constitution passed that mandated universalization of social security coverage within a decade. Although this goal was not achieved, coverage expanded to over half of the economically active population during the decade.

By the mid-1970s, the group of countries Mesa-Lago (1978) called the pioneer countries because of their comparatively early introduction of social security schemes—Argentina, Brazil, Chile, and Uruguay—had expanded coverage of these schemes to a majority of their populations.[4] Argentina covered close to 70 percent of the economically active population, Brazil about 85 percent, Chile about 75 percent, and Uruguay over 90 percent; Costa Rica lagged far behind, with just below 40 percent, but expanded coverage rapidly in the 1970s (Mesa-Lago 1994, 22).[5] Colombia, Guatemala, Mexico, Panama, Peru, and Venezuela had expanded their coverage to between 30 percent and 60 percent of the economically active population; in the remaining Latin American countries coverage remained below 30 percent.

The structure of the social security schemes resembled the Bismarckian, or conservative-corporatist type that prevailed in continental Europe (Esping-Andersen 1990). Because of the history of their development, with new schemes being developed for newly incorporated groups while the old generous schemes for privileged or strategic groups were left in place, the social security systems as a whole were stratified, fragmented, and regressive. They were built on formal-sector employment and on the male breadwinner model, typically providing pensions, health care, and family allowances. The system of social protection did not recognize a citizenship right to protection from poverty resulting from sickness, invalidity, old age, or lack of employment; that right was based on contributions made through formal-sector employment. To the extent that women without formal-sector jobs and children were protected, they were protected as dependents of formal-sector male workers. As of the 1970s, in most countries the informal sector and the rural sector remained excluded from social protection. Exceptions were Uruguay, where rural workers were included in the social security system in 1943, and noncontributory pensions for indigents and other groups had been established in 1919; Argentina, where pensions for rural workers and the self-employed were introduced in 1954; and Brazil, where noncontributory pension coverage was expanded through rural unions in 1971.

Cross-National Analysis

As outlined in chapter 2, our methodological approach is to establish the broad parameters of the associations of our hypothesized causal variables with quantitative analysis and then to make the case for causality and to uncover the causal mechanisms by examining historical sequences in selected cases. Our data series for our dependent variables begin late in the period under examination in this chapter. For social spending, data are available for almost all of our countries beginning in the early 1970s. For inequality and poverty, the data are still so spotty for this period that we do not attempt to analyze them. Since we date the end of the ISI period as 1980, the spending time series is very short. With such a short time series, one gains very little analytical leverage by conducting pooled time series analysis, since almost all of the variation is between countries, so we opt for simple cross-sectional analysis.

The selection of 1980 as the end of the ISI period is somewhat arbitrary. If one examines the Escaith and Paunovic (2004) update of the Morley et al. (1999) time series on market liberalization in Latin America, one finds that the summary index and the critical (for marking the end of ISI) trade liberalization index begin to move significantly upward in 1974. This change, however, is due to a few cases, most notably Chile under Pinochet. For most Latin American countries, the big changes do not occur until the onset of the debt crisis in 1982. The summary index moves from .40 in 1974 to .50 1982 and then to .82 in 1997, when it stabilizes.

Table 4.1 shows the data for our dependent and independent variables.[6] The data for our dependent variables are for 1980. In addition to our data on total social spending as a percentage of GDP, we have data for pension coverage and health care and maternity coverage from Mesa-Lago (1994, 22). The coverage data allow us to correct for one of the deficiencies of social spending as indicator for welfare effort (see chap. 3), namely, that unlike in OECD countries (Bradley et al. 2003), social spending is not necessarily redistributive in Latin America. In some programs and in some countries, it can be concentrated on upper-income groups. An indicator that also includes the breadth of coverage helps correct for this. Our summary index is a summation of the standardized scores for total social spending as a percentage of GDP, pension coverage as a percentage of the economically active population, and health care and maternity coverage as a percentage of the total population.[7]

Table 4.1 shows that social policy regimes cluster into three relatively clear groups (also see fig. 4.1). The top group, the advanced social policy regimes that we focus on throughout this book, consists of Argentina, Brazil, Chile, Costa Rica, and Uruguay. Among students of Latin American social policy there is almost universal agreement that Argentina, Chile, Costa Rica, and Uruguay belong in this top group (Filgueira

TABLE 4.1. **Politics and welfare in Latin America at the end of the ISI period**

	Cumulative democracy	Cumulative left political strength	GDP per capita, 1960–80	Industrial employment, 1960–80	Urban population, 1960–80	Urban working-class presence[a]	Aged population, 1960–80	Social spending	Pensions coverage, 1980	Sickness/maternity coverage, 1980	Welfare generosity[b]
Argentina	10	0.1	10,529	34.1	78.4	3.9	6.9	12.2	69	79	3.6
Brazil	9.5	5.1	5,307	20.3	56.4	0.3	3.7	8.4	87	96	3.9
Chile	16.5	10.5	6,678	28.5	74.9	2.8	5.1	15.2	61	67	3.6
Costa Rica	30.5	16.2	6,568	20.2	39.5	-0.8	4.6	15.5	68	84	4.5
Uruguay	28	14.4	6,981	28.8	82.3	3.3	9.0	14.2	81	48	3.6
Mean	18.9	9.3	7,212.9	26.4	66.3	1.9	5.9	13.1	73.2	74.8	3.8
Mexico	0	0.0	6,378	24.2	58.8	1.1	4.2	6.7	42	53	0.2
Panama	6	2.5	3,449	9.4	46.7	-2.1	4.3	11.6	52	50	1.8
Venezuela	19	17.3	11,725	25.0	71.0	2.0	2.9	7.1	50	45	0.4
Mean	8.3	6.6	7,183.9	19.5	58.8	.3	3.8	8.5	48.0	49.3	.8
Bolivia	8	10.6	3,186	20.4	40.2	-0.7	3.4	5.6	19	25	-1.9
Colombia	13	0.1	4,070	19.7	56.3	0.2	3.4	7	30	15	-1.4
Dominican Republic	3	2.4	3,168	16.4	40.2	-1.4	3.0	5.2	12	4	-3.0
Ecuador	9	0.9	3,767	19.5	40.0	-0.8	4.3	9.6	21	9	-1.3
El Salvador	0	0.0	4,296	16.4	40.3	-1.3	2.8	5.5	12	6	-2.8
Guatemala	4.5	4.5	4,273	16.3	35.3	-1.7	2.8	3.6	33	14	-2.2
Honduras	3	4.9	1,834	11.7	28.9	-2.8	2.5	5.9	14	7	-2.6
Nicaragua	0	0.0	3,588	16.8	45.8	-0.9	2.4	9.3	19	9	-1.5
Paraguay	0	0.0	4,970	19.1	37.8	-1.1	5.5	3.5	21	9	-2.9
Peru	7.5	6.4	3,167	18.4	56.5	0.0	3.5	4.1	37	16	-1.9
Mean	4.8	3.0	3,631.9	17.5	42.1	-1.1	3.4	5.9	21.8	11.4	-2.2

[a]Sum of standard scores of industrial employment and urban population.
[b]Sum of standard scores of pension coverage, sick/maternity coverage, and social spending.

2005; Huber 1996; Huber and Stephens 2010; Mesa-Lago 1989, 1994; Segura-Ubiergo 2007).[8] On our index, Brazil appears to be clearly in the top group, mainly because of its high levels of coverage. The coverage figures for Brazil jump dramatically in 1971 because of a law passed by the military government extending coverage to rural workers. The benefits to rural workers, however, were meager as can be seen from the fact that they resulted in virtually no increase in social spending. In fact, total social spending is stable in Brazil from 1970 to the return of democracy in 1985, at which point social spending doubles in a decade. Even after this large increase in spending, Filgueira (2005; also see Huber and Stephens 2010) places Brazil along with Mexico in a separate category because the benefits are deeply stratified by occupation. This arrangement fits with the fact that inequality and poverty are much higher in Brazil as well as in Mexico than they are in the four other advanced social policy regimes (see chaps. 5 and 6).[9]

Our second group—Mexico, Venezuela, and Panama—is sometimes also identified in the Latin American comparative social policy literature (Martínez Franzoni 2007b). On our index, this group is qualitatively above the next group. It may be argued that Brazil belongs in this group in the early period but converges on the higher group after the return to democracy, and yet more so, with the advent of the Lula government.[10]

Two variables that emerge from our theoretical framework, democracy and left political strength, have relatively straightforward operationalizations. Because we argue that the effects of democracy and of left political strength operate through the cumulative historical record of democracy and left strength, and not just through the political situation at the time of measurement of the dependent variable, we measure both by the cumulative record since 1945. In the case of democracy, we classify the political regimes as authoritarian regime, restricted democracy, and full democracy and score 0.5 for each year of restricted democracy and 1 for each year of democracy. In the case of left political strength, we add a score of 1 for each year of left and center-left executive and a fraction equal to the number of left and center-left seats in the lower house divided by the total number of seats in the lower house; we then divide this number by 2. These indices are found in the first two columns of table 4.1

In studies of welfare state development in OECD countries, a second measure often used to operationalize power resources theory is union density, for which there is an excellent comparable time series available for the whole postwar period for all countries (Ebbinghaus and Visser

2000). For Latin America, the union density data exist only for scattered country years, and they are of questionable quality and comparability. In any case, they are not available for this period. Our proxy for union density is "urban working-class presence," which is a summation of the standardized scores for industrial employment as a percentage of the labor force and urban population as a percentage of the total population.[11] We think most students of Latin American labor movements would agree that this is a reasonable proxy, although Brazil is probably too low on the measure and the positions of Chile and Uruguay should probably be switched.

Two variables used to operationalize the functionalist logic of industrialism theory are GDP per capita and percentage of the population over sixty-four years of age. A frequently used measure of international exposure (or "globalization") is imports plus exports as a percentage of GDP. There are two contradictory hypotheses about the effect of trade exposure for social policy. According to one, first put forth by Cameron (1978) for advanced capitalist democracies, openness creates vulnerability and thus demands for compensation by the losers in international economic competition, and consequently leads to greater social spending. Rodrik (1997) has found evidence supporting this view for developing countries. The contrary view regards the costs of generous social policy as an added labor cost and thus a disadvantage in international competition, which in turn generates a "race to the bottom" as nations exposed to trade cut social benefits in order to improve competitiveness. In his test of social policy outcomes in Latin America during this period, Segura-Ubiergo (2007, 34–37) provides a different argument about the role of trade exposure. Based on our earlier discussion of this period (Huber 1996), he argues that trade closure should promote ISI and thus expand the constituency for modern social policy, the urban working and middle classes. If this is the mechanism by which trade closure promotes generous social policy, then it is unclear why one needs a measure of trade openness, since our measure of urban working-class presence measures the presumed outcome of trade closure directly. For the record, we measured trade exposure two different ways, exports plus imports as a percentage of GDP (as Segura-Ubiergo does) and with the Morley trade liberalization index, and neither of them was significant in our analyses in the presence of our urban working-class measure.

Table 4.2 contains a correlation matrix with variables included in our analysis. As one can see, all of the independent variables are strongly

TABLE 4.2. **Correlates of welfare generosity**

Variables	(1)	(2)	(3)	(4)	(5)
1) Cumulative democracy					
2) Cumulative left political strength	.81				
3) GDP per capita	.50	.42			
4) Aged population	.52	.22	.45		
5) Urban working-class presence	.51	.32	.80	.68	
6) Welfare generosity	.71	.47	.59	.61	.63

TABLE 4.3. **OLS estimates of determinants of welfare generosity ($N = 18$)**

Variables	Model 1	Model 2	Model 3
Cumulative democracy	.166**	.156**	.162**
GDP per capita (thousands)	.329	—	—
Urban working-class presence	—	.530*	—
Aged population	—	—	.531
Constant	−3.260**	−1.449*	−3.702**
R^2	.52**	.55***	.52**

* $p \leq .05$; ** $p \leq .01$; *** $p \leq .001$.

correlated to welfare generosity with the exception of left political strength, which is only moderately (but significantly) correlated to it. In table 4.3, we regress welfare generosity on democracy, the strongest determinant according to the correlations, and the other three strong determinants. Other than democracy, only urban working-class presence emerges as a significant determinant of welfare effort. To compare the substantive effect of these two variables, we calculate the effect of a two-standard-deviation change of the independent variable on the dependent variable when controlling for the other independent variable. A change of this size in democracy is associated with a 2.9 unit increase in welfare generosity. In the case of urban working-class presence, the increase is 2.0 units. As one can see from table 4.1, the additive effect of these two variables accounts for most of the difference between the top group and the bottom group on the welfare generosity index.

We can move to the case analysis with the aid of figure 4.1. In our earlier work on social policy in Latin America (Huber 1996, 146–52), we contended that there were two paths to generous social policy regimes at end of the ISI period: a democratic path (Chile, Costa Rica, and Uruguay) and an elite-driven co-optation path (Argentina and Brazil). One can see these paths clearly in the figure. In table 4.1 one can see that all

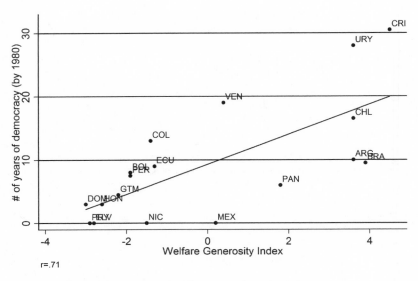

FIGURE 4.1. Years of democracy and welfare generosity, 1980

three countries following the democratic path are also characterized by high levels of left political strength, in sharp contrast to the two countries following the co-optative path. In the co-optative path, political leaders (Vargas and Perón) recognized the power potential of the urban working class, which was growing due to the ISI growth model, and acted to incorporate it into the political regimes in a top-down fashion. The table also shows that Costa Rica is distinctive among the five leaders in that the urban working class was relatively small, and indeed unions in Costa Rica were far weaker during this period than in the other four cases.

We can observe that these two paths are replicated in the second group, with Mexico following the Argentine/Brazilian path and Venezuela following the Chilean/Uruguayan path.[12] Panama, by contrast, is completely anomalous, with none of the features of either path; it is characterized by low levels of democracy, left political strength, industrial employment, urbanization, and GDP per capita.[13]

Advancement in ISI, then, was clearly an important structural factor that facilitated the development of social security systems with wide coverage. It was not a necessary condition, however, as Costa Rica demonstrates. Industrial employment reached its highest level for any country and any years in our data series (ILO 2003) in Argentina from 1960 to

1980, with 34 percent total employment. Costa Rica stood at 18 percent in 1960 and reached 23 percent in 1980, clearly behind Mexico, Uruguay, and Venezuela, in that order, and close to Chile and Brazil in that year.

Politically, longer existence of democracy was favorable for an expansion of social protection, as was the existence of a strong democratic left.[14] As noted, Uruguay, Chile, and Costa Rica fit this pattern. Yet, those were again not necessary conditions; incorporation in response to growing industrialization and strength of organized labor constituted an alternative route to expansion of a social safety net, as in Argentina and Brazil. Between 1945 and 1980, Costa Rica and Uruguay had by far the strongest records of democratic rule, followed by Venezuela and Chile (see table 4.1). Argentina and Brazil lagged behind all of them and Colombia.

Democracy tends to favor expansion of social expenditure because politicians of all political colors are responsive to their constituents. In the short run, however, the allocation of social expenditure may well reflect the interests of privileged groups. What is crucial is that in the long run, democracy affords the opportunity for groups representing the underprivileged to organize and attempt to influence policy and thus to change the nature of the social safety net and the allocation of social expenditure. The key instrument to influence policy in favor of low-income groups and the poor is the political party, more specifically political parties of the center-left or left.

Uruguay and Costa Rica were very high on our index of left political strength from 1945 to 1980, followed by Chile (table 4.1). The only other countries with scores above 10 were Venezuela and Bolivia. Although the franchise remained restricted until 1970, the preceding long period of restricted democracy offered the opportunity for Chilean parties to the left of center to grow, consolidate as organizations, build an electoral support base, and begin to influence social policy. What explains the medium level of social protection in Venezuela, despite the strong presence of a center-left party, is the fact that the ambitious reforms initiated during the three years of full democracy and rule by this party, from 1945 to 1948, were rolled back by the conservative military dictatorship that overthrew democracy and held power for the following ten years. In the decade 1958–68, political competition and latitude of action in policy remained highly constrained by the Pact of Punto Fijo, the agreement among political elites that reestablished democracy in 1958. Expansion of social protection only came back onto the agenda in the mid-1960s, so over a decade of democracy and left presence was lost compared to Chile, for instance.

Our data analysis in chapter 5 demonstrates the importance of long periods of democracy and of long-term strength of left-of-center parties for reductions in poverty and inequality. It shows that democracy drives up public expenditures on social security and welfare, health, and education. Partisanship does not make a consistent difference for the amount of expenditures. In the long run, however, democracy is associated with lower levels of poverty and of inequality, as is left partisanship. Higher levels of expenditures on social security and welfare in a democratic context are associated with lower levels of inequality.

The historical record of the expansion of the social safety net demonstrates the importance of left-of-center and left parties in government. The Colorados, inspired by reformist president Batlle (1903–7 and 1911–16), dominated in Uruguay in the 1910s, when the social security system was first established, and in the period 1948–54, when it was expanded and reorganized (Papadópulos 1992). The Partido Liberación Nacional in Costa Rica dominated the legislature in 1961 when the constitutional amendment for universalization of social security was passed (Rosenberg 1979). In Chile significant efforts to expand coverage came in the 1960s and early 1970s, in the competition between the Christian Democrats and the left and under pressure from unions (Borzutzky 2002, 48, 97–120, 139–45). In Venezuela, the short-lived Acción Democrática government in 1945–48 passed ambitious reforms, which subsequently were rolled back. As noted, Argentina illustrates an alternative path to a social security system with wide coverage, the path via populist authoritarianism and semidemocracy, driven by potential and actual labor strength. The social security system was established by Perón, and subsequently the Peronist Party and the unions became the key defenders of the system through democratic and authoritarian periods. In Brazil, Vargas's populist authoritarian regime laid the bases for urban-sector incorporation, and the military's bureaucratic-authoritarian regime extended it to the rural sector.

The two paths to high and medium levels of welfare generosity by the end of the ISI period are similar to two of Hicks's (1999) three paths to early welfare state consolidation (circa 1930) in the now advanced capitalist countries. He distinguishes between a lib/lab path in which a strong working class cooperated with liberal parties to pass social legislation (e.g., Britain and Sweden), a Catholic/labor path in which labor and Catholic parties coalesced to pass social legislation (e.g., Belgium and Netherlands), and an authoritarian co-optative path in which an authoritarian regime passed social legislation in order to co-opt the growing urban working-class movement (e.g., Germany and Austria). The two paths to early social policy leadership that we find in Latin America are similar to the lib/lab and authoritarian co-optative paths. The striking difference is that the co-optation attempts in the European cases were largely unsuccessful, whereas the Latin American leaders met with success in varying degrees.

Country Analyses

The following brief sketches of our five main cases flesh out the data and the theoretical arguments just presented. Following the chronological order of major social policy initiatives, we begin with Uruguay. Since data on organized labor are notoriously unreliable or unavailable and could not be included in our data analysis, we pay special attention to the role of unions in these sketches.

Uruguay

In Uruguay, the first legislation offering pensions for members of the military (for invalidity and for survivors), paid for out of general revenue, was passed in 1829.[15] Civil servants received pension rights in 1838. In 1884 pension benefits for old age were added to the military scheme, and in 1892 police and firemen were given the same rights. In 1896 the first real pension fund was established, for teachers and other employees in the educational system. This was the first scheme with compulsory contributions from employees and the state as employer, and a separate financial administration. Papadópulos (1992, 37) interprets the establishment of this scheme as an instrument of nation building, deployed by political elites in the context of deep political divisions between the two traditional camps—the Colorados based in the coastal region and the Blancos in the interior—and very high levels of immigration. Whatever its reasons, this action set the precedent both for the importance of public education in Uruguay and for an early expansion of social security schemes.

During his two terms in office as president of the country and head of the Colorado Party (1903–1907 and 1911–1916), Batlle consolidated the monopoly of organized force of the state and the dominant position of the urban and modernizing forces over the traditional landowners of the interior by defeating the Blanco rebellion of 1904 (Mendez Vives 1977, 87–121). This victory enabled him to consolidate his control over the Colorados, institutionalize contestation, and prepare the ground for an early breakthrough to full democracy with universal male suffrage in the 1917 constitution. Uruguay, like Argentina, exported temperate agricultural products, primarily meat (sheep and beef), hides, wool, and grain, which generated some subsidiary industrialization and, by the first two decades of the twentieth century, had already led to a comparatively high degree of urbanization and middle- and working-class formation.

In 1904, the Batlle administration established the pension fund for public employees, leaving the one for educators intact as a separate entity. Originally, only permanent employees paid by the Treasury were eligible, but over the next twenty years more and more categories of public employees were incorporated. Another crucial reform introduced by Batlle was the universalization of free secular primary education. The basic contours of the social security system were consolidated with the establishment in 1919 of the pension fund for white-collar and blue-collar employees in public utilities, both state-run and private, in railroads, trams, telephone, telegraph, water, and gas. Similar to the process of inclusion for state employees, this pension fund was widened to eventually include all private activities in industry and commerce, and the fund was renamed the pension fund for industry, commerce, and public services. Finally, in 1925 the pension fund for bank employees was established. Thus, by 1930, before the beginning of ISI, most major categories of urban workers were covered.

The urban labor movement was heavily influenced by Marxist and anarchist doctrines, instilled to a large extent by immigrants from Italy. Thus, they did not establish ties to the Colorados, nor did the Colorados attempt to incorporate labor into state-controlled institutions or a union–party alliance. The constitution of 1917 established full freedom of association, and there were no limits to collective bargaining or the right to strike (Buchanan and Nicholls 2003, 120), which allowed for the consolidation of independent unions. There is disagreement on whether unions pressed for the expansion of pension schemes. Mesa-Lago (1978, 74) argues that labor militancy increased greatly between 1916 and 1920 and that this militancy, coupled with pressures for the expansion of coverage under the existing pension plans, elicited positive responses from the Colorado governments. On the other hand, Papadópulos (1992, 47) cites evidence from a private archive in the form of articles in a communist newspaper from 1924 that demonstrates the newspaper itself and the anarchist leader of the most powerful union organization explicitly opposed the creation of a national pension fund on the grounds that it was being promoted for electoral purposes and could potentially co-opt the working class and make it lose its capacity to fight against the injustice of the capitalist system. Even if a sector of organized labor opposed the pension fund, it is clear that the presence of mobilized urban labor put the issue on the agenda and strengthened the position of the Colorado Party in its push for expansion.

Also in 1919, the Uruguayan government established a noncontributory pension for indigents who were seventy years old or invalid, a truly pathbreaking reform that recognized state responsibility for the most vulnerable members of society. After a soft authoritarian interlude from 1933 to 1942, the Colorados resumed their dominant electoral position and their leading role in expanding social security coverage and the range of benefits. Three more pension funds were established: one for notaries' employees in 1941, one for rural workers in 1943, and one for university professionals in 1954. A 1954 law finally included all workers in the private sector in social security. In 1943 family allowances were introduced for all employees in industry and commerce, and in 1958 they were extended to the unemployed. Thus, Uruguay had achieved virtually universal employment-based social security coverage and a small noncontributory safety net by the end of the 1950s. The social security system was Bismarckian, however, because of its occupational differentiation.

The key explanatory factors of the early expansion of social security coverage in Uruguay are in large part similar to those favoring the early establishment of democracy, namely, the nature of the export economy and the early thrust of subsidiary industrialization and urbanization (Rueschemeyer, Stephens and Stephens 1992). The large landowners were ranchers and thus not in need of a large cheap labor force bound to the land. Accordingly, they were not mortal enemies of democracy. In fact, parts of the coastal landowners supported the nation-building, modernization, and secularization project of Batlle and the Colorado Party. Nation building was essential in the aftermath of the final defeat of armed Blanco rebellions by Batlle. The growth of an urban labor movement and labor militancy certainly added credibility and appeal to the argument that the state had an essential role to play in promoting both economic and social development and social cohesion.

The 1917 Constitution conferred suffrage on all males (including illiterates), and in 1932 women were declared citizens by law and thus enfranchised.[16] Thus, there truly was a mass electorate, and it kept the Colorados the dominant party until the 1950s, when the Blanco Party won its first victory in an election in 1958. Both major parties were heavily factionalized, a situation facilitated by the electoral system, which allowed for multiple lists from one party, but the dominant factions in the Colorado Party maintained a commitment to an interventionist state and social integration. They were the party of the expanding urban sectors, and the expansion of social policy strengthened their support base.

With more competitive politics after the 1950s came an electoral cycle in which the value of pensions rose in election years and was eroded thereafter. At the same time, economic growth stagnated, the pension system had matured, and the ratio of contributors to pension recipients had deteriorated greatly. As a result, cost controls were already on the agenda in the 1960s. However, pensioner organizations and the labor movement, which had formed the first national confederation (Unión General de Trabajadores) in 1942, vigorously defended pension rights and the value of pension benefits (Mesa-Lago 1978, 76–77). The competition for electoral support even pushed the conservative Blanco government to introduce some additional social security programs on the eve of the 1966 elections. Nevertheless, the Colorados won this election.

In 1967, the three largest pension funds were brought under the administration of the Banco de Previsión Social with the aim of streamlining the entire system. The bureaucratic-authoritarian government of 1973–85 then pushed centralization even further by bringing virtually all social security programs under the umbrella of the Dirección General de la Seguridad Social. As a World Bank country memorandum of 1986 (cited in Papadópulos 1992, 110–12) pointed out, however, the inequalities and inefficiencies in the system were not eliminated, and the transfers from the government to the social security system were a major contributor to the huge budget deficits. Thus, social security reform became a major preoccupation for all of the democratic governments from 1984 on.

Chile

In Chile, as in Uruguay, the first pensions were established for the military and their surviving family members (in 1811 and 1855) and for civil servants (1888) (Mesa-Lago 1978). After those initial steps, though, the development of a social security system slowed. The only other group that received pension rights before 1924 were railroad workers. Unlike in Uruguay, the political system remained under the control of the oligarchy until 1920, and the oligarchy was engaged in labor-intensive agriculture as well as urban activities and totally opposed to any kind of worker or peasant rights. A militant labor movement had developed in the mining areas and spread to the urban sectors, but its political weight was not felt until the 1920s. In 1909 labor founded the Federación de Obreros de Chile, and the prominent labor leader Recabarren founded the Socialist Workers' Party in 1912, which became the Communist Party in 1922. The first president elected on the basis of a reform agenda with the support of middle and working classes was Arturo Alessandri in 1920, as candidate of the Liberal Alliance.

Alessandri proposed a labor code and a pension fund. This legislation, along with most other reform proposals, was blocked by Congress. The stalemate in Congress provoked a rebellion of younger officers in 1924, and under strong military pressure Congress rushed through various pieces of legislation, among them the labor code and a social security fund for pensions and health care for blue-collar workers. Congress did not pass the legislation as proposed by Alessandri but rather a version that was a compromise between his proposal and a more conservative one (Borzutzky 2002, 14). The labor code was restrictive and reflected an attempt to control unionization and militancy in that it restricted blue-collar unions to the enterprise level. The pension fund for white-collar workers was established in 1925, and it included life insurance. In that same year a pension fund for civil servants, one for the armed forces, and one for the police were established. The practice of covering blue- and white-collar workers and other categories with different programs followed the precedent of the already existing funds and initiated a pattern of extreme fragmentation and stratification of the social security system, which grew to over 160 programs by the 1970s (Mesa-Lago 1978, 33).

Colonel Ibáñez, who became the most powerful political figure in the wake of the 1924 military intervention and ruled in an authoritarian manner from 1927 to 1931, relied more on outright repression than social reform to deal with labor (Drake 1978b, 59). Nevertheless, he implemented the social security legislation that had been passed. These years of authoritarian rule and the Depression left the labor movement greatly debilitated. The rebuilding of the labor movement after 1932 and the turn of the Communist Party to a Popular Front strategy culminated in the formation of a new united labor confederation, the Confederación de Trabajadores de Chile in 1936 (Collier and Collier 1991, 375–76). The center-left governments headed by presidents from the Radical Party (1938–52), initially supported by the Socialists and Communists in a Popular Front alliance, heavily promoted ISI and allowed the labor movement to grow. Yet they did not develop any comprehensive new social policy approaches but instead simply extended benefits in an ad hoc manner to particularly vocal groups. In 1952, his last year in office and in the wake of greatly increasing militancy among strikers, President González reorganized the blue-collar social security system, separating income support from medical services and establishing the Servicio Nacional de Salud (SNS). The SNS took control of all public and charity health facilities and unified a variety of services both for insured blue-collar workers and the indigent. White-collar workers and the military were not integrated into the SNS, however. The comparatively limited reach of the Chilean health care system as of 1960 is underlined by the fact that it had the highest infant mortality rate at that point among our focal countries, with 120 infant deaths per 1,000 live births, almost twice the rate of Argentina and even slightly higher than that of Brazil. With the expansion of primary care under Frei, infant mortality began to decline rapidly, falling to 82 by 1970 (McGuire 2010, 311).

By the 1950s the Chilean system of social security had become so unwieldy and expensive that conservative president Alessandri (1958–64) appointed a commission to reorganize it. The commission criticized the system as highly discriminatory and regressive and recommended reforms in the direction of universalism and elimination of special privileges (Mesa-Lago 1978, 28). These recommendations, however, failed to be implemented. The same was true of attempts by Christian Democratic president Frei (1964–70) to reorganize and unify the system. The intense competition between the Christian Democrats and the left for the support of lower-income groups in urban and rural areas, though, stimulated another thrust of expansion of social security. The Frei government expanded primary health care, and the Allende government extended social security coverage to self-employed workers and small employers and increased the value of minimum pensions and blue-collar workers' pensions. The Allende government (1970–73) had a comprehensive reform plan inspired by social democratic values of universalism and solidarity that envisaged unification of social security and transition from a contributory to a tax-financed system, along with the establishment of a unified health system, but it did not control Congress and like its predecessors lacked the political power to implement its reform designs (Borzutzky 2002, 139–45). It would take the iron fist of Pinochet to reshape social security in a fundamental way.

Costa Rica

In Costa Rica, the cornerstone for the system of social protection was laid by a coalition of progressive Catholics and communist-inspired unions under President Calderón in 1941, with the passage of the law that established social security coverage to be administered by the Caja Costarricense del Seguro Social (CCSS).[17] Although it would take some two decades for a major expansion of coverage to begin, this law had important limitations and implications for the future character of the social security system. First, it restricted coverage to low- to medium-paid workers and employees by establishing a salary ceiling of 300 colones to qualify for compulsory coverage. Second, it explicitly prohibited sector-based pension programs (Rosenberg 1981, 288), which accounts for the comparatively unified nature of the Costa Rican social security system.[18] Implementation started slowly, with health coverage in the four major urban areas only. By 1950, only 8 percent of the population were covered, and by 1960, 20 percent (Barahona, Guendell, and Castro 2005).

Increasing political polarization in the 1940s was accompanied by increasing use of repression by Calderón and his ally and successor, Picado, which in turn was met with increasingly violent protests and ended in a brief civil war in 1948. It was the victor in the civil war, José Figueres, who consolidated democracy and founded the social democratic Partido Liberación Nacional (PLN), which then became the driving force behind the construction of the system of social protection.[19] The PLN-dominated Congress passed a constitutional amendment in 1961 that mandated universalization of social security coverage within a decade, which meant that the self-employed also became eligible for coverage. Achievements

fell short of the goal, but coverage expanded to over half of the economically active population during the decade and continued to expand in
the 1970s. The two PLN presidents in the 1970s (Figueres, 1970–74; and
Oduber, 1974–78) pursued policies aimed at both economic growth and
equity. In 1971, the wage ceiling for compulsory enrollment in social security was removed, which strengthened both the financial base of social
security and its redistributive profile, and in 1974 employer contributions
were raised and mandatory coverage was extended to the self-employed.
Coverage through health and maternity insurance reached 76 percent
by 1980 and continued to expand thereafter, despite the economic crisis
(Barahona, Guendell, and Castro 2005).

The 1970s saw two more important social policy innovations. First,
in 1971 a social assistance program was created for people in extreme
poverty, and in 1974 a new autonomous agency (FODESAF, or Fondo
de Desarrollo Social y Asignaciones Familiares) was created to provide
noncontributory health care and pensions and a variety of other programs (e.g., nutrition) for the poor. In contrast to social assistance programs in other countries, the funding for the Costa Rican programs accounted for a respectable 1.4 percent of GNP from the beginning (Trejos,
in Rovira 1987). Second, in 1973 an integrated national health system
was created, such that by 1980 some 95 percent of physicians had sala-
ried positions in that system. Although it was possible for physicians to
have a private practice on the side, only 14 percent of consultations were
made on a private basis (Casas and Vargas 1980). The goal of universalization of health care coverage was essentially achieved through this unified public system with heavy emphasis on primary and preventive care
and clinics in poor urban and rural areas. Coverage through the pension
system lagged behind health care, with roughly 50 percent of the economically active population (Mesa-Lago 1994), but the elderly without
coverage were eligible for social assistance pensions.

Explanations of the dynamics that drove the establishment and expansion of Costa Rican social policy vary in their emphasis. Rosenberg
(1979, 1981) emphasizes the role of one president, Calderón, and his close
advisers, and thereafter the role of bureaucrats in the CCSS and the regional context in the aftermath of the Cuban revolution. Lehoucq (2010)
argues that good policy and good governance have been a result of the establishment of a variety of semi-autonomous institutions like the CCSS,
that is, he emphasizes the effect of institutions. He also underlines, however, that the PLN was responsible for the establishment of most of these

institutions and in particular for the expansion of the welfare state. Martínez Franzoni (2010) stresses the importance of political leadership, or statecraft, which is consistent with a party-based explanation.

The actor that is conspicuously absent from all these explanations is organized labor. Clearly, the low level of industrialization and urbanization in Costa Rica and the absence of mining meant that there was no labor movement comparable to those in Argentina and Chile, for instance. Nevertheless, organized labor in the form of the General Confederation of Workers became politically active in the 1920s, forming an alliance with the Partido Reformista to support Jorge Volio in the 1924 elections on the basis of a strongly social reformist program (Rosenberg 1979). Volio lost, but the social question did not go away, and in 1926 a workmen's compensation scheme was implemented. There is no doubt that in the 1930s and 1940s the communist-led unions that had their main base in the banana plantations were crucial in bringing the issue of workers' welfare onto the agenda. It is also undisputed that Calderón actively sought support from the communists and their working-class followers along with support from the progressive Catholic leadership. Molina (2007) documents the ambiguous relationship between Calderón and the communists, going from competition in the lead-up to the 1940 elections to collaboration in mid-1941 in the promotion of social reform. Thus, it is clear that the presence of organized labor and the militancy of the banana unions in the context of competitive elections weighed in favor of reformist state initiatives. The context of competitive elections is crucial here, and the political role of organized labor contrasts sharply with the harsh repression suffered by labor in the same period in El Salvador, for instance.

The particular political alignments in the civil war led to the anomaly that the social democratic winners repressed organized labor. Figueres and his allies repressed the strongest unions because they were led by communists and allied with the Calderón camp. The PLN then promoted the formation of alternative company-based workers associations. The PLN, however, supported pro-worker policies, such as the tripartite National Wage Council that established minimum wages for different categories of private-sector employment (Sandbrook et al. 2007, 102). It also promoted the formation of all kinds of cooperatives (from production to financing and marketing) in the coffee sector, thus weakening the position of the dominant families.

In general, from the 1950s on, the PLN presided over a massive ex-

pansion of the state's role in the economy and established a great number of semi-autonomous public institutions. The promotion of ISI became a central goal in the 1960s, starting with the Industrial Protection
Law of 1959 and accelerating with the formation of the Central American Common Market. In the 1970s the state assumed a direct entrepreneurial role through the Costa Rican Development Corporation. The
corporation functioned as a huge holding company with enterprises in a
large number of sectors. By 1980, the public sector produced about one-
quarter of GDP and employed about one-fifth of the workforce (Sandbrook et al. 2007, 105). Although the level of industrial employment was
lower than in Argentina, Chile, and Uruguay, the level of social expenditure was higher.

During the period of formation and expansion of the Costa Rican social policy regime, the role of electoral competition and the presence of
first a communist party with a labor base and then the social democratic
PLN were crucial. In the period of neoliberal economic reform and pressures for retrenchment, the PLN continued to be important, and policy
legacies in the form of widespread popular support for the broad-based
social programs became very important as well.

Brazil

In Brazil, oligarchic rule, with a heavy presence of landlords engaged in
labor-intensive agriculture and therefore totally opposed to democracy,
lasted until 1930. Thus, with one exception in the case of workers located in strategic positions for the export economy, the key foundations
for the system of social protection were laid under Vargas (1930–45).
As in the other countries, however, the military, civil servants, and employees of state enterprises already received various kinds of insurance
funds. The first legislation establishing a social insurance fund for workers was passed in 1923. The legislation covered railroad workers and was
extended to dock and maritime workers in 1926. This insurance fund
covered pensions for old age (with a time-of-service provision) and invalidity and for survivors, as well as health care and funeral expenses.
The financing was tripartite, and benefits were earnings related (Malloy 1979, 41). These principles were to remain the same in the many new
pension funds established under Vargas. The 1923 legislation was passed
under the Old Republic, in the context of a still overwhelmingly rural so-

ciety in which labor organization was localized around Rio de Janeiro and São Paulo. Still, oligarchic domination came under increasing challenge from middle-class protests, localized labor militancy, and the Tenente movement, which had emerged out of a revolt of young officers in 1922. The social security legislation was a paternalistic response designed to co-opt and control the emerging labor movement.[20] As such, it was fully in line with previous state action, such as sponsorship of the Fourth National Workers' Congress in 1912, whose attendees, representatives from seventy-one associations, had their expenses paid by government authorities (Schmitter 1971, 140).

Vargas was brought to power in 1930 through a coup supported by a coalition of sectors of the military, dissident sectors of landowners, urban elite interests, and sectors of the middle classes (Skidmore 1967, 6–12). He set out to build a system of state control over economy and society designed to promote economic growth, social peace, and political stability. This attempt was strongly challenged, and political stability was not achieved until after the establishment of the clearly authoritarian and corporatist Estado Nôvo in 1937. The bases for state control over the working class were put in place in the early years of his rule, however, and the establishment of social security schemes was an important element of this strategy.[21] The Ministry of Labor defined which unions could represent which sectors of workers, and only officially recognized unions were allowed to function. Union leaders who challenged the system were repressed; those who conformed found opportunities for political advancement. The Ministry of Labor was also in charge of building the social security system.

The first groups of workers to receive social security protection under Vargas, in 1931, were all employees in public services and then in mining. Those pension funds followed the pattern of company-based pension funds set with the 1923 reform. In 1933, the pattern was changed to pension institutes covering functional groups, or national occupational categories of workers. Maritime workers received a pension institute in 1933, commercial workers and bank workers (separately) in 1934, industrial workers in 1937 (implemented in 1938), and transport and cargo workers (jointly) in 1938. The preexisting company-based pension funds were left in existence, as were the separate schemes for the military and civil servants. Benefits in all the systems were contribution related, but the rules varied within the schemes as well as between them. Moreover, benefits were not necessarily delivered in accordance with the rules. In particular, the delivery of health care services varied greatly, not only according to the category of worker but also according to geographical location. For instance, the scheme for industrial workers did not provide health care services before the 1950s, and thereafter it never provided it to more than about 30 percent of the insured (Malloy 1979, 110). The pension institutes were administered by an executive officer appointed by the president of the republic and by a council with equal representation of employers and employees, the latter selected by representatives of formally recognized unions. Beginning under Vargas and continuing during the semidemocratic period after his overthrow in 1945, the social security institutes became prime patronage employment machines and thus a strong base for official unions and the Partido Trabalhista Brasileiro (PTB), one of the two parties founded by Vargas.

Starting with a report from the Ministry of Labor in 1941, followed by a major report by experts and presented to Vargas in 1945, repeated attempts to reform the fragmented and highly stratified social security system were stymied by resistance from the members and employees of the existing system and the union leaders and politicians using the schemes for patronage . The 1945 report recommended nothing short of total overhaul, with administrative unification, universalization of coverage, and standardization of rules. Legislation was finally passed in 1960, but it only standardized rules, and even these provisions were undermined by political influences (Malloy 1979, 104). Goulart's government made further concessions to labor; in 1962 it removed the age requirement of fifty-five for retiring on the basis of thirty-five years of service. In 1963 it made an important move toward universalization by establishing an assistance scheme for rural workers, to be financed by a 1 percent tax on rural products. Thus, these years of restricted democracy (1945–64) presented a mixed picture of unsuccessful efforts at standardization, improvements of benefits in established systems in response to labor pressure, and efforts by Goulart, the president from the PTB, to expand protection to the rural sector. The thrust of the changes remained expansionary.

The bureaucratic-authoritarian government of 1964–85 then took control of the social security system as part of its strategy to weaken organized labor. It first removed the political and labor representatives from the administration and then unified the existing schemes under the

Instituto Nacional de Previdência Social in 1967. The military, federal civil servants, and state-level civil servants, however, maintained their own, more privileged systems.

The military government undertook two extensions of social security coverage, to the rural sector in 1971 and to domestic servants in 1972, the first of which was of major importance for national coverage rates. The military's main concern was with national security, which in their eyes required control of civil society. Radicalism in the rural sector was by no means an immediate major threat, but localized organization had begun to emerge, and so the military government repressed radical rural groups and then moved to preempt autonomous organizing by encouraging the formation of rural unions for workers and employers and putting them in charge of administering the services and benefits provided by the rural social security scheme, Fundo de Manutenção e Desenvolvimento do Ensino Fundamental e de Valorização do Magistério (FUNRURAL). Charged with providing health care, pensions for old age, invalidity, and survivors, and funeral expenses, FUNRURAL was the first major noncontributory scheme. The benefits were low, set at half the minimum salary, and financed by a 2 percent tax on rural products levied from wholesalers and a 2.5 percent payroll tax on urban enterprises. Health care remained largely a promise because facilities in the rural sector remained very scarce (Malloy 1979). Official national coverage rates shot up to 93 percent, however, which put Brazil way ahead of any other Latin American country (see table 4.1).

Argentina

Argentina expanded social security coverage relatively late compared to Uruguay and Chile, and even later than Brazil. As in the other countries, pensions for military veterans and various groups of civil servants, including teachers, had been introduced in the nineteenth century, and in 1915 the first strategically located group of workers, railroad workers, received a pension fund (Mesa-Lago 1978). Beef, sheep, and grain-based exports created significant subsidiary industrialization around Buenos Aires, which provided the basis for the emergence of a highly militant labor movement. At the turn of the century, strong pressures emerged from the middle classes against continued oligarchic control of the state. A sector of the oligarchy sided with the Unión Cívica Radical, the main representative of middle-class demands, to push through electoral reforms and thus create the first breakthrough to full democracy. The Radicales, led by Yrigoyen, won the 1916 elections with support from the middle classes and some sectors of the working class and remained in power until 1930. The Socialist Party won less than 10 percent of the national vote in those elections, though it was stronger in some parts of Buenos Aires (Collier and Collier 1991, 138). The labor movement up to 1919 was dominated by anarcho-syndicalists who did not engage in electoral politics and opposed state intervention. Thus, Yrigoyen did not owe the unions anything, and in fact his government unleashed severe repression in 1919 in response to the unions' greatly increasing militancy. Yrigoyen did expand social protection to middle-class sectors, however. During his first term, pensions were introduced for employees in foreign-owned utilities, in hospitals and clinics, and in the financial sector.

The labor movement entered the 1920s greatly weakened. The influence of socialists and communists grew, and in 1930 they formed the Confederación General del Trabajo, the first widely inclusive confederation. In 1928 the Radical government developed a proposal for a pension fund with wide coverage, including workers in commerce, industry, the merchant marine, and the press, but the fund was never implemented (Mesa-Lago 1978, 163). The 1929 crash critically weakened Yrigoyen, and a coup removed him and restored conservative rule. During the following period of fraudulent elections and desperate attempts to turn back the clock, the earlier pattern of spotty extension of social protection to strategic groups reasserted itself, with pensions for journalists and printers, merchant marine and civil airline employees in 1939 (Mesa-Lago 1978, 163).

The pattern up to the Depression resembles the Chilean one, with the exception of the timing of the proposal for major expansion of pension coverage. A militant labor movement was the backdrop for intense middle-class pressures for reform. Governments supported by the middle classes and sectors of the working class, but not by organized labor per se, responded to militancy with a combination of repression and reform; the reforms included social security funds. In Chile, military support for the reform proposals overcame oligarchic resistance, and the pension funds were passed in 1925; in Argentina, the proposals were developed just a few years later but fell victim to conservative resistance.

The oligarchy and its allies in Argentina were able to offer more virulent and powerful resistance, both in the form of private vigilante movements and through the seizure of state power with military support, than were their counterparts in Chile, where the balance of power within the military favored reformist interests (Collier and Collier 1991, 146–56). In neither country was the left politically strong enough to shape the emerging social security system.

The main expansion of social security coverage was undertaken by Perón. In his quest to promote industrialization and build a power base among the rapidly expanding urban labor force, he implemented, first as minister of labor in the military government from 1943 to 1945 and then as president of Argentina from 1946 to 1955 (freely elected for the first term, with fraud tainting his reelection), new programs to cover the bulk of the blue-collar labor force. Perón brought the labor movement under his control through a combination of favoring supportive unions and taking over opposing ones, and jailing or exiling their leaders. He promoted both industrialization and unionization, and the labor movement grew from roughly one-half million members in 1945 to some two million in 1950 and two and a half million in 1954 (Collier and Collier 1991, 341). As part of a whole range of pro-labor policies, he established a pension fund for industrial workers in 1946 and one for rural workers and the self-employed in 1954. He also encouraged the expansion of the mutual health insurance funds run by the unions, the *obras sociales*, and of public hospitals, and he created health insurance programs for some groups. The Eva Perón Foundation constructed public charity hospitals and clinics for the poor. Thus, Perón followed the established pattern of leaving existing programs intact and creating new ones in addition. His main concern was with building and maintaining a strong support base, not with constructing an egalitarian and solidaristic society.

In the period after Perón's overthrow, the military dominated politics, first from behind the scenes and finally by installing military regimes. Beginning in 1957 various efforts were made to unify the system in order to reduce administrative costs, but these efforts were successful only under the bureaucratic-authoritarian regime of Onganía (1966–70), when three social security funds incorporated all the others, with the exception of those for the military and police. One fund was established for blue- and white-collar workers, one for civil servants, and one for the self-employed, and within those funds rules were standardized. During his short-lived return to power in 1973–74, Perón had plans for unifying and universalizing social protection, but like Allende he lacked the power to implement those plans (Mesa-Lago 1978, 166–67).

Policy Legacies on the Eve of the Debt Crisis

By the late 1970s the contributory social security systems in Argentina, Brazil, Chile, and Uruguay faced increasingly large deficits. The systems had matured, which meant that with every cohort reaching retirement age, more people were entitled to benefits. Theoretically, the systems should have built up reserves in the period leading up to this point, when all those covered were paying into the system and only few were entitled to benefits, but in practice these reserves were not available. The reasons were varied, ranging from bad investments of the reserves; their use for other social spending (such as housing, general budget support, and huge administrative expenses resulting from patronage-based hiring); and their erosion by inflation; to evasion of contributions by employers and the state (Mesa-Lago 1989). Deficits were particularly aggravated by the more generous schemes, the bulk of whose contributions were to have been made by the state . Governments of different stripes made all kinds of efforts to streamline the systems and put them on a firmer financial basis, but a combination of stern resistance from privileged groups, the slowdown in growth resulting from the oil shocks, and repeated balance of payments crises stymied their efforts. Costa Rica was in a different situation, as the big push for expansion of social security protection was still under way and the system was much more unified.

Before 1980, the military governments in Argentina, Brazil, and Chile had imposed partial unification of the social security systems, but for the most part benefit rules had not been effectively unified and the most privileged systems were left intact. The Pinochet dictatorship in Chile was the first one to take radical action in the course of its aggressive program of neoliberal reform, privatizing the pension system and creating individual capitalized accounts—with the telling exception of the pension system for the military. In the remaining countries, far-reaching reforms were put on the agenda by the IFIs in the wake of the debt crisis. In fact, what the IFIs put on the agenda was Chilean-type privatization. Domestic resistance to privatization was strong, however, and the types of reforms finally implemented were shaped by the balance of power between proponents and opponents and by institutional factors. The struggles over social policy reform are the subject of chapter 6.

Conclusion

The evidence is clear on the importance of democracy for the expansion of social security schemes in Chile, Costa Rica, and Uruguay. The expansion of social protection in Argentina and Brazil occurred under nondemocratic regimes with incorporation designs for urban labor and later, in Brazil, for rural labor also. Left-of-center parties were directly and on a long-term basis involved in forming and expanding social security schemes in Uruguay and Costa Rica. In Chile, they only gained direct influence after 1970, but competition between them and centrist parties before then, both the Radicals and the Christian Democrats, pushed those parties toward expanding social protection and services.

As to the role of organized labor, one cannot say that social security funds were established in response to demands for them articulated by the labor movement in any of our five countries. Some unions and radical labor leaders in fact opposed them in Uruguay, Chile, and Brazil. It is also clear, however, that social security was seen by the reformist sector of the political elites as an instrument to deal with a highly militant labor movement, albeit a localized one in the case of Brazil. So, the presence of this labor movement did matter. There is no doubt that the presence of a militant labor movement was important both for the early breakthrough to full democracy in Uruguay and Argentina and for the introduction of programs of social protection in Uruguay, Argentina, and Chile. In Argentina, middle-class reformist leaders developed plans for extending social security to urban labor, though they failed to implement those plans. In other words, the distribution of power (shaped in part by the organization of lower classes) in a society matters for policy outcomes. Even if the labor movement was divided on the desirability of pension systems, the presence of a militant organized collective actor pushed moderate political elites toward finding mechanisms to incorporate this actor and thus preempt fundamental challenges to the social order. In neighboring Brazil, Vargas continued and greatly intensified a paternalistic and incorporating approach of the state toward labor. Radical labor movements in Latin America did not achieve their revolutionary goals, but their presence induced moderate political leaders to address the social question through reforms rather than (or in addition to) repression.[22] In some cases, such as Chile and Argentina in the 1920s, conservative elites managed to resist for a considerable time or roll back such reform attempts and even to weaken the labor movement itself, but with the progress of ISI the issue of labor protection reasserted itself on the agenda. In sum, this period of social policy development in the five focus countries witnessed all three mechanisms, outlined in chapter 2, by which the growing strength of labor and thus the shifting balance of power in society can affect social policy outcomes.

CHAPTER FIVE

The Determinants of Social Spending, Inequality, and Poverty

Quantitative Evidence

In this chapter, we subject the hypotheses developed in chapter 2 to statistical tests.[1] Since the quantitative data cover the period 1970–2007, they speak primarily to the period covered by the chapter on contemporary Latin America, and we do not attempt to test hypotheses (such as the role of authoritarian working-class incorporation) that pertain primarily to the formative period covered in chapter 4. Our goal in this chapter is to test whether the relationships hypothesized in chapter 2 are generalizable to all eighteen Latin American countries for the entire period covered by our data. Above all we are interested in whether democracy and left parties make a difference for social policy and poverty and inequality.

Data and Hypotheses

The data collected for this chapter represent a tremendous improvement over data available for these dependent variables just ten years ago. Unfortunately, however, they are less than ideal for our purposes, and it is useful to outline their limitations before discussing the hypotheses. We can use as our baseline the data available for advanced capitalist democracies. With regard to income inequality, enormous strides have been made in the development of comparable data for inequality during the past two decades. The Deininger and Squire (1996) World Bank study

was a watershed in this regard. The United Nations University World Institute for Development Economics Research's World Income Inequality
Database (WIID), version 2c (UNU-WIDER 2008), took over the World
Bank initiative and greatly improved on the comparability of the data. A
parallel effort by the Universidad Nacional de La Plata and the World
Bank's Latin America and Caribbean poverty group to create the Socio-
Economic Database for Latin America and the Caribbean (SEDLAC
2010) made yet more data available on income inequality for Latin America. The SEDLAC project houses the microdata from the actual household surveys on which the measures are based, thus making it possible
to render all its measures strictly comparable across country-years. By
using the information about the surveys on which the WIID are based,
we are able to partly harmonize those data to the SEDLAC standard
and control for the remaining differences (see the discussion below).

The drawback of the income inequality data then is not comparability but access: the fact that we do not have access to the microdata and
cannot calculate a measure of redistribution, which we were able to do
for OECD countries by using the Luxembourg Income Study data. This
would be our optimal strategy because it would allow us to directly measure the distributive effect of taxes and transfers. Many factors affect
income distribution other than governmental policy. Thus, our second-
best alternative is to attempt to control for the other factors identified
in the literature on the determinants of cross-national differences in income distribution.

There is, however, an upside to not measuring redistribution: government action also affects pre-tax and transfer income distribution.
As pointed out in chapter 2, "market income distribution" is not "pre-
government" because governments set the conditions under which labor
markets operate; they can set the minimum wage and the legal conditions
under which collective bargaining operates. Moreover, they can change
the distributions of market assets (land reform, education expansion),
which can have a profound influence on market income distribution.

Our second dependent variable is poverty. Here there is considerable
controversy, focused largely on the World Bank's $1 and $2 poverty measures, which we discuss later in the measurement section. We use the
CEPAL measure, which like the World Bank's is an absolute poverty
measure, but it is a significant improvement on the World Bank measure
(see discussion below). Again, here we are dealing with a post-tax and
transfer measure, so we need to try to control for factors other than gov-

ernmental redistribution which affect poverty. As in the case of income distribution, this strategy has an upside in that it will catch government affects on poverty that do not occur through taxes and transfers.

Of our dependent variables, social spending is certainly the most problematic—not as a measure of "welfare state effort" but rather as a measure of welfare state redistribution. In OECD countries, these two measures are closely related. In our study of the determinants of redistribution, we found that by far the most important explanatory variable was the sheer size of taxes and transfers (Bradley et al. 2003). As we have shown earlier in this book and will elaborate further below, in Latin American countries, social spending has much more ambiguous distributive effects. This is not a matter of spending being measured differently in Latin America than in OECD countries or our data not being comparable across countries. On both accounts all of the evidence points to our data as being high quality. Rather it is simply that social spending has very different distributive effects in Latin America, and thus social spending is not a good proxy for redistribution.

Income Inequality

DEMOCRACY. As we argued in chapter 2, there are strong theoretical reasons to expect that the length of a country's democratic experience is associated with lower inequality (Rueschemeyer, Stephens and Stephens 1992, 10). Democracy gives the powerless and underprivileged the chance to organize and use organization as a power base to gain entry into the political decision-making process. The most effective channels for underprivileged groups into the political decision-making process are political parties, as the poor lack the connections and funds to influence decision makers directly. It takes time, however, for parties to gain coherence and establish roots in social bases, as well as for legislatures to pass major pieces of legislation and for that legislation to be implemented. In particular, it takes time for parties representing the interests of less privileged groups to consolidate and gain representation in competition with parties representing privileged groups and enjoying a financial advantage.

In Latin America there is great variation in the length of time a country has been democratic, and we expect the countries with the longer democratic traditions to have lower inequality (see table 5.1). Other studies of developing countries have found such an effect (Burkhart

TABLE 5.1. **Variable descriptions and hypothesized effects**

		Hypothesized effects				
Variables	Description	Inequality	Poverty	Education spending	Health spending	Social security spending
Dependent variables						
Income inequality	Gini coefficient of household income inequality					
Poverty	Percentage of the households living in poverty		+			
Education spending	Government spending on education as a percentage of GDP	–	–			
Health spending	Government spending on health as a percentage of GDP	–	–			
Social security and welfare spending	Government spending on social security and welfare as a percentage of GDP	–/+	–			
Independent variables						
Methodological controls						
No adjustment indicator	Coded 1 for Gini observations that are calculated based on household income not adjusted for household size	–				
Gross income indicator	Coded 1 for Gini observations that are calculated using gross income or monetary gross income	+				
Earnings indicator	Coded 1 for Gini observations that are calculated using earnings	–				
Debt crisis period indicator	Coded 1 for all observations falling in 1982–89	+	+	–	–	–
1990s period indicator	Coded 1 for all observations falling in 1990–2000	–/+	–/+	–/+	–/+	–/+
2000s period indicator	Coded 1 for all observations falling in 2001–7	–/+	–/+	–/+	–/+	–/+
Panama indictor variable	Coded 1 for all Panama observations			+	+	+
Political and policy variables						
Democracy	Regime type: nondemocracy = 0, restricted democracy = 0.5, and full democracy = 1; score cumulative from 1945 to date of observation	–	–	+	+	+

Long-term democracy	Democracy −20, then set all values less than 20 to zero	−	−	+	+	+
Left political strength	([Proportion of left and center-left legislative seats cumulative from 1945 to date] + [Years of left or center-left presidency cumulative from 1945 to date])/2	−	−	+	+	−/+
Repressive authoritarianism	Regime type: repressive authoritarian regimes = 1 and all other = 0; score is cumulated for the fifteen years preceding the year of observation		−	−	−	−/+
Education (cumulative average)	Cumulative average of government spending on education as a percentage of GDP	−	−	−		
Health (cumulative average)	Cumulative average of government spending on health as a percentage of GDP	−	−	−		
Democracy and social security and welfare spending interaction term	Democracy (centered) * social security and welfare	−	−			
Average years of education	Average years of total education for the population aged 25 and older	−	−			
Market liberalization						
Capital market liberalization (Chinn-Ito)	Index of capital market openness	−/+				
Trade liberalization	Index of liberalization of trade	+				
Financial liberalization	Financial reform index	0/−				
Privatization	Privatization index	+				
Tax reform	Tax reform index	+				
Controls						
GDP per capita	Gross domestic product per capita in 1000's of constant purchasing power parity dollars	−	+			
Sector dualism	The absolute difference between the percentage of the labor force in agriculture and agriculture as a share of GDP	+				
Employment in agriculture	Employment in agriculture as a percentage of total employment	+				

(continues)

TABLE 5.1. **(continued)**

Variables	Description	Inequality	Poverty	Education spending	Health spending	Social security spending
				Hypothesized effects		
Inflation	Annual percentage change in consumer prices	+	+			
Female labor force participation	Female labor force participation as percentage of the working-age population	-/+	-	+	+	+
Youth population	Population aged 0 to 14 as a percentage of total population	+	+	+		
Elderly population	Population aged 65 and over as a percentage of total population				+	+
Urban population	Urban population as a percentage of total population	+		+	+	+
Ethnic diversity	Dummy variable coded 1 when at least 20 percent but not more than 80 percent of the population is ethnically diverse	+	+	-	-	-
Stock of foreign direct investment	Stock of inward direct foreign investment as a percentage of GDP	+	+	0/+	0/+	0/-
External debt	External debt as a percentage of GDP		+	-	-	+/-
Trade openness	Exports plus imports as a percentage of GDP	-/+	-/+	-/+	-/+	-/+
IMF	Cumulative years of IMF programs since 1970	+	+	-	-	-
Inflows of foreign direct investment	Inflows of foreign direct investment as a percentage of GDP	+	+			
Informal employment	Percentage of workers classified as informal or nonagricultural labor force	+	+			
Industrial employment	Percentage of the labor force in industry	-	-	+	+	+
Veto points	Constitutional structure veto points (see text)			-/+	-/+	-/+
Deficits	Government budget deficit as a percentage of GDP			-	-	-

1997; Reuveny and Li 2003; Rudra 2004; but see Bollen and Jackman 1985), but they have measured the immediate presence of democracy in the year of the observation of the dependent variable or the year before, not the strength of the democratic tradition, which theoretically is more appropriate. Like us, Muller (1988) operationalizes democracy by its duration, and he tests and finds support for the proposition that democracy does not have an effect on income distribution until countries have been democratic for twenty years. In his quantitative analysis of health policy and infant mortality in close to a hundred developing countries, McGuire (2010, 52–57) also finds that long-term democratic practice has a statistically significant negative relationship with infant mortality, whereas short-term democratic practice does not.

POLITICAL PARTIES.   In our theoretical chapter, we argued that in democratic settings, the prime carriers of political worldviews and corresponding policy orientations are political parties, and therefore we would expect the strength of parties of the left to be associated with the introduction of policies that affect inequality over the medium and long run. In our comparative historical and statistical analysis in chapter 4, we found support for this hypothesis. Accordingly, we would expect to see some impact of differences in the strength of left-of-center parties relative to that of right-of-center parties on the level of social expenditures and thus indirectly on income distribution. To the extent that we are not able to capture the distributive structure of public programs in our measures, we would also expect to see a direct effect of relative left party strength on inequality. In addition, we would expect a left-leaning balance of power in the legislature and executive to have a direct impact, not mediated by social spending, through legislative and administrative measures such as adjustments of the minimum wage, wage setting for public employees, and labor laws.

SOCIAL POLICIES

Social Security and Welfare Spending   The prime policy instruments for shaping the distribution of income are taxes and social expenditures. In Latin America and the Caribbean, the distributive impact of social spending is mixed and tends to be different for different kinds of expenditures, as we saw in chapter 3. Social security spending, particularly the largest share that goes to pensions, is generally regressive (Ferranti et al. 2004; Lindert, Skoufias, and Shapiro 2005). Social security schemes are typically tied to formal-sector employment and thus exclude the sizable informal sector. Moreover, social security benefits are very unequally distributed among those covered because they are earnings related and because there exists different schemes for different groups, with particular privileges for some, such as the military, police, upper-level civil servants, judges, and so forth. We have also shown, however, that social security spending, though regressive, is not necessarily more unequal than market income. Social security and welfare spending are generally reported in one category by the IMF; where disaggregated figures are available, they show that over 80 percent of the expenditures in this category go to social security. Thus, higher social security and welfare spending should have no clear effect on income inequality.

Health and Education Spending   Spending on health and education is an investment in human capital, and there is considerable lag between the moment of expenditure and returns (in the form of decreased inequality levels). The distributive effect of health and education expenditure depends on its allocation. For example, spending on primary education is more redistributive than spending on university education.[2] We do not have breakdowns for these different allocations available, but evidence from case studies cited by Ferranti et al. (2004, 263–65) and from analyses by the Inter-American Development Bank (IDB 1998, 190–97) and by Lindert, Skoufias, and Shapiro (2005), as well as by the ECLAC (2005) study cited in chapter 3, indicates that the bulk of education spending is progressive and health spending slightly progressive or neutral. Keeping in mind that even "neutral" spending, that is, when each decile receives 10 percent of a good or transfer, is generally very redistributive (as shown in chap. 3), we hypothesize that education and health spending will have an equalizing effect on income distribution.

Social Security and Welfare Spending in a Democratic Context   In a pooled time series analysis of income inequality in a worldwide sample, Lee (2005) showed that the impact of government spending on inequality is dependent on regime type. In authoritarian regimes, greater government spending is associated with greater inequality. In democracies, greater government spending is associated with less inequality. This is a very plausible hypothesis for social spending in Latin America, where the main alternative to democracy has been right-wing authoritarianism, not communism.

Education   The spread of education in the population, or the improvement of human capital, is regarded as a positive factor not only for the promotion of economic development but also for the reduction of inequality. In some sense, we can see average years of education in the population as an indicator of successful education policy, that is, education spending that keeps more students in school for longer. Thus, we expect higher levels of average education in the population to have a depressing effect on inequality in Latin America as well.

MARKET LIBERALIZATION

Capital Market Openness   Free movement of capital should attract more capital to developing countries, thus increasing the demand for labor and lowering the cost of capital, both of which should reduce inequality— unless, of course, capital is substituted for labor. Morley (2001) found a progressive effect of capital account opening in Latin America. Greater openness of capital markets has also been associated with higher volatility, however, and in downturns those with more assets can protect themselves better, which should increase inequality. Because it gives capital an exit option that labor does not have, capital mobility also increases the power of capital over labor both in wage bargaining and in the political arena. Thus, we adopt a nondirectional hypothesis.

Trade Liberalization   The standard Heckscher-Ohlin assumption was that trade liberalization in developing countries would work to the advantage of labor because these countries have abundant supplies of unskilled labor relative to the rest of the world. Spilimbergo, Londoño, and Székely (1997), however, argued that once China entered the world market, Latin America no longer had abundant supplies of unskilled and comparatively cheap labor, so one would expect, and they found, an increase in inequality as a result of trade liberalization. We adopt this result as our hypothesis.

Financial Liberalization   Morley (2001, 49) argues that the net effect of financial liberalization—elimination of controls on interest rates, low-

ering of reserve requirements, and reduced use of subsidized credit—
should be progressive but not very large.

Privatization   Privatization tended to produce windfall gains for private investors and rationalization and job losses for employees, thus increasing inequality.

Tax Reform   The essence of tax reform promoted by the IFIs during
the push to market liberal reform in the 1980s and 1990s was to lower
marginal tax rates on income and corporate tax rates, and rely more on
indirect taxes, which are generally regressive. Thus, we expect a positive
effect of tax reform on income inequality.

CONTROLS

Economic Development   Theories linking economic development and
inequality have been profoundly shaped by Kuznets's (1955) inverted-U
conjecture. Most of the Latin American and Caribbean countries are
at medium levels of development, several of them are near the peak of
the curve, and a few have passed the peak (IDB 1998, 89). Thus, for the
whole sample we would expect the relationship between economic development and inequality to be mildly negative, which is what we found in
our earlier study.

Sector Dualism   Much statistical research has been devoted to establishing and explaining the U-curve relationship between economic development and inequality (e.g., Bollen and Jackman 1985; Crenshaw
1992; Muller 1985, 1988, 1989; Nielsen 1994; Nielsen and Alderson 1995;
Simpson 1990). Alderson and Nielsen (1999) emphasize the role of labor
force shifts and sectoral dualism, along with the demographic transition
and the spread of education. Sectoral dualism refers to the coexistence
of a low-productivity traditional sector and a high-productivity modern
sector, and it is expected to contribute positively to overall inequality in
a society (Alderson and Nielsen 1999, 610).

Employment in Agriculture   Alderson and Nielsen (1999, 610), based
on Kuznets (1955), hypothesize that the shift of the labor force out of
the agricultural sector is associated with increasing inequality, because
the degree of inequality within the agricultural sector is assumed to be

lower. The assumption of lower inequality within the agricultural sector for Latin America is questionable, however. Indeed, a comparison of Gini indices based on urban and rural surveys contained in the full WIID (UNU-WIDER 2007) database (described earlier in the chapter) shows that inequality in the rural samples in Latin America is generally higher than at the national level. Therefore, we would expect the opposite in our set of countries: the larger the proportion of the labor force in agriculture, the higher the degree of inequality.

Inflation   Morley (2001, 72) argues that during periods of high inflation, labor markets adjust only with a lag, which leads to a decrease in real wages, and this decrease is particularly steep for the minimum wage. Thus, high inflation drives up inequality. The IDB (1998, 100–102) and World Bank studies (Ferranti et al. 2004, 11, 231–39) agree that macroeconomic shocks, which are typically accompanied by high inflation, have a detrimental impact on inequality.

Female Labor Force Participation   The effect on inequality of the participation of women in the labor force depends on which income groups have high female participation. If the typical pattern is for married women to stay out of the labor force if household income permits, then high levels of women's labor force participation in lower-income groups will reduce inequality. As a result of assortative mating (that is, people marrying others with similar levels of education), inequality will be greater if women from upper-income households are employed as much or more than women from other income groups. Thus, we adopt a nondirectional hypothesis.

Youth Population   Previous studies have shown a strong association between population growth and the size of the youth population, and a positive impact of population growth on inequality (Bollen and Jackman 1985; Simpson 1990). Alderson and Nielsen (1999) explain this impact by maintaining that the oversupply of young unskilled workers further depresses lower incomes and increases wage differentials. We therefore expect that an increase in the percentage of the population under fifteen years of age will push up the level of inequality.

Ethnic Composition   Scholars agree that indigenous people and people of African descent have generally lower incomes and lower educational attainment. On the other hand, studies have shown that national inequality is mostly explained by inequality within racial, ethnic, and gender groups and not by the differences among demographic groups (Ferranti et al. 2004, 85–96). Nevertheless, we include ethnic diversity among our control variables and expect a positive relationship to inequality, which is what we found in our earlier study.

Foreign Direct Investment   Previous studies have found that stock of foreign direct investment has a positive effect on inequality (Bornschier and Chase-Dunn 1985; Evans and Timberlake 1980). Tsai (1995) found that this effect is region-specific and that foreign direct investment has no significant distributional effect for Latin American countries. Reuveny and Li (2003) found that inflows of foreign direct investment have a positive effect on inequality in a worldwide sample of countries. We found that stock of foreign direct investment had a consistent positive effect on inequality in our models with politics and policy (Huber et al. 2006). We expect that stock and flows of foreign direct investment will continue to show a positive effect on inequality in Latin America because foreign investment usually brings capital-intensive production that creates comparatively few but well-paying jobs.

Trade Openness   Openness of the economy to trade theoretically should favor the abundant factor of production—unskilled labor—in developing countries. However, since more open economies in Latin America have also been exposed to competition from countries with even lower labor costs, such as China, this effect may be neutralized. Moreover, in more open economies in the information age there is a premium on higher education such that the returns to higher education may rise and inequality increase. Accordingly, we adopt a nondirectional hypothesis.

IMF Conditionality   IMF-prescribed austerity programs depress real wages, raise interest rates, and cut public expenditures, particularly on subsidies for popular consumption items and public services such as health and education. All of these measures hit lower-income groups particularly hard and thus can be expected to increase inequality. The cuts in expenditures on health and education over the longer run result in lower human capital at the bottom, a further factor accounting for inequality. Relationships between the IMF and debtor countries are mostly tense, and agreements on austerity programs are frequently broken. Therefore, we measure the number of years during which countries have been under IMF programs, and we expect more years of IMF presence to result in higher levels of inequality.

Informal Sector   The informal sector in Latin America is very heterogeneous, but low-productivity activities dominate. Accordingly, workers employed in small enterprises in the informal sector earn less than workers in the formal sector, even controlling for experience and years of schooling. The same is true for self-employed workers, the vast majority of whom are in the informal sector. Moreover, the difference between male and female earnings is larger among workers in the informal than in the formal sector and among the self-employed than among formal-sector workers (IDB 1998, 40). Thus, we expect a larger informal sector to be associated with greater overall income inequality.

Industrial Employment   Industrial jobs in Latin America on average have paid higher wages than jobs in agriculture or services. In part, this disparity reflects higher productivity. In addition, this is a result of the fact that industry, along with mining, has traditionally been the sector with the highest levels of unionization. The higher the proportion of the labor force employed in industry, the greater was the share of wage income. Thus, we expect higher levels of industrial employment to be associated with lower levels of inequality.

Poverty

As one can see from table 5.1, our hypotheses for the effects of our independent variables on poverty are, in most cases, not surprisingly, the same as our hypotheses for their effects on inequality. We do have different expectations for some variables, however, and we limit our comments here to those variables. It is reasonable to have different expectations for poverty and inequality because they measure inequality at quite different points in the income distribution. Morley (2001) points out that most of the variation in the Gini index of income distribution in Latin America is accounted for by the proportion of national income received by the top 10 percent of households. At the other end of the income distribution, an average of 38 percent of households are poor in our sample of country-years. The poverty measure is an absolute measure so, holding inequality constant, the poverty figure falls with increasing GDP per capita.

The first difference we expect is precisely related to the fact that the poverty measure is an absolute measure. We expect that there will be a much stronger association between GDP per capita and poverty than there is between GDP per capita and income inequality. Second, increased women's labor force participation will reduce poverty, but it could increase inequality if women from upper-income households increase their level of labor force participation as much or more than women from other income groups. We expect all three social spending variables unambiguously to reduce poverty. In each, part of the logic is that the poor, by definition, earn little income and thus pay little in taxes, so that what they get back in terms of services (education and health care) and transfers, even if not proportionate to their share of the population, is almost certain to be more than their share of taxes paid. In the case of transfers, the poor are the recipients of more targeted transfer programs, and as we see in the next chapter, these programs have been increasing in scope the last decade or so.

Social Spending

DEMOCRACY AND PARTIES.   Since democracy gives parties of all political colors and groups with a variety of interests the possibility to pressure the government for benefits, we expect a positive relationship between democracy and all three types of social spending. Given the generally progressive profile of the bulk of education spending and the slightly progressive or neutral profile of health spending, we expect a positive effect of left political strength on health and education spending. Given its ambiguous distributive effects, we adopt a nondirectional hypothesis for the effect of left strength on social security and welfare spending (see table 5.1). For all three types of spending, we do not expect the very strong relationship between partisan government and spending that we found in OECD countries, in part because of the ambiguous distributive effects of spending but also because of the more limited periods of democracy and the inchoate party systems of some Latin American countries.

With regard to the effect of repressive authoritarian regimes on levels of social spending, we would expect a negative effect on health and education spending. On the other hand, given that social security spending primarily benefits more privileged groups, we may see no effect on social security and welfare spending. Yet, we expect this effect to begin to fade after the replacement of the repressive regime with a democratic one. In other words, we expect that the effect of ten years of repressive authoritarian rule in the 1960s on social spending in the 1990s will be weaker than the effect of ten years of repressive authoritarian rule in the 1980s.

VETO POINTS. As we saw in chapter 2, degree of centralization versus dispersion of power through the constitutional structure has served as an explanatory variable for the ease of expansion as well as retrenchment of social policy schemes. Federalism has been held responsible for slowing the expansion of the public sector in general and the welfare state in particular. Federalism is only one aspect of power dispersion. Other institutional provisions for power dispersion, such as presidentialism, bicameralism, and popular referenda, also provide the opportunity for opponents of legislation to mobilize attempts to block its passage and thus make the adoption of important social policy schemes more difficult. By the same token these veto points also make retrenchment of existing entitlements more difficult. During our period of analysis, 1970 to 2007, both phases of expansion and retrenchment were on the agenda, so the positive and negative effects could counterbalance each other, and statistically this may result in no significant effects.

CONTROLS

Logic of Industrialism What is loosely called the logic of industrialism perspective on welfare state development has emphasized structural factors, needs, and resources, to explain patterns of social expenditures (Wilensky 1975). Industrialization brings greater affluence to a society and thus more resources for governments to allocate to a variety of social programs. Industrialization also promotes urbanization, the decline of the extended family, and the growth of the proportion of elderly people as a result of advances in life expectancy, which in turn require the construction of social safety nets and drive up social expenditures, particularly for pensions. Thus, we would expect a positive effect from industrial employment, GDP per capita, urbanization, and the proportion of the elderly population on social security and health spending in Latin American countries, as well as a positive effect from industrial employment, GDP per capita, urbanization, and size of the youth population on education spending.

Female Labor Force Participation   In advanced industrial countries, the transition to the service economy leads to rising female labor force participation, and with it a rise in demand for public social services and social transfers. We expect similar processes to occur in Latin America, with increasing women's labor force participation leading to demands for all-day school, health care for families, and cash transfers to families.

Ethnic Diversity   Ethnic diversity is associated with lower-class solidarity and lower levels of class consciousness. Thus, we expect it to have a depressing effect on social spending.

Globalization   In the past two decades, the impact of globalization on public expenditure patterns has commanded increasing attention. In developing countries, the impact of globalization has been particularly dramatic. The opening of heavily protected economies has taken place rapidly and brought significant economic dislocations. The debt crisis of the 1980s and the central role played by the IMF in dealing with this crisis have exposed these countries to strong external pressures for austerity. An opening of capital markets along with an opening to trade have made these countries vulnerable to volatility induced by rapid inflows and outflows of capital. Foreign direct investment has assumed great importance in the eyes of policy makers and thus has been able to demand concessions.

We would expect foreign direct investment, fiscal deficits, and the presence of IMF programs to have the following effects on social spending. Foreign investors want low taxes, particularly low payroll taxes, traditionally the most important source of funding for social security schemes. On the other hand, if we assume a longer time horizon, they may be interested in a better-educated and healthier labor force and thus actually favor higher expenditures on health and education, financed out of revenue generated from other than corporate taxes. Thus, we would expect a negative effect of foreign direct investment on social security spending and a neutral or weak positive one on health and education spending. Fiscal deficits sooner or later call for austerity policies, and we would expect them to have negative effects on all kinds of social expenditures. The IMF is the key enforcer of austerity through the conditionality associated with standby loans. Thus, we would expect the presence of an IMF agreement to be associated with lower levels of all kinds of social expenditures also.

Trade openness has received considerable attention in the literature and has been approached with contradictory hypotheses. A well-established view of the effect of trade openness in advanced industrial countries is that the economic vulnerabilities created by trade openness have generated demands for social protection and thus an expansion of the welfare state (Cameron 1978; Katzenstein 1985). Rodrik (1997) has made a similar argument for developing countries. The opposite hypothesis would hold that economic openness causes volatility and periodic balance of payments crises that then call for austerity and a lowering of social expenditures, which would result in a negative relationship. This negative effect would be indirect, however, and thus should be captured by measures of deficits and IMF programs. Given the contradictory nature of these expectations and previous findings, we adopt a nondirectional hypothesis for the effect of trade openness on all types of spending.

Measurement

Dependent Variables

Our income inequality variable is the Gini index of income inequality from the United Nations University's World Income Inequality Database, WIID, version 2c (UNU-WIDER 2008), and SEDLAC (2010), a Latin American partner of WIID (see table 5.A.1 for data sources on all of the variables).[3] WIID/SEDLAC were compiled using several national sources and represent a major improvement in quality over the previously most frequently used data of Deininger and Squire (1996), which they subsume. Each observation in WIID/SECLAC is coded for its quality, area of coverage, income-sharing unit, unit of analysis, and the use of a household size equivalence scale. We deleted observations with the lowest-quality rating and those with expenditure or consumption as the income concept, as well as those without coverage of the entire population.[4] In case of multiple observations for the same year, we kept observations that (*a*) have the individual as the unit of analysis and (*b*) use an equivalence scale adjusted for household size. If there were still multiple observations, we took the average of the Gini values for the year in question. We used indicator variables to control for three remaining hypothesized sources of variation due to survey methodology: no adjustment for household size, earnings as an income concept, use of gross (versus net) income, and absence of information on the use of gross versus net income. This yielded 271 country-year observations. These data cover eighteen Latin American countries (Argentina, Bolivia, Brazil, Chile, Colombia, Costa Rica, Dominican Republic, Ecuador, El Salvador, Guatemala, Honduras, Mexico, Nicaragua, Panama, Paraguay, Peru, Uruguay, and Venezuela) for the period 1971 to 2005. The data set is unbalanced with 3 to 28 observations per country and an average of 15 observations per country. There are 62 gaps in the time series for each country. Table 5.2 displays the data for three dates, 1990 through the beginning of the economic recovery period, the end of the 1990s, and the most recent available data.

The dependent variable for the analysis of poverty is the percentage of households living below the ECLAC-generated country-specific poverty line. The data are compiled from ECLAC studies, primarily the annual *Social Panorama*, and span the period 1979 through 2005, but most observations are for the period since 1990. There are 124 country-year ob-

TABLE 5.2. **Income inequality in Latin America**

	Early 1990s	1998 or 1999	Latest 2003–6
Argentina	44.4	50.2	50.7
Brazil	60.4	59.2	56.4
Chile	55.1	55.5	54.6
Costa Rica	44.0	47.1	48.2
Uruguay	44.7	44.0	45.0
Mexico	54.6	53.6	51.0
Panama	55.5	55.4	54.8
Venezuela	44.0	47.2	47.6
Bolivia	54.5	57.6	50.5
Colombia	56.7	56.2	56.2
Dominican Republic	49.0	47.5	50.3
Ecuador	53.8	49.6	53.5
El Salvador	44.7	53.4	48.4
Guatemala	54.4	54.0	49.4
Honduras	56.9	58.8	56.6
Nicaragua	—	53.8	52.3
Peru	49.1	55.5	49.8
Paraguay	41.3	55.5	53.9
Mean	50.8	53.0	51.6

Notes: Cell entries are Gini coefficients.

TABLE 5.3. **Poverty rates in Latin America**

	Early 1990s	Circa 2004
Argentina	16.2	18.7
Brazil	41.0	28.5
Chile	33.3	11.3
Costa Rica	23.6	19.5
Uruguay	11.8	11.3
Mexico	35.5	29.8
Panama	27.4	26.4
Venezuela	34.2	32.9
Bolivia	51.3	56.4
Colombia	40.8	45.2
Ecuador	55.8	41.7
Dominican Republic	—	50.4
El Salvador	—	40.4
Guatemala	63.0	52.8
Honduras	75.2	68.5
Nicaragua	—	62.9
Paraguay	36.8	57.1
Peru	52.0	40.5
Mean	39.9	38.6
Mean (data for both dates)	39.9	36.0

Notes: Cell entries indicate the percentage of individuals who live below the ECLAC-established poverty line.

servations with between 3 and 10 observations per country for the same eighteen countries as in the inequality analysis. There are many gaps in the country time series. Table 5.3 displays the data for two dates, 1990 through the beginning of the economic recovery period and the most recent available data.

We choose to use the ECLAC measure rather than the commonly employed World Bank international poverty line of two purchasing-power-parity (PPP) dollars per day. The benefit of using the two-PPP-dollars-per-day measure is that it permits unbiased cross-national comparisons (World Bank 1990; Londoño and Székely 1997; Psacharopoulos et al. 1997). Several authors, however, criticize the measure, noting that it is too static and does not consider important differences in consumption patterns and prices among countries. Minujin, Vandemoortele, and Delamonica (2002) contend that as per capita income increases, it becomes more costly to purchase goods that are necessary for day-to-day life. They argue that "the relevance of a line fixed at US$1 PPP per day is gradually eroded by economic growth and it is not even useful at one point in time to compare (or aggregate) the incidence of poverty across countries" (2002, 25). Even scholars who employ the World Bank poverty line remark on the measure's weaknesses.

Reddy and Pogge (2005, 38) criticize the World Bank poverty measure and argue that it is more useful to construct unique poverty lines, for each country, that "possess a common achievement interpretation. Each poverty line would refer to the local cost of requirements of achieving a specific set of ends." Reddy and Pogge state that if common end goals are specified, then data can be compared across time and space even when the poverty lines are country-specific. We agree with Reddy and Pogge and contend that for the region of Latin America, the measure that comes closest to this goal is that provided by ECLAC. ECLAC calculates a poverty line for each country in the region. The line is based on the cost of a basket of food and nonfood items. While the basket of goods meets a minimum nutritional requirement (that is, each has common caloric and protein end-goals), it also reflects national consumption patterns, the availability of food items, and relative prices (ECLAC 2007).

Social spending is available from two sources, the IMF and ECLAC. The ECLAC series appeared in Cominetti (1996), ECLAC (2002, 2004), and on line (http://www.eclac.cl/badeinso/Badeinso.asp). The series from the ECLAC sources are not identical, and they differ from the IMF series, especially in the case of education spending, because the IMF data are for central government only. We developed combined series using several criteria for data selection: (1) ECLAC data are preferred over the IMF series in federalist countries and other countries with significant decentralization of social spending; (2) data consistent across the various series are preferred over data that exhibit deviations; and (3) longer time series are preferred over shorter series. The data used in this chapter come from the following sources: social security and welfare spending—56 percent IMF, 44 percent ELAC; education spending—18 percent IMF, 82 percent ELAC; and health spending—51 percent IMF, 49 percent ELAC.[5] For the analysis of poverty and inequality in which the spending variables are independent variables, we used current spending on social security and welfare, and cumulative average of spending on health care and education. These data cover the same eighteen countries as the inequality and poverty analyses for the period 1970 to 2007. There are 542 country-year observations; the data set is unbalanced with 15 to 37 observations per country and an average of 30 observations per country. There are relatively few gaps in the

TABLE 5.4. **Social spending as a percentage of GDP**

	1990			2004		
	Social security and welfare	Education	Health	Social security and welfare	Education	Health
Argentina	8.1	3.3	4.0	9.3	4.2	4.4
Brazil	9.8	4.4	3.9	11.8	4.6	4.6
Chile	7.2	2.5	2	6.1	3.6	2.8
Costa Rica	4.6	4.2	7.2	5.2	4.9	6.0
Uruguay	11.7	1.9	3.1	12.2	2.6	3.3
Mexico	2.3	4.0	2.9	2.2	5.4	3.0
Panama	4.8	4.1	4.2	6.0	3.8	3.4
Venezuela	2.5	2.5	1.5	4.3	5.3	1.6
Bolivia	2.9	2.9	0.4	4.8	6.5	2.9
Colombia	2.6	3.2	1.0	6.1	4.9	2.3
Ecuador	2.6	2.7	1.6	2.1	2.6	1.2
Dominican Republic	0.5	1.1	1.0	1.7	1.7	1.9
El Salvador	0.4	1.9	1.0	2.3	2.9	3.5
Guatemala	0.8	1.6	0.9	1.1	2.5	0.9
Honduras	0.5	4.3	2.7	0.3	7.8	3.6
Nicaragua	3.0	5.1	5.1	—	4.5	3.2
Paraguay	1.1	1.1	0.3	4.2	3.7	1.6
Peru	1.0	2.5	1.0	2.3	3.2	1.1
Mean	3.7	3.0	2.4	4.8	4.2	2.9

time series for each country. The data for the three spending variables for 1990 and 2004 are shown in table 5.4.

Political and Policy Variables

POLITICAL VARIABLES The measure of democracy is taken from Rueschemeyer, Stephens, and Stephens's analysis of Latin American and Caribbean political regimes. Within their definitions, colonies and all forms of authoritarian regimes are coded as 0, restricted democracies as 0.5, and full democracies as 1. We also examined measures developed by Alvarez et al. (1996), Freedom House, and Mainwaring, Brinks, and Pérez-Liñán (2001). Not surprisingly all of these measures are highly correlated, particularly our cumulative versions of them. Alvarez et al. ends in 1990 and Freedom House begins in 1972, so these measures do not have sufficient coverage for our purposes. The Mainwaring, Brinks, and Pérez-Liñán and Rueschemeyer, Stephens, and Stephens annual measures are highly correlated (.85), and the cumulative versions of the measures are very highly correlated (.95). Thus, it is not surprising that substituting Mainwaring for Rueschemeyer yielded the same results. Each country's score is cumulated from 1945 to the year of observation. This cumulative measure is appropriate for testing the theoretical argument that it is the strength of the democratic record that allows parties representing the interests of the underprivileged to emerge, consolidate, gain entry into the legislature, and use their legislative position to shape policy. To test Muller's (1988) hypothesis that democracy only begins to have a negative effect on inequality when a country has been democratic twenty years, we measure "long-term democracy" by subtracting 20 from our cumulative democracy score and then setting all values that are less than 20 to 0.

Our political party variables are derived from Coppedge (1997).[6] In his project, he consulted country experts to classify political parties that contested elections for the lower house or constituent assemblies in eleven countries of Latin America from as far back as 1912. Classification of parties on the basis of expert surveys is a common practice also in the study of advanced industrial democracies; one of the classics is Castles and Mair (1984).[7] Coppedge's classification scheme contains two primary dimensions and several residual categories. First, it includes a left-right dimension, defined primarily in social and economic terms. He is concerned with a political party's ideology and class appeals and with its relative prioritization of growth and redistribution. This dimension is divided into five categories: left, center-left, center, center-right, and right. Second, it includes a religious dimension of two categories, Christian and secular. It distinguishes those parties that do and do not base their ideology or programs on the Catholic Church, the Bible, or religious philosophy or seek to defend the interests of the Catholic Church and to reduce the separation of church and state. Finally, his classification scheme contains three residual categories: personalist, other, and unknown. For our purposes, it is sufficient to say that these residual categories all contain parties that are not classifiable according to left-right or Christian-secular criteria.

For country-years that overlapped with Coppedge's work, we used his codings. For other country-years, we employed Coppedge's coding scheme to classify all parties that contested lower-house elections for the country-years in question. Unlike Coppedge, we did not use expert surveys. Instead, two members of our team independently consulted numerous primary and reference materials to code each political party. Then, on parties for which there was a disagreement, we consulted country experts. Finally, the entire research team convened to make a decision about each party for which there was disagreement.[8]

Coppedge's left-right and religious orientation codings refer to the parties and not the executive. We coded the executives according to the parties they represented. While this appears to be a defensible and even obvious decision, it is not without problems, which are illustrated by the Cardoso presidency (1995–2002) in Brazil. Coppedge codes Cardoso's party, the PSDB, as center-left. Cardoso, however, was elected with the support of the Liberal Front Party (PFL) and the Brazilian Labor Party (PTB), which Coppedge codes as right and center-right, respectively. The centrist Party of the Brazilian Democratic Movement (PMDB) joined Cardoso's governing coalition after the election. This broad coalition was needed because of the lack of party discipline and in part because of the PT posture of principled opposition to the government, which meant that it voted against government legislation even if it agreed that the legislation was desirable, as in the cases of the Cardoso education reforms (see chap. 6). Thus, in our comparative case analysis in chapter 6, we treat the Cardoso government as a centrist government. We nonetheless code the Cardoso presidency as center-left in the quantitative analysis. Similarly, in the quantitative analysis, we do not code the Peronist Party (PJ) presidencies according to the behavior of the president in office, but stick to the "personalist" classification derived from Coppedge's expert surveys, whereas in the comparative case analysis we treat the Menem government as center-right and the Kirchner governments as center-left.

After the classification of each party in the sample, the proportion of the seats held by each party category for every country-year in the analysis was summed.[9] During years that are nondemocratic, as defined by our democracy variable, all categories are scored as 0. In our earlier analyses of social spending, inequality, and poverty (Huber et al. 2006; Huber, Mustillo, and Stephens 2008; Pribble, Huber, and Stephens 2009), we found that the religious dimension was not related to any of the dependent variables. Thus, we combined the religious and secular categories into five categories: right, center-right, center, center-left, and left. We created three partisanship variables. First, we computed cumulative left legislative seats by adding the proportion of left and center-left legislative seats and then cumulating these scores from 1945 to the year in question. As in the case of democracy, we expect the impact of parties on the dependent variables to be long term.[10] For example, we expect inequality in a given country-year to be affected by the previous history of left partisan strength, not just by the strength of the left in that year or the previous year. Similarly, we computed cumulative left executive by adding left and center-left executives and then cumulating these scores from 1945 to the year in question. We then computed a summary variable, which we refer to as "left political strength," which is the average of the cumulative legislative and executive variables. Finally, a measure of left-center dominance was constructed: a country-year was coded as 1 if the left, center-left, and center had a majority in the legislature *and* the president was left or center-left. The score was then cumulated from 1945 to the country-year in question.[11] The results with the two different combined left legislative and executive variables were similar. We report the left political strength results in this chapter.

The final political variable tested is the presence of highly repressive authoritarian regimes. Repressive authoritarian regimes were coded as a separate category, 1 for every year the country had a repressive authoritarian regime and 0 for every year without such a regime, based on the extent of human rights violations committed or tolerated by the authoritarian government. Yearly scores were cumulated over the fifteen years prior to the year of observation, to capture the fading of the impact of repressive authoritarianism over time. The sources were country studies.[12]

EDUCATION AND HUMAN CAPITAL.   Investment in human capital is central to our theory and policy prescriptions, so we discuss the strengths and shortcomings of the available measures of human capital and its distribution in some detail here. Since the advent of new growth theory with its emphasis on human capital, the Barro-Lee measures of formal education (Barro and Lee 2000) have been used as measures of human capital in most quantitative studies of economic growth. The Barro-Lee data set contains measures of education completion at seven different levels (no schooling, some primary, completed primary, some secondary, completed secondary, some tertiary, completed tertiary) and an estimate of average years of education based on the completion data of the population aged fifteen years or older and twenty-five years or older for 140 countries at five-year intervals from 1960 to 2010.[13]

The Barro-Lee data measure the *stock* of human capital in the adult population and thus are clearly conceptually superior for studies of economic growth or income distribution than are measures of *flows* of students through the educational system, such as primary or secondary school enrollment rates. Enrollment rates only tell us what proportion of the relevant age cohorts are in school, not what the skill levels of the working-age population are. Yet further removed from the human capital levels of the working-age population are measures of educational expenditure. Indeed, to the extent that educational expenditure does not raise average years of schooling, one might expect it to have no effect on economic growth and even perverse effects on income distribution if the extra spending is used to raise the educational level of the very privileged, which—as noted—has often been the case in Latin America.

Along these same lines, it might be objected that if one raises the level of education of the privileged only, average years of education, the most commonly used measure in growth studies, will rise, yet inequality will also rise. Conceptually this is a valid argument, but empirically it is not a problem because educational inequality and average years of education are very highly negatively correlated. Thomas, Wang, and Fan (2001) calculate educational Ginis for the 140 countries in the Barro-Lee data set and find that average years of education explain 91 percent of the variation in educational inequality. In our analysis we found that the Thomas, Wang, and Fan measure of inequality of education does not predict poverty or inequality better than average years of education, so we use the conventional measure.

Unfortunately, as has been shown by the International Adult Literacy Survey (IALS), completion rates in formal education and average years of education leave much to be desired as measures of human capital and its distribution among the working-age population (OECD/HRDC 2000). They ignore the variation in school quality, which can be quite large in most of Latin America, and which varies systematically with social class. It also ignores the effect of parents' education, home environment, neighborhood, peers, and so forth, which also vary with social class, as has been established by the vast literature on the sociology of education.

The IALS has produced the best measures of the stock and distribution of human capital in the working-age population available for the twenty-four countries included the IALS, which fortunately included one Latin American country—Chile. We can use the IALS data as the gold standard by which we judge the validity of the other measures that are available for most or all the countries included in our analysis. In the

IALS, a cross-nationally comparable test of respondent skills in prose, document handling and interpretation, and mathematics (roughly analogous to the American SAT) was administered to a random sample of the adult population of twenty-four OECD countries. Figure 5.1 displays the aggregate average scores on the three tests at the 95th, 75th, 25th, and 5th percentiles and at the mean, for five countries. As Iversen and Stephens (2008) point out in their analysis of rich OECD democracies,[14] there is a correspondence between the "worlds of welfare capitalism" and "worlds of human capital," especially at the bottom of the distribution. The countries with social democratic welfare states (represented here by Sweden) rank the highest, followed by the countries with Christian democratic welfare states (represented by Germany), and the countries with liberal welfare states (represented by the United States).

Figure 5.1 shows that Portugal and Chile are distinct, having lower scores across the distribution than the advanced industrial countries, al-

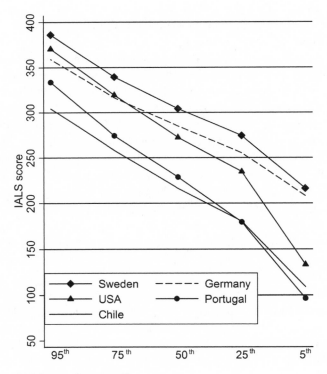

FIGURE 5.1. IALS scores by percentile

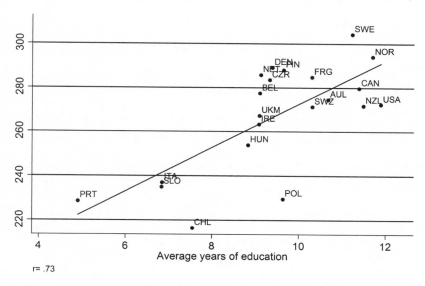

FIGURE 5.2. Mean score on IALS and average years of education

though the difference to the United States in the bottom 5 percent is surprisingly small. The scores for Chile are the lowest, except for the bottom 5 percent, where Portugal is even lower, and the 25th percentile, where Chile is tied with Portugal in the bottom spot. Inequality in human capital distribution is actually higher in Portugal than in Chile, which makes the much higher levels of income inequality in Chile all the more perplexing (see below).

Figure 5.2 shows the relationship between the Barro-Lee measure of average years of education, the most common measure of the average human capital stock in the quantitative literature, and the IALS mean score, the optimal measure. The correlation is only modest given that the two measures are supposed to be measuring the same underlying phenomenon. One can see that Chile, along with Poland, is an outlier: an additional year of education has much less payoff in these two countries than in the other countries. One interpretation, which we explore in more detail in the cross-regional comparative chapter, is that the quality of education varies greatly in Chile because private education, which accounts for fully half of total education expenditure, is much better than public education; those educated in the low-quality public schools bring down the Chilean average.

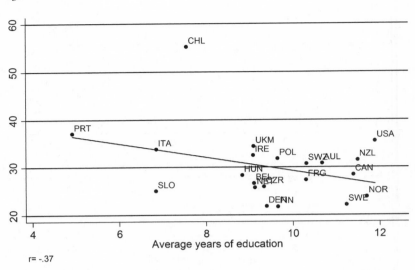

FIGURE 5.3. Average years of education and Gini index of disposable income inequality

In figures 5.3 and 5.4 we explore the relationship between our two measures of average human capital stock in the working-age population and disposable income inequality.[15] Figure 5.3 shows that average years of education is not a good predictor of income inequality and that it is particularly poor in the case of Chile. Our examination of the relationship between average years of education and IALS scores suggests that these facts might be explained by the modest relationship between the two measures of human capital stock and the fact that Chile is an outlier in that relationship.

Figure 5.4 shows that this explanation is only part of the story. The correlation between the IALS and income inequality is a respectable −.72, but Chile is still an outlier; its income distribution is much more unequal than one would expect given its average IALS score. The comparison of Chile to the two southern European countries is very instructive here. It has often been observed that one reason for the high levels of income inequality in Latin America is the high returns to formal education (e.g., see Morley 2001; Ferranti 2004), and this view is consistent with figure 5.3. Figure 5.2 suggests that the explanation is the poor quality of education at the bottom, that is, the actual differences in general skills (as measured by the IALS) between those with few and those with many years of schooling are much larger than the differences in for-mal education. This statement suggests that inequality in actual skills might explain the high returns to education in Chile and elsewhere in Latin America. A comparison of the figures for Chile and southern Eu-rope in figures 5.1 and 5.4 does not support this hypothesis. From fig-ure 5.1, one can see that level and distribution of general skill levels in Chile and southern Europe are similar, and in fact, inequality in skill levels is actually greater in Portugal than in Chile. Thus, the outlier posi-tion of Chile in figure 5.4 is *not* the result of greater inequality in the dis-tribution of general skills in the working-age population. Something else must be happening here.

Table 5.5 shows the correlation of various measures of human capi-tal—cognitive skills (test scores of students on two tests administered by UNESCO in 1997 and 2006); education completion of the adult pop-ulation (average years of education); flows of students through the edu-cational systems (primary and secondary school enrollment rates); and investment (education spending)—along with their correlations with poverty and inequality. We previously described the construction of the cumulative average of education spending variable. The cognitive test score measure was developed by Hanushek and Woessmann (2009).[16]

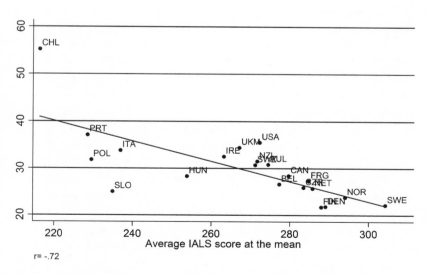

FIGURE 5.4. Average IALS scores and Gini index of disposable income inequality

TABLE 5.5. **Correlations of inequality and poverty with education measures**

	(1)	(2)	(3)	(4)	(5)	(6)
1) Income inequality, 2000 or 2001	1					
2) Average poverty, 1998–2006	.39	1				
3) Cognitive skill test scores (see text)	−.41	−.84	1			
4) Average years of education, 2000	−.20	−.69	.43	1		
5) Primary school enrollment,1990–2000	.10	−.37	.14	.73	1	
6) Secondary school enrollment, 1990–2000	−.14	−.68	.53	.90	.64	1
7) Cumulative average education spending	−.11	−.37	.28	.31	.22	.13

In their work on economic growth, Hanushek and Woessmann (2008, 2009) use the average cognitive skill scores of students as a best available proxy measure for cognitive skills of the working-age population. It is cross-sectional and only available for a time point after the end of our data series for poverty and income inequality, so it is not possible to use the measure in our pooled time series analysis. We include it in table 5.5 as a validity check on our other variables. The table also includes the correlations of the various human capital measures to the measures of poverty and income inequality used in the analyses in this chapter. The skill measure correlates only weakly with the investment, stock, and flow measures, but highly with poverty.

Table 5.5 shows that the correlation between the cognitive skill test scores and average years of education is modest, in part because the test scores stem from students and average years of education from the working-age population. On the basis of the IALS data discussed previously, however, it is probable that the modest correlation is in larger part the result of the deficiencies of average years of education as a measure of human capital stock in the working-age population. The correlation between secondary school enrollment and cognitive scores is actually somewhat higher than the correlation between scores and years of education. On conceptual grounds, it still seems that average years of education is a better measure of *stock* of human capital in the adult population than school enrollment, and in any case the education completion variable proved to be a better predictor of our dependent variables in multivariate analysis (cf. Huber et al. 2006, and Huber and Stephens 2009). So, because we do not have a skill measure available, we include average years of education and not secondary school enrollment in our analysis here.

Market Liberalization

The source for most of our data on market liberalization is Morley, Machado, and Pettinato (1999), and the update of the Morley data is Escaith and Paunovic (2004). Each index of different aspects of market liberalization is made up of two or more subindices. The capital market liberalization index measures international financial liberalization. The subcomponents measure the sectoral control of foreign investment, limits on profits and interest repatriation, and controls on external credits by national borrowers and capital outflows. The original sources for these data were World Bank country memoranda and IMF's balance of payments arrangements. The subcomponents of the trade liberalization index are the average level of tariffs and the dispersion of tariffs. The financial liberalization index measures domestic financial reform. Its subcomponents are control of borrowing rates at banks, control of lending rates at banks, and the reserves-to-deposit ratio. The privatization index is 1 minus the ratio of value added in state-owned enterprises to nonagricultural GDP. The tax reform index is the average of the maximum marginal tax rate on corporate incomes and personal incomes, the value-added tax rate, and the efficiency of the value-added tax. The efficiency of the government in collecting the value-added tax is the ratio of the VAT rate to the receipts from this tax expressed as a ratio of GDP.

Morley, Machado, and Pettinato (1999) standardize each market liberalization index such that they vary from 0 to 1, 1 being the most reformed. An increase in the index implies a reduction in government intervention. Each index is calculated following the formula $I_{it} = (\text{max} - IR_{it})/(\text{max} - \text{min})$, where I_{it} is the index value of country i at time t, IR_{it} is the raw value of the reform measure for a particular country at a particular year, and max and min represent the maximum and minimum values of a reform measure for all countries at all years, respectively. It should be noted that each country's performance is relative to the most liberalized country-year in the data set; this procedure may not result in a very high standard since, on some of the measures, no country-year was close to complete liberalization. A high value of the index, therefore, may give a misleading impression of the absolute level of reform (Morley, Machado, and Pettinato 1999). There is also some skepticism in the scholarly community regarding the validity of the cross-country differences in the index.

An alternative measure of capital market openness is available in the new data set developed by Chinn and Ito (2008). The original data source for the Chinn-Ito index is the IMF's *Annual Report on Exchange Arrangements and Exchange Restrictions*, a composite standardized index based on measures of the presence of multiple exchange rates, restrictions on current account and on capital account, and requirements of the surrender of export proceeds.

Control Variables

We employ a number of economic and demographic controls that the literature considers relevant. Gross Domestic Product in 1996 purchasing power parity dollars is taken from the Penn World Tables (version 6.3) supplemented by the World Bank's *World Development Indicators* CD (World Bank 2007).[17] Sector dualism measures the absolute difference between employment in agriculture as a percentage of total employment and agriculture as a percentage of GDP. These data come from four different sources, namely, the World Bank's *World Development Indicators* CD (2007), International Labor Organization's online labor statistics (ILO 2003), ECLAC's *Statistical Yearbook on Latin America and the Caribbean* (various years), and Alderson and Nielsen (1999). Employment in agriculture as a percentage of total employment is taken from the same four sources as sector dualism. Inflation is measured as the annual percentage change in consumer prices, taken from IMF's *International Financial Statistics* CD and Blyde and Fernandez-Arias (2004). We measure female labor force participation as a percentage of the working-age population from the World Bank's *World Development Indicators* CD (2007). From the same source we include the percentage of the population under fifteen years of age, and the percentage sixty-five and older. Also from the World Bank's *World Development Indicators* CD (2007), we include an urbanization variable, operationalized as the percentage of the population who live in areas defined as urban. We code ethnic diversity as a dummy variable, based on data presented in Ferranti et al. (2004). The variable is coded 1 when at least 20 percent, but not more than 80 percent, of the population is of African origin or is indigenous, and 0 otherwise.

The measure of stock of inward direct foreign investment is taken from two sources: United Nations Conference on Trade and Development (UNCTAD 2002) *Handbook of Statistics* and the United Nations Centre on Transnational Corporations (1985). External debt as a percentage of GDP is the sum of public, publicly guaranteed, and private nonguaranteed long-term debt, use of IMF credit, and short-term debt as measured in the World Bank's *World Development Indicators* (2007). We measure trade openness as exports and imports as a percentage of gross domestic product taken from IMF's *International Financial Statistics* CD and Blyde and Fernandez-Arias (2004). The same sources provide the cumulative years of IMF programs since 1970. Foreign direct investment inflows are measured as a percentage of gross domestic product. The data are compiled from the World Bank's *World Development Indicators* CD (2007).

We measure informal employment as the percentage of nonagricultural workers classified as informal in relation to the total labor force, as taken from International Labor Organization's online labor statistics (ILO 2003). The percentage of the labor force employed in industry, namely, industrial employment, is measured through the World Bank's *World Development Indicators* CD (2007). We code veto points only in democratic years. Each component—federalism, presidentialism, bicameralism, and the presence of popular referenda—is scored on a 0 to 2 scale; we then add the scores to obtain an additive index. Finally, we measure a central government's deficit as a percentage of gross domestic product, following IMF's *International Financial Statistics* CD and Blyde and Fernandez-Arias (2004).

Analytic Techniques

Hicks (1994, 172) states that "errors for regression equations estimated from pooled data using OLS [ordinary least squares] procedures tend to be (1) temporally autoregressive, (2) cross-sectionally heteroskedastic, and (3) cross-sectionally correlated . . . [they also] (4) conceal unit and period effects and (5) reflect some causal heterogeneity across space, time, or both." We follow Beck and Katz's (1995) recommended use of panel-corrected standard errors and imposition of a common rho for all cross-sections. To correct for serial correlation, Beck and Katz (1996) recommend inclusion of a lagged dependent variable. Achen (2000), however, has shown that the lagged dependent variable inappropriately suppresses the power of other independent variables.[18] Beck and Katz (2004, 16–17) have shown that the correction for first-order autoregressiveness includes a lagged dependent variable on the right-hand side of the equation (known as Prais-Winsten estimations). Thus, the correction deals with the problem of serial correlation but without, as our results show, suppressing the power of other independent variables. This procedure is implemented in version 10.0 of the STATA econometrics program.

Beck and Katz (1996) and others have argued for the inclusion of country dummies in order to deal with omitted variable bias. We have discussed in chapter 2 why this inclusion is inappropriate given the nature of our hypotheses and structure of variation in our data. We draw on Plümper, Troeger, and Manow (2005, 330–34) for additional reasons. They argue that the inclusion of unit dummies also (1) eliminates any variation in the dependent variable which is the result of time-invariant factors such as difference in constitutional structures, (2) greatly reduces the coefficients of factors that vary mainly between countries, (3) eliminates any differences in the dependent variable as a result of differences at $t1$ in the time series, and (4) "*completely absorb*(s) differences in the level of the independent variables across the units" (Plümper, Troeger, and Manow 2005, 331). Elaborating on this last point, they argue that if one hypothesizes that the level of the independent variable has an effect on the level of the dependent variables (e.g., democratic history and the degree of inequality), "a fixed effects specification is not the model at hand. If a theory predicts level effects, one should not include unit dummies. In these cases, allowing for a mild bias resulting from omitted variables is less harmful than running a fixed effects specification" (334). We do hypothesize (reason 1 above) effects of time-invariant factors (ethnic composition), (reason 3) effects of the levels of our dependent variables prior to $t1$, and (reason 4) effects of levels of the independent variables on levels of the dependent variable. In addition, variation in several of our independent variables, including the critical political variables, is primarily cross-sectional (reason 2). Thus, it is clear that fixed effects estimation or the inclusion of country dummies is not appropriate in this case.

Panel corrected standard errors correct for correlations of errors *within* the units. They do not correct for unmeasured factors that might affect the dependent variable in all units at the same point in time. Global economic fluctuations, such as the debt crisis period in Latin America in the 1980s, could produce such contemporaneous effects. To evaluate the potential impact of such unmeasured period specific factors we estimated the models with indicator variables for the debt crisis (1982–89) and for the 1990s (1990–2000) and 2000s (2001–7); the baseline category corresponds to the period before 1982. We hypothesize that poverty and inequality will increase and spending will decrease during the debt crisis years; we adopt a nondirectional hypothesis with regard to the differences between the pre– and post–debt crisis years.

Poverty figures were only available for varying time periods in each country, with few cases of observations in sequential years. The large number of gaps between the time observations for each country precludes correction for first-order autoregressiveness, because the common rho has to be recalculated every time there is a gap in the data. Thus, we estimate poverty with OLS regressions with panel corrected standard errors. In the case of income inequality, there are a moderate number of gaps in the data (62). To check whether this affected our results, we conducted several additional analyses for robustness. First, where possible, we added observations from Solt's (2009) Standardized World Income Inequality Database, bringing the total number of observations to 430 and reducing the number of gaps in the country time series to only eight. The results of the statistical analysis with these data were very similar to those reported in this chapter. Second, we reanalyzed the data with random effects estimation. Again the results were very similar to the ones reported here.

Cumulative record of democracy and the partisanship variables were very highly correlated ($r = .78$ for democracy and left political strength) and could not be entered into the same regression because of multicollinearity. In preliminary analyses, we found that the indicator variables for no adjustment for household size, earnings as an income concept, and absence of information on the use of gross versus net income did not have a significant impact on inequality, so we dropped them from the analyses. In the analysis of social spending, inflow of direct foreign investment was dropped because it was not correctly signed and/or not significant and made us lose 54 observations. In preliminary analyses, we also found that Panama was a significant outlier in the analyses of social spending, so a Panama indicator variable coded 1 for Panama and 0 for other cases was included in the spending analyses.[19]

Results

Tables 5.6, 5.7, and 5.8 display the regressions of education spending, health spending, and social security spending, respectively, on their hypothesized determinants. Democracy is positively associated with spending on education. Democracy beyond twenty years is not significant, indicating that education spending can be sensitive to short-term political conditions, in contrast, as we will see, to poverty and inequality. We also see that highly repressive authoritarian regimes suppress spending on education (they do not like educated masses), as do deficits. Veto points (which we would expect to matter only under democratic regimes and therefore measured only for the democratic periods) are associated with higher education expenditures. We interpret this to mean that veto points impeded cuts in education spending during the austere years of the debt crisis and early 1990s. Finally, what is interesting, particularly

TABLE 5.6. **Prais-Winsten estimates of determinants of education spending**

Variables	Model 1	Model 2	Model 3
Debt crisis	−.067	−.064	−.070
1990s	−.189*	−.190*	−.193*
2000s	−.103	−.100	−.096
Panama	.909*	.734	.727
GDP per capita	.054	.056	.059
Industrial employment	−.016	−.017	−.020
Urban population	.003	.004	.001
Youth population	.065*	.046	.037
IMF agreements	.008	.008	.006
Deficit	−.025***	−.025***	−.026***
Ethnic diversity	−.236	−.167	−.239
Female labor force participation	.011	.007	.010
Trade	−.005	−.004	−.004
Stock of FDI	.015**	.016**	.015**
Repressive authoritarianism	−.093***	−.100***	−.099***
Veto points	.076**	.081**	.082**
Democracy	.022*		
Democracy (20+ years)		.020	
Left political strength			.016
Common ρ	.79	.79	.78
Constant	.137	1.120	1.610
R^2	.31***	.30***	.31***
N	542	542	542

* $p ≤ .05$; ** $p ≤ .01$; *** $p ≤ .001$.

TABLE 5.7. **Prais-Winsten estimates of determinants of health spending**

Variables	Model 1	Model 2	Model 3
Debt crisis	−.063	−.060	−.059
1990s	−.033	−.029	−.039
2000s	.165	.169	.195
Panama	2.154**	2.282**	1.800*
GDP per capita	−.012	−.009	.012
Industrial employment	.009	.015	.005
Urban population	−.014	−.005	−.012
Aged population	−.022	−.038	.104
IMF agreements	.012	.015	.012
Deficit	−.015*	−.014*	−.015*
Ethnic diversity	−.801**	−.529*	−.746*
Female labor force participation	.011	.010	.019
Trade	−.004	−.004	−.003
Stock of FDI	.003	.004	.004
Repressive authoritarianism	−.026	−.036*	−.047*
Veto points	.013	.020	.023
Democracy	.053*		
Democracy (20+ years)		.091*	
Left political strength			.025
Common ρ	.88	.87	.88
Constant	2.143	1.851	1.644
R^2	.08***	.09***	.07***
N	542	542	542

* $p \le .05$; ** $p \le .01$; *** $p \le .001$.

in contrast to social security spending, is the vulnerability of education spending to deficits.

In table 5.7, one can see that the determinants of health spending are similar to the determinants of education expenditures, except that democracy beyond twenty years is significant, as is ethnic diversity. Veto points are positive but fall somewhat short of significance. Again, deficits depress health spending—a clearly discretionary category, like education spending.

Table 5.8 shows that the determinants of social security and welfare spending are quite different from those of health and education spending. One still sees the hypothesized effect of democracy and long-term democracy. Social security spending is highly resilient in the face of deficits; it is politically much more difficult to cut transfers (which are mostly pensions) than to cut teachers' and nurses' salaries or simply not build any new schools and clinics, and not order new textbooks or medicines, or not hire any new teachers and doctors. Veto points facilitate mobili-

TABLE 5.8. **Prais-Winsten estimates of determinants of social security and welfare spending**

Variables	Model 1	Model 2	Model 3
Debt crisis	−.017	−.011	−.012
1990s	.039	.036	.031
2000s	−.102	−.085	−.062
Panama	2.233**	2.036**	1.852*
GDP per capita	−.316[a]	−.298[a]	−.283[a]
Industrial employment	−.068	−.070[a]	−.076[a]
Urban population	.104***	.113***	.105***
Aged population	.988***	1.030***	1.126***
IMF	−.027*	−.024	−.028*
Deficit	.003	.004	.004
Ethnic diversity	.050	.298	.126
Female labor force participation	−.071[a]	−.071[a]	−.063[a]
Trade	−.005	−.004	−.004
Stock of FDI	−.004	−.002	−.003
Repressive authoritarianism	.094*	.080*	.073
Veto points	.124*	.143*	.142*
Democracy	.057***		
Democracy (20+ years)		.062**	
Left political strength			.032
Common ρ	.83	.81	.82
Constant	−2.423*	−2.776*	−2.892**
R^2	0.40***	0.43***	0.41***

[a] Significant but sign of coefficient opposite of directional hypothesis.

* $p \leq .05$; ** $p \leq .01$; *** $p \leq .001$.

zation of opposition to cuts and have a significant positive effect. Nevertheless, under prolonged IMF pressures, governments reduced social security and welfare spending. One sees how heavily social security expenditures, again in contrast to health and education spending, are driven by demographics, the sizes of the aged population and the urban population. Nevertheless, reduction can only happen once a program is in place. It is a striking contrast to our findings on OECD countries that left political strength, though correctly signed, falls short of significance on all of the social spending variables.

We can further explore the relative strength of the effects of the significant independent variables with the help of figure 5.5. The graph displays the effect of a two-standard-deviation change in the independent variables on the dependent variable.[20] Repressive authoritarianism emerges as the most important determinant of education spending followed by stock of foreign direct investment and democracy. Democracy and ethnic divisions are the most important determinants of health spending. By contrast, the effect of variations in the size of the deficit, which is highly significant in tables 5.6 and 5.7, is modest in comparison to the other independent variables. At first glance, it may seem that the absolute effect of even the strongest variables, repressive authoritarianism and democracy, are not large, only −.97 percent and 1.27 percent for education and health spending, respectively, but given means of 3.5 percent and 2.2 percent for the two dependent variables, the effect of a two-standard-deviation change is very substantial.

The pattern is very different for social security spending. Here the effects of the two demographic variables are huge. One can see that de-

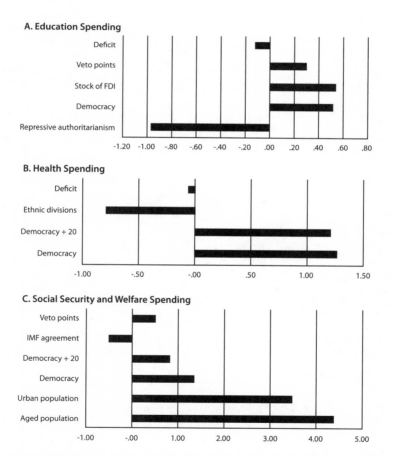

FIGURE 5.5. Estimated effect of a two-standard-deviation change in selected independent variables on social spending

mocracy is roughly of the same order of magnitude as in the case of health and education spending. Thus, it is not a question of demography squeezing out other determinants but rather of demography explaining more additional variation in the dependent variable. This can also be seen by the fact that the total variation explained is greater in the case of social security spending (table 5.8) than in the case of education spending (table 5.6) and much greater than in the case of health spending (table 5.7).

Table 5.9 displays the results of our analysis of poverty. The political variables of democracy, long-term democracy, and left political

TABLE 5.9. **Determinants of poverty (coefficients from OLS regressions with panel corrected standard errors)**

Variables	Model 1	Model 2	Model 3	Model 4	Model 5
Debt crisis	7.012***	7.566***	7.018***	8.977***	3.624***
1990s	10.000***	10.476***	9.850***	11.442***	5.335***
2000s	4.187**	4.223**	3.600**	2.232	3.983*
GDP per capita	−.931**	−.958**	−.964**	−1.057***	−1.189***
Inflation	−.001	−.002	−.001	.001	−.002*
Informal sector	.518***	.513***	.520***	.270*	.523***
External debt (% GDP)	.032***	.030***	.030***	.039***	.029**
Female labor force participation	−.727***	−.739***	−.710***	−.637**	−.645***
Youth population	.953***	1.006***	1.143***	.183	1.133***
Trade	.002	.000	.001	.055	.004
FDI inflows	−.096	−.148	−.158	−.190	−.330
Stock of FDI	.052	.038	.067	.084	.031
Ethnic diversity	7.016***	6.117***	6.706***	7.160***	3.691*
Employment in industry	−.008	−.079	−.015	−.418*	.280
IMF agreements	−.049	−.055	−.028	.036	−.018
Politics and policy					
Democracy	−.154***				
Democracy (20+ years)		−.228***			
Left political strength			−.101***		
Years of education				−2.406***	
Health (cumulativeave)				−4.604***	
Education (cumulative ave)				1.266	
Social security and welfare				−.564**	
Gini					.625***
Constant	.381	−.286	−8.381	58.509**	−42.520*
R^2	.87***	.87***	.87***	.89***	.88***
N	124	124	124	115	122

* $p<.05$; ** $p<.01$; *** $p<.001$.

strength are included in models 1, 2, and 3, respectively. All are negative as predicted and highly significant. Model 4 includes the four policy variables of spending on education, health, social security and welfare, and average years of education. Years of education, health spending, and social security and welfare are also negative as hypothesized and highly significant. The results for years of education and cumulative average health care spending can be interpreted as an outcome of successful investment in human capital in the past. It is not surprising that, once we control for average years of education, educational expenditures do not have a significant effect; that is, education spending does not matter if it does not increase the average years of education. As we hypothesized, social security and welfare spending do reduce poverty despite the fact that, as we shall see, the variable does not reduce overall inequality, unless situated in a democratic context. The targeted social assistance policies may be only a small part of overall social security and welfare spending, but they have a high impact on the poor. Not surprisingly, high levels of inequality are associated with high poverty as well. Among the control variables, informal employment, ethnic diversity, female labor force participation, external debt, GDP per capita, and youth population all have the hypothesized effect on poverty and are highly significant.

Figure 5.6 displays the effects of a two-standard-deviation change in the independent variables on poverty. In the case of ethnic diversity, the bars in the figures indicate the effect of a change from not diverse to diverse. Given that the variation explained in all regressions in figure 5.6 is very high, it is not surprising that a large number of our independent variables have strong effects on poverty. The strong effect of the size of the informal sector, which has grown in the transition from ISI to open economies, is striking. Demographic and labor force change work in the opposite direction from informalization through time as the youth population declines as a result of demographic transition and female labor force participation grows. The effect of cumulative average health spending is also very large. The other political and policy variables are more modest in strength but taken as a whole have a very substantial impact on poverty. All of the political and policy variables are positively correlated with time and thus are pushing Latin America toward less poverty through time.

The data in figure 5.6 show that democracy and long-term democracy have approximately the same effect on poverty. This finding indicates that democracy does not have an effect on poverty until countries

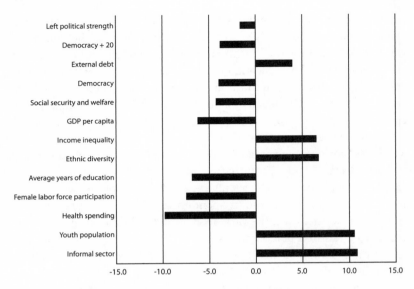

FIGURE 5.6. Estimated effect of a two-standard-deviation change in selected independent variables on poverty

have been democratic for twenty years. This is so because the long-term democracy score truncates the distribution on the explanatory variable by eliminating all values below twenty years, but the new variable (20+ years of democracy) has the same effect on the dependent variable. The effect of the partisanship variable is smaller than the effect of democracy, which indicates that the effect of democracy does not work entirely through partisan government.

Table 5.10 shows the results of the regressions of income inequality on the independent variables. All of the political variables have the hypothesized sign and are highly significant. The policy variables are entered in model 4. As in our previous analyses of inequality in Latin America (Huber et al. 2006; Huber and Stephens 2009), we find that the effect of social security and welfare spending is contingent on democracy, as the main term is positive, though not significant, indicating that spending increases inequality when democracy is 0,[21] while the interaction term with democracy is negative, indicating that social security and welfare spending developed in a democratic context reduces inequality. As in the case of poverty, average years of education have a negative effect on inequality. Again, spending on education, net of its effect on increasing the average years of education, has no effect on inequality.

Two of the control variables, industrial employment and ethnic diversity, have robust and large effects on inequality. As we have shown elsewhere (Huber and Stephens 2009), the decline in industrial employment, a byproduct of the transition from ISI to a trade open economy, was the main reason for increases in inequality in Latin America before the turn of the century.

Figure 5.7 shows the effects of a two-standard-deviation change in the independent variables on income inequality. Aside from the striking

TABLE 5.10. **Prais-Winsten estimates of determinants of income inequality**

Variables	Model 1	Model 2	Model 3	Model 4
Debt crisis	.479	.554	.650	.446
1990s	.704	.831	.677	.830
2000s	.876	.934	.328	1.005
Gross income	3.234***	2.950***	3.010***	3.000***
No household adjustment	−3.001***	−3.101***	−2.721***	−4.125***
GDP per capita	.298[a]	.207	.313[a]	.300[a]
Sector dualism	.063	.121**	.166***	.093*
Inflation	.001**	.001**	.001**	.001
Youth population	−.301[a]	−.270[a]	−.117	−.444[a]
Stock of FDI	.030	.018	.043	.047*
FDI flow	.321**	.276**	.278**	.313**
Ethnic heterogeneity	5.576***	4.342***	4.860***	3.889***
Employment in industry	−.473***	−.508***	−.399***	−.403***
Female labor force participation	−.045	−.041	−.010	.019
IMF agreements	−.058[a]	−.067[a]	−.033	−.015
External debt (% GDP)	.003	.002	.004	.005
Trade	.023*	.023*	.027*	.022
Politics and policy				
Democracy	−.191***			−.148***
Democracy (20+ years)		−.238***		
Left political strength			−.182***	
Democracy*social security welfare				−.012***
Average years of education				−1.274***
Social security and welfare				.154
Health (cumulative ave)				.172
Education (cumulative ave)				.017
Common ρ	.24	.26	.34	.20
Constant	70.503***	68.285***	57.386***	76.942***
R^2	.81***	.82***	.86***	.81***
N	271	271	271	259

[a] Significant but sign of coefficient opposite of directional hypothesis.
* $p \le .05$; ** $p \le .01$; *** $p \le .001$.

effect of ethnic diversity and the more modest effect of industrial employment, the political and policy variables emerge as the main determinants of variation in inequality within Latin America. Since the overall
variation explained is high, this means that politics is highly consequential for inequality, contrary to the received wisdom that sees inequality
in Latin America as impervious to political attempts to reduce it. As in
the case of poverty, democracy and long-term democracy have approximately the same effect on income inequality, which means that democracy does not have an effect on poverty until countries have been democratic for twenty years. As in the cases of social spending and poverty,
the effect of the partisanship variable is smaller than the effect of democracy, which indicates that the effect of democracy does not entirely
work through its effect enabling left political strength.

Table 5.11 displays the results of our analysis of market liberalization
on income inequality. Model 1 adds the Morley, Machado, and Pettinato
liberalization measures to model 2 of table 5.10. Model 2 replaces the
Morley, Machado, and Pettinato measure of capital account liberalization with the Chinn-Ito measure. The two capital account liberalization
measures are negatively related to inequality, and the tax reform measure is positively related to inequality. Both of these findings are consistent with Morley's (2001, 86) findings. We attempted to carry out a

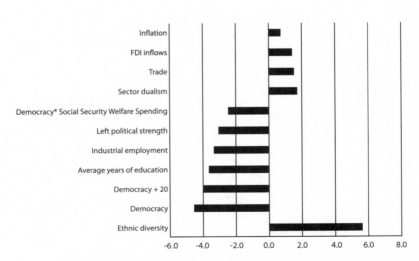

FIGURE 5.7. Estimated effect of a two-standard-deviation change in selected independent
variables on income inequality

TABLE 5.11. **Prais-Winsten estimates of the impact of market liberalization on income inequality**

Variables	Model 1	Model 2
Debt crisis	2.672**	1.773*
1990s	3.051*	1.568
2000s	−.321	.054
Gross income	2.688***	2.743***
No household adjustment	−3.474***	−3.154***
GDP per capita	.417[a]	.446[a]
Sector dualism	.138**	.137**
Inflation	.001*	.001*
Youth population	−.187	−.146
Stock of FDI	.041	.037
FDI flow	.239	.257*
Ethnic heterogeneity	4.989***	4.802***
Employment in industry	−.500***	−.529***
Female labor force participation	−.169	−.100
IMF agreements	−.069[a]	−.064[a]
External debt (% GDP)	−.019	−.021
Trade	.059***	.052**
Democracy (20+ years)	−.271***	−.272***
Capital market liberalization (Morley)	−4.383**	
Capital market liberalization (Chinn-Ito)		−.632***
Trade liberalization	−.922	−1.500
Financial liberalization	.978	1.443
Privatization	1.102	1.100
Tax reform	4.877*	5.632*
Common ρ	.05	.05
Constant	65.283***	59.828***
R^2	.71***	.72***
N	194	194

[a] Significant but sign of coefficient opposite of directional hypothesis.
* $p \leq .05$; ** $p \leq .01$; *** $p \leq .001$.

parallel analysis of market liberalization on poverty. Entering all of the measures at once as in table 5.11 creates severe multicollinearity. None of the liberalization measures was significant when entered one at a time (not shown). Our conclusion is that the *direct* net effect of overall market liberalization reforms on inequality and poverty is negligible.[22]

Conclusion and Discussion

The conventional wisdom about poverty and inequality in Latin America is that they are intractable problems, impervious to intervention by agents of change. Our analysis shows that this view seriously underestimates how much difference politics—democracy and the strength of the political left—and policies—current and past social spending and investments in education—make in explaining variation in our measures of inequality and poverty. Democracy is at the beginning of our hypothesized causal chain leading to lower levels of inequality. Democracy is a precondition for partisan effects. It has strong effects on social spending, and social spending reduces poverty and inequality, particularly if social spending is expanded in the context of democracy. Democracy enables left government, and much of its effect on poverty and inequality comes through its effect on left political strength. We found, however, that democracy had stronger effects on most of our dependent variables than left partisanship did, which we interpret to mean that its effect was partly direct, not through left political strength.

We also found support for Muller's (1989) argument that democracy's effect on income inequality was not immediate but rather took some time—twenty years in his estimation—for democracy's effect on social processes to work its way through to income inequality. We found similar long-term effects of democracy on poverty. The long-term democracy measure truncates the distribution on the explanatory variable, but the new variable (20+ years of democracy) has roughly the same effect on the dependent variables (see figs. 5.6 and 5.7). This finding alone shows that the initial years of democracy matter little for inequality and poverty, but if one considers that the standard deviation of long-term democracy is much smaller than the standard deviation of full cumulative years of democracy (7.6 versus 12.3 years in the case of the inequality analysis), our finding also shows that long-term democracy has similar effects to full cumulative democracy, but in a shorter period of time.

The mechanisms by which democracy has this delayed effect on inequality are varied. The development of a strong civil society; the formation and maturation of left parties and popular organizations; the accession of these parties to government—all of these take time; they do not happen instantaneously. In the Latin American context, new governments after the transition to democracy acted cautiously out of fear of provoking renewed military intervention, and this caution also slowed progress on egalitarian social and economic policies. It also takes time for policies to have effects. For instance, our analyses show a robust effect of average years of education on reduction of poverty and inequality. Average years of education can only be raised incrementally through time. A large expansion of secondary school enrollments takes several years to show any effect on raising average years of education and does not have its full effect for decades. This is precisely what happened in Brazil: secondary school enrollment was greatly increased in the late 1990s under Cardoso and began to have an effect on inequality after 2000 as the expanding supply of better-educated workers reduced the returns to education (López-Calva and Lustig 2010).

The implication of our finding on the long-term effects of democracy—or perhaps more precisely the absence of a short-term effect of democracy on inequality and poverty in Latin America—is clear. By 1990, only three countries in Latin America had reached the twenty-year threshold, whereas by 2000, nine countries, half of our sample, had, and by 2005 another two countries joined this group. This is consistent with the finding of López-Calva and Lustig (2010) that inequality began to decline after 2000 in eleven of the seventeen countries in their study of income inequality in Latin America.

As hypothesized, the effects of social transfer spending on inequality are ambiguous and contingent, in sharp contrast to advanced capitalist democracies, where the effects of social transfer spending on inequality are unambiguous and very large. Replicating earlier findings by Lee (2005) on a broad worldwide sample of countries and by Huber et al. (2006), we found that the effect of social security spending is contingent on democracy: the expansion of social security spending in countries with long democratic records reduces inequality, while social security spending in the absence of democracy has increased inequality.

The effects of investment in education on monetary income inequality were likewise contingent: investment in education has an equalizing effect only if it increases the average years of education of the working-age population. The effect of health spending on monetary income inequality is insignificant, probably because the inequality-reducing effects of preventative spending are cancelled out by the inequality-increasing effects of curative spending. Our income inequality data, however, certainly grossly underestimate the effect of health and education spending on the inequality of actual household consumption levels because the inequality data measure monetary income only. If education and health services for lower-income groups are improved, it does not show up in the data on income inequality in the short run. The data we presented in chapter 3 for the incidence of education and health spending in Uruguay and Brazil are fairly representative of the incidence of health and education spending in all seventeen Latin American countries in the ECLAC (2005, 143–46) study. These data indicate that health and education spending would have strong equalizing effects on household consumption levels in all of these countries. Thus, ceteris paribus, more spending on education and health results in greater equality of household consumption levels.

Social spending has different effects on poverty than on monetary income inequality, which makes sense given the differences in the measures. First, the poverty measure is insensitive to changes in the upper end of the income distribution. Second, it is a measure of absolute poverty, so it is possible for poverty to decrease, even substantially, with little change in income distribution, as happened in Chile in the 1990s. Comparing tables 5.9 and 5.10, one can see that social security and welfare spending have an unambiguous poverty-reducing effect. Although four-fifths of this spending is on social security, mainly pensions, it is the remaining fifth, primarily means-tested social assistance, that has the main poverty-reducing effect. At the bottom of the income distribution in Latin America, a small amount of spending can be highly consequential for the recipients. For example, spending on the Bolsa Família conditional cash transfer program was only 0.5 percent of Brazilian GDP but had a large effect on Brazilian poverty. As Barros et al. (2010, 154) observe in their discussion of income inequality in Brazil, "Despite representing just a tiny fraction of total household income (0.5 percent), [Bolsa Família] explains about 10 percent of the overall decline in income inequality."

Health spending had a strong negative effect on poverty but not monetary income inequality.[23] If governments simultaneously expand curative and preventative health care spending, the effects of the two types of spending on inequality might cancel each other out. The effects of such health care spending policies unambiguously reduce absolute poverty in the long run because they would improve the health and thus the employment prospects of the poor. By contrast, the impact of education on poverty is similar to its impact on inequality. We found large negative effects of average years of education on poverty and inequality, but no positive effects of educational spending, indicating that education spending that did not increase average years of education had no effect on poverty and inequality.

As in our previous work, we did not find any partisan political effects on spending (Huber, Mustillo, and Stephens 2008). Our interpretation of the lack of this effect on social expenditure was that, with few exceptions, left-of-center parties were not the creators of social safety nets. Rather, they inherited social policy regimes with heavy reliance on employment-based contributory systems, with a variety of different schemes for different occupational categories, and with unequal benefits. Governments of the right and left faced similar budgetary constraints for roughly thirty years, so neither category could greatly increase expenditures. What left-of-center governments did, however, was to shift the composition, or the structure of spending, to make it more redistributive. We have no comparable measure of structure of spending, so we need to build our interpretation on evidence from comparative historical studies and on the indirect evidence from evidence on determinants of poverty and inequality.

The constraints on spending were eased considerably by the commodities boom in the 2000s. In fact, if we run the models with partisanship for our spending variables for the 2000s only, we find a significant effect of cumulative left political strength on health and social security and welfare spending. Other conditions turned more favorable in the 2000s as well. Deficits and foreign debt declined, both variables that depressed spending and drove up poverty in our analyses. Thus, the 2000s presented more opportunities for policy innovation, and our compara-

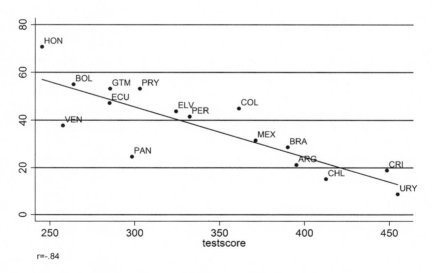

r=-.84

FIGURE 5.8. Average cognitive test scores (1997–2003) and poverty (1998–2006)

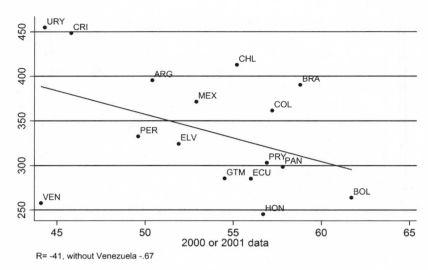

FIGURE 5.9. Cognitive test scores and Gini index of disposable income inequality

tive historical analysis in the next chapter shows how left governments took advantage of these opportunities to promote new kinds of social policies with a more universalistic and redistributive character.

Our results for market liberalization—that there was little evidence that liberalizing reforms had much direct effect on inequality or poverty—run counter to the commonplace view held by critics of neoliberal reform, who argue that the reforms have increased inequality and poverty. Other quantitative analyses of the impact of these measures with different samples of countries and years and using different estimation techniques have come to slightly different conclusions, with some of the measures being associated with more inequality and others with less, but none of them show large effects in either direction and in any case do not support the argument for unambiguous inegalitarian effects of the market liberalization measures (Morley 2001; Bogliaccini 2009, forthcoming). This does not mean, however, that the market liberalization, which was part and parcel of the transition from ISI to an open economy, had no effect on inequality in Latin America. Rather these effects are picked up by two other variables in our analyses, industrial employment and informal employment. The transition from ISI set off a process that led to deindustrialization and thus increased inequality (table 5.10 and fig. 5.7) and informalization, and thus increased poverty (table 5.9 and fig. 5.6).

In closing, let us underline the importance of human capital for our outcomes. We note again that we found average years of education are an important determinant of both poverty and inequality. It is likely that we underestimated the effects of the average levels of human capital and its distribution on both dependent variables by using average years of education as our measure of human capital. From table 5.5 we can see that the correlations of cognitive test scores with poverty and inequality are considerably higher than the correlations of average years of education with the two dependent variables. Figures 5.8 and 5.9 illustrate these relationships. Of course, the causality goes in both directions, which accounts for the strength of these correlations. This is precisely our point: it would be difficult to raise substantially the average levels of human capital in Latin American countries without simultaneously successfully reducing poverty and inequality. This is exactly why policy makers and international financial institutions, especially the World Bank, find conditional cash transfers to be such an attractive policy instrument. Hanushek and Woessmann's (2009) finding on the importance of cognitive skills for economic growth in Latin America make this line of argument all the more compelling. Thus, reducing poverty and inequality now is not just good social policy; it is also good economic growth policy.

TABLE 5.A.I. **Variable descriptions and data sources**

Variables	Sources
Gini coefficient	UNU-WIDER 2008; SEDLAC 2010
Poverty	ECLAC (see text for details)
Education spending	IMF and ECLAC (see text for details)
Health spending	IMF and ECLAC (see text for details)
Social security and welfare spending	IMF and ECLAC (see text for details)
No adjustment indicator	UNU-WIDER 2008; SEDLAC 2010
Gross income indicator	UNU-WIDER 2008; SEDLAC 2010
Earnings indicator	UNU-WIDER 2008; SEDLAC 2010
Democracy	Author codings; Rueschemeyer, Stephens, and Stephens 1992
Long-term democracy	Author codings; Rueschemeyer, Stephens, and Stephens 1992
Left political strength	Author codings; adapted and expanded by the authors from Coppedge 1997
Repressive authoritarianism	Author codings
Education (cumulative average)	IMF and ECLAC (see text for details)
Health (cumulative average)	IMF and ECLAC (see text for details)
Average years of education	Barro and Lee 2010
Capital market liberalization (Morley)	Morley, Machado, and Pettinato 1999; Escaith and Paunovic 2004
Capital market liberalization (Chinn-Ito)	Chinn and Ito 2008
Trade liberalization	Morley, Machado, and Pettinato 1999; Escaith and Paunovic 2004
Financial liberalization	Morley, Machado, and Pettinato 1999; Escaith and Paunovic 2004
Privatization	Morley, Machado, and Pettinato 1999; Escaith and Paunovic 2004
Tax reform	Morley, Machado, and Pettinato 1999; Escaith and Paunovic 2004
GDP per capita	World Bank 2007; Penn World Table version 6.3
Sector dualism	World Bank 2007; ILO 2003; ECLAC, *Statistical Yearbook* (various years); Alderson and Nielson 1999
Employment in agriculture	World Bank 2007; ILO 2003; ECLAC, *Statistical Yearbook* (various years); Alderson and Nielson 1999
Inflation	IMF, *International Financial Statistics* (various years); Blyde and Fernandez-Arlas 2004
Female labor force participation	World Bank 2007
Youth population	World Bank 2007
Elderly population	World Bank 2007
Urban population	World Bank 2007
Ethnic diversity	Coding based on data presented in Ferranti et al. 2004
Stock of FDI	UNCTAD 2002; United Nations Centre on Transnational Corporations 1985
External debt	World Bank 2010
Trade openness	Penn World Table version 6.3
IMF	IMF, *International Financial Statistics* (various years); Blyde and Fernandez-Arlas 2004
Inflows of FDI	World Bank 2007
Informal employment	ILO 2003
Industrial employment	World Bank 2007
Veto points	Author codings
Deficits	IMF, *International Financial Statistics* (various years); Blyde and Fernandez-Arlas 2004

CHAPTER SIX

Neoliberal Reforms and the Turn to Basic Universalism

In the Latin America of the 1980s, the balance of power in all three spheres—within civil society, between civil society and the state, and within the international system—was unfavorable for redistributive social policy. In fact, the quality and coverage of social policy declined considerably. At the beginning of the decade, many countries, including Argentina, Brazil, Chile, and Uruguay, were ruled by repressive authoritarian regimes, and labor and the left had been severely weakened by repression. The debt crisis then destabilized these regimes and ushered in processes of democratization, but it also greatly constrained the new democratic governments in their ability to expand and improve social policy. The IMF and the World Bank gained great leverage over Latin American countries and consistently promoted neoliberal reforms in economic and social policy.

Over the following three decades, power relations gradually shifted in a more favorable direction, and social policy assumed a more expansive and redistributive profile. Democratization opened up space for popular mobilization and citizen input into policy making. The electoral strength of left parties grew. Well before any of these parties ascended to power, party competition resulted in reforms that departed from the neoliberal orthodoxy. Where left parties gained power, they pursued policies that strengthened labor and reduced poverty and inequality. This reorientation was facilitated by economic growth, which provided increased state revenue and reduced the foreign debt, which in turn reduced the leverage of the IFIs. In this chapter, we trace these changes through a comparative historical analysis of our five cases.

First, we review the conditions that spawned the wave of neoliberal reforms, the nature and extent of these reforms, and their outcomes. We concentrate on policies in the areas of pensions, social assistance, health, and education. Second, we analyze the turn to more universalistic and solidaristic social policies under the left governments that came to power after 2000. These new policies along with economic growth contributed to a marked decline in poverty and a smaller decline in inequality between 2002 and 2007.[1] We end with an assessment of the policy legacies of the second wave of reforms.

Origins of the Neoliberal Reforms

The wave of neoliberal reforms of social policy in the 1980s and 1990s has to be understood in the context of the debt crisis and the austerity and structural adjustment policies persistently promoted by the IFIs, all of which corresponded to neoliberal blueprints in design, if not everywhere in actual implementation. Neoliberal doctrines had assumed wide policy relevance first under Thatcher and Reagan in the Anglo-Saxon world, and under Pinochet in Latin America, and they rapidly became truly hegemonic. They diagnosed the roots of the debt crisis as excessive state intervention in markets and fiscal irresponsibility. Accordingly, they prescribed reduction of government expenditures, liberalization of trade and financial markets, privatization, and deregulation as remedies. In the area of social policy, the prescriptions were partial or full privatization of social security, increasing reliance on private providers and market principles in health care and education, and targeting of the state's provision of transfers and services for the neediest groups.

Virtually every Latin American country was exposed to these policy prescriptions, as they all faced balance of payments crises, and the IMF and World Bank increasingly cooperated in imposing both austerity and neoliberal structural adjustment policies. Influence worked not only through direct conditionality but, equally importantly, through informal networks. Technocrats who held leading positions in ministries often shared educational backgrounds with IFI technocrats, and often were involved in revolving door careers, moving between a ministerial position and one in an IFI (Teichman 2001). The implementation of these prescriptions varied widely among countries, however, depending

on three factors: (1) the amount of room to maneuver, (2) the policy legacies from the ISI period, and (3) the balance of power between supporters and opponents of neoliberalism.

The room to maneuver was shaped by the size of the economy and
by the country's strategic location with regard to U.S. interests. Argentina, Brazil, and Mexico were in a stronger position to resist IFI imposition than the smaller economies, simply because a default on their part
would have been potentially catastrophic for the international financial
system. Costa Rica was in a strategic position with regard to the civil
wars in Nicaragua and El Salvador and received massive U.S. aid in the
1980s, which enabled the government to resist stringent IFI impositions.

The policy legacies from the ISI period shaped the urgency of reforms
and the degree of pressure from the IFIs. Where the pension components of the social security systems had wide coverage, had matured, and
ran big deficits that were a heavy drain on the government budget, the
reform pressures were intense (Madrid 2003). Where coverage was more
restricted and the active/passive ratio and therefore the budget picture
more favorable, there was less pressure. Health care systems underwent
reforms as well, though with more mixed motives. The IFIs had similar
goals to those they had for the pension reforms—expansion of private-
sector participation, cost savings, and efficiency, whereas other actors
pursued expansion of access and of primary and preventive care.

As to the balance of political power, arguably the crucial determinants of social policy reform were the orientation of the president, the
concentration of power in the hands of the president (be it de facto, by
constitutional structure, or by having a partisan majority in Congress),
and the mobilization capacity of opponents of neoliberal reforms. The
most radical neoliberal reforms were imposed by the Pinochet dictatorship; there neoliberal economists trained at the University of Chicago
had the ear of Pinochet himself, power was extremely concentrated, and
any opposition was brutally repressed. At the opposite end was Brazil,
where presidents other than the short-lived Collor were more pragmatic,
never enjoyed reliable partisan control over Congress, and unions had
considerable mobilization capacity to block reforms.

The economic crisis of the 1980s and the economic reforms implemented in response to the crisis greatly aggravated the problems faced
by the advanced social security systems at the end of the ISI period.
Most importantly, the changes in the labor market in the wake of liberal-

ization of trade and financial markets, that is, the loss of industrial jobs and the expansion of the informal sector, reduced effective coverage of the employment-based social security schemes and reduced the number of contributors. In addition, high inflation eroded the value of pension benefits, and governments under heavy austerity strictures were unable or unwilling to adjust the benefits. In the health sector, austerity meant not only that public-sector health service providers saw a steep decline of their real earnings but also that public hospitals and clinics lacked the funds to provide adequate services.

Extent of Reforms by 2002

In the two decades between the Chilean pension reform of 1981 and the Costa Rican reform of 2001, nine Latin American countries changed the basic structures of their pension systems.[2] Chile, Bolivia, Mexico, and El Salvador replaced their public with a fully private mandatory pension system; Peru and Colombia established a private system parallel to the public system; and Argentina, Uruguay, and Costa Rica established mixed systems, with a basic public and supplementary private component. Other countries introduced various reforms but left the basic structures of the public systems intact. Brazil was the only country among those with advanced systems of social protection that did not introduce any private components into the pension system. This was not for lack of trying on the part of presidents, but the opponents were strong enough to prevent any structural reform. In Argentina, Uruguay, and Costa Rica, long-drawn-out struggles preceded the legislation of the reforms.

Health-sector reform proliferated in the 1990s. As with pension reform, Chile was a forerunner in health-sector reform, greatly strengthening the private vis-à-vis the public sector in the 1981 reform. Unlike pension reform, in many cases there was more than one reform of the health sector, and in many cases there were unsuccessful reform attempts as well. Whereas the IFIs insisted on a number of general principles and provided loans to support reforms conforming to these principles, they did not push one blueprint as they had in pension reform. The legacies in health care were more complex and thus the number of stakeholders was greater, which made reform more difficult and required adaptation to the particular context. Still, there were reforms, and they tended to promote greater private-sector participation, more competition, lower public financing, and decentralization of responsibility for provision of health services.

Reforms in education were widespread but less dramatic. The need for educational reform was high on the agenda of the IFIs in the 1990s, not to cut costs but to promote economic development. It was also high on the agenda of the mass public, as Kaufman and Nelson (2004c, 254–56) show on the basis of survey data. The trend was toward deepening decentralization of responsibility for education to subnational levels, and the struggle was about the adequate transfer of resources from the central government (Kaufman and Nelson 2004b). Unlike pension reform, there was not a single blueprint but a wide variety of options on the reform agenda in addition to decentralization. Teachers' unions tended to be well organized and formidable opponents of reforms that would weaken their bargaining leverage, job security, and control over teacher assignments. Again, the most drastic changes occurred in Chile under a dictatorship that was determined to break the strength of unions and increase the role of the private sector. Pinochet decentralized education and turned teachers into municipal employees, which greatly weakened the unions because they could no longer bargain with one central employer. He also instituted a system of per-pupil payments that could go to purely municipal schools or private schools, which resulted in a tiered system of fully public/open admission (and therefore underfunded and low quality), publicly subsidized private/controlled admission, and fully private schools.

In the course of the 1990s, the agenda of progressive forces in Latin America changed from merely resisting neoliberal reform to a positive agenda of pressing for new inclusionary and redistributive reform. In Brazil, this process began as early as the drafting of the 1988 constitution, although the provisions regarding social policy, notably health care and social assistance, required enabling legislation which was introduced gradually over the next two decades. Argentina, Uruguay, and Brazil introduced education reforms in the 1990s that were designed to strengthen public education. In the Brazilian case they led to a major increase in primary school completion and secondary school enrollment, and in the Uruguayan case the increase in enrollment was true for preschool education. These educational investments then contributed to the decline in inequality in the 2000s (López-Calva and Lustig 2010).

Chile

Chile was the first country to radically reform its social security and health systems and became the model held up by the IFIs for both economic and social policy reform. After the 1973 coup against the democratically elected Allende government, the dictatorship first imposed a severe austerity program that led to a deep recession in 1975. It followed with a sweeping program of economic liberalization and privatization, which attracted much foreign capital and generated a boom that ended in a bust in 1981. This boom, however, was accompanied by deindustrialization; industrial employment fell from 29 percent of the labor force in 1970 to 25 percent in 1980. The bust was followed by another very deep recession with very high unemployment levels. After the economy emerged from this recession in 1984, it embarked on a trajectory of sustained growth, which made it the poster child for advocates of neoliberalism.

Along with economic liberalization, the dictatorship pursued profound changes in social policy. In 1981 it established a new statutory fully funded pension system with individual accounts and private administration.[3] The public pay-as-you-go system was closed to new entrants, and existing participants were induced to join the new system with promises of high returns and thus better benefits in the long run, lower contribution rates, and recognition bonds for past contributions. Employer contributions were abolished for both the old and the new systems. Private financial firms, the Administradoras de Fondos de Pensiones (AFPs), were put in charge of administering the new funds, and they attracted clients through advertising campaigns and masses of sales agents. The AFPs could charge fees and commissions, and the growth of the individual accounts depended on the returns on the investments made by the AFPs minus these deductions. The number of contributors to the old scheme dropped radically in the first year, to somewhere below a third of pre-reform contributors, and continued to decline gradually thereafter. The number of affiliates to the new system grew rapidly, but the number of actual contributors grew much more slowly, reflecting the instability of employment patterns in the new Chilean economy (Barrientos 1998, 170). The entire reform was extremely expensive in the transition phase because the government had to pay the pensions of those covered by the public system without the benefit of current employer contributions and employee contributions from those who joined the private system.

In the health sector, the Pinochet dictatorship established a system under which employees could direct their mandatory contributions for health insurance either to the public health system (FONASA) or private companies (ISAPRES). The ISAPRES operated with a minimum of regulation; they could charge additional premiums, differentiate these premiums according to the risk profile of individuals, and limit benefits provided. As a result, they have attracted particularly upper-income, younger, and healthier subscribers, and the Chilean health care system developed into a true two-class system by the time of the transition. Nevertheless, the democratic governments left it by and large unchanged for over a decade, except for greatly increasing public expenditures. Public expenditures as a percentage of total health care expenditures had declined from 62 percent in 1974 to 47 percent in 1989 (Borzutzky 2002, 234). By 1997, ISAPRES had 27 percent of the members of the contributory health care system (Borzutzky 2002, 235). Despite significant increases in public health care expenditures during the 1990s, the differences between the public and the private health care sectors remained large. In 1999 ISAPRES spent an estimated 177,633 pesos per person compared to 99,308 pesos per capita by FONASA (Titelman 2000, 17).

The politics of implementing these reforms were relatively simple. The dictatorship was at the height of its power right before the crash of 1981, and organized opposition was all but nonexistent. Even in health care, the reform team acted without consulting the Colegio Médico de Chile, a traditionally influential group in matters of health care. This easy imposition from above contrasts markedly with what happened to reform attempts under the democratic regimes in Argentina, Uruguay, Costa Rica, and Brazil. After the transition to democracy, the Concertación, an alliance of the Christian Democrats, the Socialist Party, and the Party for Democracy, was committed to remedying the social debt that the dictatorship had incurred, and they significantly increased social expenditures. Under the two Christian Democratic presidents, however, the basic structure of the social security and health systems remained unchanged.

The same is true for the educational system. The Concertación kept in place the financial and organizational structure of the educational system that Pinochet had established. It entailed a fixed state subsidy per student, which could be paid to private schools in the three-sector system of fully public municipal schools, publicly subsidized private schools, and fully private schools. Pinochet had decentralized education to the municipal level and thereby intentionally weakened the teachers' union.

This system obviously created major inequalities, as fully public schools in poor municipalities depended entirely on this state subsidy, whereas schools in better-off municipalities could rely on extra public subsidies or private funds. In addition to increasing the payment per student, the Concertación also instituted several programs to help the poorest schools with pedagogical materials, but the Aylwin administration significantly accentuated the built-in inequalities in the system when it passed a reform in 1993 that allowed publicly subsidized private primary schools and all secondary schools, including the fully public ones, to charge additional fees (Cox 2006). The significant increase in expenditures on education only made up for the significant cuts Pinochet had inflicted on public education; average public spending on education in Chile in the 1990s was only 3 percent of GDP, lower than in Costa Rica, Argentina, and Brazil, and only marginally higher than in Uruguay. Compared to other countries, the proportion of total education spending that is public is extremely low in Chile. According to OECD figures, in 2003 only 51 percent of total education spending was public in Chile, compared to 73 percent in the United States, 81 percent in Mexico (the only other Latin American country for which there are comparable data), and 90 percent or more in the European countries (OECD 2006).

Argentina

The military regime in Argentina that seized power in 1976 followed an economic strategy similar to the one pursued by the Pinochet regime in Chile. They first imposed a harsh economic stabilization package and then followed up with liberalization of trade and capital markets. As in Chile, this strategy caused a flood of imports, opened access to foreign loans, and created a boom that collapsed in a financial crisis. Unlike in Chile, the regime self-destructed in the wake of the 1982 Malvinas war and saddled the new democratic regime under Alfonsín with huge economic problems. Alfonsín resisted IMF austerity and further liberalization, but his government's various heterodox attempts failed and resulted in hyperinflation. After the opposition Peronists led by Menem won the 1989 elections, Alfonsín handed over power early. Menem then immediately made a 180 degree turn away from his campaign promises and embarked on a harsh orthodox stabilization program and an aggressive program of liberalization, privatization, and reduction of public-sector employment, accompanied by convertibility of the currency in

1991. These measures brought inflation under control and attracted foreign capital, which revived economic growth.

Pension reform was essential to bring down the public deficit. The system had accumulated a significant debt to pensioners, as the value of real pensions declined by 25 percent from 1981 to 1988 and another 30 percent from 1988 to 1991 (Mesa-Lago 1994, 149). This decline generated law suits, a declaration of emergency within the pension system in 1986, and subsequent steps to pay up, but the basic problem remained unresolved (Isuani and San Martino 1993, 34–39). The Menem administration's belief in the importance of solving the social security problem is underlined by the fact that in 1991 the Ministry of the Economy took over the Secretariat of Social Security, which before had been under the Ministry of Labor (Madrid 2003, 112). A team of economists, some of whom had been hired as consultants on a World Bank study of social policy in Argentina, created the privatization proposal that was presented to Congress in June 1992. These economists had also been in close contact with Chilean pension experts (Madrid 2003, 114–16). Nevertheless, the proposal presented was for a mixed system, with a public and a private component. The reasons for this choice were twofold. Given the high pension liabilities, full privatization would have been a great drain on the budget. Moreover, the experts anticipated strong opposition to full privatization (Madrid 2003, 117). They were certainly correct, as even the proposal for the mixed system encountered strong opposition and underwent many modifications.[4] Ultimately, it passed because the government controlled a majority of seats in the Senate and a near majority in the Chamber of Deputies, the major labor confederation was tied to the party, and the government made concessions to the unions.

Under the new system, all insured were to receive a pension benefit from the public system based on length of contributions only, not previous salary. The public system was financed by employer contributions (with the self-employed, whose coverage was mandatory, paying the employer's portion of the contribution), special earmarked taxes, and proceeds from the sale of the state oil company (Mesa-Lago 1994, 152–55). Employees could then choose whether to direct their own contributions to the public system for a supplementary pension or to the private system, which consisted of private individual accounts that would work like the Chilean ones. Employees who chose the private system would be compensated for past contributions to the public system at the time of retirement. Employees who did not make a choice were automatically allocated to the private system. In contrast to Chile, private pension funds could be administered not only by private firms but also by nonprofit organizations, including unions and cooperatives.

The public health system in Argentina had been suffering from underfunding since the 1960s, and by the 1980s the quality of public health services was very poor. Beginning in the 1970s, responsibility for public hospitals was transferred to the provinces. In the 1990s this process accelerated and transferred full financial responsibility to the provinces or to self-managed hospitals, with the result that services for the uninsured poor became even less available. The bulk of the employed population was covered by *obras sociales*, the health insurance schemes administered by the unions. Membership was compulsory in the particular *obra social* that corresponded to an employee's workplace; there was no freedom of choice. Pensioners were covered by a separate scheme. With the increase in unemployment and informal employment and the decline in real wages, income of the *obras sociales* declined and quality of coverage deteriorated as well. Private insurance and provision began to grow in the 1980s and accelerated in the 1990s. The Menem administration attempted to introduce competition among the *obras sociales*, and between them and private insurers, in order to increase efficiency and reduce the burden on payroll taxes, but the unions strongly resisted the loss of their monopoly rights. Eventually, workers obtained the right to choose, as the administration managed to divide the union movement, but competition with private insurers was thwarted and the ability of workers to switch remained de facto constrained (Lloyd-Sherlock 2004a, 102–8). Thus, the Argentine health system remained largely unchanged.

The Menem government's one clear and important departure from neoliberal social policy, made in a progressive direction, was its educational policy reform.[5] The first phase of the reform process, the Transference Law of December 1991 that mandated decentralization of all primary and secondary education to the provincial or municipal level, was completely consistent with the World Bank's Washington Consensus recommendations. The next round of reform concerned the services and resources the federal government would guarantee to the provinces. It pitted the provinces, which wanted maximal guarantees, against the Economics Ministry, which wanted minimal guarantees. The Ministry of Education was standing in-between: it wanted to raise school quality, but it was obvious this could not be done without resources. The provinces found allies among the teachers' union, which favored large increases in education spending, and citizens' groups, which were concerned that the Menem government might extend its privatization efforts to education. The provinces and the teachers' union were very ambitious in that the former wanted to increase education spending from 3.3 percent to 6 percent of GDP, and the latter wanted the goal set at 8 percent of GDP.

In part because of the governors' strong influence in the senatorial nomination process, the Peronist faction in the Senate, which was in the majority, sided with the provinces. The Senate proposals called for a 6 percent of GDP target, ten years of compulsory schooling (rather than the current seven—which the Ministry of Education continued to favor), and the continuation of free schooling. The Chamber of Deputies, led by Rodríguez, a member of the Education Commission and a progressive Peronist who wanted the government's social policy to have a human face to balance its neoliberal economic policies, emerged as the mediator. The provisions of the 1993 Federal Education Law were close to the Senate proposal: free schooling, ten years of compulsory education, and a doubling of education spending (in absolute levels, not as a percentage of GDP) in five years. Education spending as percentage of GDP did increase from 3.3 percent in 1991 to 4.9 percent in 1999, the year Menem left office.

Uruguay

In Uruguay economic growth had been sluggish since the 1950s, and the country faced frequent balance of payments problems. The military government of 1973–85 imposed stringent austerity and significant liberalization of trade and financial markets. Indeed, by 1985 Uruguay even ranked ahead of Chile on Morley et al.'s general index of market reform (.79 for Uruguay and .61 for Chile) (Escaith and Paunovic 2004). The debt crisis led to a severe recession and renewed harsh austerity. The country, however, managed to avoid hyperinflation, and further liberalization proceeded more slowly; by 2000 the index of market reform in Uruguay was lower than in Chile, and even below that in Argentina and Costa Rica.

The struggle over pension reform was protracted.[6] With the relative generosity and wide coverage of the pension system, the aging of the population, and the deficit in the system, concerns over the drain on the budget pushed the issue of pension reform to the top of the agenda of not only the IMF but also the democratic governments of both traditional parties. The 1985 IMF agreement included a commitment to pension reform, but it was precisely the wide coverage of the system that galvanized a broad-based opposition to any reform that would reduce security and generosity of pension benefits. Institutional factors facilitated this mobilization. Constitutional provisions made it possible for a coalition of pensioner organizations, unions, and left opposition parties to force a referendum in 1989 that improved pension benefits and indexed them to public-sector salaries. The referendum received the overwhelming support of some 80 percent of voters.

As a result of the referendum, which left the expensive privileged schemes in place as well, pension expenditures increased markedly and kept the issue of pension reform high on the political agenda. In the first half of the 1990s, various modest reform bills failed in the legislature, and one that passed was overturned by a large majority in another referendum in 1994. Finally, a reform was passed in 1996, after much negotiation with a large spectrum of stakeholders and with the support of both traditional parties. It established a mixed system with a public and a private pillar, but the mandatory private pillar was small, affecting only higher income earners. Contributions to the private pillar were mandatory for all those with incomes above $800 per month who were under forty years of age at the time of the reform and for all new entrants to the labor force. All employer contributions and all employee contributions up to a specified income limit ($800 per month when the reform was passed) continued to go to the public system. Pension benefits from the public system were calculated on the basis of earnings of the best twenty years.

Uruguay's health care system was similar to Argentina's and proved equally difficult to reform. It covered the bulk of the population through a combination of *mutuales* (IAMCs), to which the mandatory contributions of employees are directed; the public sector, which suffered from underfunding; and a private sector, which grew by default. Public expenditures on health were increased after the transition to democracy but declined again as economic problems mounted. Increasing costs and concerns over uneven quality of services and inefficient coordination between the public sector and the IAMCs generated several reform attempts, but none of them managed to gain sufficient support in the legislature. In particular, physicians are very influential in Uruguay as some of them hold seats in the legislature, and they resisted a reduction of public subsidies to the health care system. Thus, in Uruguay, a combination of the strength of civil society, including but not limited to unions, the strength of the left opposition, policy legacies of wide coverage, and the constitutional provisions for referenda prevented the imposition of neoliberal reforms in social policy.

As in Chile, education expenditures had seriously declined during the military government, from 3.5 percent of GDP in 1970 to 2.5 percent in 1985, but unlike in Chile there had been no structural reform. The growth of private school enrollment happened by default, not by design as in Chile, and remained at much lower levels, with just over 80 percent of students attending public schools in 1992, a figure that rose to 87 percent by 2000 (Pribble 2008). Primary and secondary school enrollment was comparatively high and continued growing after the transition, but the quality of education suffered from underfunding, and dropout rates in secondary education were high. An education reform launched in 1995 introduced universal mandatory preschool, an expansion of full-day schools in high-risk areas, various adjustments to improve secondary schools, and attempts to improve and standardize teacher training (Pribble 2008). This reform was not anchored in legislation, and implementation proceeded by way of pilot projects. The economic crisis of 2002 put some projects on hold, but the point is that no Uruguayan government attempted to undermine the principle of public education and follow in Chile's footsteps. Policy legacies from the long democratic period survived the military government and were more favorable for public education, as was the balance of power, with a strong teachers' union, the persistence of some progressive factions within the Colorados, and the growing strength of the left's opposition.

Costa Rica

Costa Rica was able to delay radical austerity and structural adjustment measures in the1980s to some extent, mainly as a result of its strategic location vis-à-vis the Central American conflict. Funds from USAID provided a temporary cushion, but at the same time USAID was a strong promoter of neoliberal reforms that gained traction by the end of the 1980s. When special U.S. funds began to dry up in the early 1990s, the World Bank became the main agent of external pressure, and liberalization of trade and financial markets continued. As of 1985, Costa Rica's liberalization index was .48, lower than those of Uruguay (.79), Chile (.61), and Argentina (.61), and the same as that of Brazil (.48). By 1998,

Costa Rica's index had risen to .85, very similar to those of Argentina (.87), Chile (.84), and Uruguay (.83) and higher than that of Brazil (.77). Thus, the extent of structural adjustment between 1985 and 1998 was greater than in any of the other four countries, with an increase of .37 in the index (Escaith and Paunovic 2004). In contrast to Argentina, however, the main areas of liberalization in Costa Rica were trade and finance, whereas privatization remained highly limited (Seligson and Martínez 2010). Similarly and importantly, the neoliberal reform impulse in social policy was much weaker.

Social policy underwent only marginal changes in the 1980s, and those changes were decidedly not neoliberal but rather were designed to strengthen the financial base of the social security system.[7] They included increased contributions for health services from employers, employees, and the government, and increased support for the pension system by the government, along with an increase in the retirement age. In a step toward further unification, the special system for civil servants was closed to all new entrants. In the 1990s, pressures for reform of both the health care and pension systems mounted. The PLN government under Figueres (1994–98) pushed through a reform of the essentially bankrupt teachers' pension system but withdrew a proposal for reform of the general pension system in the face of widespread protests. Unions and other civil society organizations vigorously opposed any curtailment of benefits. The center-right government under Rodríguez (1998–2002) then pushed pension privatization but proceeded with wide consultation in an inclusive policy-making process.

The result of this process was a mild reform and a mixed system that began operations in 2001. The majority of employer and half of employee contributions, along with a state subsidy, continue to go to the public system. The mandatory contributions to the individual fully funded accounts can be directed to public or private funds. The default is the public fund administered by the Banco Popular, and this fund administered the large majority of all accounts as of 2002.

As in the rest of the region, the real value of public funding for the health system declined in the 1980s, while costs kept rising because of an aging population and increasing demand for sophisticated medical technologies. The rise in illegal Central American immigrants, principally from Nicaragua, put an additional strain on the unified health system. The result was increased waiting times for appointments and treatment, which triggered an exit of those who could afford it to private care. The share of private health expenditures rose to 26 percent of total health expenditures in 1991, which continued to increase to 32 percent in 2000 (Martínez Franzoni and Mesa-Lago 2003).

The center-right administration of Calderón (1990–94) appointed a bipartisan commission to come up with a proposal for health-sector reform, and it also initiated negotiations with the World Bank for a loan to finance reform of the health sector (McGuire 2010). The World Bank invited Chilean consultants and proposed a reform that entailed the creation of private insurers and providers along the lines of the Chilean ISAPRES. The Costa Ricans, though, particularly the representatives of the CCSS (Caja Costarricense del Seguro Social), were mainly concerned with the quality and accessibility of primary care and rejected that model. The negotiations lasted some two years and resulted in a compromise weighed toward the Costa Rican preference of reforming primary care (Clark 2004). The reform established primary care teams around the country, financed by payment based on the number of people for which the teams were responsible. The reform involved a transfer of personnel and facilities responsible for public health from the Ministry of Health to the CCSS, as preventive and primary care were being unified and the basic health care teams came to serve as a gateway to the entire health care system (McGuire 2010, 81). Despite the closeness of the presidential elections, the reform received support from both major parties in the legislature and was implemented by the opposition PLN candidate Figueres after his election. Here was a case of strong policy legacies and bipartisan cooperation in resisting World Bank designs and pursuing a more universalistic path.

In education, expenditures had reached over 6 percent of GDP by the end of the 1970s but fell radically to an average of about 4.5 percent in the 1980s. As in Uruguay, the overwhelming proportion of students attend public schools. The cuts fell particularly on the secondary level and had a detrimental impact on the quality of education. Expenditures did not recover to pre-crisis levels despite a constitutional amendment passed in 1997 that mandated a minimum level of 6 percent of GDP for the funding of public education (Trejos 2008). In the 1980s and 1990s, however, various governments promoted reforms to improve the quality of education through measures such as standardized testing, an increase in the number of school days, and a strengthening of the curriculum. As elsewhere, the teachers' union was an obstacle to many such reforms, and concerns about the quality of education remained considerable. As of 2006, 89 percent of the students had completed primary education but only 42 percent secondary education. On the positive side, the gap between completion rates of low-income and high-income students had begun to narrow after the mid-1990s (Trejos 2008).

Brazil

The military government in Brazil turned to the IMF in 1982 and imposed several rounds of harsh austerity policies. The new civilian government that came to power in 1985, though, resisted pressures for more of the same and attempted to deal with high inflation through a heterodox program aimed at avoiding a recession.[8] After a temporary success, inflation returned and increased to ever higher levels. Despite the government's heterodox approach to economic stabilization, it proceeded with significant structural adjustment; the general structural reform index climbed from .48, among the lowest of the major Latin American countries, in 1985 to .69 in 1990, about the level of Chile (Escaith and Paunovic 2004). Collor's attempts to bring inflation under control with an orthodox approach combining harsh austerity and aggressive liberalization were cut short by his impeachment. His cuts in social expenditure, however, made a deep mark on health and education services. It was Cardoso's successful policies as minister of the economy under Franco that finally tamed inflation and prepared the ground for his election as president in 1994. Under his presidency, fiscal discipline along with liberalization of trade and financial markets continued, but in a more gradual manner than in Argentina and without the costs of steep deindustrialization.

Brazil's pension system had wide coverage and, for some sectors, generous eligibility conditions and benefits at the time of transition to democracy. The 1988 Constitution included specific provisions regulating the pension system and increasing benefits, which had two sets of implications. It meant that the Brazilian pension system would confront serious financial problems by the 1990s, and that the system would be difficult to change because it would require a constitutional amendment.[9] Like elsewhere in the region, the World Bank pushed privatization through consultants, technical assistance, studies of the system, and so forth, but unlike elsewhere there was little domestic support for privatization outside of some circles of economists and business leaders. On the other side, there was strong opposition from the PT (Partido dos Trabalhadores) and the unions to any neoliberal reform proposals. Thus, legislative proposals for reform were all aimed at putting the existing system on a firmer financial base.

Cardoso presented a proposal for pension reform early in his administration, and it immediately ran into strong opposition in parliament and from unions. The proposal contained provisions to limit early retirement, eliminate particularly costly privileges, and equalize conditions for public- and private-sector workers. Because Cardoso's party controlled a small share of seats in the Chamber of Deputies and the Senate only and that coalition building and coherence were hampered by the low degree of party discipline, and because of the complexities of the legislative process for constitutional amendments, the bill that was finally passed at the end of 1998 contained only minor modifications and did nothing to solve the financial problems of the social security system. In particular, the special programs for teachers and public employees were left intact and provisions for early retirement only included a minimum age. Allied with other public-sector unions, the teachers' union turned into a particularly influential lobbying force, one that Lula would have to contend with during his presidency as well.

The rural scheme of noncontributory pensions underwent a major expansion and improvement in the wake of the adoption in 1991 of legislation that implemented provisions contained in the 1988 Constitution. The pension age was reduced to 60 for men and 55 for women; women were entitled to their own pension, independent of the male head of household, and benefits were raised to one minimum wage. This provision doubled the value of the old-age pension (OIT 2002, 75). The 1988 Constitution also provided a benefit, equal to one minimum wage, for all poor, aged, and disabled persons. Enabling legislation for this benefit, Benefício de Prestação Continuada (BPC), was passed in 1991.

In health care, Chilean-style reforms were not even seriously on the table. A movement of progressive health professionals and academics, the *sanitaristas*, had already begun working to universalize reforms during the military regime and had managed to access important positions at various levels of the state after the transition (McGuire 2010, 161ff.). The 1988 Constitution enshrined the right to health care for all citizens, but the implementation of this principle was slow and uneven across the country. The creation of a unified and decentralized health care system, with better coordination between the Ministry of Health and the health care functions of the social security system, and transfer of responsibilities to the state and municipal levels were undermined and delayed by state governments, whose officials used transferred resources for purposes other than those intended (Weyland 1996). Moreover, little progress was made in curtailing the influence of private hospitals and drug companies on the health care services in the social security system and thus in containing rising costs. The logjam on health reform was broken in 1998 when Jose Serra became health minister (Arretche 2004, 176–80). Like Cardoso, Serra was from the center-left PSDB (Partido da Social Democracia Brasileira) and enjoyed the confidence of the president. The Cardoso government managed to push forward with a significant reorganization of the health care system by bypassing governors and dealing directly with municipalities on the transfer of responsibility and resources for the provision of preventive and primary care services through two programs, the Health Community Agents Program and the Family Health Program (Programa Saúde da Família, or PSF) (Arretche 2004, 177). Ideological orientation played a role at the subnational level also, because municipalities with left-of-center executives were more likely to adopt the new PSF scheme, which was designed to make basic care more universally available in poor areas (Sugiyama 2008).

The most important progressive social reforms in Brazil undertaken before the Lula government were the education reforms of the Cardoso government. A series of laws that affected mainly primary education were passed, the most important of which was passage of FUNDEF, the Elementary Education and Teacher Valorization Fund, in 1998 (Draibe 2004). Together these laws decentralized the administration of elementary schools to the provincial or municipal level, increased funding of education, increased average spending per student, transferred funds to poor regions of the country, and improved teachers' salaries. The transfer of education funds from the central government was large, 1.5 percent of GDP (Draibe 2004, 401). Although these reforms were aimed at primary education, secondary school enrollment increased steeply from 20 percent in 1994 before Cardoso took office to 75 percent in 2002, arguably, in part, the result of the increase in primary school completion during this period. As to the politics of the reform, Draibe (2004) argues that it was a top-down affair. The minister of education, Paulo Renato Souza, a former university dean, and a member of the PSDB's progressive wing, was part of Cardoso's inner circle and also had the strong support of the first lady, who was a former university professor. The close relationship to Cardoso allowed Souza to insulate the new educational programs from the Finance Ministry's economizing efforts on several occasions. The proposal for FUNDEF had strong support from congressional committees on education, including individual members of the Workers' Party, who, however, voted against the final bill, in keeping with the party's consistent status as opponent to the government.[10]

Impact of the Reforms

The 1980s in Latin America are appropriately called the Lost Decade in terms of economic and social development. The debt crisis led to negative growth and macroeconomic instability, which was accompanied by hyperinflation in a number of countries. Both high unemployment and high inflation hit the poor disproportionately. In addition, the debt crisis catalyzed the dismantling of ISI, which generated a process of skill-biased technological change as some low-skill, low-productivity import-substituting industries closed doors and others shed labor and invested in labor-saving machinery and technology. The result was deindustrialization and informalization, which increased inequality and poverty.

Argentina, Brazil, Costa Rica, and Uruguay, like most of the rest of Latin America, all had negative average economic growth rates, whereas Chile grew at an annual average of 1.1 percent of GDP per capita. In the early 1990s, more than 40 percent of the Brazilian population lived below the ECLAC poverty line, along with about a third of Chileans, somewhat below a quarter of Costa Ricans, about 16 percent of Argentines, and 12 percent of Uruguayans. Similarly, inequality had risen to a Gini of over .55 in Brazil and Chile, and .44 in Argentina, whereas Uruguay and Costa Rica had remained more or less stable between .42 and .44 (see chap. 5). In the 1990s, deindustrialization, informalization, and skill-biased technological change continued to exert an upward pressure on inequality, but the return of growth and the move toward macroeconomic stability caused poverty to decline in most countries and the increase of inequality to level off in some countries. By 2000 inequality had remained at unchanged high levels in Chile, had increased in Argentina, Costa Rica, and Uruguay, and declined only marginally in Brazil. Argentina had undergone the most serious economic crisis and the most radical program of liberalization, resulting in the most serious deindustrialization, with a loss of 10 percentage points in industrial employment between 1980 and 2000. The effect was the most dramatic increase in poverty and inequality among our focal cases. Comparing the trajectory of economic and social indicators for seventeen Latin American countries during the period 1982 to 1995, one can make the general statement that countries that underwent drastic reform episodes performed more poorly in a variety of areas, including poverty and inequality, than did countries that liberalized more slowly (Huber and Solt 2004).

As just noted, the rise in poverty and inequality was largely the result of the economic crisis and the rising unemployment and informalization of the labor market, resulting from the dismantling of ISI and the accompanying skill-biased change (Morley 2001). Skill-biased change in production increased the returns to education and thus led to increased wage dispersion. Brazil was the only one of our five countries that managed to keep industrial employment as a percentage of the labor force stable between 1980 and 2000; in the following few years it also suffered a decline of 2 percentage points (see table 7.7). The neoliberal social policy reforms did little to counteract these trends. On the contrary, after the structural reforms, coverage rates in social security programs fell everywhere except Costa Rica. In 2004, coverage based on active contributors to pension systems, excluding members of separate schemes such as the military and civil servants, was 59 percent in Uruguay, 57 percent in Chile, 47 percent in Costa Rica, 45 percent in Brazil, and only 24 percent in Argentina (Mesa-Lago 2008, 38). Health coverage rates through the public and social insurance systems remained roughly constant in the 1990s, but estimated private expenditures in the form of out-of-pocket payments and private insurance (including ISAPRES in Chile and IAMCs in Uruguay) had reached over 50 percent in all of our focal countries except for Costa Rica, where it accounted for 21 percent (Mesa-Lago 2008, 295). Clearly, this change had detrimental consequences for quality and equality of access.

It was not only in coverage rates that the results of pension privatization were disappointing but also in the amount of benefits accumulated. In most cases, the reforms were too recent to make much of an assessment, but the Chilean system had been in existence for two decades by 2001, and people who had previously contributed to the public system and switched to the private one began to retire and discovered that their pension income was way below expectations. Throughout most of this period, Chilean economic growth had been exceptional, and thus claims by the AFPs regarding returns on pension investments were extravagant. The system of commissions and flat-rate fees weighed particularly heavily on lower-income earners and significantly lowered the real rate of return compared to the one claimed by the AFPs (Mesa-Lago and Arenas de Mesa 1998, 69). In general, administrative costs in the private systems were much higher than in the public systems. According to Mesa-Lago (2008, 99), administrative costs accounted for 37 percent of the total wage deduction for the private pension system in Argentina and 19 percent in both Chile and Uruguay in 2005. Not surprisingly, many new retirees in Chile complained about their inadequate pension income. For other countries, projections also indicated that a significant percentage of the population would not contribute sufficient funds to finance more than a minimum pension, in addition to the fact that many would not even contribute for a sufficient number of years to obtain a minimum pension.

Clearly, the central problem from the point of view of combating poverty was that the traditional social policy regimes in Latin America that had provided reasonable if incomplete protection under conditions of high levels of formal employment lost their effectiveness in tandem with informalization and increasing precariousness of the labor market. An additional set of social changes reinforced the incapacity of the traditional social security schemes to provide adequate protection. These schemes were built on the male breadwinner model, in which women and children were covered as dependents. With an increase in divorce rates, a growing number of women and children were deprived of access, based on social security, to pensions and health care. An increase in women's participation in the labor force has not helped much in expanding coverage, since women are disproportionately represented in informal-sector jobs that lack social security coverage.

If anything, the neoliberal reforms reinforced the tendency toward reduced access and more unequal access because they forced greater reliance on private contributions and expenditures. Noncontributory safety nets, or social assistance, had long been underdeveloped, but the poor were not organized and did not constitute an effective pressure group, least so under authoritarian regimes. As of the early 1990s, not enough attention had been paid to adapting social protection to the new realities. Since democracy had been (re)installed, however, politicians began to pay more attention to the poor as potential voters. Particularly, but by no means exclusively, left-of-center parties began to present policy proposals to address poverty more effectively. Some of these proposals were picked up by nonleft governments, and many others would become policy after the left won elections in the first decade of the twenty-first century.

All of our focal countries had some sort of social assistance pensions, but benefits were low, eligibility was restricted to the very poor, and not everyone who would formally qualify in fact received it. In Chile, the value of a social assistance pension in 2001 was the equivalent of $50 per month, in Costa Rica in 2000 it was $33.50, in Argentina after the devaluation of January 2002 it was $50, in Brazil in 2000 it was $77, and in Uruguay in 2000 it was $120 (OIT 2002, 20). Uruguay was the only country in which the social assistance pension was set at 45 percent of the average pension in the general system, and thus comparatively generous. De facto budget limitations meant, for instance, that in 2003 in Costa Rica only about 45 percent of the target population received the benefits, and some 11,000 people were on the waiting list (Martínez Franzoni and Mesa-Lago 2003). Chile had waiting lists as well (OIT 2002). The Brazilian rural pension scheme was a noncontributory scheme based on number of years of employment in agriculture, with benefits such as the minimum social assistance pension.

For the working-age poor and their children, social assistance was minimal.[11] Social assistance budgets overall were a fraction of social security budgets before 2000: on average below 1 percent of GDP. Unemployment insurance did not exist or, where it did exist, covered only a small percentage of the labor force. Severance payments linked to length of service were in place instead of unemployment insurance, but they were a major obstacle to greater flexibilization of labor markets and provided little protection in more flexible markets. In short, there was no safety net to effectively protect people from poverty during normal economic times in the neoliberal era, not to speak of economic crises. The most common forms of safety nets in times of economic crisis were emergency employment programs, but their reach and duration were highly limited. Some improvements in this picture began in the 1990s, for instance, in Brazil, where legislation was passed to implement the progressive principles enshrined in the 1988 Constitution. During the first decade of the twenty-first century, however, improvements accelerated rapidly, particularly in those countries in which left-of-center governments came to power. Social assistance expanded considerably, and the state reassumed more responsibilities in the privatized social security systems.

The most promising developments in the 1990s were educational reforms in Brazil, Argentina, and Uruguay. The Brazilian government's improvements of public primary and secondary education were to contribute to the decline in inequality in the 1990s. The Uruguayan government greatly expanded preschool education and attempted to improve the quality of secondary education particularly in poorer areas, both of which helped to reduce inequality in educational attainment. In Argentina, compulsory schooling was extended to ten years, and the principle of free schooling was upheld.

The Turn to the Left and Basic Universalism

By the turn of the century, popular discontent with the effects of economic and social policies spurred a backlash against neoliberalism and gave more legitimacy to alternative views. Discontent with the policies pursued by incumbents also generated a set of victories for left-of-center opposition parties. Filgueira et al. (2011) compellingly argue that the combination of experiences of electoral participation but deficient representation, in the context of increased urbanization, labor market participation, exposure to new consumption patterns, and education, combined with persistent high inequality and social exclusion, created a crisis of incorporation whose political expression was the shift to the left.[12]

An important symbolic milestone in the reorientation of social policy in Latin America was a 1999 World Bank conference paper "Rethinking Pension Reform: Ten Myths about Social Security Systems," by World Bank chief economist Joseph Stiglitz and Peter Orszag, debunking ten assumptions on which the Chilean pension model was based (Orszag and Stiglitz 1999). Critics had raised similar points before (Huber 1996), but the fact that a leading official of the institution that had so strenuously advocated pension privatization publicly criticized the model clearly signaled that those pressures had lost their force. A further important contribution to the debate in the IFIs was the publication by the Inter-American Development Bank of the volume *Universalismo básico* (Molina 2006). The contributions to this volume advocated that social policy be oriented toward providing basic income support and access to social services, particularly in health and education, of high quality on a universalistic basis, as a social right guaranteed by the state.

In arguing for basic income support, the proponents of basic universalism accepted the need to target cash transfers to lower-income groups.

Targeting, of course, has a long tradition as a social policy instrument in advanced industrial countries as well. What distinguished their concept of targeting in basic universalism from neoliberal targeting is the breadth of the target population. Neoliberal prescriptions were to target narrowly on the most needy groups, as part of an effort to reduce social expenditures. Basic universalism targets large groups (60 percent in the case of Chilean pensions, about one-third of the population in the case of Plan Equidad in Uruguay) as part of an effort to pursue an inclusive and solidaristic model of social policy. A related crucial difference is that neoliberal targeting often entailed determination of eligibility for benefits on the basis of availability of resources and waiting lists for benefits, whereas basic universalism bestows benefits as social rights.

Despite its appeal as an alternative to neoliberal targeting, basic universalism is a contested concept. There are different views of its role in the development of social policy regimes. Proponents of basic universalism see it as a first and necessary step toward the construction of truly universalistic social policies, an essential building block constructed in a context of resource constraints and deficient tax systems. Critics see it as a dangerous and dead-end path toward a two-class system of social protection and social services—basic and public for the poor and working class, and better and private for the middle and upper classes. In transfers the issue is relatively clear-cut; better-off sectors do not need basic income support. In health and education, however, everyone needs primary and secondary education and preventive and primary care, and the challenge is to improve the quality of public primary and secondary education and preventive and primary care such that the middle classes do not seek private alternatives. In order to avoid the dead-end trap, efforts to improve the quality in the public sector need to be complemented by an avoidance of subsidizing an exit from the public sector through tax breaks and vouchers. This problem is particularly difficult where a significant private sector exists and enjoys such kinds of support, because its stakeholders will mobilize to defend their resources. This is precisely what has made education and health-sector reform so difficult in Chile and health-sector reform so difficult in Brazil.

In Chile, Brazil, and Uruguay, the new left governments took major initiatives toward universalizing access to health care and greatly expanding income support on a social rights basis, along with wage policies favorable toward the lower-paid categories of workers. At the same time they were careful to maintain macroeconomic stability. The picture was different in Costa Rica and Argentina. In Costa Rica, Arias was able to work with universalistic policy legacies, so his main initiative was to increase the value of noncontributory benefits. In Argentina the Kirchners also undertook bold policy reforms of the pension system and social assistance, but sustainability was much more questionable. All these governments were greatly helped by the commodities boom of 2002–7, and they managed to accumulate reserves during this period that would help them weather the global financial crisis of 2008 better than any financial crisis before.

Chile

The presidency of Ricardo Lagos prepared the ground for an important pension reform by his successor, Michelle Bachelet. Lagos himself implemented an important health-sector reform (see below), but arguably his most crucial reform achievement was the constitutional reform of August 2005. In its waning moments, the Pinochet dictatorship had enshrined a number of authoritarian enclaves in the constitution that would preserve preponderant influence for the right. It took one and a half decades for the democratic governments to eliminate most of them. Central among these constraints was the provision of appointed senators, which kept the Concertación parties from obtaining control of the Senate and forced them to negotiate with the opposition on all important legislation. The constitutional reforms—among other measures—eliminated the appointed senators, gave the president the power to remove the chiefs of the branches of the armed forces, and curtailed the powers of the National Security Council.[13]

Lagos prepared the ground for the pension reform in still another way. Like the Concertación governments of the 1990s, he adhered to the unwritten rule of fiscal responsibility, which required that all new expenditures had to be financed with new revenue. The rule stipulated that the primary balance should yield a surplus of 1 percent under conditions of expected growth and "normal" copper prices (Muñoz 2007). In September 2006 he actually put the rule in writing with the fiscal responsibility law (law 20128), which established the following: (1) a requirement that each president, at the beginning is his or her term, establish the bases of fiscal policy for the new administration and spell out the implications of this policy for the structural balance; (2) a contingency program to combat unemployment; (3) a Reserve Fund for Pensions; (4) a Fund for Eco-

nomic and Social Stabilization; and (5) capital transfers to the Central
Bank. The structural surplus was to be channeled into these funds and
the Central Bank. The existence of the Reserve Fund for Pensions then
allowed Bachelet to launch her pension reform and protect it during the
recession following the financial collapse in the United States. The Fund
for Economic and Social Stabilization also allowed her in January 2009
to fund an economic stimulus package worth 2.8 percent of GDP (Mof-
fet 2009).[14]

As noted earlier, by the turn of the century it had become abun-
dantly clear that fewer than half of Chileans would contribute regularly
enough to receive more than a subsidized minimum pension and a significant portion would not even make contributions for a sufficient number of years to acquire the right to a minimum pension. Therefore they
would depend on a state-financed social assistance pension, which was
means-tested and thus only available to the poor. Moreover, only a certain number of such pensions were available, and the waiting lists were
long (Mesa-Lago and Arenas de Mesa 1998, 65).

Bachelet had campaigned on the promise of a pension reform and was
able to institute a system that offers two kinds of solidaristic pensions for
old-age, disability, and survivor benefits to individuals who have lived at
least twenty years in Chile, including four of the five years immediately
preceding their request for the pension, and are sixty-five years of age or
older. One type is a basic universalistic pension, intended for all those
who have not contributed to a private pension fund and who are in the
bottom 60 percent of income earners; the other is a solidaristic supplementary pension for all those whose accumulated pension funds yield a
pension below a defined limit. All benefits were phased in between 2008
and 2012. The basic universalistic pension in 2008 was set at 60,000 pesos per month, the equivalent of $120, with the total supported by a sol-
idaristic supplementary pension at 70,000 pesos. In 2009 the basic pension increased to 75,000 pesos and the supplementary pension was paid
to persons with pensions lower than 120,000 pesos; pensions supported
by a supplementary pension will reach 255,000 pesos in 2012. There remains, therefore, a strong incentive for people to contribute to the pension system. The reform also contains some tax incentives for members
of the middle classes whose pensions are above the limits that would en-
title them to a supplementary pension—a politically important provision
to garner cross-class support for the reform.

The basic and supplementary solidaristic pensions are financed by general revenue and by the Pension Reserve Fund set up under the Financial Responsibility Law. The reform also contains a bonus for time lost in the labor market by women due to the birth of a child, an important gender egalitarian provision. It further abolishes fixed commissions charged by the AFPs which weighed particularly heavy on low incomes; it requires more transparency from the AFPs; and it allows them to invest more abroad. The original bill approved by the Chamber included the establishment of a state-run AFP, but that provision was eliminated by the Senate.

The basic solidaristic pensions constituted an important move toward noncontributory basic income security for the elderly and disabled. Lagos had also promoted Chile Solidario, a comprehensive program that included noncontributory income security and access to a variety of social services for the extremely poor. This program responded to his concern that poverty had been reduced significantly but that extreme poverty seemed to persist (Pribble 2008). Indeed, between 1996 and 2000 the share of individuals living in extreme poverty in Chile had remained constant, while overall poverty levels had continued to decline. Chile Solidario provided a small cash benefit, counseling, access to in-kind benefits, in short a comprehensive attempt at integrating these families into a support network (Serrano and Raczynski 2004). Participating households must fulfill several commitments outlined in a social contract, so the program belongs to the category of conditional cash transfers. Evaluation studies indicated an increased uptake of social assistance benefits, improved school attendance, and an expansion in the use of primary health care services among Chile's most vulnerable citizens (Galasso 2006). Its highly targeted nature, however, ensured that its reach remained limited. President Bachelet then attempted to expand the program to include the homeless.

A final important innovation adapting the social safety net to the new labor market conditions, introduced in 2002, was unemployment insurance (Muñoz 2007, 223). It is funded by contributions from employers, employees, and the state. Under current labor market conditions, however, coverage will not grow to more than about half the labor force because the program is restricted to formal-sector employment. Even in the formal sector, job instability is high, so workers do not easily accumulate the necessary length of service to qualify for meaningful benefits.

As noted earlier, the first two Concertación governments left the architecture of Pinochet's health care system in place. Coverage limits of

ISAPRES often caused their subscribers to seek treatment in the public sector when they became seriously ill, which burdened the public sector with the heavy expenses while depriving it of the regular subscriber fees of these patients. Those patients relying exclusively on the public sector often faced long waiting lists for treatments because of the lack of capacity resulting from the many years of underfunding. Lagos launched a health care reform called AUGE, conceived as universal coverage for the most common illnesses for users of both public- and private-sector health care. It was to be financed in part by directing a share of everyone's health care contributions to a national solidarity fund.

The government launched the proposal in 2002, but negotiations delayed adoption until 2004 and forced several curtailments. Originally, 56 illnesses were to be covered immediately, but in the end they were covered gradually, beginning with 25 illnesses in 2005 and reaching the full 56 in 2007. A crucial curtailment was the elimination of the solidarity fund and its replacement with an inter-ISAPRES risk-pooling fund. Sectors of the Christian Democrats opposed the fund internally, and of course the ISAPRES and the parties of the right opposed it strenuously (Dávila 2005). A one percentage point increase in the value-added tax and new copayments replaced the originally proposed financing through a tax on alcohol and cigarettes (Espinosa, Tokman, and Rodriguez 2005). The reformers, however, managed to protect the lower-income sectors by putting income-related caps on the total copayments for AUGE illnesses (Pribble 2008). The law also gave new powers to the regulatory agency of the health sector (Superintendencia de Salud) to enforce the guarantees of timely treatment of these illnesses. The Bachelet administration then extended the number of illnesses covered under AUGE to 62 by 2008 and 69 by 2010. AUGE certainly constitutes a big step toward guaranteeing universal, affordable health care to all Chileans, but it has three serious limitations. First, it failed to correct the inequitable allocation of mandatory contributions to the health care system and thus to do away with the two-class health care system. Second, it only covers the designated illnesses and does not help those who fall ill with something else. Finally, it left a hole in coverage in so far as the poor enjoy free access to public health care, but informal-sector workers above the poverty line who mostly do not contribute to FONASA are left out of the system.

Progress under Lagos and Bachelet on moving education toward basic universalism was much more limited. Lagos successfully pushed through a reform to make twelve years of schooling mandatory, as did Bachelet for kindergarten. Bachelet attempted to implement a comprehensive reform of the educational system, including elimination of extra fees and admissions criteria for publicly subsidized private schools, but she had to abandon many crucial elements of her reform in the face of determined opposition. She managed to provide increased funding for schools with high at-risk student populations, and eliminate previous academic performance and socioeconomic background as admissions criteria for primary and secondary subsidized schools (but not for subsidized high schools). She significantly expanded preschool education (Pribble 2008), which is important because it prepares children from underprivileged backgrounds to learn when they enter school. Moreover, it also frees poor mothers to enter the labor market. Thus, expansion of preschool education was a step toward reducing class and gender inequality. Yet the key structural inequalities built into the three-tiered Chilean education system remained intact.

An additional dimension of policy, although one not generally included under social policy but closely related to it, be it through links to benefits or simply through its impact on the primary income distribution, is wage policy. Wage policy can take the form of government intervention in collective bargaining or adjustments of the minimum wage. In Chile, the minimum wage was the key instrument to influence earnings. The Concertación governments increased the minimum wage annually after the transition, nearly doubling its value (in real purchasing power) by 2005 (Marinakis and Velasco 2006, 171). The Lagos administration contributed strongly to these increases, raising the value of the minimum wage from US$200 to US$255 between 2001 and 2005 (Government of Chile 2001, 2005). Bachelet continued the policy of annual increases, and as of 2008 the wage had reached US$318 (Government of Chile 2008).

Uruguay

When the Frente Amplio (FA) came to power in 2005, it found more favorable policy legacies for moving in a universalistic direction than Lagos and Bachelet faced in Chile. Privatization of social policy had been limited, so private insurers and service providers constituted less powerful obstacles to policy reform than they did in Chile. The legitimacy of basic state responsibility for the welfare of citizens had not been battered by neoliberals to the extent it had been in Chile and Argentina.

The pension system continued to be a drain on resources, but not much could be done about it because the referendum had firmly anchored the benefits in the compensation system of public employees. Moreover, the minimum pensions and social assistance pensions compared favorably in coverage and benefits with those in the other more advanced Latin American countries. The way the FA attempted to deal with the cost burden of pensions was to tax them under the new income tax system they introduced. Pensioners, however, won a constitutional complaint in the Supreme Court and forced a modification of the legislation, in the end exempting some 87 percent of pension recipients from taxation (Castiglioni 2010). Nevertheless, this legislation enabled the government to tax the most generous pensions, an important achievement.

The introduction of a new and progressive income tax system was arguably the most important policy reform of the FA for the long run, along with the unification of the health system, the expansion of preschool education, and the revival of the wage councils. Tax reform had been an issue in the 1999 campaign already, and after coming to power in 2005, the FA lost little time in presenting a sweeping overhaul of the tax system. Another crucial reform which addressed the poverty of the present generation and the human capital of the next one was the Plan Equidad.[15] The plan was the successor to the emergency antipoverty program that had been in effect for the first two years of the FA's term in government. It significantly increased the value of family allowances and lowered the age for receipt of the noncontributory pension to sixty-five. Family allowances under the contributory social security program had existed in Uruguay since 1943. In the late 1990s and early 2000s, a noncontributory version was added, but the value of the benefit remained extremely low (Pribble 2008). The Plan Equidad almost tripled the value of the benefit for children under thirteen and more than tripled it for children aged thirteen to eighteen, with the stipulation that they attend school. The benefit is means tested but not narrowly targeted: it includes about one-third of Uruguayan families, which means about half of all children (Amarante et al. 2009). The benefit is the same whether access is obtained through the contributory or noncontributory path. The plan also provides incentives for children to enroll in preschool and to stay in secondary school. Further, it extends the availability of nutrition cards, used to obtain food, and subsidies for electricity and water costs for poor households. It also provides subsidies to private firms that hire previously unemployed members of poor households. In sum, it constitutes a comprehensive approach to combating poverty and lack of educational attainment.

Health-sector reform in Uruguay had long been on the agenda but long stymied by the multiplicity of stakeholders. The IAMCs operated as not-for-profit institutions and worked in partnership with the public sector, using public hospitals under contracts. Overall, however, coordination was deficient, and therefore the use of resources inefficient and the quality of health care unequal. The financial crisis of 2002 brought about declining contributions to the IAMCs, and more of their subscribers came to rely on the public sector by default. As are result, health reform was one of the central campaign commitments of the FA and one of its major early projects. The reform unified the financing of the health care system, though not its delivery.[16] A national health care fund was established to which mandatory employee and employer contributions are directed; that fund then provides a per capita payment either to the public sector or the IAMC of choice. The IAMCs may not reject individuals or provide only partial coverage. In addition, the government significantly increased funding for the public sector and expanded the net of primary care facilities throughout the country. Health care for the poor continues to be financed by the state, but now the per capita payment for everyone is on the same scale, adjusted for the individual's risk profile. An important aspect of this reform was the mandatory expansion of coverage to the children of insured employees, through contributions based on income level and the number of children. Also, copayments are limited and assessed according to income. Overall, this arrangement is close to a universalistic health care system, with affordable access to the same quality health care for all. Private insurance and services, though, remain an option for high-income earners. Also, as in Chile, the one category that remains excluded from this system is nonpoor informal-sector workers.

An improvement of the educational system was high on the agenda of the FA government as well, but meaningful reform eluded it, just as it had its predecessors. The government did substantially increase public expenditure on education, however, setting a goal of 4.5 percent of GDP, to be reached before the end of the FA's first term. Moreover, it significantly expanded preschool attendance from 70 percent of three- to five-year-olds in 2005 to 79 percent in 2008; similar 9 percent increases had taken six years under the previous governments (Presidencia de la República 2009, 41). The close relations between the FA and the teachers' union, however, narrowly circumscribed the options for reform. While in opposition, the FA had sided with the teachers' union against aspects of the 1995 reforms, with the result that changes in the curriculum, in the assignment of teachers, and in teacher training had stalled. While in government, the FA could not muster the internal consensus to formulate a comprehensive reform that would address these areas (Pribble 2008). Still, the FA government became the first government in the world to guarantee each child a portable computer, an Internet connection at school, and thus new ways of learning in the information age (Castiglioni 2010).

Uruguay used to have a system of tripartite wage councils in different sectors of the economy,[17] but they stopped functioning when the right-leaning President Lacalle withdrew governmental participation in the early 1990s. The FA government reinstated them and achieved not only a more coordinated process of wage setting and an improvement of real wages, but also an increase in unionization. Unions in the private sector had become extremely weak under previous governments, but they added some 100,000 new members after the reinvigoration of the wage councils (Midaglia 2009, 158).

Argentina

Unlike in Chile and Uruguay, where new reforms were added to improve the pension system for those without sufficient contributions but the basic structure of the (partially) privatized system was left in place, in Argentina the government actually reappropriated the entire pension system. The takeover occurred gradually, and the financial crash of 2001 was an important precipitating factor. Indeed, one of the myths about pension privatization, the myth that it would insulate pension funds from political manipulations, was shown to be dead wrong within the first decade of the reformed system in Argentina. As the financial crisis was unfolding in late 2001, the government first pressured the private pension funds to accept a debt swap. After those negotiations failed, the government forced the pension funds to purchase Treasury notes in December 2001. At the beginning of January 2002 the government defaulted on its international debt and then devalued the peso. The government debt that was originally denoted in U.S. dollars was converted to Argentine pesos, and then the government defaulted on that debt, which resulted in a precipitous drop in the value of pension fund investment (Kay 2009).

When the government declared the default, pension funds held about 64 percent of their portfolio in state bonds (Arza 2009). In 2005, negotiations on debt restructuring were finally concluded and the government issued new debt instruments, but only three years later the government announced the takeover of pension funds and the reunification of the pension system into a public pay-as-you-go system.

The renationalization of the private pension funds was preceded by two reforms in 2005 and another one in 2007, all three of which shifted the public–private balance of coverage to the former. The first one allowed early retirement with reduced benefits for unemployed persons who had made the full thirty years' worth of required contributions but were five years short of retirement age; the second one allowed enrollment for all workers of retirement age who lacked the full thirty years of contributions. These workers had to accept responsibility for the contributions they still owed and agree to a payment plan; in return they began to receive pension benefits from which the contributions due were deducted. Enrolling for pension benefits would also enroll them in the health care system for pensioners, the PAMI. These reforms reversed the roughly 10 percent decline of pension coverage among the elderly that had occurred over the previous decade and brought coverage back up to 77 percent by 2007 (Arza 2009, 16). Benefits were low, particularly after the deduction of contributions owed, but this enrollment opportunity was particularly important for women who had had shorter histories of paid work. Benefits were low not only for those newly enrolled workers but for everyone, as indexation had essentially been abandoned with the economic crisis and therefore the real value of benefits had fallen steeply. The government decreed periodic adjustments of the minimum pension only, with the result that the distribution of pension benefits became more equal. By 2008 the mean benefit was worth only 33 percent of the mean wage (Arza 2009, 22).

The 2007 reform made it possible for workers enrolled in private pension funds to return to the public system every five years. It also changed the rules for the default allocation of new contributors to make them affiliates of the public system rather than one of the private funds, and it transferred all workers within ten years of retirement who did not have sufficient accumulated private funds back to the public system. It also reactivated the special programs for teachers, scientists, diplomats, and judges and transferred them to the public system. Finally, it raised the replacement rate from 0.85 to 1.5 percent per year of contribution. Naturally, all the assets of these workers were transferred to the public system with them. Ominously from the point of view of future financial viability of the system, these assets were classified as social security contributions in 2007 and used to finance the increased commitments in the short run (Vuolo and Seppi 2009). Thereafter current surpluses were transferred to reserve funds.

In 2008 the government of Cristina Fernández de Kirchner announced a plan to dissolve the private pension funds and transfer all their assets back to the public social security system, and within three weeks both chambers of the legislature passed the legislation. Given the complexity of the issues involved, this move is astounding and testifies to the lack of trust in the private system. The government assured all workers whose pensions were transferred that they would have the same rights as if they had been contributing to the public system all along; the same applied to pensioners who were receiving annuities. The assets were transferred to a reserve fund administered by the social security administration, and a parliamentary oversight commission was created, but the regulatory framework remained a contested political issue. Given the history of pension management—public and private—in Argentina and the lack of transparency in accounting in the public sector,[18] it is difficult to be confident about the future of the pension system as an effective safety net. The renationalization of the pension system per se did not affect the noncontributory system. In 2003, however, the government had also expanded the system of noncontributory pensions to include some 500,000 elderly people.

The economic crisis of 2001 gave rise to several policy innovations in social assistance and health care.[19] Duhalde, the Peronist who assumed the interim presidency in the middle of the crisis, created the Plan Jefes y Jefas de Hogar Desocupados (PJJHD) as an emergency conditional cash transfer (CCT) program. It provided the equivalent of roughly US$40 per month to unemployed heads of household with children under the age of eighteen, contingent on vaccination of the children and participation by the adult in workfare training. At its peak in 2003 the program covered over 2 million beneficiaries. There are, however, estimates that some 1.8 million additional households would have been eligible but missed the deadline for registration. Targeting worked reasonably well in that 80 percent of the benefits were given to the poorest two quintiles (World Bank 2009), although there was also some degree of political manipulation of the territorial allocation of benefits (Giraudy 2007). Along with the PJJHD, the Duhalde administration also put in place a highly targeted program of food assistance, but it remained much smaller in coverage.

Once the crisis subsided, three new social assistance programs were established to which some of the beneficiaries of the PJJHD were transferred. The Plan Famílias, a CCT contingent on regular medical checkups and school attendance by the recipients' children, targeted the most vulnerable families among the beneficiaries of the PJJHD. The Seguro de Capacitación y Empleo provides a small cash transfer for up to two years along with training and assistance in finding a job.[20] The number covered under this program remains comparatively low. The most ambitious of the social assistance programs is the Asignación Universal por Hijo para Protección Social, created in 2009. It covers all under- or unemployed persons who earn less than minimum wage and have children under the age of eighteen. This program reached 3.4 million children by March 2010, some 2 million of whom had previously received benefits under another program. Benefits are conditional on health and educational requirements and calculated on the basis of family size. The significant increase in social assistance spending required by this program was financed by the pension system.

In health care there were no structural reforms after 2000 to the *obras sociales* or to health care delivery through the public sector, but in response to the economic crisis the Duhalde government launched two emergency programs. The first one, originally financed by an IDB loan and later shifted to general budgetary support, provided for free basic medicines to be distributed by the central government directly to the primary health care centers, and by those centers to the population in need, that is, people below the poverty line and without health insurance. This program grew to benefit some 15 million people by 2006 (Niedzwiecki 2010a). The second program was originally funded by the World Bank and entailed resource transfers from the central government to the provinces to fund health care for pregnant women and for children under six years old who had no health care coverage.

Educational reform under the Kirchners was of limited importance. The state did reaffirm its responsibility to provide universal free education to all children from age five through secondary school. It also committed to expanding gradually free preschool for four-year-olds, without specifying a time table. And it established the same structures for education in all regions and set a minimum level of pay for all public school teachers (Pribble, forthcoming).

In short, under the two Kirchner presidencies, the Argentine state greatly expanded its responsibilities in the areas of social protection and health services. Noncontributory programs for transfers in cash and in kind became available to millions of poor children and parents. In addition, the minimum wage was increased, and pro-union policies helped unions regain lost strength in some sectors. The result was a strong decline in poverty but no impact on inequality, which remained at stubbornly high levels. Two concerns about these policies and programs arise. First, the entire approach to social policy in Argentina is very much a patchwork (Vuolo 2009a), rather than oriented toward universalism as was the health care reform in Uruguay or the pension reform in Chile. Second, the big question is the sustainability of social assistance expenditures, once the windfall from the pension renationalization has been exhausted.

Brazil

Expectations (and fears) were high when Luiz Inácio Lula da Silva, better known as Lula, won the 2002 elections as the candidate of the clearly left-wing PT.[21] Lula had started his career as a blue-collar worker and became one of the major labor leaders under the military government, from which he rose to leadership of the PT. The fears around his election required him to reassure financial markets strongly that he would continue with Cardoso's macroeconomic policies, which he did. The three major achievements of the Lula administration in social policy were a pension reform (though less far-reaching than intended), a significant expansion of Bolsa Família, and a significant increase in the minimum wage. In health and education, he mostly continued with the policies pursued under Cardoso but increased health expenditures and intensified the push to expand primary care.

Lula launched the pension reform in his first year in office. It was politically very difficult because it affected the interests of members of public-sector unions, a major support base of the PT. Moreover, the PT had staunchly opposed all pension reform proposals presented by previous administrations, so this constituted a policy reversal. The reform that Lula managed to pass increased the minimum retirement age and imposed higher penalties for early retirement, reduced survivor benefits, strengthened limits on benefit ceilings, taxed the benefits of the most affluent pension recipients, and equalized benefits for new entrants in the public and private sectors. Thus, it reduced the fiscal drain of the system and it improved the distributive profile, particularly for the future.

In the area of social assistance, Lula's first major initiative, touted as his top priority, was a Zero Hunger program. It involved a number of subprograms directed at those living in extreme poverty, but it encountered lots of obstacles in its implementation. Eventually it was abandoned and replaced by a new CCT program created out of the merger of previously existing programs and named Bolsa Família. It was similar in concept to the Bolsa Escola program originated simultaneously by the PT governor of Brasilia and two city administrations in 1995 and then picked up by a number of municipalities in 1997–98 (Soares 2011, 3). In 2001, the Bolsa Escola was federalized by the Cardoso government and came to cover 5.1 million families at its peak (Fenwick 2009, 112; Hunter and Sugiyama 2009b). It provides a cash payment to poor families on the condition that they keep their children in school and that children under seven years of age undergo regular health checkups. The payment is higher for families in extreme poverty and is dependent on the number of children. Lula's innovations in the renamed Bolsa Família were a major expansion of the program, to the extent that it reached 12.4 million families by 2009, or 22 percent of Brazilian households (Soares 2011), and the creation of a new registry of beneficiaries to bypass local political brokers and thus insulate the program from clientelism. By all accounts, the program operates surprisingly free of political interference and patronage abuse (Hunter and Sugiyama 2009a), which is a huge step forward for social assistance policies in Brazil.[22] Expenditures on social assistance grew significantly under Lula; federal expenditures on social assistance were 0.14 percent of GDP in 1995 and .83 percent in 2005; federal, state, and municipal expenditures in this category combined grew from 0.41 to 1.04 percent of GDP in the same period (Araújo Teixeira 2009). Though the budget for social assistance is still dwarfed by the budget for social security, at the federal level, where Lula had most direct influence, it grew much more rapidly than any other category of social expenditure.

As in Chile, the legal minimum wage in Brazil is an important reference point, and it increased significantly under both Cardoso and Lula, but much more so under Lula. Since some transfers targeted at the poor are valued as a minimum wage, changing the minimum wage also raised the transfer income of low-income households. The real minimum wage in 1995 stood at R$242 (in constant R$), and in 2002, the last year of the Cardoso administration, at R$289; by 2008 it had grown to R$424 (Kingstone and Ponce 2010, 113). This is clearly one reason why the income of the poorer sectors grew at a time when the income of the top quintile declined; between 2001 and 2005, the income of the lower half of the population grew by 16 percent, while the income of the top 20 percent declined by 0.5 percent (Hunter and Power 2007, 16).

In health care the Lula administration increased funding in comparison with the Cardoso years. In particular the government promoted improved access to primary and preventive care. It promoted the establishment of pharmacies in poorer areas, and it continued to emphasize the role of community health agents. It tied transfers of resources to agreements negotiated with states and municipalities for the provision of health services and the achievement of health outcomes. Lula's successor, Dilma Rousseff, issued a decree in 2011 to make these agreements legally binding (Osterkatz 2011). In 2008 the Lula government launched a health program in schools, with the aim of reaching 26 million students with health services by 2011, including distribution of glasses and hearing aids.

In education, there was more continuity than change from the Cardoso administration. The Lula government presented a plan in 2007 to promote teacher education, and it set a national minimum for teacher salaries. Expenditures on education as a percentage of GDP remained at the levels reached under Cardoso, however.

Costa Rica

In Costa Rica, policy did not change much structurally in a more progressive or universalistic direction after 2000. One of the obvious reasons for the lack of major change is that policy was already more universalistic in Costa Rica than anywhere else in Latin America outside of Cuba. The other reason, though, lies in party political developments. Internal fights in the PLN over democratization of internal party life, for instance with regard to candidate selection, led to a split and the formation of a new party, the Citizens' Action Party, which won 25 percent of the vote in the 2002 elections (Lehoucq 2005). In the presidential runoff, PUSC candidate Pacheco won, for the second PUSC (Partido Unidad Social Cristiana) presidency in a row. Thus, one would not have expected major redistributive social policy initiatives during this period. Moreover, with the presence of a larger number of parties in the legislature, policy making became more difficult and major departures from the status quo less likely. A 2005 reform, preceded by lengthy negotiations involving business, unions, and other civil society groups, introduced a gradual increase in social security contributions over many years, and it replaced a flat with a progressive replacement rate for pension benefits (Martínez Franzoni 2007a).

There is a debate about whether any ideological differences between the PUSC and the PLN remained by the beginning of the new century. Critics contend that the PLN ceased to be a center-left party during the 1980s and that the only left-of-center party after 2000 was the Citizens' Action Party. It is clear that there were few ideological differences between the PUSC and the PLN in the area of economic policy; both parties had subscribed to liberalization and macroeconomic stability in the 1980s. The PUSC, however, remained more market friendly in the areas of privatization of state-owned enterprises and in social policy, whereas the PLN remained more concerned with the universalistic nature of social policy. Still, neither party used the minimum wage to improve labor incomes at the bottom; the minimum wage remained essentially stagnant for two decades after 1990 (Castro and Martínez Franzoni 2010).

PLN president Arias (2006–10) then increased overall social expenditures significantly from 15 percent of GDP in 2005 to 17 percent in 2008, and he emphasized the priority of social expenditures, increasing them from 65 percent to 71 percent of total government expenditures in the same period (Estado de la Nación 2009, 113). He massively improved the value of the benefit of the noncontributory pensions, close to 300 percent between 2005 and 2008 (Estado de la Nación 2009, 131). He also implemented a conditional cash transfer program targeted at adolescents to reduce secondary school dropout rates, funded by FODESAF (Martínez Franzoni 2010). By 2008 this program covered about a third of all secondary school students and 43.5 percent of students enrolled in public secondary schools; 62 percent of those receiving the transfer belonged to the lowest 30 percent of income-earning households (Estado de la Nación 2010, 108).

Perhaps most important for long-term survival of Costa Rica's system of social protection and investment in human capital is the challenge to strengthen tax collection. As elsewhere, with the liberalization of trade, an important source of state income—taxes on foreign trade—dried up.

In 2007–8, Costa Rica's tax burden, including social security contributions, was roughly the same as Uruguay's, significantly below those of Brazil and Argentina, and higher by a couple of percentage points than Chile's. Unless funding can be increased to guarantee quality health care through the public system, for instance, the drift to de facto privatization is likely to continue, with highly predictable consequences for equality of access.

Poverty and Inequality in the Wake of the Reorientation

The trajectory of poverty and inequality since the debt crisis is not the same in all of our focus countries. Still, two trends are clear. Between the early 1990s and 2008–9, poverty declined steeply in Chile, Brazil, and Costa Rica. In Uruguay and Argentina the crisis of 2002 had increased poverty rates dramatically, and by 2006 they were still higher than they had been in the early 1990s by some 2 percentage points in the SEDLAC data. As to inequality, between the early 1990s and 2008–9, it fell in Brazil and Chile, increased clearly in Costa Rica and marginally in Uruguay, and was at roughly the same level in Argentina, after having peaked there in 2002. Clearly, a variety of factors contributed to these developments: high economic growth rates, particularly as a result of the post-2002 commodities boom; the different phasing of restructuring economies, particularly of skill-biased change; and increasing labor and nonlabor incomes at the bottom. These developments in turn were heavily influenced by various policies.

In a recent UNDP study, López-Calva and Lustig (2009, 2010) point out that, between 2000 and 2006, inequality declined in twelve of seventeen Latin American countries for which they have data, which is historically unprecedented development for the region. They and their collaborators analyze microdata to pin down the causes of this reversal for four countries: Argentina, Brazil, Mexico, and Peru. Labor income inequality declined primarily as a result of the decline in the skill premium, which they link to the petering out of skill-biased technological change and to the expansion of education in the previous decade or so, which increased the supply of workers with secondary and tertiary education. Increased minimum wage and changes in labor regulations in favor of organized labor played a role in some cases. Nonlabor income inequality fell primarily as a result of the increase in transfers aimed at lower-income groups.

This increase includes but is not limited to conditional cash transfers to poor families. It seems likely that the decline in inequality in the other eight Latin American countries was the result of factors similar to those in the four countries included in the analysis of the microdata.

We now turn to our focal cases in an attempt to pin down the causes of the changes in inequality and poverty and to link them to changes in policy outlined in this chapter and in turn to our hypothesized anteced-ent cause of policy change, particular democracy and partisan govern-ment. Figures 6.1 and 6.2 show the changes in inequality and poverty in the five countries during the period since 1980. The year of transition to democracy and partisan color of the executive are indicated in the fig-ures.[23] For the period 2001–6, the UNDP analysis of microdata for Ar-gentina (Gasparini and Cruces 2010) and Brazil (Barros et al. 2010) al-lows us to pinpoint what factors caused the declines in inequality and poverty for those two countries in that period. For the other countries and for other periods we cannot be so precise, but we have sufficient evi-dence from Morley (2001), López-Calva and Lustig (2010), Lustig (2009), and our own data, so we can be fairly confident about the processes that led to the changes in poverty and income inequality observed in fig-ures 6.1 and 6.2.

At the outset of our discussion of the cases, it is useful to remind the

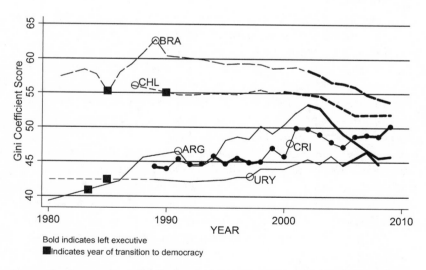

FIGURE 6.1. Income inequality in five Latin American countries, 1980–2010. *Source:* SEDLAC 2010.

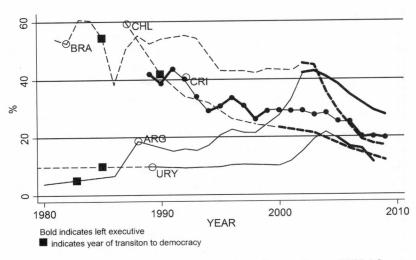

Bold indicates left executive
■ indicates year of transiton to democracy

FIGURE 6.2. Poverty in five Latin American countries, 1980–2010. *Source*: SEDLAC 2010.

reader of some of the complexity of how social and economic policies affect inequality and poverty. First, both our inequality and poverty figures are based on the monetary income of the household. This means the figures do not include publicly provided or subsidized services, such as education and health care. As we showed in chapter 3, in Latin America these services are generally much more equally distributed than transfers, so our figures underestimate the redistributive effect of government in Latin America. More to the point, the immediate distributive effect of the education and health care reforms discussed in this chapter does not show up in the data represented in the two figures. Health and education reforms are investments in human capital, and as such they also have a long-term effect potentially more important than the short-term effect on household consumption, at least in the case of education. Indeed, as we have seen from the UNDP studies, one of the major reasons for the egalitarian turn of income distribution in Latin America after 2001 was the rapid expansion of education during the previous period. One therefore has to credit the previous governments that carried out the education reform with part of the equalizing trend that occurred later in time.

In Argentina, inequality and especially poverty had increased greatly in the 1980s (figs. 6.1 and 6.2). During this period, the informal sector grew from 26 percent to 48 percent of the labor force, but industrial employment was stable at 32 percent of the labor force. The 1990s was another decade of steeply increasing inequality (fig. 6.1). Skill-biased technological change is the most important reason for this increase, because the increasing returns to education account for half of the increase in the Gini (Gasparini and Cruces 2010). The neoliberal policies of the Menem government are arguably at the root of these changes. The rapid opening of trade and the privatizations resulted in rapid declines in industrial employment, which fell from 32 percent to 23 percent of the labor force. Deindustrialization and labor market deregulation also decreased the strength of organized labor in wage bargaining. Despite the economic recovery and GDP growth in the 1991–2000 period, poverty continued to increase as a result of the increase in inequality (fig. 6.2). The crisis of 2001–3 further exacerbated the situation and, as GDP and employment fell sharply, resulted in increased inequality and poverty.

As one can see from figures 6.1 and 6.2, after 2002, Argentina experienced a significant decline in inequality. A large part of this was the result of the economic recovery and the commodities boom, as GDP per capita in constant dollars increased from $11,274 in 2002 to $15,275 in 2007. But the social and economic policies of the Kirchner governments contributed to the trends (Gasparini and Cruces 2010). They expanded the conditional cash transfer program, PJJHD, raised the minimum wage, and strengthened the hand of organized labor with pro-union policies. In addition, Gasparini and Cruces (2010) argue that skill-biased technological change had run its course and no longer exerted a strong upward pressure on the skill premium in wages. In addition, the education reforms of the Menem government arguably increased secondary school enrollment substantially, which should have increased the supply of medium-skilled workers and thus reduced the skill premium.[24] The combination of these processes contributed to the stabilization of industrial employment. Because of a combination of economic growth and the decline in inequality, poverty declined dramatically during this period.

Barros et al. (2010) do not provide an analysis of the causes of changes in inequality in Brazil based on microdata before 2001, but it is easy to account for the changes one sees in figures 6.1 and 6.2 for this period. There is a spike in inequality between 1986 and 1993 and a spike in poverty between 1986 and 1995. These spikes correspond to a period of declining GDP per capita and hyperinflation (an average of over 1,000 percent) as well as of increasing informal employment from 30 percent in

1985 to 57 percent in 1994. The taming of inflation and restoration of growth under Cardoso goes far in explaining the decline in poverty in the mid-1990s.

Figures 6.1 and 6.2 show that Brazil experienced a decline in inequality and poverty after 2001. On the basis of their analysis of microdata on household income distribution, Barros et al. (2010) conclude that the decline in income inequality between 2001 and 2007 was the result of (1) a decreased educational premium in wages and decreased inequality in education levels, (2) increasing spatial and sectoral integration of labor markets, and (3) increased generosity of contributory and noncontributory government transfers. They attribute (1) to the earlier expansion of education, and we credit the Cardoso reforms with most of that increase. López-Calva and Lustig (2009, 16) note that raising the minimum wage, which was increased by Cardoso and then more steeply by Lula, certainly played a role in not only reducing the skill premium but also in increasing the value of transfers, since many transfers, notably the BPC, are indexed to the minimum wage. Poverty declined steeply after 2001 as a result of the decline in inequality and growth of per capita GDP. Since it is targeted at the poor, Bolsa Família contributed disproportionately to the decline in poverty.

As figures 6.1 and 6.2 show, in Chile during the period of Concertación governments led by a Christian Democratic president, poverty declined but inequality was stable. This was possible because the average rate of growth of per capita GDP in constant currency was 6.2 percent, so with stable distribution, economic growth lifted many households out of poverty. Moreover, the marked increases in the minimum wage contributed to the decline in poverty.

By contrast, both poverty and inequality fell during the Socialist-led Concertación governments of the 2000s. These declines cannot be attributed to the signature reforms of the two presidents. Lagos's health care reform would not show up in these figures because they only cover monetary income and thus are not government-provided or -subsidized services. The Bachelet pension reform was phased in beginning in 2008 and so could only have affected the last numbers in the figures. On the other hand, Lagos's Chile Solidario reform almost certainly resulted in a decline in poverty and possibly inequality. As noted earlier, the reform was aimed at the extremely poor, and Lustig (2009, 12) shows that extreme poverty in Chile declined by 46.9 percent between 2003 and 2006.

Moreover, the increase in the minimum wage continued to make a contribution to lowering poverty. Eberhard and Engel (2009) show that wage inequality among males declined because of a decline in the skill premium. They attribute this to an increase in tertiary enrollment which occurred primarily since 1990 and thus to the greater supply of educated workers. We think it is probably much broader than that, as SEDLAC education data for Chile show large increases at every level from 1990 to 2006: primary completion increased from 83 percent to 95 percent; secondary enrollment from 71 percent to 87 percent; and tertiary enrollment from 17 percent to 36 percent. We note that education spending as a percentage of GDP increased only modestly during this period, from 2.5 percent to 3.5 percent, although with the rise in GDP per capita due to the strong Chilean economy, the increase in spending per student was larger than that. Thus, despite the fact that public spending on education as a percentage of GDP in Chile was somewhat lower than the average in Latin America, and despite the continuing disparities in the quality of education, we think it likely that the expansion of education under the Concertación governments contributed to the decline in inequality and poverty after 2000.

The income inequality data for Uruguay show a modest increase in inequality from the mid- to late 1990s to 2004, and then stability or even a slight decline (fig. 6.1). Uruguay experienced the same underlying economic developments that pushed up inequality elsewhere in Latin America: a reduction of trade barriers, rapidly from 1977 to 1985 and then more slowly from 1985 to 1995, followed by deindustrialization mainly in the 1990s (33 percent to 25 percent of the labor force). It is a good guess that this triggered a process of skill-biased technological change, as occurred elsewhere in the continent, but we cannot be sure, in the absence of analyses of income distribution microdata for several points in time. What is amazing is that the economic crisis induced by Argentina's collapse in 2001, which led to a decline in GDP per capita in Uruguay of 14 percent in 2002 alone, appears to have had no effect on income distribution. It did have a marked effect on poverty, as one can see from figure 6.2. Growth resumed in 2003, and GDP per capita finally returned to its pre-crisis level in 2006, which helped to bring down poverty. Frente Amplio policies contributed to the decline also. Forteza and Rossi's (2009) analysis of microdata on household income distribution shows that family allowances reduced income inequality in 2005, and this was before the introduction of Plan Equidad, which greatly increased the benefits of noncontributory, means-tested family benefits. The revival of the wage councils also likely helped increase the wages of poor workers.

The trend in inequality in Costa Rica is different from that in the rest of Latin America. On the whole it remained stable (at a low level for Latin America) until the mid-1990s, then moved upward in the late 1990s, and stabilized at a higher level after the turn of the century (fig. 6.1). The reason for the difference is that trade liberalization occurred later in Costa Rica: Morley et al.'s trade liberalization index does not increase until 1985, and then it moves up sharply and stabilizes at a high level in the mid-1990s. As a result, deindustrialization occurred primarily after 1995, and the accompanying process of skill-biased technological change continued into the new century. Thus, the education wage premium increased until 2006, when it began to decline slightly (Estado de la Nación 2009, 102).

The combination of stable inequality and declining poverty from the late 1980s to the late 1990s indicates that the main factor pushing down absolute poverty was the increase in GDP per capita from $7,461 in 1989 to $9,043 in 1998 (Penn World Tables 6.3). As one can see from figures 6.1 and 6.2, the upturn in inequality after 1998 was accompanied by and probably caused an increase in the poverty rate. The stabilization of inequality and the return of economic growth in 2003 after three years of minimal growth led to declines in poverty. The Arias social reforms mentioned earlier certainly contributed to the decline in poverty, but without analyses of microdata on household income distribution at several points in time across the decade, it is not possible to say how large the effect was.

Conclusion: Democracy, Partisanship, and Globalization

We know from our data analysis that democracy and left strength in the long run are associated with lower poverty and inequality. We also know that they are statistically virtually impossible to disentangle because they are highly correlated. Our case analyses make it possible to identify causal relationships. On the face of it, it is not easy to make the case that democracy per se is responsible for improvements in social policy. After all, Menem was democratically elected and yet pushed through a painful program of liberalization and privatization in economic and social policies that allowed poverty and inequality increase to levels unprecedented in Argentina. On the other hand, Menem's plans were tempered by opposition from the unions and their allies in his own party, whose votes he needed to pass the reform. It is unthinkable that a democratic president in one of our focal cases would have been able to push through reforms as radical as those imposed by Pinochet. All of the countries in our study had periods of democracy before the authoritarian breakdowns and therefore parties and organizations in civil society with some roots and experience, and thus the capacity to resist radical reforms.

In other cases, it is apparent that democracy acted as a break on neoliberal designs pushed by the IFIs. In Uruguay, pension reform with a private system for upper-income earners only was preceded by a referendum that protected the value of pension benefits by linking it to remuneration of public-sector employees. In Brazil, the 1988 Constitution was clearly a democratic product and was very progressive in the area of social rights. Implementation was slow, but the direction was set; Collor was not able to push through his neoliberal designs and was removed by democratic means. In Costa Rica, as the democracy with the longest uninterrupted record, radical neoliberal social policy proposals never even made it into parliament. Finally, spurred on by high public concern with the quality and accessibility of education, nonleft governments in Argentina, Brazil, and Uruguay introduced important educational reforms that increased both secondary and preschool enrollment and thus had potentially important long-range downward effects on inequality.

Democracy was particularly important as the context in which civil society organizations and parties to the left of center could grow and gain influence on policy. These processes were most important in Brazil, Uruguay, and Chile. In Brazil, the PT was able to prove itself in local administration; implement policies, such as forerunners to Bolsa Família; run candidates in elections at all levels; and eventually win the presidency. Another example is the growing influence of the *sanitaristas*, who were appointed to various administrative leadership positions and took advantage of these positions to promote health-sector reform. In Chile, the Socialists could reestablish themselves by distancing themselves from the Allende period as loyal and effective partners in the center-left Concertación, hold important ministries and eventually win the presidency. In Uruguay the FA managed to grow in strength gradually and to break the domination of the two traditional parties. In Costa Rica the PLN was founded by the winners of the civil war, and the subsequent long period of democracy allowed it to consolidate and exercise political power for prolonged periods, clearly leaving its imprint on the universalistic orientation of the welfare state. Finally, Argentina is a special case because the Peronists as a party do not have a unified ideological commitment independent from the leader of the day and thus are difficult to classify on a left–right spectrum. They are internally split, but a Peronist president generally manages to get support from Peronist members of the legislature, often after significant concessions and modifications. This is particularly true if the president pursues policies adverse to the interests of labor, as Menem did with the pension reform.

Of course, even if left parties grow stronger under democracy and eventually gain legislative and executive power, the policy outcomes are not necessarily the same. The strategic choices that parties make differ, as do the institutional obstacles to implementation of their choices. Although left parties generally share an ideological commitment to solidarity and equality and thus to redistributive social policy, they do not all choose the same policy instruments. Ideology includes not only abstract values and a vision of a desirable society, but also an analysis of what is wrong with society as it exists, and what is needed to improve it. It is here, in the strategic vision, that parties and individual party leaders may differ considerably. These differences are a product of personal experiences, policy legacies, party structures, and political institutions.

Among our focal cases, we can contrast the leadership of the Chilean Socialist Party and Party for Democracy (PPD), on the one hand, with the leadership of the Uruguayan FA and the Brazilian PT on the other hand. The former went through the traumatic experience of the Allende years and exile, whereas the latter spent their formative political years in opposition. Much of the time in exile was spent analyzing what went wrong under Allende, and one of the conclusions was that popular pressures had pushed the Allende government to do too much too fast (Roberts 1998). Moreover, some of the members of the Socialist leadership spent part of their exile in Communist countries and experienced first-hand the inefficiencies of the state sector there (Pribble 2008). These experiences caused the Chilean leadership to refuse to reestablish close relationships with unions and popular organizations, to keep popular mobilization low, and to hesitate to expand the state's role not only in the economy but also in social policy. The party structures themselves are very elite-centered, allowing for little input from the rank and file, which means that there is little effective pressure from below for far-reaching reforms (Pribble 2008).

The PT and FA, in contrast, were founded in opposition to the military regime and the dominant parties, respectively, and they were from their origins closely linked to unions and other social movements. The FA ran for the first time in 1971 and received 18 percent of the vote (Lanzaro 2011); the PT was founded in 1980 by a grassroots coalition of labor leaders, Christian base communities, and left intellectuals, and it won its first few seats in the 1982 congressional elections (Hunter 2007). In both cases, the leadership moderated its radical political views in response to electoral constraints and the constraints of governing in the presence of powerful international financial markets (Hunter 2010). They did not, however, move as far from reliance on statist models as the Chileans did, nor did they sever their relations to unions and other civil society organizations (Pribble 2008). As a result, their policy initiatives tended to be more sweeping in some areas (Uruguayan health reform versus AUGE; Bolsa Família versus Chile Solidario; wage councils in Uruguay versus lack of significant departures from the restrictive labor code in Chile) but also heavily constrained in others (education reform) where their allied unions were stakeholders.

The PLN leadership had an entirely different set of formative experiences. The party was founded in 1951 by the winners of the 1948 civil war, led by José Figueres, as a successor to the Social Democratic Party that had been formed in 1945 (Yashar 1995). It adopted a social democratic view of the state and society, but did not build a social base typical of social democratic parties. Because the communists were dominant in the labor movement and were allied with the other side in the civil war, Figueres repressed the largest union confederation in the wake of the civil war. Catholic-inspired unions persisted but the attempt to build a PLN-allied union movement failed, with the result that unions were overall weak and never constituted a major base for the PLN. The PLN dominated electoral politics into the 1980s, until the opposition united into the PUSC, and it lost organizational strength independent of its elected representatives as it came more and more under the control of the top leadership (Yashar 1995). Arias was the first PLN president not from the generation of the 1940s, formed in the context of a politically

powerful and ideologically social democratic party. While under tremendous pressure to liberalize economically, he and the party remained
committed to protecting the social achievements of his predecessors.

Policy legacies made it more or less difficult for left parties to advance
with redistributive reforms. Here the contrast between Costa Rica and
Chile is instructive. In Costa Rica, the health-sector reform could build
on the unified health care system and expand the network of primary
care without encountering effective opposition from private providers.
In Chile, the Pinochet legacies in pensions, health, and education meant
that private provider interests in all three sectors were strong and determined opponents of equity-enhancing reforms. Particularly in the
health sector, the for-profit ISAPRES fought very hard against the fund
that was to redistribute financial resources between the public and private sectors, and they found support in the business community at large
and the allied parties of the right (Dávila 2005; Pribble 2008). In education, the publicly subsidized private schools and the fully private schools
fought equally hard (and to a large part successfully) to defeat Bachelet's attempt to eliminate copayments and discretionary admissions in
the publicly subsidized private schools. In the end, the pension reform
did not even attempt to redistribute resources from the private accounts
but simply added on the supplementary and basic solidarity pensions.
The one proposal that affected the interests of the AFPs was to establish a public AFP to compete with the private ones. This proposal was
strenuously opposed by the private AFPs and ended up on the chopping
block.

In Brazil, private insurers and health care providers also constituted a
formidable opposition to a unification of the health care system. Accordingly, the public sector frequently contracted private providers of health
care services. In the pension system, the government was able to curtail some privileges, but improvements for the poorer sectors came in
the form of additions to the existing system, not as part of a sweeping
overhaul.

The Uruguayan and Argentine situations were in between the ex-
tremes of Costa Rica and Chile. The health care sector was dominated
by private but not-for-profit insurers and providers. Thus, in Uruguay the
FA was able to implement a health-sector reform that centralized and
equalized financing but left the system of providers intact. The problem
in Argentina was that the health care institutions are run by the unions,
and the Peronist governments did not want to pick an all-out fight with

the unions, so the system survived a serious reform attempt under Menem largely unchanged. In general, despite the significant changes in social policy in the first decade of the twenty-first century in all our cases, the nature of these changes was constrained by path dependency in the form of the constellation of interests created by previous reforms.[25] In the language of the recent literature on institutional change, the process of change was one of layering, not displacement (Streeck and Thelen 2005).

Institutional constraints further explain different policy initiatives and outcomes under left governments. Essentially, constitutional provisions that disperse power or require supermajorities for changing certain policies are major obstacles to equity-enhancing changes; they offer veto points to opponents of change and may shape the kinds of reforms that are even attempted by left governments. Federalism is an institutional feature that disperses power, and it proved to be an important obstacle to the implementation of the unified health system in Brazil, as various governors did not comply with the national guidelines.[26] The constitutional anchoring of essential parts of the pension system made pension reform particularly difficult. The existence of popular referenda provides another veto point.[27] The pension referendum in Uruguay in 1989 that linked pension benefits to public-sector wages made it extremely difficult to bring costs in the contributory pension system under control and to direct more social expenditures to the poor of working age and their children.

Party systems and the internal coherence of parties also shape the degree of power concentration or dispersion. The more fragmented the party system and the less disciplined the individual parties, the more difficult it is for the executive to obtain a reliable majority in the legislature. Brazil has long been notorious for party system fragmentation and lack of party discipline (Mainwaring 1999; Ames 2001), and indeed Lula ran into corruption scandals related to payments to representatives from other parties in exchange for their support for government initiatives.[28] Party discipline has also been a long-standing problem in Costa Rica. The prohibition of reelection of both the president and the members of the legislature means that the party leadership and the president have little control over the members of the legislature. Indeed, early in the term of the incumbent the legislators start positioning themselves favorably in relation to the president's possible successor (Carey 1996). Since 2002, the problem of the president lacking a reliable majority in the leg-

islature has been aggravated by the greater number of parties represented in the legislature. This problem tends to have a moderating influence on the policy agenda, as incumbents are reluctant to attempt major
departures from the status quo. In Chile, institutional constraints on the
left presidents consisted of dependence on coalition partners and, in the
case of Lagos before his constitutional reform, the presence of the appointed senators.

In the initial period covered in this chapter, circa 1980–2000—the
Washington Consensus era—transnational structures of power had a
huge impact on social policy in Latin America. Just how important this
influence was is underlined by our comparison in the next chapter with
Spain and Portugal, where international power structures were very different. It is important to address the questions of how much market liberalization was truly necessary for establishing a viable economic model,
how much market liberalization was inevitable because of the power of
the IFIs and the United States, and how much room for choice Latin
American countries actually had. To answer fully, however, involves
some counterfactual speculation, so we hold that discussion for the conclusion to the book. Suffice it to say here that we will argue that ISI had
exhausted itself and thus the transition to a more open trading system
was a necessity. Macroeconomic stability, and thus control of inflation
through monetary and fiscal discipline, was a necessity also, but achieving it through cutting social policy rather than tax increases was not and
was counterproductive for long-run economic development.

The Washington Consensus social policy prescription in this era was
to cut overall social spending in order to cut budget deficits, increase the
targeting of spending by increasing means testing, decentralize spending and administration to regions/states/provinces or municipalities, and
privatize the pension system. In the wake of the debt crisis, most Latin
American countries, including all five of our focal countries, were forced
to go to the IMF and accept austerity programs that typically involved
cutting social spending. In addition, the IMF increasingly worked with
the World Bank to impose structural adjustment policies, and the World
Bank pushed for increasing reliance on the market and private providers
in social policy.

With regard to the pension system, the World Bank recommended a
three-tier model with a first tier of basic pensions, a second tier of compulsory, fully funded, contributory, individual accounts along Chilean
lines, and a third tier of voluntary funded individual accounts. In the

World Bank formula, the main tier, which was to provide retirement income for most, was the second tier, the compulsory individual accounts. This formula was pushed across Latin America, but, as we saw was only fully implemented in Chile, Mexico, Bolivia, El Salvador, and the Dominican Republic. Elsewhere push back from domestic social forces resulted in compromises in the form of parallel systems (Peru, Colombia) or mixed models (Argentina, Uruguay, Costa Rica) or no structural change (Brazil and the rest of Latin America). We discuss the failure of the individual account systems in more detail in the conclusion of the book, but it should have been clear from the outset that such a system could not provide adequate retirement income for the bulk of the population of Latin American countries for the simple reason that a minority of households are headed by a wage or salary earner who spends his or her entire career in a formal-sector job. Neoliberal ideology, not sound policy, motivated the promotion of pension reforms with this configuration.

After the turn of the century, the Washington Consensus began slowly to crumble as the neoliberal model failed to deliver on its promises, and nowhere was its failure more apparent than in the area of social policy. By the end of the decade, the World Bank had abandoned the Chilean pension model in favor of the Swedish Notional Defined Contribution (NDC) PAYG model and was vigorously promoting investment in human capital: health and educational reforms and conditional cash transfers. This turn afforded all governments, but particularly the new left governments, more latitude for action. In addition, the responsible macroeconomic policies meant that they could avoid going to the IMF for "help" and the attendant conditionality. Although this fiscal restraint constrained governments in the short run, it clearly increased the governments' freedom of action in the long run. In other words, big budget deficits can allow a government to fund a lot of social policies in the short run, but they will come back to haunt that government in the form of macroeconomic instability and IMF conditionality.

Iberia and the Advanced Latin American Social Policy Regimes

Explaining the Different Trajectories

We now turn to a comparison of the development of the size and structure of the welfare state in Portugal and Spain versus our Latin American focus countries in order to further support our theoretical claims about the importance of social policy for distributive outcomes and of democracy and left political strength for social policy. Spain and Portugal have shared a common history with Argentina, Brazil, Chile, and Uruguay over the past fifty years in terms of democratization and the opening of their economies, and in terms of policy legacies in the form of a Bismarckian welfare state. Nevertheless, the size and structure of their welfare states and the outcomes in terms of inequality at the end of the twentieth century are markedly different (tables 7.1 and 7.2).

In 1970, before the transitions to democracy, the Iberian countries were similar to their Latin American counterparts in welfare effort and welfare state structure. They all had occupationally based and highly stratified systems of social protection. Spain was comparable to the higher spenders in South America and Portugal to the lowest. By the end of the twentieth century, Spain and Portugal were outspending all of the Latin American countries; only Uruguay came close to their spending levels. More important, their spending had a much stronger distributive profile. The Portuguese tax and transfer system reduced the Gini by more than ten percentage points, the Spanish even somewhat more, whereas the Latin American tax and transfer systems lowered it by one to two percentage points only (Goñi, López, and Servén 2008). If social

TABLE 7.1. **Income inequality**

	1970	1980	1990	2000	Latest 2006–9
Argentina	36.4 [a]	40.8	44.4	50.4	45.8
Brazil	59.0 [a]	56.0	60.4	58.7	53.7
Chile	46.0 [a]	53.2	55.1	55.2	51.9
Uruguay		42.5 [a]	42.4	44.3	44.7
Average	47.1	48.1	50.6	52.2	49.0
Portugal	40.1 [a,c]	34.1	32.9	34.7 [b]	38.0 [b]
Spain	34.1 [c]	34.0	31.6	34.5	31.0 [b]
Average	37.1	34.1	32.3	34.6	34.5

*Notes:*Cell entries are Gini indices.
[a] Not adjusted for household size.
[b] Adjusted for square root or OECD, otherwise adjusted for per capita.
[c] 1973.

TABLE 7.2. **Government social spending in 1970 and 2000**

	Education		Health		Social security and welfare		Total	
	1970	2000	1970	2000	1970	2000	1970	2000
Argentina	1.0	5.0	0.3	5.0	5.0	10.1	6.3	20.1
Brazil	1.2	4.9	1.3	3.9	6.5	11.2	9.0	20.0
Chile	3.9	3.7	1.7	2.8	6.1	7.2	11.7	13.7
Uruguay	3.6	2.8	0.5	3.1	12.8	15.7	16.9	21.6
Average	2.4	4.1	1.0	3.7	7.6	11.1	11.0	18.9
Portugal	1.4	5.4	1.4	9.4	3.1	12.1	5.9	26.9
Spain	1.9	4.3	2.3	5.2	8.6	12.3	12.8	21.8
Average	1.7	4.9	1.9	7.3	5.9	12.2	9.4	24.4

Notes: Cell entries are percentage of GDP.

services were included in this calculation, particularly health care, the difference in the redistributive nature of social policy would be even greater.

Our task, then, is to explain why the development of social policy in the two sets of countries took such different forms. We begin with an examination of possible explanations based on structural differences. Most of them fail to be supported by evidence; the exceptions are economic growth and location in Europe, in the sphere of influence of the European Union. These, however, were not sufficient reasons. The main driv-

ing forces behind expansion and reforms of the welfare state were democratic party competition and the commitment of left-of-center parties to
social inclusion and the fight against poverty and inequality. The differences in length of democratic rule and in the strength of the left make a
major contribution to the explanation of the differences in social policy
and its redistributive impact between the two sets of countries.

We center our discussion on a systematic comparison of the South
American cases with Spain and Portugal, because this allows us to hold
timing of the transition to democracy and cultural factors constant.
Costa Rica, Italy, and Greece are used for selective comparisons; Italy
and Costa Rica are partly different because they have the longest uninterrupted democratic records, and Greece has different historical and
cultural roots.

Potential Structural Explanations

The economists' answer to the question of why welfare states and inequality look so different in Iberia than in South America is that the former enjoy a higher level of economic development and therefore can afford to spend more. There is certainly some truth to this answer, but it is
far from the whole story. Chile's GDP per capita in 2000 was roughly the
same as Portugal's in 1990 (see table 7.3); Chile in 2000 spent 14 percent
of its GDP on total social expenditures, whereas Portugal in 1990 spent
19 percent. Other plausible hypotheses are that the two sets of countries
started out at different levels of development and different levels of expenditure at the time of democratization and that the Iberian countries
initially had more equal distributions of assets. The data do not support
these hypotheses; in 1960 Spain's and Portugal's GDP per capita were
lower than those of Argentina and Uruguay, and their total social policy expenditure in 1970 was comparable to that of the South American
countries (table 7.2).

The data for inequality of income distribution in 1970 are spotty.
They suggest that with a Gini of 40.1 in 1973, Portugal was similar to Argentina and Uruguay. They also suggest that with a Gini of 34.1, Spain
in 1973 already had a more equal distribution of disposable income than
Latin America.[1] What is clear, however, is that Portugal reduced inequality up to 1990 and that both countries managed to keep their levels of income inequality significantly below those of the South American

TABLE 7.3. **GDP per capita and growth**

	GDP per capita						Growth of GDP per capita (%)				
	1960	1970	1980	1990	2000	2007	1960s	1970s	1980s	1990s	2000s
Argentina	8,825	10,879	12,054	9,432	12,528	15,273	2.8	1.1	-2.4	2.9	3.0
Brazil	3,067	4,761	8,482	7,818	8,405	9,644	4.7	6.0	-0.7	0.7	2.0
Chile	5,860	7,039	7,885	8,630	14,300	18,380	2.7	1.4	1.1	5.2	3.7
Uruguay	6,555	6,774	9,234	8,550	11,442	12,921	0.6	3.2	-0.6	3.0	2.1
Average	6,077	7,363	9,414	8,608	11,669	14,055	2.7	2.9	-0.7	3.0	2.7
Portugal	4,071	7,692	11,071	15,065	19,666	20,123	6.7	4.0	3.2	2.7	0.4
Spain	5,879	11,585	14,733	19,085	24,928	31,443	7.3	2.5	2.6	2.7	3.4
Average	4,975	9,639	12,902	17,075	22,297	25,783	7.0	3.3	2.9	2.7	1.9

TABLE 7.4. **Asset distribution circa 1960**

	Ginis	
	Land	Education
Argentina	81.4	34.4
Brazil	78.7	62.8
Chile	86.5	41.3
Uruguay	79.1	38.8
Average	81.4	44.3
Portugal	75.6	58.2
Spain	79.1	37.9
Average	77.4	48.1

countries. The distribution of assets, land and education, around 1960 does not show clear differences between the Iberian and Latin American countries (table 7.4). Land distribution in Spain and Portugal showed Latin American degrees of inequality, very close to those in Brazil and Uruguay. Education in 1960 was almost as unequally distributed in Portugal as in Brazil, the most unequal of all; Spain was comparable to Uruguay and Argentina.

In a further search for possible structural causes of the different trajectories of the welfare state and inequality in Iberia and South America, we might hypothesize that three important structural transformations that all these countries went through in the second half of the twentieth century were less far reaching and therefore less disruptive in Iberia: the decline of agricultural employment, the opening of the economies, and deindustrialization. Disruption would manifest itself in higher levels of unemployment and informality and a lower tax base and therefore lower fiscal capacity of the government to expand the welfare state and redistribute income. Table 7.5 shows Portugal and Spain in an intermediate position with regard to the proportion of the labor force employed in agriculture in 1970, below Brazil but above the other three South American countries. By 2000, Spain and Uruguay had fallen to single digits and Portugal was comparable to Argentina and Chile. The decline in Spain, of 23 percentage points, was the steepest.

Opening highly protected economies to world markets poses a problem for the fiscal base of governments not only indirectly through changes in the structure of production and the labor market, but also directly

TABLE 7.5. **Agricultural employment**

	1970	2000
Argentina	16.0	12.5[a]
Brazil	45.0	24.2
Chile	23.2	13.7
Uruguay	18.6	4.1
Average	25.7	14.0
Portugal	29.2	12.7
Spain	29.4	6.6
Average	29.3	9.7

Notes: Cell entries are a percentage of the labor force employed
in agriculture.
[a] 1990.

through the decline of revenues from import and export taxes. Ideally, we would measure this opening with data on tariffs and nontariff barriers, but comparable time series of such data are not available. Therefore, we use trade flows as an indicator. Both Spain and Portugal increased imports and exports as a percentage of GDP by roughly 50 percentage points, slightly less than did Chile and slightly more than Uruguay (table 7.6). Similarly, their levels of openness were not systematically different so as to explain a different trajectory of social policy and inequality. Brazil is a big outlier on this dimension, remaining much less dependent on exports and imports due to its large internal market.

Industrial employment in 1970 was highest in Spain, but only 3 percentage points higher than in Argentina (table 7.7). The level of industrial employment in Portugal was lower than in Argentina and higher by somewhat more than 3 percentage points than in Chile and Uruguay. By 2004 the difference had grown, with Spain's and Portugal's levels of industrial employment about 8 percentage points higher than those in the South American countries. The level of industrial employment is important in so far as traditional social security schemes are based on formal employment, and thus higher industrial employment, which is mostly formal, means that a higher proportion of the population is protected. If, however, we see deindustrialization as an indicator of economic disruption, and we look at the change from the highest level reached in each country to the level in 2004, we find roughly a 5 percentage point decline in Spain, Portugal, and Chile, a 7 percentage point decline in Uruguay,

214

CHAPTER SEVEN

TABLE 7.6. **Economic openness**

	1960	1970	1980	1990	2000	2007
Argentina	15	14	22	23	43	47
Brazil	13	10	11	13	23	25
Chile	24	26	40	47	63	80
Uruguay	21	24	30	36	53	63
Average	18	19	26	30	46	54
Portugal	23	30	30	45	61	72
Spain	8	14	19	28	53	59
Average	16	22	25	37	57	66

Notes: Cell entries are exports plus imports as a percentage of GDP.

TABLE 7.7. **Industrial employment**

	1970	1980	1990	2000	2004
Argentina	34.3	33.7	32.4	22.7	23.0
Brazil	20.0	23.9	23.0	23.4	21.0
Chile	29.3	25.4	25.4	23.4	23.6
Uruguay	29.1	28.2	27.1	24.7	21.9
Average	28.2	27.8	27.0	23.6	22.4
Portugal	32.7	36.6	34.5	34.7	31.4
Spain	37.2	35.3	32.6	31.1	30.6
Average	35.0	36.0	33.6	32.9	31.0

Notes: Cell entries are a percentage of the labor force employed in industry.

but only a 3 percentage point decline in Brazil. Argentina suffered the most, with a decline of over 11 percentage points. Again, it would be difficult to detect a systematic pattern of difference that could be held responsible for the different trajectories of social policy and inequality in the two sets of countries. If anything, the higher levels of industrial employment should have induced Portugal and Spain to be more complacent about changing their inherited welfare state structures, based on traditional social security schemes. The opposite was the case; as we show, Portugal and Spain added protections earlier and on a larger scale for those outside the formal labor market or with only intermittent connections to it, than did the South American countries.

Where we find a systematic pattern of difference is in economic growth. The divergence already starts in the 1960s, is less pronounced in the 1970s, when only Argentina and Chile grow at a clearly slower pace than Spain and Portugal, but turns dramatic in the 1980s (table 7.3). The 1980s were the decade of the debt crisis, aptly called the lost decade, during which Latin America became a net exporter of capital and saw its GDP per capita decline markedly. Only Chile managed an average growth of about 1 percent per year, whereas Spain and Portugal continued growing at an average rate of close to 3 percent. Still, economic growth improves the potential fiscal base of the government but does not necessarily translate into better social policy or into lower inequality. The 1990s are a case in point; they were a decade of significant growth in Latin America, but also a decade of considerable neoliberal reforms of economic and social policy and of growing inequality in many countries, including Argentina and Uruguay (table 7.1).

The Politics of Social Policy

As we just demonstrated, the only systematic and significant structural difference between the Iberian and South American countries is the record of economic growth and therefore the level of GDP per capita reached. A higher level of societal affluence, however, only makes policy innovation possible; it does not generate the forces that carry it out. Therefore, explanations based on economic and social structural factors are clearly insufficient to explain the different trajectories of social policy and of levels of inequality in those two sets of countries. Rather, we have to introduce three political variables to understand those trajectories: the record of democracy, the political strength of the left and organized labor, and the influence of the European Union.

Spain and Portugal democratized some seven or eight years before Argentina, Brazil, and Uruguay, and some fourteen years before Chile (table 7.8). In Spain, Portugal, and Argentina, the military remained a threat in the early years, but after the failed coup attempt of 1981 in Spain and the constitutional revision of 1982 in Portugal, the issue was settled, whereas in Argentina it was only under Menem in the 1990s that the military finally was firmly brought under civilian control.[2] Moreover, the new democracies in Brazil and Chile were saddled with authoritarian legacies. In Brazil, the first direct presidential election took place in 1989, and in Chile the existence of the designated senators, which

TABLE 7.8. **Year of transition to democracy**

Country	Year
Argentina	1983
Brazil	1985
Chile	1990
Uruguay	1985
Portugal	1976
Spain	1977

assured the right a veto power, could only be eliminated with the constitutional reform of 2005. Thus, democratic governments in Spain and Portugal were able to put social policies at the center of their attention and use their full democratic powers to implement reforms at least a decade earlier than the governments in the South American countries.

Equally if not more important were the legacies of the transitions and the partisan distribution of political power. The Portuguese transition was a revolutionary one and constituted a clean break with the previous political elite (Fishman 2011). This shifted the entire political spectrum to the left, such that the opposition to the right of the Communist and Socialist parties was more centrist than rightist in orientation. The left already held a majority of parliamentary seats in the early years in Portugal and more than 40 percent of seats in Spain; the left's share of seats in the lower house never fell below 40 percent in either country and, in some periods, surpassed half in both of them (table 7.9). The picture in South America was entirely different. In Uruguay and Brazil the left emerged with roughly one-third of the seats and in Chile with slightly above a quarter. The highest levels were reached after 2000, and they were just above a third in Chile, just below half in Uruguay, and 45 percent in Brazil. Thus, the left never fully controlled the legislative levers of power but rather remained dependent on allies and had to make major compromises. At the level of the executive, we have a total absence of the left in South America before 2000, compared to 10 years of left incumbency in Portugal and 14 years in Spain (table 7.10). Between 2000 and 2010, left executives were in power for 5 years in Uruguay, 8 years in Brazil, and 10 years in Chile. Whereas we accept the majority opinion of scholars of Argentine politics that the Peronists (PJ) are not a programmatic party at all and cannot be classified on a left–right scale, we would argue that Nestor Kirchner and Cristina Fernández de Kirchner clearly

TABLE 7.9. **Left legislative seats (%)**

	1970s	1980s	1990s	2000–2008
Argentina	0	2	4	7
Brazil	0	4	32	45
Chile	0	0	27	34
Uruguay	0	14	34	49
Average	0	5	23	32
Portugal	53	42	49	56
Spain	41	55	48	45
Average	47	49	49	51

TABLE 7.10. **Left executive after (re)democratization**

Country	Years	Total	President or prime minister
Argentina	2002–present	10	Kirchners
Brazil[a]	2002–present	10	Lula, Rousseff
Chile	2000–2010	10	Lagos, Bachelet
Uruguay	2005–present	7	Vazquez, Mujica
Portugal	1975–78, (1983–85), 1995–2002, 2005–present	15 (17)	Soares, (Soares), Guterres, Socrates
Spain	1982–96, 2004–2011	21	Gonzalez, Zapatero

[a] See the text on the classification of the Cardoso government.

campaigned on left-of-center appeals and thus can be classified as such. Accordingly, the figure for legislative seats held by the left and center-left is only 7 percent, whereas the years of left executive incumbency are 8. Adding the years since 2000, the total years under left executives since democratization were 17 in Portugal and 21 in Spain, which makes the Spanish record twice that of the strongest Latin American record, the Chilean one.

As discussed in chapter 6, it is precisely during the first decade of the twenty-first century that the most far-reaching redistributive policy innovations were introduced in Chile, Uruguay, and Brazil, and they were introduced by left-of-center governments. In Chile and Brazil, however, these executives did not control a majority of seats in the lower house, which forced them to make major concessions. In Spain and Portugal, such reforms were introduced earlier and mostly under governments with a parliamentary majority, which gave the reforms a more far-reaching character.

An additional difference between the advanced South American and the Iberian countries that helped propel welfare state expansion more in the latter was the strength of organized labor and its close relationship to parties of the left. The exception here is Brazil, where unionization and the relationship to the PT were comparable to the situation in Iberia. Initially, unionization rates were high in Portugal, falling from well over half of wage and salary earners around 1980 to some 30 percent a decade later. In Spain, unionization rates remained much lower, reaching only 18 percent in 1995, but the unions had an important presence at the enterprise level and a high mobilization capacity, and the Spanish governments and employers also participated in the search for social pacts with the unions (Encarnación 2008b).

On the one hand, unions in Spain and Portugal fiercely resisted curtailment of members' benefits, which was a big issue in pension reform; on the other hand, they helped to push welfare state policy in a more generous and universalistic direction, particularly in the areas of health care and protection for the unemployed. For instance, the socialist UGT (General Union of Workers) in Spain agreed to some labor market flexibilization on the condition of improvements in unemployment protection. The labor movement in both countries was politically split, but the competition for the unions allied with the socialist parties came from the left, from unions allied with the communist parties. The UGT broke relations with the Socialist Party (PSOE) in 1988 and moved closer to the Communist union confederation, but the labor movement as a whole remained a militant defender of generous social policy.

In contrast, in Chile and Uruguay the unions were much weaker, with 13 percent (Chile) and 12 percent (Uruguay) of wage and salary earners registered as union members in 1995.[3] In Chile, they had emerged as a largely irrelevant actor from the Pinochet dictatorship, hampered by the legacies of physical suppression and a repressive system of labor legislation that allowed for replacement of striking workers. The rationalization of enterprises and deindustrialization in the 1990s further diminished their ranks. Moreover, the member parties of the Concertación, including the Socialists, deliberately kept their distance from the unions. In Uruguay, deindustrialization in the 1990s and the economic crisis of 2001 greatly weakened organized labor, before the period of growth from 2003 on and the coming to power of allied governments helped them recover some strength. It is important to note here that the FA government in Uruguay reinstated centralized bargaining and included previously excluded sectors, thus strengthening the position of unions. In Argentina, labor remained comparatively strong up to the crisis of 2001, with a membership rate of some 35 percent of wage and salary earners, but it also remained politically split, and its main political ally was the Peronist Party and government, which in the 1990s pursued a neoliberal agenda. Under the Kirchners they did regain strength, particularly in sectors where production was growing rapidly (Etchemendy and Collier 2007). In Brazil, union density in the 1990s was about a quarter of wage and salary earners, and though the union movement was split into several confederations, an important sector retained close ties to the PT, whose leadership had come from the union ranks. This union leadership very clearly had a comprehensive left vision of social change, emphasizing not only the interests of those who were already union members but also the need to organize the rural sector and engage in community organizing in order to build a broad-based progressive coalition. Brazilian unions have particularly emphasized the need for increases in the minimum wage, which affect a large array of social assistance benefits, and they have supported the expansion of Bolsa Família.

Clearly, the influence of the European Union on the development of social policy in Spain and Portugal has been major. Democratization and Europeanization were intertwined goals in the minds of the political elites leading the transitions. In Portugal, these were the alternative to the project of Portuguese socialism pushed by the Communist Party (PCP) during and after the revolution (Guillén, Álvarez, and Adão e Silva 2003). In Spain, the goal of democratization was linked to economic and social modernization, which meant becoming part of Europe. Accordingly, catching up with Europe was an important motivation for the early and continued expansion of social expenditures. After Spain acceded to membership in 1986, EU influence was supported by the flow of resources. Revenue from the structural and cohesion funds was an average of 0.7 percent of GDP over the period 1989–93, 1.5 percent in 1994–99, and 1.3 percent in 2000–2006 in Spain, and 3 percent, 3.3 percent, and 2.9 percent, respectively, over the same periods in Portugal (Balmaseda and Sebastián 2003, 213). These funds greatly facilitated the increases in social expenditures in Portugal. They did not, however, determine the allocation of these expenditures in an equity-enhancing manner.

EU influence on the structure of social policy began in the 1980s with three successive poverty programs and the establishment of an Observatory on National Policies to Combat Social Exclusion in 1990. A resolution adopted in 1992 and the 1997 Treaty of Amsterdam made the fight against poverty and exclusion an official goal of the EU. After 2000, in the wake of the Lisbon Summit's declaration on fighting poverty and social exclusion, the Open Method of Coordination required member countries to formulate national action plans to meet this goal, though actually implementing the plan was not compulsory (Ferrera 2005, 2–3). These plans focused attention on those outside the reach of the traditional social security system and stimulated innovation in noncontributory social protection programs. Yet, as Adão e Silva (2009) demonstrates convincingly in the case of the minimum insertion income, European recommendations were only implemented if the domestic constellation of forces was favorable. Indeed, the 1992 recommendation on providing sufficient resources for the fight against poverty was adopted during the Portuguese presidency of the EU, but the centrist/center-right Social Democratic Party (PSD) government whose representative signed the recommendation at the European level refused to implement it at home.[4] The PSD government defeated two parliamentary proposals to that effect from the Socialist Party (PS) and the Communist Party (PCP). Only when the PS campaigned on this issue and mobilized support from Catholic action groups involved in the fight against poverty and from the unions, and after the party won the 1995 elections, could the minimum insertion income be introduced in Portugal.

In Spain, the Socialist government supported the fight against poverty, but the responsibility for social assistance was under the competence of the regions. Between 1989 and 1995 the regions introduced minimum income programs, but they varied widely in coverage and generosity (Arriba and Moreno 2005). The Greek and Italian examples further demonstrate that European funds and influence could not guarantee policy innovation in a more universalistic and redistributive direction, if domestic forces were not supportive. In Italy, the center-left government under Prodi established an expert commission and, acting on the recommendations of this commission, launched an experiment in 1998 with a minimum income and insertion component in 39 municipalities, extending it in 2001 to 306 municipalities (Sacchi and Bastagli 2005). In 2000 the government presented a new law for social assistance, but the 2001 constitutional revision undermined the framework of this law by putting social assistance under the exclusive authority of the regions. The center-right led by Berlusconi won the 2001 elections, and since his government had no interest in pursuing a minimum income program, he froze the experiment at the end of 2003.

In Greece, social policy remained very heavily biased toward pensions, with particularly generous provisions for public employees, and progress in a universalistic direction was stymied by the organizational weakness and personalistic nature of the left party and the concentration of unions in the public sector (Matsaganis 2005). There was a Socialist government in power between 1993 and 2004, but that government remained preoccupied with meeting the Economic and Monetary Union criteria and decided not to expand the basic safety net. The party was split, as a third of the Socialist members of the legislature signed a draft law for a minimum income, but they could not get the support of their leadership. Moreover, the socialist leader of a trade union confederation also took a position opposing the introduction of a minimum income (Matsaganis 2005).

There is no doubt that the domestic constellation of forces was decisive for progress toward more inclusive and universalistic welfare states. It is also clear, however, that the proposals put on the domestic agendas by the European social model since the 1990s were fundamentally different from the proposals put on the domestic agendas of the Latin American countries in that same period by the IMF, the World Bank, and USAID. Europe was promoting a comprehensive, inclusive, and universalistic model, whereas the neoliberal residualist model dominated in Washington and the IFIs.

The Development of the Welfare State in Spain and Portugal

The social policy legacies from the Franco regime in Spain consisted of a fragmented system with public and private elements.[5] There was one scheme for dependent workers and many additional schemes for various professional categories. Even within the supposedly unified public system, different rules existed for different occupational categories. The system was completely employment-based and built on the male breadwinner model, providing pensions, sickness insurance, and family allowances. Social assistance for those outside the formal labor market was minimal, provided by a small program of noncontributory pensions and by the Social Charitable Protection Fund on a highly discretionary basis (Arriba and Moreno 2005). Social security was almost exclusively financed by employer and employee contributions; state transfers to social security were only 0.43 percent of GDP in 1975, compared to an OECD average of 12 percent (Guillén 1992). The tax system was regressive and highly inefficient. Various reforms beginning in the 1960s had expanded benefits, so that by the time of the transition there was a system that provided benefits and services to the bulk of the population, albeit generally of low quality. In short, at the time of transition the structure of the system of social protection looked like the structure in the advanced South American countries, but the state's contribution to it was lower.

The Spanish transition to democracy happened in the context of an economic crisis. The old regime had failed to adjust to the new economic situation after the first oil shocks, so inflation rose to 24 percent in 1977. The economic problems added to the political problems of the transition, and radical innovation of social policy as in neighboring revolutionary Portugal was out of the question. The Pact of Moncloa of 1977 tied wage restraint to a government commitment to introduce a progressive tax system and an expansion of social security coverage, but expansion was slow until after the victory of the PSOE in 1982. Even then, the economy shaped government priorities. The government reduced the previously high tariff protection, which led to a process of industrial restructuring. With unemployment reaching 21 percent by 1985, expenditures for unemployment compensation and disability pensions, which served as an early retirement scheme as elsewhere in continental Europe, continued to rise. Despite these constraints, the government made major efforts to move the structure of the welfare state in a more universalistic direction. In 1983, a first wave of labor market flexibilization measures allowed for greater use of temporary contracts in order to lower unemployment. In 1984, the government followed up with the introduction of unemployment assistance, for people not or no longer entitled to unemployment insurance. The use of temporary contracts proliferated rapidly, coming to account for roughly a third of all labor contracts.

In 1985 the government passed a pension reform that reduced the replacement rate by basing the calculation on eight instead of two years preceding the claim and lengthened the minimum contributory period from ten to fifteen years (Guillén, Álvarez, and Adão e Silva 2003). This reform was heavily resisted by the unions because it affected benefits of their members and constituencies. The union movement was split between the Communist Workers' Commissions (CCOO) and the General Union of Workers (UGT), which was extremely close to the PSOE and participated in a variety of pacts after the transition (Royo 2000). Union membership was comparatively low, with 18 percent of wage and salary earners enrolled as union members in 1995. Collective contracts, however, covered union members and nonmembers alike, and union mobilization capacity reached much further than the membership. Spain inherited a dual system of representation from the Franco period, with factory councils serving as bargaining agents with the ability to call strikes. If a union obtained a majority of seats on the factory council, then the union became the bargaining agent (Burgess 2004). Thus, unions were considerably more powerful than the low union density figures indicate, and governments often sought tripartite agreements on important matters. Union rivalry, however, weakened the weight of organized labor because it often prevented the articulation of a coherent position of the labor movement.

In 1985 the CCOO called a general strike against the pension reform of that year. The UGT did not join the strike but vocally opposed the reform and began to change its position from one of critical support to one of opposition to the government (Burgess 2004). The 1986 factory council elections showed losses for the UGT, which were attributable to the support the union had shown for the government during the period of austerity and high unemployment. When the 1988 budget did not show the increase in social expenditures that the UGT had pushed for, the union officially broke with the government and joined a general strike in December 1988 to protest a youth employment plan (Burgess 2004). As a result, tripartite negotiations ceased until after the election of the conservative Partido Popular (PP) government in 1996, when the unions feared unilateral action on the part of the new government (Royo 2000).

Welfare state expansion in social services was important and highly redistributive (Maravall and Fraile 2001, 306). The Constitution of 1978 devolved authority for social services and social assistance to the regions, while preserving social security as a national-level program. Devolution, however, took place in stages; each region negotiated with the central state. Between 1982 and 1993, the regions established systems of social services in a concerted effort to get as much autonomy as possible, in the context of a tripartite system of financing from the national, regional, and municipal levels. In fact, the regions resisted the efforts of the PSOE government at national legislation of social services (Ferrera 2005). Despite such resistance, the government passed a law in 1986 establishing a national health system, with services to be provided by the regions and coordinated by the central state. Medical associations (like elsewhere), employers' associations, and the conservative party in opposition opposed establishment of the national health system, but they were unable to block the coalition of the PSOE government, the unions, and the regional governments that favored it (Guillén 2010). In 1989 previous beneficiaries of poor relief were incorporated into the public health system, and by the end of the 1980s almost 70 percent of financing came from tax revenue (Guillén 2002). Given the shared system of financing, there has been considerable variation in the quality of services offered across regions, despite financing through block grants from the central government.

After the accession to membership in the European Union in 1986, the economic picture improved, in line with a general period of economic growth in Europe, but unemployment only fell slowly. To fight the consequences of this problem, the government expanded unemployment coverage to reach 82 percent of the unemployed by 1992. It also indexed pension benefits to past inflation in 1988, and it adopted a number of reforms to offer support to those without a sufficiently long record of sufficiently remunerated employment. Noncontributory means-tested retirement and disability pensions were introduced in 1991; supplements to minimum pensions grew; family allowances for poor families became universal in 1990; and the regions began to introduce minimum-income schemes linked to efforts at integrating recipients into the labor market (Guillén, Álvarez, and Adão e Silva 2003). Initially, the noncontributory pensions were financed through the social security system, but under the Toledo Pact (see below) their financing was shifted to general revenue (Arriba and Moreno 2005). Unions were strongly in favor of the noncontributory pensions and these minimum income schemes, and negotiated with regional governments to promote their introduction (Guillén 2010).

In 1992, the Spanish economy entered a deep recession, which prompted successive devaluations in 1992, 1993, and 1995, a renewed rise in unemployment, and efforts at cost control in the welfare state. First to be cut were unemployment benefits. Replacement rates and duration were reduced and qualifying periods lengthened, which meant that a larger number of unemployed had to rely on unemployment assistance with yet lower benefits. Soon thereafter, active labor market policies were stepped up, with subsidies for employment of young people, those over forty-five, and the long-term unemployed, and for part-time employment. Also, nonprofit private employment agencies were authorized to operate. In 1996, under the new conservative PP government, the unions agreed to a social pact that promoted the creation of open-ended contracts, placed part-time and temporary contracts on the same basis as permanent contracts with regard to social security rights, and reduced severance payments (Guillén 2010). In other words, the previously rigid labor market with high employment protection legislation was made more flexible, but in contrast to Chile and Argentina, these reforms were followed up with a strengthening of the social safety net for those with nonpermanent, non-full-time contracts.

The deteriorating economic situation and the need to meet the criteria for joining the European Monetary Union caused serious concerns about the current costs and the future sustainability of the pension system. A parliamentary commission studied the issue and formulated a series of recommendations that became the basis for the tripartite Toledo Pact of 1995 and subsequent reforms. The reforms changed the indexing rules and increased the number of years for calculating the replacement rate, and they separated out the financing of contributory income support from noncontributory transfers and health care and other social services—the former to be financed by contributions and the latter by general revenue. At the same time, they raised the minimum pension for widows and orphans (Guillén, Álvarez, and Adão e Silva 2003). They also improved the situation of workers with a long history of temporary contracts in the calculation of pension benefits (Guillén 2010). Overall, the PSOE government had set a path of welfare state expansion and labor market flexibilization, linked to efforts at cost control and restructuring of the corporatist welfare state in a more social democratic direction, with an expansion of noncontributory benefits and a national health system. The conservative government of 1996–2004 continued with reforms of the social security system negotiated through pacts with unions and employers, reforms that combined cost controls with an improvement of the position of nonstandard workers (Guillén 2010).

After the PSOE's return to power in 2004, reform efforts intensified. Reforms of the labor market and of pensions were again reached through negotiations with unions and employers' associations. Incentives were put in place to encourage working beyond the legal retirement age, and benefits in special professional schemes were further equalized. The position of women in the labor market and the social security system was improved in the pursuit of gender equality. And in 2006 a national system of care was established for all people in need of it, mainly the elderly and disabled, funded by a combination of public funds and out-of-pocket payments adjusted to income (Guillén 2010). Thus, some thirty years after the pacted transition, the left was still working on overcoming the structural legacies of the inegalitarian and deficient welfare state edifice left by the Franco regime and turning it into a more comprehensive, universalistic, and service-oriented edifice. All these piecemeal reforms, however, transformed the Spanish welfare state from one that looked very Latin American and hardly reduced inequality at all to one that today looks very European and reduces the Gini by some 12 percentage points (Goñi, López and Servén 2008).

Clearly, the burden on the welfare state has been great during the entire democratic period because of the high levels of unemployment. The democratic governments inherited an economy with noncompetitive manufacturing and dependence on raw-material-based exports and tourism. They also started out with low average educational levels. Despite high economic growth, an opening of the economy, and a massive shift in the structural composition of employment, the basic structure of exports did not change much. What did change was that Spanish companies became major investors abroad, particularly in Latin America. Employment in agriculture declined radically, from 29 percent of the labor force in 1970 to 7 percent in 2000, and employment in industry declined from 37 percent of the labor force in 1970 to 31 percent in 2004, with the service sector growing correspondingly. Much of the economic growth from the 1990s on was stimulated by construction and thus came to a halt with the world economic crisis of 2008.

The Portuguese system of social protection at the time of the revolution was much weaker than those of our focal countries in Latin America.[6] It consisted of three different funds: one for wage earners in trade and industry, a second one for farmworkers, and a third for seamen/fishermen. Workers in trade and industry were covered by sickness insurance and health care, pensions for old age and disability, unemployment insurance, and later also family allowances. Their coverage was financed through contributions from employers and employees. Farmworkers had coverage only for medical care and sick pay and a death allowance, and fishermen only for medical care. The schemes for farmworkers and fishermen were funded by contributions from members and occasional donations only. In addition, there were special retirement and welfare funds for subordinate workers in certain companies and sectors of activity, financed by compulsory contributions from workers and employers. The government did not run or finance any of these social insurance funds, and they were based on a capitalization system. There were various funds for state employees, some of them voluntary, with varying risk coverage and benefits. By the end of 1959, some 30 percent of workers in industry and 40 percent of family members had no coverage, and only 20 percent of farmworkers were covered. Expenditures on social security and welfare amounted to 2.8 percent of GDP (Capucha et al. 2005, 210). In the 1960s the system was changed to a mix of pay-as-you-go and capitalization, more money was allocated to sickness and maternity allowances, and the situation of farmworkers saw some improvement. Still, coverage and benefits remained very low; by 1970 only 60 percent of the economically active population were covered.

The revolutionary period of 1974–76 dramatically expanded social services and social protection, along with other rights and policies such as a national minimum wage, a land reform, and nationalization of the main financial-economic groups. The value of minimum pensions was doubled and a limit was set on maximum pensions, a noncontributory regime was set up, and unemployment benefits were extended to include some previously not covered and medical care for family members. By 1975, 78 percent of the working population were covered by social protection schemes as contributors, and 86 percent of the population had access to health care. Expenditures for social protection reached 7.5 percent of GDP (Capucha et al. 2005). From 1976 on, the key task became stabilization and macroeconomic austerity, as the country dealt with huge deficits, high inflation, and a steep rise in unemployment, from 1.7 percent in 1974 to 7.9 percent in 1978, as a result of the return of some 700,000 people from the African colonies (Silva Lopes 2003). In 1977 the country concluded an agreement with the IMF that included crawling-peg devaluations over a three-year period.

Despite the IMF agreement, expansion of social expenditures and innovation in social policy continued, driven by the left and organized labor. Expenditures on social protection climbed to 11 percent of GDP by 1980. The center-left Socialist Party (PS) had won the 1976 elections with a commitment to joining Europe and building a welfare state. At the time of the revolution, the labor movement was dominated by the General Confederation of Portuguese Workers (CGTP) allied with the Communist Party (PCP); in 1978 the Socialists formed a second union confederation, the UGT, which then became a major partner in concertation agreements. Exact and reliable figures on union density over time are not available (Stoleroff 2001). Nickell and Nunziata's (2001) database puts it at 61 percent of wage and salary earners during 1975 to 1984, declining to 51 percent by 1986, 41 percent by 1988, and 32 percent by 1990, where it stays until 1995. Stoleroff (2001, 194) cites a source that he considers high, with 52 percent in 1974–78, rising to 59 percent in 1979–84, before declining to 44 percent in 1985–90 and 36 percent in 1991–95. Considering that in 1985 some 60 percent of employees worked in enterprises with more than fifty workers (figures from the Ministry of Labor, cited by Stoleroff 2001, 185), and considering the intensely politicized revolutionary era, it is not unreasonable to accept that close to half the employed labor force was unionized until 1985. It is further clear that the process of rationalization of enterprises after the entry into the EU reduced the bases of union membership.

A unionization rate of roughly half the wage and salary earners is comparatively high—much higher than in Spain and Latin America. Moreover, unions were more oriented toward national-level political action and national- and sectoral-level bargaining than the enterprise level. Thus, they asserted themselves as important political actors and supported the improvement of the social safety net and social services. Even after the economic crisis of 1982–85 and the subsequent restructuring of the industrial base took their toll on union membership and mobilization capacity, the union confederations retained an important role at the national level. Tripartite concertation became a frequently used political strategy to deal with economic and social policy matters.

Although the opposition center/center-right Social Democrats (PSD) won the 1978 elections, legislation on a national health system was adopted in 1979. This legislation had been in the works under the Socialist government, and there was bipartisan consensus on its importance. During the revolutionary period, local hospitals and hospitals owned by charity funds were integrated into the public system, and the 1976 Constitution guaranteed the right to health care and obliged the state to establish a universal national health service. In 1977, medical services for the poor were integrated into the national system. Implementation of a universal national health system remained deficient, however, as the government did not effectively counter opposition from private health funds and the medical profession. Existing health funds were left intact, financing was on a contributory basis rather than out of general revenue, and doctors continued to be paid on a fee-for-service basis. In fact, the private sector expanded, coming to cover 17 percent of the population, with about another quarter of the population covered by various professional funds. Still, the national health system owned most hospitals and was accessible to all residents (Guillén 2002), so universal coverage was achieved, but not necessarily equality of access to quality services.

After a temporary improvement, Portugal faced a new balance of payments crisis in 1981–82, followed by IMF agreements. In 1982, the two major parties joined forces in a grand coalition government with the goal of implementing the austerity program and meeting the conditions for EU membership. Notwithstanding austerity, in 1984 the coalition government adopted a major new law on social security with contributory, noncontributory, and social action components. They also institutionalized a tripartite social dialogue structure, the Permanent Council for Social Dialogue (CPCS), although the CGTP refused to sign agreements (Guillén, Álvarez, and Adão e Silva 2003).

As in Spain, the period after 1986 was one of economic growth and further expansion of social expenditures. The flow of resources through the EU's structural and cohesion funds was more significant than in Spain, accounting for an average of 3 percent of GDP per annum in 1989–2006 (Guillén, Álvarez, and Adão e Silva 2003, 213). While social expenditures climbed significantly, the basic structure of the system was left unchanged until after the return of the PS to power in the 1995 elections, which were fought with a program of changes in social policy. In fact, the minimum insertion income played a central role in the campaign. The PS and the PCP had presented legislative proposals for its implementation under the PSD government, which had been rejected by the parliamentary majority. In the 1995 campaign, the PS profiled itself with the promise to implement such a program if elected, and the party successfully reached out to progressive Catholics involved in the fight against poverty. The UGT also supported the campaign and the minimum income proposal (Adão e Silva 2009).

Arguably, establishment of the minimum insertion income in 1996 was the most important innovation introduced by the PS government. This program provides a means-tested cash transfer to poor individuals and households, which is tied to the requirement to be available for job training and placement—the insertion component. Other important innovations introduced by the PS government were improvements in the minimum benefits in social programs, improvement in social protection for those with nonstandard attachments to the labor market, improvements in administration, and emphasis on active labor market policies.

For instance, the value of the minimum noncontributory pension rose by 42 percent between 1995 and 2000 (Capucha et al. 2005). The Institute for Solidarity and Social Security unified the administration of contributory and noncontributory programs and at the same time reduced the autonomy of regional structures providing income support and thus local clientelistic practices; oversight in the sickness program in particular was tightened to reduce widespread abuses. The financing of the contributory pension system was solidified, and the benefit calculation formula changed. Many of these reforms were agreed on in social pacts, as the government emphasized a widening of the social dialogue.

The Portuguese labor market shows, on the one hand, a comparatively high labor force participation rate, particularly for women, but on the other hand high levels of fragmentation. Up to the late 1990s, unemployment in Portugal was comparatively low, not rising above 10 percent, and much lower than in Spain. As in Spain and South America, employment protection legislation was traditionally strong, but a significant percentage of the labor force is either self-employed or employed in small or medium enterprises where such legislation is not enforced. Thus, there is considerable flexibility in the Portuguese labor market (Silva Lopes 2003). Since the late 1990s, fixed-term contracts have increased, rising to about 20 percent by 2009 (Adão e Silva 2010). Unemployment insurance and active labor market policies were only greatly strengthened after 1995. Despite the introduction of unemployment insurance and unemployment assistance in the revolutionary period, as late as 1989 only about 20 percent of the unemployed received benefits. By 2004, this figure had risen to 86 percent (OECD figures, cited in Adão e Silva 2010). Unemployment protection has three components: the regular contribution-based insurance, tax-financed unemployment assistance for those not meeting the requirements for insurance or having exhausted insurance benefits, and the minimum insertion income as a last resort. In 2000 the minimum income reached some 4 percent of the population (Capucha et al. 2005).

In line with the EU Open Method of Coordination, Portugal elaborated a National Action Plan for Inclusion for the period 2001–3. Poverty as measured at 60 percent of median income, the EU poverty line, stood at 20 percent, compared to an EU average of 15 percent. The plan emphasized a move from the passive to a more active welfare state, with particular emphasis on training. Despite improvement in the average years of education of the adult population, Portugal was still an economy relying on industry with low skills, low productivity, and low wages. For instance, the proportion of eighteen- to twenty-four-year-olds with less than a secondary education and not in school or training was 45.5 percent in the early 2000s (Capucha et al. 2005). Wage inequality remains very high, which puts a high burden on the welfare state for redistribution.

Reforms in Comparison

To compare the progress of reforms in accordance with the principles of basic universalism in Iberia and South America, we find it useful to focus on three types of reforms: the health system, contributory pensions, and social assistance. For a reform to qualify as having a basic universalistic character, it must move in a significant way toward (1) including all people or at least a large majority of those in need of the transfer or service, (2) providing the same quality of transfer or service, under the same rules, and (3) granting the transfer or service as a right guaranteed by the state, not as a discretionary benefit. Classic universalism of the Nordic social democratic variety means that everyone gets the same thing, regardless of need. Flat-rate citizenship pensions going to every citizen regardless of other income are a key example. Where tax systems are efficient, the benefits that go to people with good incomes from other sources can be reclaimed through taxation. Where tax systems are not efficient and public resources scarce, it may be more practical to select out the 20 or 30 percent of the population who clearly do not need the benefits. This is how the Australian pension system operated, for instance, from 1970 on, when coverage had reached over two-thirds of the aged (Palme 1990, 47).

All these reforms were discussed in more detail either in chapter 6 or earlier in this chapter. The purpose here is to establish what categories of reforms were introduced in the different countries, at what point in time, and by what kinds of governments, in order to explain the more comprehensive and redistributive nature of the welfare states in Spain and Portugal. For the substance of the reforms, the reader will have to refer back to these earlier discussions.

Table 7.11 offers an overview of reforms of the health care systems that were designed to extend health care as a right to larger sectors of the population. Clearly, the most far-reaching measure in this regard is the

TABLE 7.11. **Major health care reforms**

Country	Year	Reforms	Party
Spain	1986	NHS, universal; tax financed, delivery by regions	PSOE
Portugal	1979	NHS, insurance funds left intact, fee-for-service payment	PSD
Argentina	1990s	Failed reform attempts	PJ
	2002	Plan Remediar	PJ (Kirchner)
	2002	Plan Nacer	PJ (Kirchner)
Brazil	1988	NHS, unification of compulsory social security and public health; special funds left intact; gradual implementation	Constitution
Chile	2004	AUGE	PS
Uruguay	2007	NH fund; contribution based, per capita payment	FA

establishment of a national health service (NHS), as was done in Spain. In Portugal, as noted, the implementation of the reform has been somewhat deficient, but coverage of health care is universal. Among our focus cases, this is the only health-sector reform with a universalistic character passed under a nonleft government, although plans for it were developed under the Socialist government.

Brazil enshrined the right to health care in the 1988 Constitution and formally established the Unified Health System by terminating compulsory contribution-based health insurance and offering free access to the tax-financed public health system. Implementation, however, was slow and uneven (Weyland 1996). Decentralization and cofinancing from state and municipal sources brought significant geographical divergence in the quality of care offered. Moreover, the quality of care provided is not considered adequate for civil servants and the military, as they have access to private providers paid for by general revenue. Also, many enterprises offer additional contribution-based voluntary health insurance to their employees, such that approximately a quarter of the population has supplementary private health insurance (Mesa-Lago 2008). Under Lula, major efforts were made to push states and municipalities to improve their health services. The federal government began to use negotiated health plans to set targets for health outcomes in the municipalities and states, and the transfer of resources became conditional on compliance with these plans (Osterkatz 2011). Also, an oral health program and a program of subsidies for basic medicine were added (Niedzwiecki

2010b). Thus, the legal parameters are there, but movement toward de facto universal health care remains a work in progress.

The Uruguayan reform established a single-payer system. All payroll contributions go to a central fund, which pays a per capita fee adjusted for the risk profile of patients to public and private providers. Patients have a choice between the traditional nonprofit private providers and the public system. They may also join a private insurance plan and pay the difference between the state subsidy and whatever premiums that private insurer demands. The poor have free access to the public system. This reform is going a long way toward equalizing quality of access and care.

It is worth noting here that the only Latin American country that implemented an NHS before 2000 is Costa Rica. The program was introduced after some twenty years of democracy by the center-left PLN government in 1973, and it propelled Costa Rica to the forefront of Latin America in basic health indicators (McGuire 2010).

In Chile, the existing system, divided between the public and the private health care sectors, both of which are payroll contribution funded, was left intact. Plans for moving in a more universalistic direction were first stymied by concerns within the Concertación over costs; then the proposed equalization fund between the public and private sectors was killed by resistance from the private sector and the right-wing parties. Thus, the guaranteed treatment of the illnesses covered by AUGE is an important step in that it equalizes access for patients with these illnesses, but the reform falls far short of equalizing quality of access and care for all.

The least far-reaching reforms are those in Argentina, where the unions have been allied with the governing party and staunch and effective defenders of the existing system of union-controlled health care funds. Thus, the economic crisis gave rise to two additional programs designed to address crucial immediate needs. Plan Remediar supplies basic medicines to primary care centers, which in turn distribute them to poor families. This program has become quite important, growing to benefit about 40 percent of the population by 2006 (Ministry of Health figures, cited in Niedzwiecki 2010a). Plan Nacer provides basic health services to pregnant women and children under the age of six who do not have health insurance.

Table 7.12 provides an overview of reforms of contributory pension systems. To be included in the table, the reforms must be parametric re-

TABLE 7.12. **Major parametric pension reforms**

Country	Year	Reforms	Party
Spain	1985	Raised minimum contribution	PSOE
	1988	Reduced replacement rate	PSOE
		Index to past inflation	
	1995	Change replacement rate	Toledo Pact
Portugal	1974–76	Minimum increased, ceiling on top	Revolution
	1984	New rules	Coalition
	1995–	Financing solidified	PS
Argentina	2008	Renationalization	PJ (Kirchner)
Brazil	1998	Minimum retirement age for public sector	PSDB
	2003	Reduce benefits in public system	PT

forms of the existing public pension system, which were a necessity because the parameters of the pay-as-you-go systems in all of these countries were not financially viable. We exclude the reforms whose primary
aim was to privatize or partially privatize the public pension system, because those reforms went in a direction directly opposite of universalism. In a striking difference with our South American cases, privatization was not on the agenda in Portugal and Spain, despite the fact that
their defined-benefit pay-as-you-go pension systems faced the same economic and demographic pressures as the systems in the Latin American
countries faced. Again this difference can be linked to the difference in
transnational structures of power: the Iberian countries were not subject to the same neoliberal pressures that the Latin American countries
were subject to. We do include in the table parametric reforms that the
government passed in order to bring the pension system into fiscal balance, even if these reforms made the pension systems less generous by
reducing the replacement rate or raising the retirement age. The common driving force behind these reforms other than the Portuguese ones
in 1974–76 was fiscal pressure; pension expenditures weighed heavily on
government budgets, and reforms were necessary to keep the systems viable. Reform of the contributory system was not necessarily egalitarian,
but in most cases it involved efforts to reduce special benefits or to standardize rules, and it was a prerequisite to freeing resources for other important social policy initiatives.

The reforms in Portugal during the revolutionary period were clearly
equity-oriented, improving benefits at the bottom, putting a ceiling on
high benefits, and expanding protection. Under the constraints of economic austerity, the grand coalition government (1983–85) introduced

new rules for the contributory system, at the same time as it strengthened the noncontributory system in 1984. The imperative of strengthening the financial base of the pension system led to a further round of reforms under the post-1995 Socialist government.

In Spain, the new democratic constitution guaranteed the right to social welfare, and coverage began to increase under the centrist government of Suarez and accelerated under the Socialist government in the
1980s. With huge pressures to increase unemployment protection, keeping pension costs under control became a constant preoccupation, leading to the pension reforms of 1985 and 1988, both of which were aimed
at lowering benefits and increasing contributions. The 1988 reform, however, was followed by an improvement of benefits in the form of indexing
to past inflation.

As we mentioned, the privatizing pension reforms in Chile, Argentina, and Uruguay are not included in table 7.12. The most drastic reform
was the full privatization of pensions in Chile under Pinochet. It was
implemented by a brutal dictatorship, which simply did not care about
beating down resistance. In the short run it was very costly for the state,
because the state had to pay pension obligations to existing pension recipients and recognition bonds for previous contributions to future retirees without the benefit of contributions from the current working population, but in the long run it was expected to ease the financial burden on
the state. This reform could be imposed under a dictatorship willing to
forget about all those unable to accumulate sufficient contributions for
even a minimum pension, but under a democracy this approach was not
a viable option.

In the 1990s the Chilean model of privatization was put on the table by reformers with a neoliberal bent everywhere in Latin America,
but resistance from the political left, from unions, and from pensioners
made the model hard to implement in a democratic context. So, governments were forced to find compromises. In Argentina, the compromise
was a basic public tier for everyone and a choice between a supplementary public or funded private option, with policy steering people toward
the private option. In Uruguay the compromise was the preservation of
the public system but a supplementary private funded tier for higher-
income earners. The Uruguayan system proved viable, whereas the financial crisis of 2001–2 greatly weakened the Argentine system and prepared the way for eventual renationalization of the pension funds.

In Brazil reform was made difficult by the fact that changes to social security entitlements entailed changing a constitutional provision that required special majorities in the legislature. Efforts in the direction of establishing a fully funded pillar were cut short by the impeachment of Collor. Cardoso proposed a parametric reform to limit early retirement, equalize eligibility between the public and private sectors, and eliminate provisions for specific privileged categories of employees, but legislative amendments neutralized many of the provisions (Madrid 2003). A second attempt in 1998 dealt mainly with the system for workers in the private sector and left the costly system for public-sector workers unchanged. Finally, Lula managed to obtain support for a reform that changed the public-sector scheme, making early retirement costly, putting a cap on tax-exempt benefits, and equalizing conditions between future employees in the public and private sectors.

What is immediately obvious here is that a mix of parties is implementing these reforms, left and center and coalitions. They all had to deal with opposition, and one good strategy was to try to get a societal agreement, or a social pact, as happened in Spain. Overall, Spain and Portugal had a stronger capacity to implement reforms that were painful but that made the systems more sustainable. We attribute this ability to the stronger parties and the stronger tradition of concertation or tripartite negotiation, both of which again can only develop under democratic regimes. So, the capacity to reform is an important contributor to the formation of better-quality social policy, which in the case of contributory pensions meant to put the systems on a sustainable financial basis.

The capacity to shape better-quality social policy also means the capacity to provide income support systems for those unable to earn a sufficient income to support themselves and their families and to achieve social protection through contributory systems. This task is performed through noncontributory income transfers. Table 7.13 gives an overview of the most important policies in this area.

Three facts spring out from this table. First, the only noteworthy reforms that occurred in this area in Latin America before 2000 were the introduction of the noncontributory rural pensions and the basic social assistance pension (BPC) in Brazil. The rural pensions in Brazil were introduced by the military government to strengthen the political control of the official rural unions, as those unions were in charge of administering the benefits. These pensions also became an important patronage resource for the official pro-government party ARENA (Weyland 1996, 100). The value of the benefits was "truly minimal" (Weyland 1996,

TABLE 7.13. **Noncontributory transfer reforms**

Country	Years	Reforms	Party
Spain	1984	Unemployment assistance	PSOE
	1988–90	Noncontributory pensions/social assistance	PSOE
	1989–95	Minimum income	Regions
Portugal	1974–76	Social pension	Revolution
	1984	Reorganization; noncontributory	Grand Bloc
	1996–97	Minimum income	PS
Argentina	2001–3	PJJHD	PJ
	2003–6	Noncontributory pensions	PJ (Kirchner)
	2006	Famílias, Seguro de Capacitación	PJ (Kirchner)
	2009	Child allowances	PJ (Kirchner)
Brazil	1971–77	FUNRURAL: rural pensions/ health	Military
	1988	BPC: transfers to poor, aged, and disabled; gradual implementation	Constitution
	2002	Bolsa Família	PT
Chile	2004	Chile Solidario	PS
	2007	Solidarity pensions	PS
Uruguay	2005–7	PANES/Equidad	FA

91). Subsequently, benefits were increased so that, by the early 2000s, benefits were sufficient to pull families out of extreme poverty (Hunter and Sugiyama 2007, 10). Thus, it could be argued that the Rural Workers' Assistance Fund (FUNRURAL) should not be credited to the military government as it is in the table. This is also a problem with other initially small programs that were subsequently improved. For example, the 1988 Constitution enshrined the right to social assistance for "whoever may need it, regardless of contribution to social security" (Haggard and Kaufman 2008, 282). Legislation establishing the BPC (see chap. 6) was passed by the Franco government, and the benefit was linked to the minimum wage. Its value was greatly increased by Cardoso and Lula, who raised the minimum wage by 14 percent and 47 percent, respectively. By the late 2000s, BPC had made a significant contribution to the reduction of poverty and inequality (Barros et al. 2010). So in this case it is again unclear which government should be credited for its success.

Second, every single reform except for the rural pensions and BPC in Brazil was implemented by a left-of-center government, or at least a coalition with a strong left-of-center presence, which explains why the reforms in Latin America were delayed until the turn to the left happened in the 2000s. If we add Costa Rica to this comparison, we find that FODESAF was set up in 1974 and put in charge of a variety of noncontributory programs. FODESAF was set up after some twenty years of democracy and under the first of the two consecutive PLN presidencies in the 1970s that pushed redistributive reforms, when the national health service was established as well and social security coverage greatly expanded (Martínez Franzoni 2010).

Argentina is again a somewhat special case. The noncontributory conditional cash transfer programs were first established in response to the economic collapse of 2001–2 but then maintained and eventually transformed, with a transfer of beneficiaries to two new programs, Famílias and Seguro de Capacitación, under the left-leaning Kirchner presidencies. Fernández de Kirchner also introduced the child allowances. Plan Jefes y Jefas, however, was subject to at least some political manipulation (Giraudy 2007), and it remains to be seen how much of this will be present in the distribution of the child allowances. Moreover, the funding of the child allowances needs to be put on a sustainable basis outside of the pension funds.

The third important fact is that, whereas noncontributory pensions have been established in all of these countries, none of the Latin American countries has introduced a minimum income for working-age people, although the family allowances in Uruguay point in this direction.

Conclusion

We have shown how democratic competition in the presence of a strong left propelled the expansion of the welfare state in Spain and Portugal, and we have explained the differences between these two countries and those South American countries with longer periods of democracy, the presence of stronger left parties, and location in the European Union sphere of influence rather than in that of the United States and the IFIs. Whereas the right-of-center parties did not roll back welfare programs that the left had established and even continued with some plans that were in the making, such as passage of national health service legislation in Portugal, they did not necessarily fully implement these plans, as the same example shows, nor were they innovators in noncontributory programs.

None of these conditions was sufficient by itself. Greece has had a similarly long history of democracy and the same location with regards to the EU, but it has also had a left party that is clientelistic and personalistic more than programmatic and committed to redistribution. Costa Rica has had an even longer record of democracy and a strong left-of-center party but was subject to numerous austerity and structural adjustment programs with a strong neoliberal bent. Although the various governments resisted major neoliberal reforms in social policy, significant expansion of income support programs along the lines of a minimum insertion income were off the agenda, and the redistributive impact of the tax and transfer system remained much more limited than in Spain and Portugal.

We analyzed and rejected hypotheses about structural factors as explanations for the differences in the welfare states of the Iberian and Latin American countries. The Iberian countries had better economic growth performance, but they did much better in the area of social policy than did the Latin American countries at comparable levels of GDP per capita. As we have stressed continually, the key is not overall social expenditures, where the differences were not great by the 2000s, but the allocation of these expenditures, which has a more universalistic and solidaristic character in Spain and Portugal. In particular, these two countries have minimum income schemes and national health services, which none of our South American cases do. As noted, the tax and transfer systems in Spain and Portugal lower the Gini in income distribution by ten points or more, as opposed to two points in our Latin American cases (Goñi, López, and Servén 2008).

We have highlighted the importance of location in the European versus the American sphere of influence. This difference was crucial not only in the negative sense, with regard to the intensity of pressures for austerity and neoliberal reforms, which were much weaker in Spain and Portugal. The difference was also crucial in the positive sense, with regard to the model to be imitated, which was Social Europe versus the residualist liberal welfare state model in the United States. The EU programs and resolutions strengthened the position of the left parties and made it more difficult for nonleft parties to resist the implementation of social policies designed to achieve the goals of social inclusion and solidarity. The differences in external influence were particularly stark in the area of pension reforms, to which we return in the next chapter.

CHAPTER EIGHT

Conclusion

A t the beginning of the second decade of the twenty-first century, there is reason for cautious optimism that Latin America may indeed be able to "break with history" and reduce inequality.[1] Despite the weight of historical structural conditions going back to the concentration of wealth and power in colonial times and perpetuated in the form of enduring social hierarchies and predominantly authoritarian or clientelistic politics into the second half of the twentieth century, not only poverty but also inequality has finally shown a downward trend in many Latin American countries. We have explained this departure with the increased strength of political forces promoting redistributive reforms. Democracy has taken hold and—despite its deficiencies—has enabled parties committed to egalitarianism and solidarity to grow, participate in political power, and shape policy in a redistributive direction. There have also been remarkable differences in inequality and poverty between countries for a considerable time. These differences can similarly be explained with the longevity of democracy and the strength of parties to the left of center. Our evidence supports the view that inequality is not immutable in Latin America but rather that politics can make a big difference for the distribution of life chances.

We begin this chapter by reviewing the results of our quantitative and comparative historical analyses. After drawing lessons from our findings, we reflect on the viability of the left project in the twenty-first century and on strategies for the pursuit of redistributive social policy regimes. These reflections involve a discussion of other left governments in Latin America. Our third task is to reflect on some methodological issues. We end the book by drawing out the implications of our findings for theories of redistribution and social change.

Recapitulating Our Central Findings

Quantitative Results

The quantitative analyses in chapters 4 and 5 strongly support our theoretical claims that democracy and left political strength had significant effects on the development of social policy, especially redistributive social policy, in Latin America in the past century. In the cross-national analysis of the development of social policy in the ISI period in chapter 4, we found urban working-class presence and democracy to be strongly associated with welfare generosity in 1980. Left political strength was not statistically significant in this analysis because by this point in time the left had held power in too few cases without being followed by authoritarian regimes that rolled back social policy gains, as the comparative historical analysis later in chapter 4 shows.

The much larger number of cases in the pooled time series analysis of data from 1970 to 2005 allowed us to test our hypotheses in a more nuanced fashion in chapter 5. Democracy emerged as the most important variable in this analysis, in part because of its direct effects, but mainly because it was at the beginning of a causal chain that influenced all of the dependent variables in our analysis—social spending, inequality, and poverty. Democracy had a strong direct influence on all three spending variables (health, education, and social security and welfare), on poverty, and on inequality. The polar opposite of democracy, repressive authoritarianism, had negative effects on education spending. Democracy made left political mobilization possible, and left political strength had important effects on inequality and poverty. Democracy pushed up spending on education, which had strong indirect effects on inequality and poverty through its effect on the average educational level of the population. Finally, social security and welfare spending had a negative effect on inequality but only if it developed in a democratic context.

We found support for Muller's (1989) argument that the effect of democracy on inequality appears only after some twenty years of democracy. We also found a similar relationship with poverty. This finding is important because only three countries in the analysis had reached this threshold by 1990; eight more had reached it by 2005. Our comparative historical analysis suggests some reasons for why democracy would have a delayed effect on inequality and poverty. Once a country becomes democratic, it takes time for social groups to organize, for civil society to strengthen, and for left parties to form and mobilize. For example, most Latin American countries democratized or redemocratized in the 1980s, but the left did not gain executive power until the turn of the century or afterward. Some reforms take time to have an effect on income inequality and poverty. For example, many democratic governments of the 1990s, notably those of Argentina, Brazil, and Uruguay among our focal countries, carried out reforms of their education systems, which increased the supply of educated workers after the turn of the century and thus lowered the skill premium. These reforms, as a result, were partly responsible for the historically unprecedented decline in income inequality in most of Latin America after 2000.

Our measures of left strength and democracy were collinear and could not be entered in the same equation. We found, however, that the effect of a two-standard-deviation change in democracy was larger than the effect of the same change in left strength on all of our dependent variables. This indicates that the effect of democracy did not operate entirely through enabling the growth of left political forces. We discuss the other mechanisms through which democracy had effects on social welfare outcomes in our summary of the comparative historical evidence below.

In sharp contrast to our findings for developed democracies (Bradley et al. 2003), we found that social spending did not have unambiguous negative effects on inequality in Latin America. Given this result, it is not surprising that we found little evidence of left political effects on the level of social spending, again in sharp contrast to our finding for developed democracies (Huber and Stephens 2001a). Since left strength did affect inequality, we surmised that left political strength affected the composition of spending. We found strong evidence of this in the comparative historical analysis.

Our quantitative analysis showed little net effect of the market liberalization measures developed by Morley, Machado, and Pettinato (1999) and updated by Escaith and Paunovic (2004) on inequality or poverty. This may seem surprising but it is consistent with findings of Morley (2001) and Bogliaccini (2009). It does not mean, however, that the transition from ISI to open economies had no effect on poverty and inequality. The dismantling of ISI led to deindustrialization and informalization of the labor force, which our analysis showed increased inequality and poverty, respectively. Moreover, earlier analyses showed that radical reform episodes were particularly detrimental for poverty and inequality (Huber and Solt 2004).

Finally, it is worth underlining the importance of investment in human capital for lowering poverty and inequality in Latin America. Our analysis showed strong negative effects of average years of education on both poverty and inequality as well as strong effects of health spending on poverty. The relationship almost certainly involves some feedback. We found that average cognitive scores of secondary school students were very highly correlated to poverty levels in the country ($r = -.84$). The reciprocal link between poverty and human capital investment is clearly recognized by the design of the conditional cash transfer programs discussed below.

Latin American Systems of Social Protection in the Construction Phase

Our qualitative comparative analysis of the most advanced Latin American social policy regimes and those of Spain and Portugal served to elucidate the mechanisms through which democracy, left strength, urban labor, and globalization affected social policy, poverty, and inequality from the phase of initial construction through the phase of neoliberal reforms to the universalistic reorientation. To begin with the construction phase, in Uruguay, Chile, and Costa Rica, democracy opened the way for leaders committed to the welfare of the majority of the population to win elections and produce early legislation on social security schemes for ordinary working people. Batlle in Uruguay was by far the earliest political leader in Latin America to be democratically elected and then, during his two terms in office (1903–7 and 1911–16), to initiate the construction of a welfare state and universalize free secular public education. Alessandri in Chile (1920–25) became the second such leader to institute a social security scheme for blue-collar workers. In Costa Rica, it was a democratically elected progressive Catholic president, Calderón, supported by the communists, who in 1941 passed the first legislation for a social security scheme that was to cover the working population. Implementation was slow until the PLN, founded and led by Figueres after his victory in the brief civil war of 1948, used its control of the legislature to mandate universalization.

More important in the longer run, civil and political rights made it possible for these leaders and others to build political parties to represent the interests of the lower classes, and for these parties to win elections and shape policy to expand social protection and investment in human capital. By 1980 Uruguay and Costa Rica had the longest records of full democracy in Latin America, followed by Chile with more restrictions, and they also had the strongest record of left-of-center political presence in the legislature and executive. The Colorados were dominant in Uruguay from the 1910s to 1958, and the PLN in Costa Rica from the 1950s to the 1980s. In Chile, the left did not achieve executive power until 1970, but it had been present in the legislature since the 1930s and in the cabinet under the Popular Front beginning in 1938. For instance, the intense competition with the left spurred the Christian Democrats' attempts in the 1960s to expand primary health care.

Historical assessments of the role of organized labor in pushing for the introduction of social protection programs under democratic governments are ambiguous. Labor did not necessarily speak with one voice, and there were radical groups that saw social policy as elite attempts to co-opt and demobilize the working class. It is clear, however, that a strong and militant labor movement put the social question on the agenda and kept it there, and that workers were a potential political support base. These were reasons for democratic political leaders concerned with social integration, such as Batlle and Alessandri, to propose protective labor and social policy legislation. In Uruguay, the labor movement was not allied with the Colorados, nor was the Chilean labor movement allied with Alessandri's Liberal Alliance, but workers did provide electoral support to those presidents.[2] In the case of Costa Rica, the communist movement based in the unions in the banana plantations allied with Calderón and pushed for the implementation of social security. The expansion of social security in Costa Rica, though, happened on the initiative of the PLN and without labor pressure, as the strongest unions had been repressed after the civil war.

The presence of a labor movement that was growing in strength and militancy but was not integrated politically constituted a crucial force inducing nondemocratic or semi-democratic leaders to attempt an incorporation from above by means of labor and social legislation. This was the case for Vargas in Brazil and Perón in Argentina, both of whom extended social security protection to the bulk of the urban labor force. In fact, Vargas followed a precedent set by governments dominated by the oligarchy in the 1920s, which had set up insurance funds for railroad, dock, and maritime workers, for the same purpose of preempting and controlling labor militancy. Interestingly, the Brazilian bureaucratic-authoritarian government of 1964–85 followed suit again by extending noncontributory pensions and health care to the rural sector through the rural *sindicatos*, in an attempt to preempt emerging rural radicalism. Perón began to court organized labor as minister of labor under the military government from 1943 to 1945 and continued to do so as president. Extension to industrial labor of a social security scheme and promotion of the *obras sociales* were part of this strategy.

The development pattern of social protection systems, including health care, in Latin American countries during the ISI phase was essentially similar, whether it occurred under more or less democratic auspices. Protection came in the form of employment-based contributory systems, based on employer and employee contributions with greater or smaller contributions from the state, and new systems were added to already existing ones, with different rules governing eligibility and benefits. Once this pattern had been set, it became exceedingly difficult for democratic governments to change it because of the political influence of beneficiaries of privileged systems. The exception was the establishment of a unified health care system in Costa Rica. In our other focus countries, the military governments imposed some unification with varying degrees of success. It was the debt crisis that catalyzed more far-reaching reforms, driven by the high deficits of the pension systems that aggravated the burden on the public budget.

There are only scarce data and analyses of the impact of the social security schemes and of the health care systems on poverty and inequality in the pre-1980 period. Mesa-Lago (1991b, 105–7) reviewed a number of studies and concluded that the Chilean, Brazilian, and Costa Rican systems overall were somewhat progressive among the insured sectors. If we take into account the excluded rural and urban informal sectors, the systems were clearly regressive. As noted, the main sources of financing were employer and employee contributions, but the state was the employer of those sectors with the most privileged systems—the military and civil servants. These sectors required financing from general revenue and thus from indirect taxes, particularly import taxes, which were paid by those not covered or covered under less generous systems. Contributions from employers in the private sector were generally high, but when the contributions were paid (rather than evaded) the cost was passed on to consumers, which again affected not only those covered by social security.

The impact on poverty was more positive, though it was largely confined to the urban sector, where a larger share of the population was covered. Although benefits outside the privileged schemes were low, pensions made an important contribution to the budget of extended households. Family allowances had a similar effect. Social assistance pensions for disability, survivors, and old age in Uruguay, and a variety of programs directed at the poor in Costa Rica, such as nutrition assistance, also helped to alleviate poverty. All these various programs contributed to keeping poverty levels in Chile, Costa Rica and Uruguay below what one would have predicted on the basis of GDP per capita (Huber and Stephens 2010, 176).

The Debt Crisis and Beyond

The impact of democracy on social policy manifested itself again very clearly in the phase of neoliberal reform. The Chilean model of pension privatization and greater reliance on private insurers and providers in health and education was put on the agenda by the IFIs everywhere, but in stark contrast to the Pinochet dictatorship, the democratic governments that embraced this model had to make concessions to the opposition (Argentina and Uruguay), and other democratic governments sought alternative reforms from the beginning (Brazil and Costa Rica). The results were mixed systems with a choice in Argentina, mixed systems with a robust basic tier and a smaller capitalized tier in Costa Rica and Uruguay, and a reformed public system in Brazil. In contrast to Chile, in all these cases, employer contributions were continued, which together with the minimum pension guarantee in the public tier preserved a certain degree of solidarity. Democracy, however, did not always work unambiguously in the direction of equity. In Brazil, the beneficiaries of the privileged systems mobilized strong opposition against a curtailment of their benefits, under Cardoso as well as Lula, and in Uruguay the pension referendum tied up a large part of social expenditures in transfers to the elderly, to the detriment of the poor of working age and their children. In the end, though, it mattered that democracy made it possible for opponents of full privatization to block it and to prevent the emergence of powerful private pension administrators as in Chile, which then made it impossible to tap the pension contributions of higher-income earners for redistributive purposes in the future.

Democracy made it possible for left-of-center parties to gain representation in the legislatures and to field candidates in presidential elections and thus to put up resistance against neoliberal reforms in social policy. The FA and the PT were consistent and strident opponents of reform proposals presented by the nonleft incumbents—both proposals with a neoliberal bent and proposals that actually had some good provisions but in the left's opinion did not go far enough in a redistributive direction. When in government, the left at times pursued economic liberalization. This was particularly the case for the PLN in Costa Rica, but even Lagos continued with the promotion of free trade agreements. The left did not pursue neoliberal reforms in social policy, however; on the contrary, they attempted to strengthen universalistic and solidaristic systems.

Our comparative historical analysis allowed us to trace the mechanisms behind the statistical finding that democracy only has a strong effect on inequality after about twenty years. For instance, in Costa Rica the rapid expansion of social security coverage and the establishment of FODESAF, the agency in charge of noncontributory benefits, happened under the PLN governments in the 1970s, some two decades after the PLN had been founded. For the more recent period, analyses of microdata showed that two key factors accounted for the decline in inequality after 2000. The first was a decline in wage dispersion, which in turn was linked to the greater supply of workers with more education and increases in the minimum wage. The second was less inequality in nonlabor income, which in turn was mainly a result of the spread of noncontributory social assistance programs and increases in the benefits of these programs, which in many cases were linked to the minimum wage. Increases in education spending and educational reforms happened under democratic governments of a variety of political stripes, but they took time to filter through to the composition of the working-age population and thus to reduce the wage dispersion. The spread of noncontributory social assistance programs was most consistently promoted by left governments, but the left did not win executive power until some ten (in Chile) or twenty (in Uruguay) years after the transition to democracy.

Skeptics might argue that the decline of inequality after 2000 is overdetermined. Transitions to democracy took place during the lost decade of the 1980s, which was followed by another decade of economic turmoil. It was not until after 2000 that economic stability was achieved, which more or less coincided with the achievement of twenty years of democracy. In addition, the commodities boom made major amounts of resources available to governments. There is no doubt that the commodities boom facilitated policy innovation. However, the benefits from this growth could have accrued mainly to upper-income earners, as they did under Pinochet from 1985 to 1989 or during the Brazilian economic miracle of 1968–73. Instead, pressures from left-of-center parties, first in opposition and then in government, managed to shape social policy increasingly according to the principles of basic universalism.

Our statistical results did not show a significant effect of left strength on social expenditures, but they did show one on poverty and inequality. We hypothesized that this could be explained with the fiscal constraints in the 1980s and 1990s on all governments and the difference between left and right governments in the allocation of social expenditures. Again, our case studies provide the evidence for our claim that the left allocated spending in a more progressive manner. The Chilean government under Bachelet passed a major pension reform that greatly expanded and improved basic and supplementary solidaristic pensions, and it expanded the reach of Chile Solidario. The Brazilian government under Lula unified and greatly expanded various social assistance programs as Bolsa Família, and it significantly raised the minimum wage, which in turn increased benefits in social assistance pensions. The Uruguayan government under Vazquez implemented Plan Equidad with expanded coverage and improved benefits of noncontributory family allowances and pensions. The Argentine governments under the Kirchners consistently improved the value of minimum pensions, and they expanded conditional cash transfers. The PLN in Costa Rica had already set up FODESAF as the agency in charge of social assistance in the 1970s, and the second Arias administration used it to implement a conditional cash transfer directed at secondary school students. He also massively increased the value of the noncontributory pensions.

We found similar universalistic and egalitarian trends in health policy. In Chile, Lagos succeeded in introducing guaranteed coverage for a large number of illnesses and attempted but failed to link it to a fund that would have equalized financing between the public and private sectors. In Argentina, Plan Remediar started as a response to the 2001 crisis with a loan from the Inter-American Development Bank to distribute free basic medicine to health centers in poor areas, and it was expanded under the Kirchners to reach more than 40 percent of the population by 2006 (Niedzwiecki 2010a). In Uruguay, the FA government virtually universalized coverage and unified payments in the health system. In Costa Rica, the PLN had unified the health system in the 1970s and implemented the reform in the 1990s that strengthened the primary care networks. This reform had received support from both major parties in the legislature, but it was implemented by Figueres. In Brazil, a slow and uneven implementation of the unified national health system that had been enshrined in the 1988 Constitution began under Collor but picked up steam under Cardoso and Lula.

The reorientation toward more basic and universalistic programs in social policy had a clearly beneficial effect on lowering poverty and inequality. Of course, economic growth, particularly the comparatively very high growth rates from 2002 to 2008, was a major factor in lowering poverty, but far from sufficient. In Chile, Brazil, and Costa Rica, increases in the minimum wage were important, and in Uruguay the revival of the wage councils. In Brazil, Argentina, and Uruguay the conditional cash transfers made an important contribution to lowering poverty, as did the increases in minimum pensions and social assistance pensions in Argentina, Brazil, and Costa Rica. The basic and supplementary solidarity pensions in Chile began to do the same. In Chile, extreme poverty was lowered significantly through Chile Solidario.

Moreover, growth in the 1990s had been accompanied by rising inequality, whereas inequality was lowered after 2000. The end of the major skill-biased economic transformations that had accompanied the transition from ISI to open economies meant that inequality would be less likely to rise further; to actually lower it, however, appropriate social policies were crucial. Education policies that increased the supply of persons with secondary schooling lowered the skill premium. This was particularly important in Brazil, where secondary enrollment jumped from 20.5 to 51.5 percent of the age population between 1993 and 2005. The increases in the minimum wage, the conditional cash transfers, and the improvements in noncontributory pensions not only lowered poverty but also inequality, because they reduced inequality in both labor and nonlabor income.

If we widen our focus beyond monetary income and include social services, then the redistributive profile of social expenditure becomes stronger than if we just look at taxes and transfers. Calculations based on national surveys done in the late 1990s provided by the Inter-American Development Bank in the ECLAC Social Panorama 2005 show the following picture: spending on education, health, and social security lowered the Gini of the after-tax income distribution by 11 percentage points in Argentina, 7 percentage points in Brazil, 8 in Costa Rica, and

2 in Uruguay. Using the same expenditure categories, social spending accounted for more than half of the total income of households in the lowest quintile in Argentina (65 percent), Brazil (62 percent), and Costa Rica (56 percent), and 32 percent in Uruguay (no data for Chile). Certainly, with the reorientation toward improvements of transfer benefits for those with the lowest incomes, and with more universalistic and egalitarian tendencies in health care after 2000, these redistributive and poverty-lowering effects grew stronger.

In the construction phase of the systems of social protection, we saw that a notable presence of a militant urban labor movement constituted an incentive for democratic and nondemocratic leaders alike to appeal to this movement for support by extending social security schemes. During the debt crisis, the following period of neoliberal reform, and even in the new century, the situation was different. Labor had emerged greatly weakened from the repression under authoritarianism in Chile and Argentina and was further weakened in all countries by the structural adjustment measures that shrank the industrial sector and formal employment more generally. Thus, organized labor was overall less of a significant actor in social policy formation in the post-ISI period. The exceptions were the resistance to the proposed pension reforms in Argentina, Brazil, and Uruguay, particularly among unions of public-sector employees, and the resistance of unions to the reforms of the *obras sociales* in Argentina. In Argentina, opposition from the unions and their allies in the legislature forced Menem to make major concessions in pension reform, and the unions were able to essentially block the implementation of the reform that was to allow competition in the health sector. In Uruguay, the unions joined with the pensioners in mobilizing for the pension referendum that tied the value of pensions to remunerations, and in opposing more far-reaching privatization. In Brazil, public-sector unions strenuously opposed a reform of their privileged pension regime. Thus, in the cases of Uruguay and Brazil, the role of organized labor with regard to the pension reform was actually conservative in that they defended the benefits of all those who were covered, including those in the privileged programs. On the other hand, labor was supportive of progressive reforms in Uruguay, particularly the health care reform that universalized coverage, equalized resources among providers, and set a progressive schedule of contributions linked to income and family status. In Brazil, the unions strongly supported the minimum wage and noncontributory transfers.

Latin America and Iberia Compared

The comparison of our Latin American focus countries with Spain and Portugal in the period after their respective transitions to democracy provides further evidence in support of our contention that a longer record of democracy and greater strength of the left result in a stronger social policy effort, more redistributive allocation of social expenditures, and lower poverty and inequality (see chap. 7). Spain and Portugal had consolidated their democracies by 1982, and in both countries political forces to the left of center were strong and controlled the executive and a majority in the legislature for extended periods of time. That they managed to reduce absolute poverty to lower levels than the Latin American countries did is not surprising, given the growing differences in GDP per capita. That the same is true for income inequality is surprising, however, given the initial similarities in the distribution of land and skills and continuing similarities in the distribution of skills in the 1990s. The greater redistributive capacity of taxes and transfers in Spain and Portugal goes a long way toward explaining this difference. In Argentina, Brazil, and Chile, direct and indirect taxes and transfers reduced the Gini by an average of 1.5 percentage points, and in Spain and Portugal by more than 10 percentage points (Goñi, López, and Servén 2008). As noted earlier, if we include health and education spending, the reduction in inequality is higher, but this is true for the Latin American and Iberian countries alike.

The comparison between Latin America and Iberia brought into relief a factor that was a constant among the Latin American countries but significantly shaped the differences in the social policy trajectory between the two sets of countries—their different location in the international system of power. Being located in the U.S. versus European sphere of influence meant being exposed to different impositions and incentives. In Latin America the IMF, the World Bank, and the U.S. government, mostly through USAID, all worked together throughout the 1980s and 1990s to promote not only structural adjustment of the economies but also neoliberal reforms of social policy. In contrast, neoliberalism remained confined to economic reform in Spain and Portugal, whereas the model for social policy was Social Europe, with a concern for social inclusion through transfers and services. The European Union began to engage in the fight against poverty in the 1980s with three poverty reports in sequence, followed by the establishment of the Observatory on National Policies to Combat Social Exclusion in 1990. It was not until a decade later that the IFIs seriously began to worry about social exclusion and inequality in Latin America.

Pension reform in Spain and Portugal was aimed at fixing the public system, not introducing privatization. It included a significant expansion of minimum and noncontributory pensions. In Spain unemployment insurance was greatly expanded as well. Both Spain and Portugal moved toward national health systems in the 1980s, and the national government introduced a minimum income scheme in Portugal in 1995, whereas in Spain the individual regions moved in this direction.

Globalization and Neoliberalism

This comparison of the effects of location in the world system leads us to a discussion of the effects of globalization on social policy. As noted, an analysis of the effects of globalization needs to differentiate between economic and political forces and between real and perceived constraints. Economic constraints forced the countries in both regions to open their economies in the form of lowering barriers to trade and to capital flows. The old ISI model was exhausted, which required an opening to trade. In addition, as economically weaker countries they had to follow suit in the liberalization of international capital flows. This opening entailed costs of deindustrialization, rising unemployment, and a growth of the informal sector, and it greatly increased vulnerability to volatile capital flows, with boom and bust cycles. However, the speed of transformation and the extent of accompanying neoliberal reforms, such as deregulation of economic activities and privatization of enterprises, did not respond to economic constraints, as they varied considerably between countries. Nor did neoliberal reform of social policy respond to economic constraints. Yes, social security systems needed to be reformed, but they did not need to undergo privatization, and social policies did not need to move toward residualism.

Here, weakness in the form of high indebtedness and thus high exposure to pressures from the IFIs was crucial. In the IFIs, neoliberalism was hegemonic, and neoliberal ideology penetrated the policymaking circles in many Latin American (and even European) countries that were in the closest contact with the IFIs, that is, in Ministries of Finance. There is clearly a material base to the hegemony of neoliberalism in the form of control by advanced countries of the IFIs and the reaction of international banks and governments in advanced countries to the debt crisis. Thatcher and Reagan made their imprint on the IMF and the World Bank, which consistently insisted on those neoliberal solutions. Additional material channels for influence were the common educational background of many technocrats in the IFIs and national financial bureaucracies, and the revolving doors that allowed technocrats from Finance Ministries in Latin America work for a while in the IFIs.

In addition, though, one should not underestimate the power of the ideas themselves. Neoliberalism offered a closed system of thought with easy solutions in a very complex and rapidly changing world, where easy answers were hard to come by. The diagnosis was that state intervention inevitably caused rent-seeking behavior and thus blocked and distorted development, and that the solution was to shrink the state and let the market rule in all aspects of policy making. It was the repeated financial crises in the 1990s and the very limited progress in poverty reduction even in periods of significant economic growth in the 1990s that forced a rethinking of these facile solutions. The change from Reagan/Bush to Clinton and even more so from Thatcher to Blair also facilitated a transition to more pluralist views. The failures of neoliberal reforms to produce the promised results spurred an interest in inequality and alternative approaches to social policy in the IFIs and among Latin American governments. A signal event was the publication of the "ten myths" about pension reform by the World Bank in 1999. In this article, Stiglitz—Nobel Prize winner and chief economist of the World Bank—in collaboration with Orszag, offered a devastating critique of the assumptions underlying the pension privatization schemes promoted by the bank earlier.

Structure of Left Parties, Power of the Opposition, and Policy Legacies

Our comparative historical analysis brought into relief some factors that we had not been able to explore in the statistical analysis—the organizational structure of left parties, the power of the right, policy legacies, and institutional factors. Left parties vary in the degree to which they resemble mass parties versus electoral-professional parties, and in the closeness of relations to civil society organizations, most prominently unions (Pribble 2008; Levitsky and Roberts 2011). Mass parties with close ties to unions tend to be more aggressively redistributive and universalistic in their policy proposals, whereas elite electoral parties without ties to mass organizations tend to be more cautious. The PT in Brazil and the FA in Uruguay belong to the former type, and the Socialists in Chile and the PLN in Costa Rica to the latter. As a result, the policy reorientation under the left governments was more dramatic in Brazil and Uruguay than in Chile and Costa Rica.

Of course, there are additional factors that account for the moderation of the governments in Chile and Costa Rica. In Chile, the Socialist presidents led coalition governments with the Christian Democrats, and some sectors of the Christian Democrats were not very supportive of strengthening the role of the state; in particular, they strongly preferred a large private-sector participation in education and also in health. Moreover, until the constitutional reform of 2005 the Lagos government had to contend with the appointed senators who gave the right undue (from the point of view of their electoral strength) influence. As a result, the government was constrained in its policy options; a case in point is Lagos's failure to get the equalization fund between the public and private health care systems accepted. In Costa Rica, the social policy regime had been built up along more universalistic lines, and therefore there was less need for radical innovation. Pribble's (2008) interview evidence suggests that the Chilean left leadership was more technocratic and sympathetic to neoliberalism than the Uruguayan, and more skeptical with regard to a comprehensive state role in the provision of transfers and social services. These views were also represented among the Uruguayan leadership, but the sectors of the party leadership that wanted a more comprehensive approach were stronger precisely because they could mobilize mass support if needed.

Left parties with a mass base and close links to unions and other popular organizations are also more likely to remain programmatic and committed to redistribution than are elite electoral parties. If leaders stray from these commitments and become too sympathetic to neoliberalism or pursue personal interests, it is more likely they will be censured or pressured back onto the left path by the party base and affiliated mass organizations. One could see the development of the PLN to some extent as resulting from a lack of mass participation and linkages. Neoliberal factions gained the upper hand in the 1980s, and several high-level leaders became entangled in corruption cases. Whereas the PLN protected and adapted the welfare state as it had been constructed, it did not develop any major new initiatives after 2000. Arias did establish a conditional cash transfer program to reduce the dropout rate of second-ary school students, and he significantly increased the value of noncon-tributory pensions, but inequality slowly drifted upward.

When assessing the latitude of action for a government committed to redistribution, one should also look at the organizational structure and strength of the opposition. Here the Chilean Socialist governments were clearly most constrained. There are only two Chilean right parties, but they are highly disciplined, have formed a coalition, and have close rela-tions to a well-organized business community.[3] One of them is extremely right wing, defending to this day the Pinochet dictatorship. The strength of this opposition coalition goes a long way toward explaining the inabil-ity of the left governments to increase direct taxation in a meaningful way (Fairfield 2010a). In Brazil, Argentina, Costa Rica, and Uruguay, the right is not as cohesive and conservative, and business is not nearly as well organized as in Chile. In Brazil the right is highly fragmented; in Uruguay the two traditional parties are uncomfortable allies out of ne-cessity, and the Colorados still have progressive factions; in Argentina there is no real right-wing party; and in Costa Rica the opposition to the PLN is internally heterogeneous. None of these countries has a national peak organization that can speak for business.

The importance of policy legacies as obstacles to reform—positive and negative for redistribution—became apparent in several cases. The most detrimental to redistributive reforms were coalitions of beneficia-ries of inegalitarian systems. An extreme example is the ability of the co-alition of ISAPRES and their upper-income subscribers, supported by business and the right, to prevent a proposal for unification of the health care system from even getting onto the political agenda in Chile, and their ability to kill the proposal for a solidarity fund between the pri-vate and public systems. Also, private insurers, hospitals, and drug com-panies continue to fight the implementation of the unified health system in Brazil. Another example is the opposition of public-sector unions in Brazil to a reform of the special pension system for civil servants. On the positive side, the widespread support of the Costa Rican health care system by its beneficiaries induced politicians from all parties to reject World Bank proposals for an increased role for private provision and in-stead to search for ways to strengthen universal access to primary care. So, the general rule is that private for-profit providers of social services oppose universalistic reforms and, where their role is large, may wield veto power. In contrast, legacies of systems with a very broad base of beneficiaries with the same entitlements provided by the public sector are more hospitable toward further universalistic reforms.

Various institutional factors constituted obstacles to redistributive reforms in different countries. Federalism has long been shown in the literature to be associated with slower welfare state development (Obinger, Leibfried, and Castles 2005). Certainly, in Brazil the role of the states in the decentralization of responsibility for health services complicated the implementation of the unified health system. In the beginning, several governors used federal transfers destined for implementation of this system for other purposes (Weyland 1996). Thus, the governments in the 1990s began to bypass the state level, and the Cardoso and Lula governments eventually signed contracts with thousands of individual municipalities for the type of health care responsibilities they were ready to take on in exchange for resource transfers.

The incorporation of a wide range of aspects of the pension system into Brazil's 1988 Constitution meant that it would take a supermajority of 60 percent of the votes in the legislature to change them. Cardoso tried hard to deconstitutionalize major provisions, but he consistently failed to reach the necessary 60 percent (Hunter and Sugiyama 2009b). Accordingly, he was only able to pass minor reforms. A further example of a constitutional feature that complicated social policy reform is the provision for referenda in Uruguay. Research in Switzerland, where frequent use of referenda is a regular feature of the political process, has shown that it is a conservatizing feature. It makes departures from the status quo more difficult, as it opens the opportunity for highly mobilized groups to spread fear and confusion and thus get voters to stay home or reject the proposal (Neidhart 1970). In the Uruguayan case, the decision that was approved visibly improved the status quo for present and future pension recipients, but it imposed a heavy financial burden on the state budget, which made it difficult to find resources for social policy needs that were arguably more pressing from the point of view of the human capital of future generations.

Finally, among the authoritarian enclaves left in the Chilean constitution by the exiting military dictatorship, the appointed senators were a major obstacle to redistributive reforms. They gave the right a veto power in the senate at least until the early 2000s and thus forced the government to get the acquiescence of the opposition to major reform initiatives. Right after the transition, the government reached an agreement with the right on a temporary tax increase to begin to address the social debt, but after this agreement expired, the right strenuously and successfully opposed any major tax increases. As a result, Chile still has the lowest percentage of its GDP devoted to social policy among our focal countries.

Viability of the Left Project

Incrementalism

Our findings suggest a number of strategic implications for the pursuit of redistributive policy. Perhaps one of the most crucial is incrementalism—a prescription often derided as demonstrating lack of courage and imagination by members of left parties. Reforms that change things too fast are likely to suffer from deficient management and harsh political polarization, both of which contribute to macroeconomic imbalances, economic decline, and loss of support for democratic governments. In other words, the changes are not sustainable economically and politically. These were the experiences of the French Popular Front, Allende in Chile, and Manley in Jamaica, among others. In contrast, the left in the Nordic countries built welfare states step by step and over the span of some forty years (1945–85) and managed to achieve the lowest levels of poverty and inequality among advanced industrial countries. Our analysis shows that incrementalism works in new democracies in the developing world as well.

Costa Rica was the pioneer in constructing a lasting democracy and gradually expanding health care in a universalistic direction. Similarly, the country established an agency in charge of noncontributory transfers and in-kind benefits and services comparatively early on, and invested in basic education. Despite the severity of the economic crisis and the depth of structural adjustment, Costa Rica was able to protect these policies and still performed significantly better on basic human development indicators than did countries with higher levels of GDP per capita in Latin America. In the Southern Cone countries and Brazil, gradual increases in the minimum wage, expansion of coverage and improvement of benefits for participants in noncontributory social assistance programs, and investment in education all contributed to the lowering of poverty and inequality over the past two decades. Similarly, the push toward expansion of universalistic health care systems with equal access to preventive and primary care has improved health outcomes for the underprivileged.

In a context of continued scarcity of resources, incrementalism needs to be oriented by the principles of basic universalism—that everyone should have the right to basic subsistence and to quality health care and education. Basic universalism is different from classic universalism in that it does not provide the same basic transfers to everyone in the society, regardless of income, but that it broadly—not narrowly—focuses on those who need the transfers. In the Latin American context, broadly focused means all those in poverty or vulnerable to poverty, which includes between 40 percent and 70 percent of the population, depending on the country. If tax systems were to improve, noncontributory transfers could move from basic to classic universalism, with the same benefits for all income groups but subject to taxation. In the area of health and education, basic universalism starts with massive investment in public primary and secondary education and preventive and primary health care, in order to provide everyone with access to quality education and health care. The ultimate goal is to improve public health care and education to the point where the middle classes stay with or return to the public system. This is politically essential because participation by the middle classes not only reduces their reluctance to pay taxes for services they do not utilize, but it also harnesses extra energies and contributions to education from middle-class parents. Again, such changes take time; improvements of public services have to be substantial, and perceptions of them among the middle classes have to spread to the point where they change attitudes and behavior.

Incrementalism and basic universalism help to make reforms sustainable, but they do not guarantee that the policies and their effects will be sustained. Policy legacies are important, as arguments about path dependence suggest (Pierson 2001), but they do not lock in gains forever. Financial commitments to transfers and social services need to be renewed periodically, and policies need to be adapted to preserve a universalistic character under new demographic and economic conditions. This statement implies that developing a solid system of taxation is a crucial component of an incrementalist and sustainable strategy of redistribution. The tax systems have remained a weak point in all of our focus countries, which raises concerns for the period after the high-growth episode driven by demand for raw materials in Asia. It is no exaggeration to say that the weak tax systems may be the Achilles' heel of most Latin American welfare states in the making.

The need to renew financial commitments and adapt welfare states further implies that long-term incumbency of left parties is crucial. No matter how well constructed a welfare state and how strong popular support for it is, if the left is shut out of governmental power for prolonged periods, it becomes possible for governments to slowly allow the welfare state to atrophy. Hacker (2002) has diagnosed the phenomenon of welfare state shrinkage or privatization by omission in the United States, and of course the same can occur elsewhere. In the eight years that the PLN was out of power in Costa Rica, inequality crept up very slowly, in contrast to the decline in most other Latin American countries.

Investment in Human Capital

The evidence that investment in human capital is the key to any successful development path and thus to a lowering of poverty in the long run is by now overwhelming. This was a central insight of new growth theory and has been supported in quantitative studies of economic growth that use the Barro-Lee measure, average years of education, as the measure of human capital (e.g., see Barro 1991, 1997). As we pointed out in chapter 2, Hanushek and Woessmann (2008, 2009) have shown that these studies grossly underestimate the effects of the level of human capital because of error in the measure of human capital, average years of education, and that actual cognitive skills yield even higher estimates for the effect of human capital on growth. Investment in human capital is the most essential measure in a strategy to put Latin American countries on a development path that results in moving up the product cycle through industrial upgrading. This path is the one followed by the backward economies of early twentieth-century Europe, such as Finland, and then replicated by the East Asian newly industrialized countries (Vartiainen 1999). The East Asian countries began with labor-intensive products like textiles and apparel and then moved up the product cycle, taking over export production in industries like shipbuilding, which the Nordic countries no longer do competitively, and then moving on to automobiles and electronics. To bring about this expansion, these countries needed a highly skilled workforce, and thus this path required government investment in mass education. As we pointed out in chapter 2,

Evans's (2008) reconceptualization of the developmental state highlights the importance of investment in human capital for East Asia's spectacular development, and he argues that investment in human capabilities and the generation of intangible assets—ideas, skills, and networks—will be even more critical in the twenty-first century.

Our quantitative analysis showed that higher average years of education are strongly related to lower levels of poverty and inequality in Latin America. The link between inequality and mass education is inextricable. A World Bank study by Thomas, Wang, and Fan (2001) shows that there is an extremely high correlation between inequality of education as measured by the Gini index and average years of education, suggesting that it is almost impossible to increase significantly the average level of education without increasing equality in the distribution of education. The relationship between the level of human capital, and poverty and inequality is almost certainly reciprocal. In chapter 5, we showed that the correlation between poverty levels and average cognitive skills of secondary school students in Latin America is very high, −.84. From this and microlevel studies of school achievement, we surmise that it would be difficult to raise the average level of human capital without doing anything about poverty. Thus, a development strategy aimed at raising human capabilities in order to achieve industrial upgrading must almost inevitably be an egalitarian strategy.

The future challenge for Latin America in this area is clear. López-Calva and Lustig (2010, 18) argue that a barrier to the continuing decline in inequality in Latin America is the poor quality of the public education received by children of the poor and middle classes, in comparison to those in the top 10 percent, who usually attend private schools. This makes it very difficult for them to compete for admission to tertiary education institutions. For instance, in Chile, a student who has attended only municipal schools has a dramatically lower chance of receiving a score on the nationwide university entrance exam that is high enough to obtain admission into one of the eight best universities.[4] It is essential that investing in public education to improve the quality of mass education be high on the agenda of any government committed to national development and integration.

Intimately related to improvements in education is the need to increase investment in research and development in the pursuit of industrial upgrading. This book has looked at social policy and social development, not economic policy and economic development. Of course, the two are linked. It remains true that the best protection against poverty is a job with a good wage. The job with the good wage, however, is not available to people without skills. Where economic and social policy meet is in investment in education. The contributions of economic development to social development have long been emphasized; the reverse causality began to be recognized in new growth theory and is at the center of the current rethinking of the developmental state.

Party Building and Election Campaigns

Another crucial set of implications has to do with the political infrastructure and playing field. We have demonstrated the importance of the strength of left political parties for successful redistributive social policy. We have also pointed to the difference between elite electoral parties and mass parties with close ties to mass organizations as a determinant of the depth and breadth of redistributive reforms. These observations imply that party building and movement building are important components of strategies of equity-oriented social change. Parties and mass organization are not necessarily simply emerging from below; they can be heavily influenced by state policy. Public subsidies for parties and rules that protect labor organizers and facilitate the formation of unions are clearly supportive of the development of organizational strength. Given the greater availability of private financial support for parties that protect interests of the privileged, public support for parties should be an important agenda item for governments committed to equity-oriented change. The same observations apply to campaign finance legislation. Public support for election campaigns needs to be accompanied by rules putting limits on private financing of campaigns and by strict enforcement of these rules in order to level the playing field for parties representing the interests of the underprivileged.

The Left Economic Model and Market Liberalization

There is widespread agreement among scholars of Latin American political economy that the ISI model of economic development was exhausted by the 1970s and that a turn to open trade markets was essential. As we have pointed out, this turn had the negative consequence in the transition period that inequality and poverty rose as a result of deindustrialization and informalization and skill-biased technology, which in turn were caused by closure of uncompetitive low-skill enterprises and the shedding of low-skilled labor by the survivors. By the turn of the century, however, this process had run its course. Moreover, ample evidence suggests that open trade markets are compatible with low levels of inequality and poverty, as the examples of the Nordic countries and Taiwan and Korea show. Indeed, these cases lend support to the argument that low levels of inequality and poverty and high levels of investment in human capital are necessary characteristics of an economic model that leads to rising levels of per capita income through industrial upgrading and a move up the product cycle into higher technology and a more-skill-intensive production of goods and services.

The necessity of open trading is one of the few areas of agreement we have with the neoliberal formula of the Washington Consensus era. The second area is the necessity of balancing the budget across economic cycles. Commitment to low tariffs and budget balance is characteristic of the successful social democratic models in Europe in the Golden Age (1945–72) and more recently (Huber and Stephens 2001b). In Latin America in the 1980s and 1900s, the neoliberal formula also prescribed elimination of international capital controls, deregulation of domestic capital markets, cuts in social spending and residualization of social policy, tax "reform," and privatization of state enterprises. In the light of the 2008 financial crisis, it does not even seem necessary to argue that the deregulation of domestic and international capital markets has huge downsides. Even the IMF concedes this point (Stiglitz 2011). As we have repeatedly stated with regard to social spending, the IFIs, particularly the World Bank, have abandoned their Washington Consensus position and now advocate investments in human capital and reductions in poverty and inequality.

The neoliberal formula for tax reform has been reduction of marginal rates on labor and capital income, greater reliance on indirect taxes, and reduction of the overall tax burden. By contrast, we have argued that Latin American countries are lightly taxed and that taxation should be increased to fund investments in human capital and redistributive social policy. With regard to privatization, we take a pragmatic view. On the one hand, there is an argument that private and public enterprises in tradable goods sectors in open economies will not behave differently because they are constrained by competition. On the other hand, in public service monopolies, the argument for private ownership is weak, and the experience of advanced industrial democracies with privatization of these enterprises has not been favorable. Regulatory capacity in Latin America is lower, which is even greater reason for concern. In any case, the European experience indicates that a large state sector is not an essential element of an egalitarian model, and low levels of inequality and economic success in the Golden Age were achieved in countries with large state sectors (Norway, Austria, and Finland) and small state sectors (Denmark and Sweden).

In his prescriptions for a "new developmentalism," Bresser Pereira (2009) recommends low interest rates and competitive (that is, not overvalued) exchange rates combined with conservative fiscal policy to contain inflation. We concur and add that some measure of external capital controls would facilitate exchange rate and interest rate management and would reduce the risk of financial crises precipitated by capital flight. Interestingly, this combination of low interest rates, capital controls, budget surpluses, and competitive exchange rates was the macroeconomic model of Norway and Sweden during the Golden Age of postwar capitalism.

The Other Left

Our focus cases in this volume were those Latin American countries with the most developed social policy regimes which had been built in the context of comparatively long histories of democracy and had consolidated party systems with strong left-of-center parties. There are governments of another sort pursuing a left project in Latin America at the beginning of the twenty-first century. These governments came to power in countries with shorter histories of democracy, less institutionalized party systems, and weaker left parties. They are headed by charismatic leaders: Hugo Chávez in Venezuela, Evo Morales in Bolivia, Rafael Correa in Ecuador, Daniel Ortega in Nicaragua, Mauricio Funes in El Salvador, and Fernando Lugo in Paraguay.[5] Not only do these governments find themselves in circumstances different from those in our core cases, but they also differ from each other. In particular, Ortega and Funes came to power in post–civil war situations, and together with Lugo they preside over small countries with weak economies, which sets them apart from the countries with oil and gas exports—Venezuela, Bolivia, and Ecuador. The governments in the former set of countries are highly constrained by low resource availability, whereas those in the latter have significant latitude of action and have introduced some major social policy innovations. Thus, we restrict our comments to the latter set of countries.

The governments of Chávez, Morales, and Correa share with the left parties and governments in our focus cases a commitment to egalitarianism and solidarity, but they are less incrementalist than the governments in our cases.[6] They have a broader program of transformation, extending to the economic model and political institutions. They have all championed state ownership and regulation of the economy. They also called constituent assemblies that modified political institutions. The rationale given for these institutional changes was the goal to deepen democracy by providing more opportunities for popular participation and for direct input of the population into the policy-making process. By the same token, the reforms served to strengthen the leader's power base by centralizing power in the hands of the executive. In the case of Venezuela, the reforms arguably went as far as to undermine democracy.[7] In contrast, in Bolivia and Ecuador Morales and Correa have been able to break the cycle of presidents being forced to resign by extra-institutional means and to bring a measure of democratic stability to their countries. In the case of Bolivia, accountability of the leader to the social bases that brought him to power has remained strong. The relationship between the leader and the base exhibits a complex mix of mobilization from below with cooptation attempts by a charismatic leader (Anria 2010, 122). Finally, these leaders have engaged in militant rhetoric, promising to move toward socialism and attacking capitalism as a system and capitalists as the enemies of the people, which is counterproductive in a mixed economy that depends on private investment to generate growth and employment.

The combination of changes in political institutions, economic regulations, and rhetoric has radicalized large sectors of the opposition and alienated investors. Opposition forces have used judicial procedures, recall attempts, and a variety of extraparliamentary protests and massive strikes to stop government initiatives. In Venezuela, they went as far as staging a short-lived coup against Chávez (McCoy 2010). Investors have withheld funds and exported capital, which is clearly detrimental to prospects for growth. In the short run, these governments have been able to use export windfalls from oil and natural gas to keep their economies growing. Export revenues have also enabled them to avoid the severe macroeconomic imbalances that beset the Allende government, for instance. Periods of declining oil prices revealed the weaknesses of the

Venezuelan economy, however, and inflation and unemployment have been way above the regional average since 1999 (Corrales 2010, 46).

Export windfalls have also been the basis for the financing of a whole host of new social programs. Some of them are transparent and important advances, such as the basic citizenship pension, the Renta Dignidad, and the conditional cash transfer program to elementary school children, the Bono Juancito Pinto, in Bolivia (Gray Molina 2010; Anria and Niedzwiecki 2011). Others lack transparency and accountability, such as the many new social service programs established under the name of Misiones in Venezuela. The Misiones certainly have been doing some good by bringing health and education services to previously neglected populations, but critics point to patronage use of the programs and corruption (Penfold-Becerra 2007). These programs are run by the presidency outside existing ministerial and legal structures, with a view to building political bases (Ellner 2008). Supporters claim that the traditional ministries were too inefficient and lacked commitment to the implementation of these policies. This may largely be true, and setting up new institutions may have been necessary given the desired speed of implementation. Duplication of institutions is costly, however, because personnel in both old and new institutions need to be paid, and over the longer run coordination problems occur. A more gradual approach to policy innovation, accompanied by efforts to improve the efficiency of existing state institutions and articulate the old with new agencies, would have been less costly and potentially more effective in the longer run.

The crucial question that will not be answered until sometime after these leaders lose political power is the nature of their policy legacies. On the positive side, they leave institutions that guarantee basic social rights and social programs that benefit large sectors of the population; the beneficiaries come to see access to these transfers and services as their right and mobilize as voters to defend them from cuts by future governments. The constitution and the Renta Dignidad in Bolivia are good candidates for such a legacy because of the constitutional provisions on social rights and the universalistic character of the basic pension. On the negative side, the programs are poorly anchored in legislation and have a strong partisan identification in that they are perceived as patronage handouts from the leader and his political machine; this perception may legitimize attempts by future opposition governments to cut funding for the programs. Chávez's Misiones are prime candidates for this scenario. To the extent that the efforts of these leaders to deepen democracy, increase popular participation, and strengthen citizenship are real and successful, a positive legacy appears more likely. To realize the positive potential of their legacies, however, the nature of the political parties that the leaders leave behind is crucial. Mobilized voters need a party to vote for that can be trusted to protect the policies the voters want—a party that is both strong enough and committed enough to do so. Historically, charismatic Latin American political leaders do not have a good track record when it comes to building strong political parties that would become organizational actors independent of those leaders.[8] Chávez, Correa, and Morales still have to break the mold.

Methodological Reflections

As in our previous work on the development of the welfare state in advanced capitalist democracies (Huber and Stephens 2001a), our methodological approach in this book has been to bring quantitative analysis and comparative historical analysis of selected cases into a dialogue with one another. In comparison to the earlier work, this work deepens that dialogue. Specifically, we bring our case knowledge and theoretical frame to bear on the selection of estimation technique in the quantitative analysis. Because our hypotheses specify that levels of our independent variables (e.g., duration of democracy) cause variation in levels of our dependent variables (e.g., poverty rates) and because our theory is designed to explain both variations through time within countries and variations between countries, it is inappropriate to employ a fixed effects specification, that is, country unit dummies. By the same token, since much of the variation we explain in the statistical analysis is between countries, we forego one advantage of the time structure of pooled time series data, that is, using the time sequence in the data to make claims about causality. We do not think we lose much in doing this because, for the reasons outlined in the next paragraph, we make our claims to have uncovered causal relations through examining the historical sequence in the comparative historical analysis. The role of the quantitative analysis is to demonstrate that these relations hold over a large number of cases over long periods of time. Our goal in the quantitative analysis is to establish strong and robust patterns of co-variation and to eliminate possible rival explanations, not to establish cause between our dependent variables and the independent variables that appear as strong predictors of our dependent variables in the analysis.

The reason we think it is nearly impossible to tap into causality with statistical analysis is that we view causality in the world as being highly complex. All of the following occur frequently in the real world: multiple paths to the same outcomes, complex interaction effects (cases in which the causal effect of one factor is dependent on one or more other factors), path-dependent effects, reciprocal causality, and diffusion (events in one case affecting other cases). As Hall (2003) points out, if this is what the real world is like, then we are not likely to get at causal processes with techniques such as multiple regression or any other statistical technique for that matter. That does not mean quantitative analysis has no role in empirical inquiry. As we have argued in Rueschemeyer, Stephens, and Stephens (1992) and Huber and Stephens (2001a), if quantitative analysis produces a robust association between two variables, then good comparative historical analysis has either to provide an explanation for the association or to provide evidence that it is a spurious association.

The past decade has witnessed major advances in the literature on the methodology of comparative qualitative analysis (Brady and Collier 2004; Mahoney and Rueschemeyer 2003). We chose our cases to represent the high end of the distribution on social policy effort, a procedure that has been heavily criticized as producing selection bias. Collier, Mahoney, and Seawright (2004) correctly argue that no selection bias occurs if one is conducting within-case analysis (i.e., if one is examining historical sequences or tracing processes). We examine historical sequences over long periods of time, seven or more decades, and across this span of time the outcomes we are interested in (poverty, social welfare effort, and, to a lesser extent, inequality) vary greatly within the cases; all of our hypothesized explanatory variables (e.g., democracy, urban working-class presence, left political strength, average educational levels) also vary greatly within the cases.

If we had attempted to demonstrate our causal argument with the Millian method of difference by use of our five focal cases, selection bias would have been a problem precisely because the cases are selected on the basis of high outcomes on social policy effort and success in reducing poverty. But we don't do this. We use the comparative method to trace different paths to the same outcome, that is, the paths taken to early social policy advance (chap. 4). In our comparison of Iberia and the four

South American countries, the two groups of countries vary on the outcome variables, and we use a most similar systems design to explain these different outcomes (chap. 7).

By examining the historical sequences in the cases, we attempt to uncover the causal mechanisms that link the independent variables that appeared as determinants of the dependent variables in the statistical analysis of the latter. For instance, in the statistical analysis, we found that cumulative record of democracy was strongly associated with less inequality but that this association only appeared after the record of democracy passed a threshold of twenty years. In the comparative case studies, we identified two mechanisms by which democracy had this delayed effect on inequality. First, we found that a number of Latin American governments expanded secondary education in the wake of democratization, including very important reforms in two of our five cases, Argentina and Brazil, in the 1990s. In both of these cases, entrepreneurial politicians within nonleft governments successfully promoted educational reform. The expansion of secondary education during this period increased the supply of educated workers after the turn of the century, which lowered the skill premium and was partly responsible for the decline in inequality in this period. Second, we argued that building left parties takes time; it does not happen spontaneously with democratization. This argument is consistent with the fact that the left executives came to power in our four cases of redemocratization only after the turn of the century. These left governments variously expanded conditional cash transfers to the poor, raised the minimum wage which in turn raised transfers that were indexed to the minimum wage, and changed labor laws to strengthen organized labor and strengthen its position at the bargaining table. These measures all contributed to the decline in inequality.

Reflections on Theories of Redistribution and Social Change

Our theoretical framework, fashioned in our studies of the development of democracy across world regions (Rueschemeyer, Stephens, and Stephens 1992) and the development of the welfare state in advanced capitalist democracies (Huber and Stephens 2001a), travels well to the topic of the development of social policy regimes in Latin America. Our book on democracy showed that our power constellation theory explains emergence and survival of democracy in Latin America well, and in this present book we use it to explain the formation and reforms of welfare states in the region. In those works, we argue that one needs to understand power relations within society, the power distribution between society and state, and the power distribution in the international system.

With regard to power within society, the first power cluster, we found that democracy was important for the outcomes we attempted to explain. Both the quantitative analysis and the comparative case studies indicated that formal political equality and party competition per se mattered, but the most important effect of democracy was the result of its allowing the underprivileged to organize. The organizational power of these groups and their allies was the support base for left parties, and left party government was critical for the egalitarian reforms that have occurred since the turn of the century. In the chapter on the development of social policy regimes in the ISI period, we identified an alternative constellation of power that led to early social policy innovation: in Brazil and Argentina, the presence of strong but politically unincorporated labor movements led to efforts of political elites to co-opt the working class with social policy initiatives.

As we pointed out in chapter 2, power resources theory, the theoretical foundation of our first cluster of power, predicts that inequality and redistribution will be inversely related, the exact opposite of the rational choice–based Meltzer-Richard theory of redistribution (Meltzer and Richard 1981). One reason for this difference is the difference in a basic assumption about political equality. The Meltzer-Richard theory assumes real political equality, that is, that in democracies, all citizens have close to exactly the same influence in the process of governmental decision making. Power resources theory makes the opposite assumption—that, even in a democracy, political resources are asymmetrically distributed, and greater inequality in material resources in society leads to greater inequality in political resources. The second reason for this difference is that we view class interests as socially constructed, while rational choice political economy makes the simplifying assumption that interests can be read off from position in the income distribution. Unions and left parties do not simply mobilize voters; they also shape their opinions and thus shape the distribution of preferences in society. As we pointed out in chapter 2, the basic premise of the Meltzer-Richard theory is implausible. It asserts that a major feature of social structure, the very system of stratification of society, is self-negating. The usual assumption in sociology, political science, and anthropology is that social structures reproduce themselves—from day to day, from year to year, from generation to generation. Inequality today will produce inequality tomorrow, next year, and in the next generation. Even in the most unequal of societies (e.g., Brazil), however, subordinate class organization can change the balance of power in domestic society, provided that the polity is democratic. It is consistent with power resources that the decline in inequality in Latin America since the turn of the century was accomplished by simultaneous decline in market income inequality and an increase in governmental redistribution.

The second cluster of power, the balance of power between the state and civil society, was more important in our explanation of social policy development in Latin America than it was in our explanation of developments in OECD countries (Huber and Stephens 2001a). In the initial years after democratization in Latin America (and Spain), progressive political actors acted with great moderation for fear of provoking renewed military intervention. Only after they became convinced that the military was under civilian control did they dare to propose bolder policies. In an earlier period of social policy development, the state–society power balance also figured strongly in our "Bismarckian co-optation cases," Argentina and Brazil, where state elites acted to co-opt emergent urban working-class forces through the use of incorporative social policy. The bureaucratic-authoritarian government in Brazil followed the same pattern in the 1970s with the establishment of FUNRURAL to confront the threat of rural radicalism.

With regard to the policy-making role of state bureaucrats, we agree that they were generally the immediate authors of state policy, but we argue that they acted within the power constraints of the three clusters of power. To our knowledge, no scholar has even proposed, much less demonstrated, that the differences in long-term trajectories of social policy in a given group of countries (e.g., Latin American, Europe) can be explained by the activities of bureaucrats; indeed, no scholar has ever shown this explanation in quantitative analysis. The studies making far-reaching claims about the influence of bureaucrats tend to be case studies or comparative studies of countries in a restricted time frame in which the structures of power vary little. Broadening the time frame or range of comparative cases (as in our comparison with Iberia) allows us to see how the structures of power restrict the range of options considered by policy-making bureaucrats.

The third cluster of power, transnational structures of power, also figured much more prominently in our explanation of social policy development in Latin America and Iberia than it did in our work on advanced capitalist democracies. During the debt crisis of the 1980s, virtually all Latin American countries sought support packages from the IMF, and most signed on to structural adjustment loans from the World Bank. This activity occurred during the neoliberal Washington Consensus era, and the social policy prescriptions from the IFIs were narrowly targeted transfer programs tied to cuts in total social spending, privatization of pensions—that is, the replacement of public defined benefit pay-as-you-go pensions with statutory funded, individual account, privately administered systems inspired by the Chilean reform under Pinochet— and increasing room for private providers in health and education. In the wake of democratization, civil society actors, stakeholders in the old pension regimes, and parties of varying political colors resisted the neoliberal agenda with varying success in different countries. As the debt crisis receded, a positive agenda of redistributive reform emerged promoted by center-left and left parties and civil society groups, such as the *sanitaristas* in Brazil, in the mid- and late 1990s, but it was only after the turn of the century that this alternative agenda reached full flower, enabled by the accession of left governments to power and a combination of alleviation of the debt burden and the shift of the IFIs, particularly the World Bank, from neoliberalism to a social investment approach to social policy.

Our most similar systems comparison of Portugal and Spain and the four South American countries further demonstrated the importance of transnational structures of power. In 1970, these six countries were very similar in terms of social policy. By 2000, the Iberian countries' social policy regimes were more generous and much more redistributive than those of the four South American countries, and poverty and inequality were much lower. Part of the difference is explained by earlier democratization, greater left strength, and more rapid economic growth in Iberia, but there is no question that position in the world economic and political system explains an important part of the difference. During the 1980s and 1990s, international actors pushed social policy in diametrically opposed directions in the two regions, as the IFIs promoted a neoliberal agenda in Latin America, and the European Union promoted and, after accession, subsidized the development of the European Social Model in Portugal and Spain.

Notes

Chapter 1. Introduction

1. We focus on class inequality. Of course, there are other important dimensions of inequality, most prominently gender and ethnicity. Class inequality, though, is relevant for gender and ethnic inequalities because it aggravates these other dimensions of inequality. Ethnic minorities typically belong to the lower classes, and the greater class inequality, the greater are ethnic disparities. Blofield (2006) has shown how greater class inequality has rendered the pursuit of women-friendly policies on divorce and abortion more difficult.

2. See our discussion in chapter 2 of why this case selection for our comparative historical analysis, which selects cases at one end of the scale on the dependent variable, is not subject to charges of selection bias.

Chapter 2. Theoretical Framework and Methodological Approach

1. For early statements of the power resources approach, also see Korpi (1978) and Stephens (1976). In addition to Korpi and Stephens, Esping-Andersen (1985) and Esping-Andersen and Korpi (1984) are most often associated with the power resource explanation of welfare state development. Other earlier neo-Marxist influenced contributors to power resources theory include Hicks, Friedland, and Johnson (1978) and Friedland (1977). Forerunners include Martin (1973) and Lenski (1966, esp. 316–25). See Shalev (1983) for a review of the early contributions to power resources theory or the "social democratic model," as he calls it. For other recent discussions and revisions of power resources theory, see Korpi (2000) and Brady (2009).

2. The big exceptions here are the National Health Services in Britain and New Zealand, which were implemented under the post–World War II Labour governments and became very popular and thus politically resilient.

3. In 1950, the ratio of GDP per capita (at purchasing power parities) of the richest of these countries, the United States, to the poorest, Japan, was five to one. By 1990, that ratio (now United States to Ireland) was two to one.

4. We say "production related" rather than "economic" because only relationships and activities that are strictly necessary for the production and distribution of goods and services are excluded from this concept of civil society; employers' organizations and unions are part of civil society.

5. For a more elaborate discussion of the social construction of class interests, see Rueschemeyer, Stephens, and Stephens (1992, 51–63).

6. Levitsky and Roberts (2011, 5) take the same position in their conceptualization of left parties at the beginning of the 2000s: "For the purposes of this study, the Left refers to political actors who seek, as a central programmatic objective, to reduce social and economic inequalities." Similarly, Weyland (2010, 5) defines the left "in ideological terms, characterized by the determined pursuit of social equity, justice, and solidarity as an overriding priority." For a discussion of classification procedures of political parties for our quantitative analysis, see chapter 5.

7. Note that APRA in Peru was heavily based on the workforce in the sugar sector in the north of Peru, not on miners, even though Peru was also a mineral-export economy. APRA is also different from the other parties in this category because it was founded and remained dominated by a populist leader, Haya de la Torre.

8. See the related discussion of structural limitation later in the chapter.

9. As noted previously, we (Huber and Stephens 2001a, 3) call the theory developed in Rueschemeyer, Stephens, and Stephens (1992), and Huber and Stephens (2001a), "power constellations theory" to differentiate it from "power resources theory," which focuses entirely on one of our three clusters of power, domestic class relations (see n. 1). Since this excursus focuses on domestic class relations, we refer to the theory as "power resources theory."

10. We say "our version" because social construction of class interests and the accompanying concepts of hegemony and counterhegemony are not central in Korpi's (1978, 1983) version of the theory.

11. In his discussion of the limitations of rational action theory (rational choice), Rueschemeyer (2009, chaps. 2–6) distinguishes not only norms and preferences but also cognition (ignorance and knowledge) and emotions as determinants of social action.

12. For an expanded discussion of social capital, see Rothstein and Uslaner (2005).

13. See chapter 4 for a discussion of the International Adult Literacy Survey.

14. We are adopting the terminology "production regime" from the literature on varieties of capitalism (Hall and Soskice 2001), where it is widely used. It denotes national systems of political economy, or the institutions that govern the behavior of and the relations among governments, firms, and labor.

15. As we point out in the next section, the task for progressive governments in the region in the future is to transcend the current low-wage, low-benefit equilibrium by investing in human capital in order to move up the product cycle in export industries and create a new set of complementarities between more generous social policy and a higher-skill, higher-wage production regime.

16. For recent analyses of emerging models of capitalism in Latin America, see the contributions to Martínez Franzoni, Molyneux, and Sánchez-Ancochea (2009).

17. Haiti and Suriname were dropped because of missing data.

18. Freedman (2008, 15) argues that Goertz is wrong to neglect these negative cases, but his point only holds if one is carrying out the qualitative analysis in the absence of the prior quantitative analysis.

19. Of the case selection strategies outlined by Seawright and Gerring (2008), this comes closest to their extreme case, though "extreme" would not appear to be a good description for five cases out of a universe of eighteen.

20. See Pierson (2003) for an insightful discussion of the pitfalls of focusing on short-term change.

21. As Lieberman (2005, 442) observes, "in a highly structural argument, actors may not be very aware of the circumstances that shape their actions, and so evidence of large-scale processes and events will be more appropriate than in the cases of agent oriented models, in which we would expect evidence of individual-level calculations and deliberate action."

22. By sampling at the high end of the distribution we get this variation, whereas if we had taken a random sample of cases, we would have some cases (e.g., El Salvador, Guatemala) with little variation through time.

23. The reason reviewers give for insisting on a fixed effects specification is that it deals with omitted variable bias. They often ask for a Hausman test in order to demonstrate that it is permissible to employ a random effects specification. This is, of course, an error. A Hausman test simply tells one whether the two estimators are different, not whether one is better. Only if one makes the a priori assumption that fixed effects is the better estimator can one conclude that the test shows whether it is permissible to employ a random effects specification.

Chapter 3. Strategy for Redistribution and Poverty Reduction

1. We made the basic argument of this chapter in a contribution to a volume sponsored by the World Bank (Huber, Pribble, and Stephens 2009). We thank Antonio Estache for comments on our ideas while we were working on that contribution.

2. To calculate the quasi-Gini (ECLAC's 2005 term), income units are ranked according to the size of gross income, and then the income in question is distrib-

uted along this continuum. The index varies from −1 to 1, with −1 indicating that the poorest income group received all of the income of this type, 0 indicating that all income groups received the same amount, and 1 indicating that the richest income group received all of this type of income.

3. Our labels for the class categories are slightly different from those used by Portes and Hoffman (2003).

4. The collection of essays in Blofield (2011) offers a compelling overview of the many obstacles to redistribution in Latin America.

Chapter 4. The Development of Social Policy Regimes in the ISI Period

1. One of the classic studies of the development of social security in Latin America argues that it was driven by pressure groups and power politics (Mesa-Lago 1978). It began with schemes for the military, top-level civil servants, and the judiciary, and was gradually expanded to crucial sectors in the middle and working classes, such as bank workers, teachers, railroad and port workers, miners, and finally middle- and working-class employees in the public and private urban sectors more broadly. This is a largely correct chronology for the pioneer countries, but among the later developers of social security Costa Rica developed a small number of special schemes and a unified health system. Mesa-Lago's work (particularly 1978, 1989, 1994) is fundamental and provides much factual detail on the development of social security schemes. Huber (1996) traces the politics of welfare state development in Argentina, Brazil, Chile, and Costa Rica; Segura-Ubiergo (2007) offers an overall analysis of welfare state development in Latin America and separate discussions of Chile, Argentina, Brazil, and Costa Rica; and Haggard and Kaufman (2008, 79–113) provide a general framework and brief political analyses of the development of welfare policy in the major Latin American countries.

2. In addition to the broadly comparative works cited in note 1, there are a number of important country monographs on which this chapter draws heavily. For Uruguay see Papadópulos (1992), Filgueira (1995), and Castiglioni (2005); for Chile see Borzutzky (2002) and Castiglioni (2005); for Costa Rica see Rosenberg (1979); for Argentina see Isuani (1985); for Brazil see Malloy (1979).

3. By 1934, Uruguay had instituted three of the five programs Hicks examines (pensions, work injury, and unemployment insurance). Hicks's (1999, 53) criteria for classification as an "early program consolidators" among fifteen now-advanced capitalist democracies is that the country has three programs by 1930 and that these programs were "binding and extensive." Uruguay appears to meet the binding and extensive condition for pensions and work injury insurance but possibly not unemployment insurance. In any case, even if it did not qualify for

designation as an "early consolidator," it was more advanced in social policy than about half of the countries Hicks examines.

4. Mesa-Lago also included Cuba in the group of pioneer countries, but the revolution took policy there in a different direction, so we do not include it in our study.

5. These figures are drawn from Mesa-Lago and are somewhat on the high side, because he looks at legal coverage. Other scholars look at actual contributors to social security schemes. Isuani (1985, 95) gives coverage for Argentina in 1970 as 68 percent and Chile as 69 percent, and Papadópulos for Uruguay as somewhat over 80 percent (1992, 55ff.).

6. See chapter 5 for a more detailed discussion of the measurement of the variables and for the data sources.

7. An alternative index adding the two coverage variables, and thus weighing coverage and spending equally, yielded almost identical results in the regression analysis.

8. Typologies employing outcome measures, such as infant mortality rates, yield slightly different clusterings (Martínez Franzoni 2007b; Pribble 2008).

9. Chile is an exception here in that it is characterized by low poverty but relatively high inequality.

10. Pribble (2008) identifies similar groups of countries in her cluster analysis of poverty regimes in Latin America. She distinguishes between risk prevention (through health and education policies) and risk coping (through pension policies). She finds through cluster analysis that around 2000, Argentina, Chile, Costa Rica, and Uruguay were the most advanced countries in both risk prevention and risk coping; Brazil, Mexico, and Panama were high in risk coping but medium in risk prevention; Peru, Colombia, Ecuador, and Paraguay were medium on both indicators; and El Salvador, Guatemala, Nicaragua, and the Dominican Republic were low on both. She explains the paths to these rankings generally with industrialization in the case of risk coping and democracy in the case of risk prevention and develops a nuanced comparative historical analysis that emphasizes different sequencing of regimes and industrialization as determinants of social policy formation.

11. Here "industrial employment" includes mining and quarrying (including oil production), manufacturing, electricity, gas and water, and construction. Segura-Ubiergo (2007, 45) develops an index of left-labor power, based on a principal components factor analysis of four indicators of potential strength of organized labor (value added by the manufacturing sector in 1960, per capita supply of electric energy, percentage of population in urban areas, and small/medium/large informal sector—the last three without specification of the time period). These are very crude indicators, but the index has face validity. Argentina ranks highest on the standardized labor strength index with 100, followed by Chile

with 91 and Uruguay with 82, the next closest being Venezuela with 51, Brazil with 42, and Costa Rica with 38. He then constructs an additive index consisting of his labor strength index and the average percentage of votes received by left and center-left parties in the 1945–79 period (based on Coppedge's coding). On this combined index, Uruguay ranks highest with 128.5, followed closely by Chile with 128 and Argentina with 126; then come Venezuela with 120 and Costa Rica with 90; Brazil falls back to 53.

12. Although there are clear similarities between Cárdenas and Vargas, and Perón, Dion (2010) shows that the innovations in social policy in Mexico actually came in the presidency of Cárdenas's successor, Ávila Camacho.

13. Unfortunately, we have been unable to find any scholarly work covering the historical development of social policy in Panama. Our hypothesis is that the Canal Zone had an effect in part as a result of the high levels of employment of Panamanians in the Zone.

14. Haggard and Kaufman (2008) find weak results for economic development measured as GDP per capita in cross-regional regressions testing for determinants of social expenditure. For Latin America, however, they also argue that the advance of ISI and democracy were the driving forces of welfare state expansion. They do a comprehensive survey of social insurance and services initiatives from 1945 to 1980 and find that "democracies and semi-democracies were more likely than authoritarian governments to undertake a broadening of social insurance and services" (2008, 84). Segura-Ubiergo (2007) examines level of development as measured by GDP per capita and trade openness separately and finds that both of them are associated with stronger welfare state efforts in the period 1973–2000, although not perfectly. He also argues that democracy was an important factor facilitating welfare state development, and he adds the importance of the strength of labor and the left.

15. Unless otherwise noted, the information on the historical development of Uruguay's welfare state is drawn from the detailed study by Papadópulos (1992).

16. As in Argentina, a significant proportion of the population was foreign born and thus excluded from suffrage. Nevertheless, those two countries experienced the first breakthroughs to full formal male democracy in Latin America.

17. Rosenberg (1979, 1981) argues that the project of introducing a social security scheme was actually conceived by President Calderón, who was inspired by Catholic social reformism. The policy-making process was closed, and the communists were not consulted, nor were they the driving force. The law was passed in November 1941, and Calderón did not begin actively to seek worker support until 1942. Rosenberg, however, bases his arguments mostly on interviews with participants close to Calderón, and he does note that the communists themselves took credit for creating the conditions under which social security was introduced. Other accounts (e.g., Molina 2007) give more weight to the role of the communists.

18. Nevertheless, in the 1980s there were nineteen special programs in the public sector (Martínez Franzoni and Mesa-Lago 2003).

19. Bowman (2002) argues convincingly that the abolition of the military by Figueres was crucial for his ability to consolidate democracy because it deprived his opposition of what was perhaps the most effective weapon to overthrow him. Moreover, the elimination of military expenditures freed resources in the longer run for economic and social investment.

20. Malloy (1979, 45) makes essentially the same argument, by "interpreting the beginnings of social insurance policy in Brazil as an elite-designed response to a general political crisis and, more specifically, as an attempt to dampen social protest and weaken radical labor organizers by preempting the ability to define a significant aspect of the 'social question.'" He adds that radical labor leaders saw the legislation in precisely this manner.

21. Unless otherwise noted, this section relies primarily on Malloy (1979) for information on the expansion of social security schemes.

22. We see clear parallel developments in Europe. The groundwork for the Bismarckian welfare state was laid by a conservative political leader, but in response to a militant labor movement (Hicks 1999, chap. 2). Indeed, there is no doubt that some Latin American reformers looked to Europe in their attempts to address the social question.

Chapter 5. The Determinants of Social Spending, Inequality, and Poverty

1. This chapter updates our previous quantitative analyses of social policy, poverty, and inequality in Latin America (Huber et al. 2006; Huber, Mustillo, and Stephens 2008; Pribble, Huber, and Stephens 2009; Huber and Stephens 2009). The present analysis adds additional data beyond 2000 to these previous works and substantially improves on the income inequality data. These publications provide more extensive discussion of the control variables and of the previous literature.

2. To take the example of Mexico, López-Calva and Lustig (2009) report that the ratio of spending per student in tertiary education versus primary education reached a historic high in 1983–88 of 12 to 1 and then dropped to 6 to 1 by the end of the century. By contrast, the same ratio in rich OECD countries is around 2 to 1. Considering that overrepresentation of students from upper-income families in tertiary education is stronger in Latin America than in rich OECD countries, the regressive nature of spending on tertiary education becomes even starker.

3. The data used in this chapter are collected in an updated version of the Huber et al. (2008) data sets, which are available at http://www.unc.edu/~jdsteph/common/data-common.html. The updated version of the data sets will be made available at that web site once the updating is complete.

4. Following Londoño and Székely (1997), we used urban data for Uruguay since (1) it was the only data available; (2) Uruguay is heavily urban; and (3) for the few years in which rural data for Uruguay are available, there are small differences between the Ginis for the urban and rural samples.

5. Precise criteria used in the case of the 2008 data set are available in the Huber et al. (2008) codebook. The new updated codebook contains the criteria used for the updated series. The sources for individual points are indicated by data source variables in the data sets.

6. See Coppedge (1997) for detailed category descriptions; available at www .nd.edu/~mcoppedg/crd/criteria.htm.

7. For a general defense of the validity of expert surveys in assessing party positions, see Hooghe et al. (2010).

8. For details of the party codings, see Huber et al. 2008.

9. Our procedure of tallying seat shares differs from that of Coppedge (1997), who tallied vote shares. We make this choice on the grounds that seat shares are more consequential for policy than vote shares.

10. This is consistent with the cumulative measure of partisan effects in our quantitative analysis of social policy in OECD countries. See Huber, Ragin, and Stephens (1993); Huber and Stephens (2000a, 2001a); Bradley et al. (2003); and Moller et al. (2003).

11. In earlier works, we measured legislative seats and executive using a center-of-gravity score that utilized the full range of left/right party positions (Huber et al. 2006; Huber, Mustillo, and Stephens 2008; Huber and Stephens 2009; Pribble, Huber, and Stephens 2009). We found that the measures described here performed somewhat better than the center-of-gravity scores.

12. A table with the regime codings is available on the authors' web site.

13. For the multivariate analysis, average years of education for the years between the five-year intervals were interpolated.

14. Southern Europe was not included in Iversen and Stephens's (2008) discussion of the IALS data.

15. The income inequality data in these figures are from LIS wave IV, if available; for Chile, from SEDLAC; New Zealand, SWIID; and Portugal, WIID.

16. Hanushek and Woessmann combine scores on math and reading tests of two different studies, one of fourth graders (nine countries) and one of sixth graders (thirteen countries), by rescaling them so that they have comparable means and standard deviations to produce comparable scores for sixteen Latin American countries.

17. Penn World Table Version 6.3 (2009).

18. In these data, the lagged dependent variable explains 98 percent of the variation in the dependent variable.

19. Many scholars of Latin America argue that unequal land distribution explains why income distribution is so unequal in Latin America, and Frankema

(2009) has recently demonstrated this in a cross-regional statistical analysis. Within Latin America, however, there is no great variation in land distribution; the available data show that land inequality is high in all countries. In previous analyses with the few observations available, we found that land inequality was not significantly related to income inequality, so we do not include it here (Huber et al. 2006).

20. Variables are included in this figure if they are significant in two-thirds of the models in which they appear and are correctly signed.

21. Recent literature on the interpretation of main terms in the presence of interaction terms warns that the main term coefficient has limited value because it indicates the effect when the other main term included in the interaction term is 0, which is often a null set (Brambor, Clark, and Golder 2006). In this case, nineteen of our observations have values of 0 on democracy.

22. We contend, however, that market liberalization has had large indirect effects on inequality and poverty in its capacity as part and parcel of the transition from ISI to a trade open economy. See our discussion in the conclusion of this chapter.

23. In this paragraph we are referring to monetary household income both in the cases of poverty and inequality. The inclusion of in-kind use of health services and education would reduce poverty and inequality in all cases, so, again, ceteris paribus, more spending would result in greater reductions of poverty and inequality.

Chapter 6. Neoliberal Reforms and the Turn to Basic Universalism

1. The effects on the South American countries of the 2008 economic crisis that started within the U.S. financial system were surprisingly muted; it is not clear yet how they affected poverty and inequality.

2. Cruz-Saco and Mesa-Lago (1998) and Mesa-Lago (2008) provide extensive and detailed overviews of all the reform processes in social security, both pensions and health. The contributions to Kaufman and Nelson (2004a) analyze reforms in health and education in a large number of countries. Kay and Sinha (2008) offer lessons from the pension reforms.

3. There is a voluminous literature on pension reform in Chile; see, for instance, Barrientos (1998), Mesa-Lago and Arenas de Mesa (1998), Borzutzky (1998), and Kay (1999).

4. Madrid (2003, 127) provides a concise overview of these modifications. Brooks (2009) discusses the financial motives of the reformers.

5. The primary source for this discussion of 1990s reform in education in Argentina is Corrales (2004).

6. The discussion of reforms in Uruguay draws on Kay (1999), Papadópulos (1998), and Castiglioni (2005).

7. The section on Costa Rica draws mainly on Wilson (1998), Clark (2001, 2004), Martínez Franzoni and Mesa-Lago (2003), and Martínez Franzoni (2010).

8. Bresser Pereira (2009) provides an insider's view of economic management under the democratic governments.

9. This discussion draws heavily on Madrid (2003), Weyland (1996), and Kay (1999); see also Brooks (2009). Changes to constitutional provisions require supermajorities of 60 percent in both chambers in two consecutive sessions of each body; moreover, if 10 percent of deputies requested it, specific provisions of a reform bill would be voted on separately and subject to the same constitutional requirements as the entire bill. This made it possible for relatively small groups of opponents to drag out the reform process almost indefinitely and take out the most controversial points (Madrid 2003, 149–50).

10. Cardoso's strong support for these education and health reforms, which had a clear redistributive profile, raises the question whether the Cardoso government should be classified as a center-left rather than a center government. Coppedge classifies his party, the PSDB, as center-left, as we do in the quantitative analysis, but, in the case analysis, we treat the Cardoso government as centrist because center-right parties were included in his cabinet. As noted in the text, the PT was not a possible coalition partner. This is consistent with our handling of Argentina in that we treat the Kirchner governments as center-left governments but do not classify the PJ as center-left. This treatment in turn is consistent with most scholars working on Argentina (e.g., see Levitsky and Roberts 2011).

11. There were some programs of in-kind assistance in most countries; Costa Rica had the most developed system of social assistance, and Brazil introduced limited conditional cash transfers in the 1990s (see below).

12. Mainwaring and Scully (2010b, 370–72) argue that market-oriented economic policies were necessary but not sufficient for economic success, and that the prolonged economic stagnation in the region from 1998 to 2002 shattered the hegemony of the Washington Consensus.

13. Agüero (2006) and Funk (2006) analyze these reforms and their significance. The electoral system is another Pinochet legacy that has not been changed yet, but the reforms made it easier to change; see Alcántara and Ruiz (2006) for an in-depth analysis of electoral institutions and outcomes in post-Pinochet Chile.

14. See Huber, Pribble, and Stephens (2010) for an analysis of economic and social policies and their determinants under Lagos and Bachelet.

15. Sources on the Plan Equidad are Campodonico (2007), Cuenca (2007), Pribble (2008), and Castiglioni (2010).

16. The main source for the Uruguayan health-sector reform is Pribble (2008).

17. The wage councils, which date back to the early 1940s, were abolished by the military government and reestablished under civilian rule.

18. See, e.g., the controversy over inflation figures under the Fernández de Kirchner administration.

19. The following discussion relies heavily on the overview of policy reforms by Niedzwiecki (2010b).

20. Seguro is a misnomer, as this is a noncontributory program. There is also a contributory unemployment insurance for formal-sector workers, but its coverage is highly restricted.

21. This section relies on Haggard and Kaufman (2008), Hunter and Sugiyama (2009b), Hunter (2010), and Kingstone and Ponce (2010).

22. On the basis of an analysis of individual and aggregate data on electoral behavior in Brazil, Zucco (2011) also concludes that Bolsa Família has not been captured by clientelistic machines.

23. The data in both figures are from SEDLAC, and they are the same data that are the basis for López-Calva and Lustig (2009, 2010) and Lustig (2009). Most of the recent data points in our analysis of inequality in chapter 5 come from this source. The poverty data are not the same as the data in our analysis. We use the ECLAC household poverty figures that adjust the poverty line for the cost of a basket of food and nonfood items in each country-year (see chap. 5). The SEDLAC poverty figures are similar to World Bank figures for poverty, which control for overall purchasing power parities but not for the cost of specific items consumed by the poor. The SEDLAC data have the advantage of having more data points and more recent data. Since our focus here is on changes through time within the countries, possible differences in measures between the countries are not of great concern. Both ECLAC and SEDLAC measures are measures of absolute poverty; thus it is possible for poverty to decrease while income distribution is stable if the economy grows in per capita terms, as one can see from the figures for the 1990s for Brazil and Chile in the two figures.

24. According to SEDLAC data (2010), secondary school enrollment in Argentina increased from 63 percent in 1992 to 81 percent in 2000. Although not all of this increase can be attributed to the educational reforms of the period, they certainly contributed to it. In addition, given the large increase in education expenditure (from 3.3 percent to 4.9 percent of GDP, and even greater in absolute terms given the rise in GDP per capita), one can assume that the skill level of the workforce in Argentina after 2002 was greater than ten years earlier.

25. Dion (2009) and Hunter and Sugiyama (2009b) make similar arguments with regard to Latin American social policy reforms.

26. In Brazil, as in Argentina, federalism entails a high degree of fiscal decentralization. In 1995, Brazilian states accounted for 28 percent of all public expenditures and municipalities for 16 percent. Less than 60 percent of fed-

eral transfers to states and municipalities were tied to specific purposes; some 30 percent were tied to health and education but not to specific programs (Samuels and Mainwaring 2004, 95–96). This decentralization makes it difficult for the federal government to ensure implementation of policies oriented by basic universalism.

27. Of course, veto points are also obstacles to neoliberal changes, as in the case of the Uruguayan pension reform. They are favorable for maintenance of the status quo.

28. This view has been challenged, and there is a vigorous debate about the trajectory of the Brazilian party system. Lucas and Samuels (2010) offer an overview of this debate and argue that the PT remains an exception; no other party can claim more than 5 percent of voters as partisans, and the positions of the other three main parties do not differ systematically from each other so as to offer the voters an ideologically differentiated set of choices.

Chapter 7. Iberia and the Advanced Latin American Social Policy Regimes

1. The unequal distribution of assets in Spain at that point (see below) and the fact that the tax system was weak and regressive by the time of the transition cast doubt on the validity of the 1973 Gini coefficient. The capitalist authoritarian countries that had relatively equal income distributions were Korea and Taiwan, both of which had carried out land reforms and invested heavily in primary and secondary education.

2. Stepan (1988, 122) compares the degree of military prerogatives and of military contestation in Argentina, Brazil, Uruguay, and Spain, and he shows that by 1987 Spain had established by far the strongest civilian control over the military among these countries. Chile of course was still under military rule at that point.

3. Data on union density are notoriously questionable with regard to reliability and comparability. The data for Portugal and Spain come from Nickell and Nunziata (2001), who cite Ebbinghaus and Visser (2000), and those for Latin America from Roberts (2002), who cites various ILO, U.S. government, and Latin American governmental sources.

4. It is not clear-cut how one should classify the PSD. As Fishman (2010) argues, the revolution shifted the entire political spectrum to the left. So, compared to the right in Spain, for instance, the PSD is much more centrist, but within the Portuguese political space the PSD takes positions to the right of the Socialists and represents the better-off sectors of Portuguese society, so a center/center-right classification seems more accurate. The health-sector reform is a case in point illustrating a nonright position of the PSD.

5. This discussion draws heavily on Arriba and Moreno (2005), Guillén (1992, 2010), Guillén, Álvarez, and Adão e Silva (2003), and Royo (2000).

6. The discussion of the Portuguese case relies heavily on Adão e Silva (2009), Capucha et al. (2005), Silva Lopes (2003), Guillén (2002), and Guillén, Álvarez, and Adão e Silva (2003).

Chapter 8. Conclusion

1. This is the subtitle of the World Bank study of inequality in Latin America by Ferranti et al. (2004).

2. We are not arguing that workers were the decisive electoral support base. In Uruguay, a large percentage of the urban workforce were immigrants and not even able to vote, and in both countries the urban middle classes were important support bases for these reformist presidents also, but workers contributed to the electoral victories.

3. Schneider (2004, 209ff.) argues that business associations in Chile were much stronger than in Argentina and Brazil and made greater contributions to economic governance and democratic governability. By the same token, this greater organizational strength made business a more formidable opponent of reforms in social policy that the business community perceived as affecting its interests negatively.

4. See http://prontus.ivn.cl/cambio21/site/artic/20110107/pags/20110107194058 .html.

5. Venezuela is the exception in this group in terms of longevity of democracy. The formerly consolidated party system broke down (Morgan 2011), however, and Chávez essentially stepped into a power vacuum and created his own political machine. The inclusion of Ortega's government in Nicaragua might be contested, because it appears that the ideological commitments of the FSLN were weakened under his leadership.

6. They have variously been labeled as populist (Panizza 2005; Castañeda 2006), radical/constituent (Luna 2010), and contestatory (Weyland 2010). Levitsky and Roberts (2011) also distinguish between established party organizations and new parties or movements, and they further distinguish among these newer lefts on the basis of the concentration of power—concentrated in the hands of the leader in the populist cases (Chávez and Correa), versus resting in social movements to which the leader remains accountable in the cases of the movement-based left (Morales). Thus, they do not use policy orientation as a classification criterion. Beasley-Murray, Cameron, and Hershberg (2010, 9) argue against the use of dichotomies on the grounds that "dichotomizing the left into radical populists and social democrats conveniently reproduces the old cleavage

between revolution and reform within the new context of democracy and global-ization." Our interest is not so much in coming up with a classification as in un-derstanding differences in policy orientation and their likely consequences for long-run success in the construction of redistributive policy regimes.

7. Corrales (2010), and Corrales and Penfold-Becerra (2007) label the regime as competitive authoritarian.

8. As with any generalization, there are exceptions. The key exception here is Cárdenas in Mexico.

References

Acemoglu, Daron, and James A. Robinson. 2006. *Economic Origins of Dictatorship and Democracy*. New York: Cambridge University Press.
———. 2008. "Persistence of Power, Elites, and Institutions." *American Economic Review* 98 (1): 267–93.
Achen, Christopher. 2000. "Why Lagged Dependent Variables Can Suppress the Explanatory Power of Other Independent Variables." Paper presented at the annual meeting of the Society for Political Methodology, UCLA.
Adão e Silva, Pedro. 2009. "Waving the European Flag in a Southern European Welfare State: Factors behind Domestic Compliance with European Social Policy in Portugal." Ph.D. dissertation. Florence, Italy: Department of Political and Social Sciences, European University Institute.
———. 2010. "Protecting the Unemployed in Portugal: Recent Trends with Special Focus on Precarious Market Participation." Paper prepared for the seminar "Social Protection and Labour Markets: Latin America and Southern Europe Compared." Torino, May 20.
Agüero, Felipe. 2006. Democracia, gobierno y militares desde el cambio de siglo: Avances hacia la normalidad democrática. In *El gobierno de Ricardo Lagos*, edited by Robert L. Funk, 49–68. Santiago, Chile: Universidad Diego Portales.
Ahmad, Ehtisham, Jean Dréze, John Hills, and Amartya Sen, eds. 1991. *Social Security in Developing Countries*. New York: Oxford University Press.
Alcántara Sáez, Manuel, and Cristina Rivas. 2006. "The Left–Right Dimension in Latin American Party Politics." Paper delivered at the annual meeting of the American Political Science Association.
Alcántara Sáez, Manuel, and Leticia M. Ruiz-Rodríguez. 2006. "Instituciones y elecciones en Chile." In *Chile: Política y modernización democrática*, edited by Manuel Alcántara Sáez and Leticia M. Ruiz-Rodríguez, 13–33. Barcelona: Ediciones Bellaterra.

Alderson, Arthur S., and François Nielsen. 1999. "Income Inequality, Development, and Dependence: A Reconsideration." *American Sociological Review* 64 (4): 606–31.

Alesina, Alberto, and Dani Rodrik. 1994. "Distributive Politics and Economic Growth." *Quarterly Journal of Economics* 109 (2) (May 1): 465–90.

Alvarez, Michael, Antonio Cheibub, Fernando Limongi, and Adam Przeworski. 1996. "Classifying Political Regimes." *Studies in Comparative International Development* 31: 3–36.

Amarante, Veronica, Rodrigo Arim, Gioia de Melo, and Andrea Vigorito. 2009. "Family Allowances and Child School Attendance: An Ex-Ante Evaluation of Alternative Schemes in Uruguay." Montevideo: Universidad de la Republica.

Ames, Barry. 2001. *The Deadlock of Democracy in Brazil*. Ann Arbor: University of Michigan Press.

Anria, Santiago. 2010. "Bolivia's MAS: Between Party and Movement." In Maxwell A. Cameron, ed., *Latin America's Left Turns: Politics, Policies, and Trajectories of Change*, 101–26. Boulder, CO: Lynne Rienner.

Anria, Santiago, and Sara Niedzwiecki.2011. "Social Movements and Social Policy: The Case of the Renta Dignidad." Unpublished paper. Department of Political Science, University of North Carolina at Chapel Hill.

Araújo Teixeira, Zuleide. 2009. Consenso progresista desde el Sur. In *Consenso progresista: Las políticas sociales de los gobiernos progresistas del Cono Sur*, edited by Yesko Quiroga, Agustín Canzani, and Jaime Ensignia, 47–84. Santiago, Chile: Fundación Friedrich Ebert.

Arretche, Marta. 2004. Toward a Unified and More Equitable System: Health Reform in Brazil. In *Crucial Needs, Weak Incentives: Social Sector Reform, Democratization, and Globalization in Latin America*, edited by Robert R. Kaufman and Joan M. Nelson, 155–88. Baltimore: Johns Hopkins University Press.

Arriba, Ana, and Luis Moreno. 2005. "Spain: Poverty, Social exclusion, and Safety Nets." In *Welfare State Reform in Southern Europe*, edited by Maurizio Ferrera, 110–62. London: Routledge.

Arza, Camila. 2009. "Back to the State: Pension Fund Nationalization in Argentina." Ciepp: Centro Interdisciplinatio para el Estudio de Politicas Publicas, December.

Balmaseda, Manuel, and Miguel Sebastián. 2003. "Spain in the EU: Fifteen Years May Not Be Enough." *South European Society and Politics* 8 (1): 195–230.

Barahona, Manuel, Ludwig G. Guendell, and Carlos Castro. 2005. *Política social y reforma social "a la tica": Un caso paradigmático de heterodoxia en el contexto de una economía periférica*. Geneva: United Nations Research Institute for Social Development.

Barreix, Alberto, Martin Bes, and Jeronimo Roca. 2009. *Equidad fiscal en Cen-*

troamerica, Panama y Republica Dominicana. Washington, DC: BID-Euro Social.

Barrientos, Armando. 1998. *Pension Reform in Latin America.* Aldershot, UK: Ashgate.

Barro, Robert J. 1991. "Economic Growth in a Cross Section of Countries." *Quarterly Journal of Economics* 106 (2): 407–43.

———. 1997. *Determinants of Economic Growth: A Cross-Country Empirical Study.* Cambridge: MIT Press.

Barro, Robert, and Jong-Wha Lee. 2010. *International Data on Educational Attainment: Updates and Implications.* http://www.cid.harvard.edu/ciddata/cid data.html.

Barros, Ricardo, Mirela de Carvalho, Samuel Franco, and Rosane Mendonça. 2010. "Markets, the State, and the Dynamics of Inequality." In *Declining Inequality in Latin America: A Decade of Progress?* edited by Luis F. López-Calva and Nora Lustig, 134–74. Washington, DC: Brookings Institution Press.

Bartolini, Stefano. 2000. *The Political Mobilization of the European Left, 1860–1980: The Class Cleavage.* New York: Cambridge University Press.

Beasley-Murray, Jon, Maxwell A. Cameron, and Eric Hershberg. 2010. "Latin America's Left Turns: A Tour d'Horizon." In *Latin America's Left Turns: Politics, Policies and Trajectories of Change,* edited by Maxwell A. Cameron and Eric Hershberg, 1–20. Boulder, CO: Lynne Rienner.

Beck, Nathaniel, and Jonathan N. Katz. 1995. "What to Do (and Not to Do) with Time-Series Cross-Section Data." *American Political Science Review* 89 (3): 634–47.

———. 1996. "Nuisance vs. Substance: Specifying and Estimating Time-Series-Cross-Section Models." *Political Analysis* 6 (1) (January): 1–36.

———. 2004. "Times-Series-Cross-Section Issues: Dynamics, 2004." Unpublished paper. New York University.

Bermeo, Nancy Gina, ed. 2001. *Unemployment in the New Europe.* New York: Cambridge University Press.

Blofield, Merike. 2006. *The Politics of Moral Sin: Abortion and Divorce in Spain, Chile and Argentina.* New York: Routledge.

———, ed. 2011. *The Great Gap: Inequality and the Politics of Redistribution in Latin America.* University Park: Penn State University Press.

Blofield, Merike, and Juan Pablo Luna. 2011. "Public Opinion on Income Inequalities in Latin America." In *The Great Gap: Inequality and the Politics of Redistribution in Latin America,* edited by Merike Blofield, 147–81. University Park: Penn State University Press.

Blyde, Juan, and Eduardo Fernandez-Arias. 2004. *Economic Growth in the Southern Cone.* Washington, DC: Inter-American Development Bank, Regional Operations Dept. 1.

Bogliaccini, Juan. 2009. "The Effect of Liberalization Policies on Inequality in Latin America." Paper presented at the Latin American Studies Association (LASA) Conference. Rio de Janeiro, Brazil.

———. Forthcoming. "Trade Liberalization, Deindustrialization and Inequality: Evidence from Latin American Middle-Income Countries." *Latin American Research Review.*

Boix, Carles. 2003. *Democracy and Redistribution.* New York: Cambridge University Press.

Bollen, Kenneth A., and Robert W. Jackman. 1985. "Political Democracy and the Size Distribution of Income." *American Sociological Review* 50 (4): 438–57.

Bonoli, Giuliano, and André Mach. 2000. "Switzerland: Adjustment Politics with Institutional Constraints." In *Welfare and Work in the Open Economy. Volume II. Diverse Responses to Common Challenges,* edited by Fritz W. Scharpf and Vivien A. Schmidt, 131–74. New York: Oxford University Press.

Bonvecchi, Alejandro, and Agustina Giraudy. 2007. "Argentina: Crecimiento económico y concentración del poder institucional." *Revista de Ciencia Política* (Santiago) 27: 29–42.

Bornschier, Volker, and Christopher K. Chase-Dunn. 1985. *Transnational Corporations and Underdevelopment.* New York: Praeger.

Borzutzky, Silvia. 1998. "Chile: The Politics of Privatization." In *Do Options Exist? The Reform of Pension and Health Care Systems in Latin America,* edited by María Amparo Cruz-Saco and Carmelo Mesa-Lago, 35–55. Pittsburgh: University of Pittsburgh Press.

———. 2002. *Vital Connections: Politics, Social Security, and Inequality in Chile.* Notre Dame, IN: University of Notre Dame Press.

Bourguignon, Francois. 2002. "The Growth Elasticity of Poverty Reduction: Explaining Heterogeneity across Countries and Time Periods." In *Growth and Inequality,* edited by T. Eichler and S. Turnovsky. Cambridge: MIT Press.

Bowman, Kirk S. 2002. *Militarization, Democracy, and Development: The Perils of Praetorianism in Latin America.* University Park: Penn State University Press.

Bradley, David, Evelyne Huber, Stephanie Moller, François Nielsen, and John D. Stephens. 2003. "Distribution and Redistribution in Postindustrial Democracies." *World Politics* 55 (2) (January): 193–228.

Brady, David. 2009. *Rich Democracies, Poor People: How Politics Explain Poverty.* New York: Oxford University Press.

Brady, Henry E., and David Collier. 2004. *Rethinking Social Inquiry: Diverse Tools, Shared Standards.* Lanham, MD: Rowman and Littlefield.

Brambor, Thomas, William Roberts Clark, and Matt Golder. 2006. "Understanding Interaction Models: Improving Empirical Analyses." *Political Analysis* 14 (1): 63–82.

Bresser Pereira, Luiz Carlos. 2009. *Developing Brazil: Overcoming the Failure of the Washington Consensus.* Boulder, CO: Lynne Rienner.

Brooks, Sarah Marie. 2009. *Social Protection and the Market in Latin America: The Transformation of Social Security Institutions.* New York: Cambridge University Press.

Brown, David S., and Wendy Hunter. 1999. "Democracy and Social Spending in Latin America, 1980–92." *American Political Science Review* 93 (4) (December): 779–90.

———. 2004. "Democracy and Human Capital Formation: Education Spending in Latin America, 1980 to 1997." *Comparative Political Studies* 37 (7): 842–64.

Buchanan, Paul G., and Kate Nicholls. 2003. *Labour Politics in Small Open Democracies: Australia, Chile, Ireland, New Zealand, and Uruguay.* New York: Palgrave Macmillan.

Bucheli, Marisa, Alvaro Forteza, and Ianina Rossi. 2007. "Work History and the Access to Contributory Pensions: The Case of Uruguay." *SSRN eLibrary* (October). Http://papers.ssrn.com/sol3/papers.cfm?abstract_id=1625308.

Burgess, Katrina. 2004. *Parties and Unions in the New Global Economy.* Pittsburgh: University of Pittsburgh Press.

Burkhart, Ross E. 1997. "Comparative Democracy and Income Distribution: Shape and Direction of the Causal Arrow." *Journal of Politics* 59 (1): 148–64.

Calvo, Ernesto, and Maria Victoria Murillo. 2004. "Who Delivers? Partisan Clients in the Argentine Electoral Market." *American Journal of Political Science* 48 (4): 742–57.

Cameron, David R. 1978. "The Expansion of the Public Economy: A Comparative Analysis." *American Political Science Review* 72 (4): 1243–61.

Campodónico, M. 2007. "Bajan edad para cobro de pension a la vejez." *Diario el Observador,* December.

Capucha, Luis, Teresa Bomba, Rita Fernandes, and Gisela Matos. 2005. "Portugal: A Virtuous Path towards Minimum Income." In *Welfare State Reform in Southern Europe,* edited by Maurizio Ferrera, 204–65. London: Routledge.

Cardoso, Fernando Henrique. 2009. "New Paths: Globalization in Historical Perspective." *Studies in Comparative International Development* 44 (4): 296–317.

Carey, John M. 1996. *Term Limits and Legislative Representation.* New York: Cambridge University Press.

Casas, Antonio, and Herman Vargas. 1980. "The Health System in Costa Rica: Toward a National Health Service." *Journal of Public Health Policy* 1 (3): 258–79.

Castañeda, Jorge G. 2006. "Latin America's Left Turn." *Foreign Affairs* 85 (May):28–43.

Castiglioni, Rossana. 2005. *The Politics of Social Policy Change in Chile and Uruguay: Retrenchment versus Maintenance, 1973–1998*. New York: Routledge.

———. 2010. *Las políticas sociales de la nueva (vieja) izquierda uruguaya*. Gobernabilidad Democrática y la "Nueva Izquierda." Washington, DC: Woodrow Wilson International Center for Scholars (Latin American Program).

Castles, Francis. 1982. *The Impact of Parties*. Beverly Hills, CA: Sage Publications.

———. 1999. "Decentralization and the Post-War Political Economy." *European Journal of Political Research* 36 (1): 27–53.

Castles, Francis, and Peter Mair. 1984. "Left–Right Political Scales: Some 'Expert' Judgments." *European Journal of Political Research* (12): 73–88.

Castro, Mauricio M., and Juliana Martínez Franzoni. 2010. "Un modelo social extitoso en la encrucijada: Limites del desencuentro entre el regimen laboral y el bienestar en Costa Rica." *Revista Centroamericana de Ciencias Sociales* 7 (1): 79–122.

Chinn, Menzie, and Hiro Ito. 2008. "A New Measure of Financial Openness." *Journal of Comparative Policy Analysis* 10 (3): 309–22.

Clark, Mary A. 2001. *Gradual Economic Reform in Latin America: The Costa Rican Experience*. Albany: State University of New York Press.

———. 2004. "Health Sector Reform in Costa Rica: Reinforcing a Public System." In *Crucial Needs, Weak Incentives: Social Sector Reform, Democratization, and Globalization in Latin America*, edited by Robert R. Kaufman and Joan M. Nelson, 189–216. Baltimore: Johns Hopkins University Press.

Collier, David, Henry E. Brady, and Jason Seawright. 2004. "Critiques, Responses, and Trade-Offs: Drawing Together the Debate." In *Rethinking Social Inquiry: Diverse Tools, Shared Standards*, edited by Henry E. Brady and David Collier, 195–228. Lanham, MD: Rowman and Littlefield.

Collier, David, James Mahoney, and Jason Seawright. 2004. "Claiming Too Much: Warnings about Selection Bias." In *Rethinking Social Inquiry: Diverse Tools, Shared Standards*, 85–102. Lanham, MD: Rowman and Littlefield.

Collier, Ruth Berins, and David Collier. 1991. *Shaping the Political Arena: Critical Junctures, the Labor Movement, and Regime Dynamics in Latin America*. Notre Dame, IN: University of Notre Dame Press.

Colomer, Josep M., and Luis E. Escatel. 2004. "The Left–Right Dimension in Latin America." Working Paper SDTEP 165. Mexico City: Centro de Investigación y Docencia Económicas.

Cominetti, Rossella. 1996. "Social Expenditure in Latin America: An Update." Santiago, Chile: CEPAL Technical Department.

Conference on Social Policies in the 1980s, and Organisation for Economic Co-operation and Development (OECD). 1981. *The Welfare State in Crisis: An Account of the Conference on Social Policies in the 1980s, OECD, Paris,*

20–23 October 1981 [i.e. 1980]. Paris: OECD Publications and Information Center [distributor].

Coppedge, Michael. 1997. *A Classification of Latin American Political Parties.* Helen Kellogg Institute for International Studies, University of Notre Dame.

Corrales, Javier. 2002. *Presidents without Parties: The Politics of Economic Reform in Argentina and Venezuela in the 1990s.* University Park: Penn State University Press.

———. 2004. "Multiple Preferences, Variable Strengths: The Politics of Education Reforms in Argentina." In *Crucial Needs, Weak Incentives: Social Sector Reform, Democratization, and Globalization in Latin America,* edited by Robert R. Kaufman and Joan M. Nelson, 315–49. Baltimore: Johns Hopkins University Press.

———. 2010. "The Repeating Revolution: Chavez's New Politics and Old Economics." In *Leftist Governments in Latin America: Successes and Shortcomings,* edited by Kurt Weyland, Raúl L. Madrid, and Wendy Hunter, 28–56. New York: Cambridge University Press.

Corrales, Javier, and Michael Penfold-Becerra. 2007. "Venezuela: Crowding Out the Opposition." *Journal of Democracy* 18 (2): 99–113.

Cott, Donna Lee van. 2000. *The Friendly Liquidation of the Past: The Politics of Diversity in Latin America.* Pittsburgh, PA: University of Pittsburgh Press.

Cox, Cristián. 2003. "Las políticas educacionales de Chile en las últimas dos décadas del siglo XX." In *Las políticas educacionales en el Cambio de Siglo,* edited by Cristián Cox. Santiago, Chile: Editorial Universitaria.

———. 2006. "Policy Formation and Implementation in Secondary Education Reform: The Case of Chile at the Turn of the Century." Education Working Paper No. 3. Washington, DC: World Bank.

Crenshaw, Edward. 1992. "Cross-National Determinants of Income Inequality: A Replication and Extension Using Ecological-Evolutionary Theory." *Social Forces* 71 (2): 339–63.

Cruz-Saco, Maria Amparo, and Carmelo Mesa-Lago. 1998. "Conclusion: Conditioning Factors, Cross-Country Comparisons, and Recommendations." In *Do Options Exist? The Reform of Pension and Health Care Systems in Latin America,* edited by María Amparo Cruz-Saco and Carmelo Mesa-Lago. Pittsburgh, PA: University of Pittsburgh Press.

Cuenca, A. 2007. "Plan de equidad subsidiará agua y luz de hogares pobres." *Diario el Observador,* December 13.

Cusack, Thomas R., and Susanne Fuchs. 2002. "Documentation Notes for Parties, Governments, and Legislatures Data Set." Wissenschaftszentrum Berlin.

Dávila, Mireya. 2005. "Health Reform in Contemporary Chile: Does Politics Matter?" Ph.D. dissertation. Chapel Hill: University of North Carolina at Chapel Hill.

Deininger, Klaus, and Lyn Squire. 1996. "A New Data Set Measuring Income In-equality." *World Bank Economic Review* 10 (3): 565–91.

Dion, Michelle. 2009. "Globalization, Democracy, and Mexican Welfare, 1988–2006." *Comparative Politics* 42 (1): 63–82.

———. 2010. *Workers and Welfare: Comparative Institutional Change in Twentieth-Century Mexico*. Pittsburgh, PA: University of Pittsburgh Press.

Draibe, Sônia. 2004. "Social Policy Reform." In *Reforming Brazil*, edited by Mauricio A. Font, Anthony Peter Spanakos, and Cristina Bordin, 71–92. Lanham, MD: Lexington Books.

Drake, Paul W. 1978a. "Corporatism and Functionalism in Modern Chilean Pol-itics." *Journal of Latin American Studies* 10 (1): 83–116.

———. 1978b. *Socialism and Populism in Chile, 1932–52*. Urbana: University of Illinois Press.

———. 1996. *Labor Movements and Dictatorships*. Baltimore: Johns Hopkins University Press.

Duverger, Maurice. 1954. *Political Parties, Their Organization and Activity in the Modern State*. New York: Wiley.

Ebbinghaus, Bernhard, and Jelle Visser. 2000. *Trade Unions in Western Europe since 1945*. London: Grove's Dictionaries.

Eberhard, Juan, and Eduardo Engel. 2009. "The Educational Transition and Decreasing Wage Inequality in Chile." United Nations Development Pro-gramme: Regional Bureau for Latin America and the Caribbean.

ECLAC [Economic Commission on Latin America and the Caribbean]. 1999. *Social Panorama of Latin America 1999–2000*. Santiago, Chile: United Na-tions Economic Commission for Latin America and the Caribbean.

———. 2002. *Social Panorama of Latin America*. Santiago, Chile: United Nations Economic Commission for Latin America and the Caribbean.

———. 2004. *Social Panorama of Latin America*. Santiago, Chile: United Nations Economic Commission for Latin America and the Caribbean.

———. 2005. *Panorama social de America Latina*. Santiago, Chile: United Na-tions Economic Commission on Latin America and the Caribbean.

———. 2007. *Social Panorama of Latin America*. Santiago, Chile: United Nations Economic Commission on Latin America and the Caribbean.

———. 2010. *Economic Survey of Latin America and the Caribbean: The Distrib-utive Impact of Public Policies*. Santiago, Chile: United Nations Publication.

———. Various years. *Statistical Yearbook on Latin America and the Caribbean*. Santiago, Chile: United Nations Economic Commission on Latin America and the Caribbean.

Ellner, Steve. 2008. *Rethinking Venezuelan Politics: Class, Conflict, and the Chávez Phenomenon*. Boulder, CO: Lynne Rienner.

Elster, Jon. 1985. *Making Sense of Marx*. New York: Cambridge University Press.

Encarnación, Omar Guillermo. 2008a. "Reconciliation after Democratization: Coping with the Past in Spain." *Political Science Quarterly* 123 (3): 435–60.

———. 2008b. *Spanish Politics: Democracy after Dictatorship.* Cambridge, UK: Polity Press.

Escaith, Hubert, and Igor Paunovic. 2004. "Reformas estructurales en América Latina y el Caribe en el periodo 1970–2000: Indices y notas metodológicas." Economic Commission for Latin America and the Caribbean (ECLAC).

Esping-Andersen, Gøsta. 1985. *Politics against Markets: The Social Democratic Road to Power.* Princeton, NJ: Princeton University Press.

———. 1990. *The Three Worlds of Welfare Capitalism.* Princeton, NJ: Princeton University Press.

Esping-Andersen, Gøsta, and Walter Korpi. 1984. "Social Policy as Class Politics in Post-War Capitalism: Scandinavia, Austria, and Germany." In *Order and Conflict in Contemporary Capitalism: Studies in the Political Economy of Western European Nations,* edited by John Goldthorpe, 179–208. Oxford: Oxford University Press.

Espinosa, Consuelo, Marcelo Tokman, and Jorge Rodriguez Cabello. 2005. "Finanzas publicas de la reforma." In *Reforma de la salud en Chile: Desafíos en la implementación.* Santiago: Universidad de Andres Bello.

Estado de la Nación. 2009. *Decimoquinto informe estado de la nación en desarrollo humano sostenible.* Pavas, Costa Rica: Programa Estado de la Nación.

Estevez-Abe, Margarita, Torben Iversen, and David Soskice. 2001. "Social Protection and the Formation of Skills: A Reinterpretation of the Welfare State." In *Varieties of Capitalism: The Institutional Foundations of Comparative Advantage,* edited by Peter A. Hall and David Soskice, 145–83. New York: Oxford University Press.

Etchemendy, Sebastián, and Ruth Berins Collier. 2007. "Down but Not Out: Union Resurgence and Segmented Neocorporatism in Argentina (2003–2007)." *Politics and Society* 35 (3): 363–401.

Evans, Peter B. 2008. "In Search of the 21st Century Developmental State." Centre for Global Political Economy, University of Sussex.

Evans, Peter B., and Michael Timberlake. 1980. "Dependence, Inequality, and the Growth of the Tertiary: A Comparative Analysis of Less Developed Countries." *American Sociological Review* 45 (4): 531–52.

Ewig, Christina. 2010. "Health Policy and the Historical Reproduction of Class, Race, and Gender Inequality in Peru." In *Indelible Inequalities in Latin America: Insights from History, Politics, and Culture,* edited by Paul Gootenberg and Luis Reygadas, 53–80. Durham, NC: Duke University Press.

Fairfield, Tasha. 2010a. "Business Power and Tax Reform: Taxing Income and Profits in Chile and Argentina." *Latin American Politics and Society* 52: 37–71.

———. 2010b. "Taxation and Inequality in Modern Latin America." Paper presented at the annual meeting of the American Political Science Association.

Fearon, James, and David Laitin. 2008. "Integrating Qualitative and Quantitative Methods." In *The Oxford Handbook of Political Methodology*, edited by Janet Box-Steffensmeier, Henry Brady, and David Collier, 756–78. Oxford: Oxford University Press.

Fenwick, Tracy B. 2009. "Avoiding Governors: The Success of Bolsa Família." *Latin American Research Review* 44 (1): 102–31.

Ferranti, David M. de, Guillermo E. Perry, Francisco H.G. Ferreira, and Michael Walton. 2004. *Inequality in Latin America: Breaking with History?* Washington, DC: World Bank Publications.

Ferrera, Maurizio. 1996. "The 'Southern Model' of Welfare in Social Europe." *Journal of European Social Policy* 6 (1): 17–37.

———. 2005. *The Boundaries of Welfare: European Integration and the New Spatial Politics of Social Protection*. Oxford: Oxford University Press.

Filgueira, Carlos, and Fernando Filgueira. 2002. "Models of Welfare and Models of Capitalism: The Limits of Transferability." In *Models of Capitalism: Lessons for Latin America*, edited by Evelyne Huber, 127–58. University Park: Penn State University Press.

Filgueira, Fernando. 1995. *A Century of Social Welfare in Uruguay: Growth to the Limit of the Batllista Social State*. Notre Dame, IN: University of Notre Dame Helen Kellogg Institute for International Studies.

———. 2005. "Welfare and Democracy in Latin America: The Development, Crises and Aftermath of Universal, Dual and Exclusionary Social States." Paper prepared for the UNRISD Project on Social Policy and Democratization.

Filgueira, Fernando, Luis Reygadas, Juan Pablo Luna, and Pablo Alegre. 2011. "Shallow States, Deep Inequalities, and the Limits of Conservative Modernization: The Politics and Policies of Incorporation in Latin America." In *The Great Gap: Inequality and the Politics of Redistribution in Latin America*, edited by Merike Blofield, 245–77. University Park: Penn State University Press.

Finch, M. H. J. (Martin Henry John). 1981. *A Political Economy of Uruguay since 1870*. New York: St. Martin's Press.

Fishman, Robert M. 2010. "Rethinking the Iberian Transformations: How Democratization Scenarios Shaped Labor Market Outcomes." *Studies in Comparative International Development* 45 (3): 281–310.

———. 2011. "Democratic Practice after the Revolution: The Case of Portugal and Beyond." *Politics and Society* 39 (2): 233–67.

Font, Mauricio A., Anthony Peter Spanakos, and Cristina Bordin, eds. 2004. *Reforming Brazil*. Lanham, MD: Lexington Books.

Forteza, Alvaro, and Ianina Rossi. 2009. "The Contribution of Government Transfer Programs to Inequality: A Net-Benefit Approach." *Journal of Applied Economics* 12 (1): 55–67.

Frankema, Ewout. 2009. *Has Latin America Always Been Unequal? A Compar-*

ative Study of Asset and Income Inequality in the Long Twentieth Century. Boston: Brill.

Freedman, David A. 2008. "Rejoinder." *Qualitative and Multi-Method Research* 6 (2): 14–16.

Friedland, Roger. 1977. "Class Power and the City." Ph.D. dissertation. University of Wisconsin.

Fuentes, Claudio. 2004. *El costo de la democracia.* FLACSO-Chile. Santiago.

Funk, Robert L. 2006. "¿Un destape chileno? Reformas políticas y cambio social durante el gobierno de Ricardo Lagos." In *El gobierno de Ricardo Lagos*, edited by Robert L. Funk, 27–48. Santiago, Chile: Universidad Diego Portales.

Galasso, Emanuela. 2006. "With Their Effort and One Opportunity: Alleviating Extreme Poverty in Chile." Washington, DC: Inter-American Development Bank. http://www.iadb.org/res/publications/pubfiles/pubS-001.pdf.

Garretón, Manuel Antonio. 2005. "Coping with Opacity: The Financing of Politics in Chile." In *The Financing of Politics: Latin American and European Perspectives*, edited by Eduardo Posada-Carbo and Carlos Malamud, 160–68. London: Institute for the Study of the Americas.

Gasparini, Leonardo, and Guillermo Cruces. 2010. "A Distribution in Motion: The Case of Argentina." In *Declining Inequality in Latin America: A Decade of Progress?* edited by Luis F. López-Calva and Nora Lustig, 100–133. Washington, DC: Brookings Institution Press.

Geddes, Barbara. 1991. "Paradigms and Sand Castles in Comparative Politics of Developing Areas." In *Political Science: Looking to the Future*, edited by William Crotty, 2:45–76. Evanston, IL: Northwestern University Press.

Gibson, Edward L. 1997. "The Populist Road to Market Reform: Policy and Electoral Coalitions in Argentina and Mexico." *World Politics* 49 (3): 339–70.

Giddens, Anthony. 1973. *The Class Structure of Advanced Societies.* London: Hutchinson.

Giraudy, Agustina. 2007. "The Distributive Politics of Emergency Employment Programs in Argentina (1993–2002)." *Latin American Research Review* 42 (2): 33–55.

———. 2009. "Subnational Undemocratic Regime Continuity after Democratization: Argentina and Mexico in Comparative Perspective." Ph.D. dissertation. Chapel Hill: University of North Carolina.

Goertz, Gary. 2008. "Choosing Cases for Case Studies: A Qualitative Logic." *Qualitative and Multi-Method Research* 6 (2): 11–14.

Gómez-Sabaini, Juan Carlos. 2006. *Cohesión social, equidad y tributación.* Santiago, Chile: United Nations.

Goñi, Edwin, Humberto López, and Luis Servén. 2008. "Fiscal Redistribution and Income Inequality in Latin America." World Bank Policy Research Working Paper Series No. 4487. *SSRN eLibrary* (January 1). Http://papers.ssrn.com/sol3/papers.cfm?abstract_id=1087459.

Gootenberg, Paul. 2010. "Latin American Inequalities: New Perspectives from History, Politics, and Culture." In *Indelible Inequalities in Latin America: Insights from History, Politics, and Culture*, edited by Paul Gootenberg and Luis Reygadas, 3–22. Durham, NC: Duke University Press.

Government of Chile. 2001. *Law Number 19.729: Reajusta el monto del ingreso mínimo mensual*. Valparaiso, Chile.

———. 2005. *Law Number 20.039: Reajusta el monto del ingreso mínimo mensual*. Valparaiso, Chile.

———. 2008. *Report: Sistema de pensiones solidarios*. Valparaiso, Chile. Http://www.gobiernodechile.cl/reforma_previsional/sistema.html. Accessed January 4, 2008.

Gray Molina, George. 2010. "The Challenge of Progressive Change under Evo Morales." In *Leftist Governments in Latin America: Successes and Shortcomings*, edited by Kurt Weyland, Raúl L. Madrid, and Wendy Hunter, 56–76. New York: Cambridge University Press.

Guillén, Ana. 1992. "Social Policy in Spain: From Dictatorship to Democracy (1939–1982)." In *Social Policy in a Changing Europe*, edited by Zsuzsa Ferga and Jon-Eivind Kolberg, 119–42. New York: Westview.

———. 2002. "The Politics of Universalisation: Establishing National Health Services in Southern Europe." *West European Politics* 25 (4): 49–68.

———. 2010. "Defrosting the Spanish Welfare State: The Weight of Conservative Opponents." In *A Long Goodbye to Bismarck? The Politics of Welfare Reform in Continental Europe*, edited by Bruno Palier,183–206. Amsterdam: Amsterdam University Press.

Guillén, Ana, Santiago Álvarez, and Pedro Adão e Silva. 2003. "Redesigning the Spanish and Portuguese Welfare States: The Impact of Accession into the European Union." In *Spain and Portugal in the European Union*, edited by Sebastian Royo and Paul Christopher Manuel, 231–68. Portland, OR: Frank Cass.

Gurr, Ted Robert. 2000. *Peoples versus States: Minorities at Risk in the New Century*. Washington, DC: United States Institute of Peace Press.

Hacker, Jacob S. 2002. *The Divided Welfare State: The Battle over Public and Private Social Benefits in the United States*. New York: Cambridge University Press.

Haggard, Stephan, and Robert R. Kaufman. 2008. *Development, Democracy, and Welfare States: Latin America, East Asia, and Eastern Europe*. Princeton, NJ: Princeton University Press.

Hagopian, Frances. 2004. "Economic Liberalization, Party Competition, and Elite Partisan Cleavages: Brazil in Comparative (Latin American) Perspective." Paper prepared for Workshop on the Analysis of Political Cleavages and Party Competition. Department of Political Science, Duke University, April 2–3.

Hall, Peter A. 2003. "Aligning Ontology and Methodology in Comparative Politics." In *Comparative Historical Analysis in the Social Sciences*, edited by James Mahoney and Dietrich Rueschemeyer, 373–406. New York: Cambridge University Press.

Hall, Peter A., and David W. Soskice. 2001. *Varieties of Capitalism: The Institutional Foundations of Comparative Advantage*. New York: Oxford University Press.

Hansen, Erik Jørgen. 1993. *Welfare Trends in the Scandinavian Countries*. Armonk, NY: M. E. Sharpe.

Hanushek, Eric A., and Ludger Woessmann. 2008. "The Role of Cognitive Skills in Economic Development." *Journal of Economic Literature* 46 (3): 607–68.

———. 2009. *Schooling, Cognitive Skills, and the Latin American Growth Puzzle*. Cambridge: National Bureau of Economic Research. Http://ideas.repec.org/p/nbr/nberwo/15066.html.

Heclo, Hugh. 1974. *Modern Social Politics in Britain and Sweden: From Relief to Income Maintenance*. New Haven: Yale University Press.

Hicks, Alexander. 1994. "Introduction to Pooling." In *The Comparative Political Economy of the Welfare State*, edited by Alexander Hicks and Thomas Janoski, 169–88. New York: Cambridge University Press.

———. 1999. *Social Democracy and Welfare Capitalism: A Century of Income Security Politics*. Ithaca, NY: Cornell University Press.

Hicks, Alexander, Roger Friedland, and Edwin Johnson. 1978. "Class Power and State Policy: The Case of Large Business Corporations, Labor Unions and Governmental Redistribution in the American States." *American Sociological Review* 43 (3): 302–15.

Hicks, Alexander, and Joya Misra. 1993. "Political Resources and the Growth of Welfare in Affluent Capitalist Democracies, 1960–1982." *American Journal of Sociology* 99 (3): 668.

Hill, Barrington. 2009. Dissertation proposal. Department of Political Science, University of North Carolina at Chapel Hill.

Hoffman, Kelly, and Miguel Angel Centeno. 2003. "The Lopsided Continent: Inequality in Latin America." *Annual Review of Sociology* 29 (December): 363–90.

Hooghe, Liesbet, Ryan Bakker, Anna Brigevich, Catherine de Vries, Erica Edwards, Gary Marks, Jan Rovny, and Marco Steenbergen. 2010. "Reliability and Validity of Measuring Party Positions: The Chapel Hill Expert Surveys of 2002 and 2006." *European Journal of Political Research* 4:684–703.

Huber, Evelyne. 1996. "Options for Social Policy in Latin America: Neoliberal versus Social Democratic Models." In *Welfare States in Transition: National Adaptations in Global Economies*, 141–91. London: Sage Publications.

———. 2006. "Un nuevo enfoque para la seguridad social en la región." In *Universalismo básico: Una nueva política social para América Latina*. Washington, DC: Inter-American Development Bank.

Huber, Evelyne, Thomas Mustillo, and John D. Stephens. 2004. "Determinants of Social Spending in Latin America." Paper delivered at the Meetings of the Society for the Advancement of Socio-Economics, Washington, DC, July 8–11.

———. 2008. "Politics and Social Spending in Latin America." *Journal of Politics* 70 (2): 420–36.

Huber, Evelyne, François Nielsen, Jenny Pribble, and John D. Stephens. 2006. "Politics and Inequality in Latin America and the Caribbean." *American Sociological Review* 71 (6): 943–63.

Huber, Evelyne, Jennifer Pribble, and John D. Stephens. 2009. "The Politics of Effective and Sustainable Redistribution." In *Stuck in the Middle: Is Fiscal Policy Failing the Middle Class?* edited by Antonio Estache and Danny Leipziger, 155–88. Washington, DC: Brookings Institution Press.

———. 2010. "The Chilean Left in Power: Achievements, Failures, and Omissions." In *Leftist Governments in Latin America: Successes and Shortcomings*, edited by Kurt Weyland, Raúl L. Madrid, and Wendy Hunter, 77–97. New York: Cambridge University Press.

Huber, Evelyne, Charles Ragin, and John D. Stephens. 1993. "Social Democracy, Christian Democracy, Constitutional Structure and the Welfare State." *American Journal of Sociology* 99 (3): 711–49.

Huber, Evelyne, Dietrich Rueschemeyer, and John D. Stephens. 1997. "The Paradoxes of Contemporary Democracy: Formal, Participatory, and Social Dimensions." *Comparative Politics* 29 (3): 323–42.

Huber, Evelyne, and Frederick Solt. 2004. "Successes and Failures of Neoliberalism." *Latin American Research Review* 39 (3): 150–64.

Huber, Evelyne, and John D. Stephens. 2000a. "Partisan Governance, Women's Employment, and the Social Democratic Service State." *American Sociological Review* 65 (3): 323–42.

———. 2000b. "The Political Economy of Pension Reform: Latin America in Comparative Perspective." Geneva: United Nations Research Institute for Social Development.

———. 2001a. *Development and Crisis of the Welfare State: Parties and Policies in Global Markets*. Chicago: University of Chicago Press.

———. 2001b. "The Social Democratic Welfare State." In *Social Democracy in Neoliberal Times: The Left and Economic Policy since 1980*, edited by Andrew Glyn, 276–311. New York: Oxford University Press.

———. 2009. Globalization and Inequality in Latin America and the Caribbean. In *Challenges of Globalization*, edited by Andrew C. Sobel, 127–53. New York: Routledge.

———. 2010. "Successful Social Policy Regimes? Political Economy, Politics, and Social Policy in Argentina, Chile, Uruguay, and Costa Rica." In *Democratic*

Governance in Latin America, edited by Scott Mainwaring and Timothy Scully, 155–209. Stanford, CA: Stanford University Press.

Huber, Evelyne, John D. Stephens, Thomas Mustillo, and Jennifer Pribble. 2008a+b "Latin America and the Caribbean Political and Welfare Datasets, 1945–2001." Chapel Hill: University of North Carolina.

Hunter, Wendy. 2007. "The Normalization of an Anomaly: The Workers' Party in Brazil." *World Politics* 59 (3): 440–75.

———. 2010. *The Transformation of the Workers' Party in Brazil, 1989–2009*. New York: Cambridge University Press.

Hunter, Wendy, and Timothy J. Power. 2007. "Rewarding Lula: Executive Power, Social Policy, and the Brazilian Elections of 2006." *Latin American Politics and Society* 49 (1): 1–30.

Hunter, Wendy, and Natasha Borges Sugiyama. 2009a. "Building Citizenship or Reinforcing Clientelism? Contributions of the Bolsa Família in Brazil." Paper prepared for presentation at the annual meeting of the American Political Science Association, Toronto Canada, September 3–6.

———. 2009b. "Democracy and Social Policy in Brazil: Advancing Basic Needs, Preserving Privileged Interests." *Latin American Politics and Society* 51 (2): 29–58.

IDB [Inter-American Development Bank]. 1998. *Facing up to Inequality in Latin America: Economic and Social Progress 1998 Report*. Washington, DC.

ILO [International Labor Organization]. 2003. *Online Labor Statistics*. Available at http://laborsta.ilo.org.

Immergut, Ellen M. 1992. *Health Politics: Interests and Institutions in Western Europe*. New York: Cambridge University Press.

International Monetary Fund. Various years undefined. *International Financial Statistics Yearbook*. Washington, DC.

Isuani, Ernesto Aldo. 1985. "Social Security and Public Assistance." In *The Crisis of Social Security and Health Care: Latin American Experiences and Lessons*, edited by Carmelo Mesa-Lago. Latin American Monograph and Document Series. Pittsburgh: University of Pittsburg, Center for Latin American Studies.

———. 2006. "Importancia y posibilidades del ingreso ciudadano." In *Universalismo básico: Una nueva política social para América Latina*, edited by Carlos G. Molina, 189–212. Washington, DC: Inter-American Development Bank.

Isuani, Ernesto Aldo, and Jorge A. San Martino. 1993. *La reforma previsional Argentina: Opciones y riesgos*. Buenos Aires: Miño y Dávila.

Iversen, Torben, and John D. Stephens. 2008. "Partisan Politics, the Welfare State, and Three Worlds of Human Capital Formation." *Comparative Political Studies* 41 (4–5): 600–637.

Jorratt, Michael. 2010. "Equidad fiscal en Chile: Un análisis de la incidencia distributiva de los impuestos y el gasto social." In *Equidad fiscal en Brasil, Chile, Paraguay y Uruguay*. Equidad Fiscal en América Latina del BID series. Washington, DC: Inter-American Development Bank.

Kangas, Olli, and Joakim Palme. 1993. "Statism Eroded? Labor-Market Benefits and Challenges to the Scandinavian Welfare States." In *Welfare Trends in the Scandinavian Countries*, edited by Erik Jorgen Hansen, Robert Erikson, Stein Ringen, and Hannu Uusitalo, 3–24. Armonk, NY: M. E. Sharpe.

Katzenstein, Peter. 1985. *Small States in World Markets*. Ithaca, NY: Cornell University Press.

Kaufman, Robert R., and Joan M. Nelson, eds. 2004a. *Crucial Needs, Weak Incentives: Social Sector Reform, Democratization, and Globalization in Latin America*. Washington, DC: Woodrow Wilson Center Press.

——. 2004b. "Introduction: The Political Challenges of Social Sector." In *Crucial Needs, Weak Incentives: Social Sector Reform, Democratization, and Globalization in Latin America*, edited by Robert R. Kaufman and Joan M. Nelson, 1–22. Baltimore: Johns Hopkins University Press.

——. 2004c. "The Politics of Education Sector Reform: Cross-National Comparisons." In *Crucial Needs, Weak Incentives: Social Sector Reform, Democratization, and Globalization in Latin America*, edited by Robert R. Kaufman and Joan M. Nelson, 249–82. Washington, DC: Johns Hopkins University Press.

Kaufman, Robert R., and Alex Segura-Ubiergo. 2001. "Globalization, Domestic Politics, and Social Spending in Latin America: A Time-Series Cross-Section Analysis, 1973–97." *World Politics* 53 (4): 553–87.

Kay, Stephen J. 1999. "Unexpected Privatizations: Politics and Social Security Reform in the Southern Cone." *Comparative Politics* 31 (4): 403–22.

——. 2009. "Political Risk and Pension Privatization: The Case of Argentina (1994–2008)." *International Social Security Review* 62 (3): 1–21.

Kay, Stephen J., and Tapen Sinha. 2008. *Lessons from Pension Reform in the Americas*. New York: Oxford University Press.

Keck, Margaret E. 1992. *The Workers' Party and Democratization in Brazil*. New Haven: Yale University Press.

Kersbergen, Kees van. 1995. *Social Capitalism: A Study of Christian Democracy and the Welfare State*. New York: Routledge Kegan and Paul.

King, Gary, Robert O. [Owen] Keohane, and Sidney Verba. 1994. *Designing Social Inquiry: Scientific Inference in Qualitative Research*. Princeton, NJ: Princeton University Press.

Kingstone, Peter R., and Aldo F. Ponce. 2010. "From Cardoso to Lula: The Triumph of Pragmatism in Brazil." In *Leftist Governments in Latin America: Successes and Shortcomings*, edited by Kurt Weyland, Raúl L. Madrid, and Wendy Hunter, 98–123. New York: Cambridge University Press.

Kitschelt, Herbert, and Steven Wilkinson. 2007. *Patrons, Clients, and Policies:*

Patterns of Democratic Accountability and Political Competition. New York: Cambridge University Press.

Korpi, Walter. 1978. *The Working Class in Welfare Capitalism: Work, Unions, and Politics in Sweden.* London; Boston: Routledge and Kegan Paul.

———. 1983. *The Democratic Class Struggle.* Routledge Kegan and Paul.

———. 2000. "Faces of Inequality: Gender, Class, and Patterns of Inequalities in Different Types of Welfare States." *Social Politics: International Studies in Gender, State and Society* 7 (2): 127–91.

Korpi, Walter, and Joakim Palme. 1998. "The Strategy of Equality and the Paradox of Redistribution." *American Sociological Review* 63 (5): 661–87.

Kuipers, Sanneke. 2006. *The Crisis Imperative: Crisis Rhetoric and Welfare State Reform in Belgium and the Netherlands in the Early 1990s.* Amsterdam: Amsterdam University Press.

Kuznets, Simon. 1955. "Economic Growth and Income Inequality." *American Economic Review* 45 (1): 1–28.

Lanzaro, Jorge Luis. 2004a. "La izquierda se acerca a los uruguayos y los uruguayos se acercan a la izquierda. Claves de desarrollo del Frente Amplio." In *La izquierda uruguaya entre la oposición y el gobierno,* edited by J. Lanzaro. Montevideo: Editorial Fin de Siglo.

———, ed. 2004b. *La izquierda uruguaya entre la oposición y el gobierno.* Montevideo: Editorial Fin de Siglo.

———. 2011. "Uruguay: A Social Democratic Government in Latin America." In *The Resurgence of the Latin American Left,* edited by Steven Levitsky and Kenneth Roberts, 343–98. Baltimore: Johns Hopkins University Press.

Lee, Cheol-Sung. 2005. "Income Inequality, Democracy, and Public Sector Size." *American Sociological Review* 70 (1): 158–81.

Lehoucq, Fabrice Edouard. 2005. "Costa Rica: Paradise in Doubt." *Journal of Democracy* 16 (3): 140–54.

———. 2010. "Political Competition, Constitutional Arrangements, and the Quality of Public Policies in Costa Rica." *Latin American Politics and Society* 52 (4): 53–77.

Lenski, Gerhard Emmanuel. 1966. *Power and Privilege: A Theory of Social Stratification.* New York: McGraw-Hill.

Levitsky, Steven. 2003. *Transforming Labor-Based Parties in Latin America: Argentine Peronism in Comparative Perspective.* New York: Cambridge University Press.

Levitsky, Steven, and Kenneth M. Roberts, eds. 2011. *The Resurgence of the Latin American Left.* Baltimore: Johns Hopkins University Press.

Lieberman, Evan S. 2005. "Nested Analysis as a Mixed-Method Strategy for Comparative Research." *American Political Science Review* 99 (3): 435–52.

Lindert, Kathy, Emmanuel Skoufias, and Joseph Shapiro. 2005. "Redistributing

Income to the Poor and the Rich: Public Transfers in Latin America and the Caribbean." Discussion draft (October 24). World Bank, Washington, DC.

Lloyd-Sherlock, Peter. 2004a. "Ambitious Plans, Modest Outcomes: The Politics of Health Care Reform in Argentina." In *Crucial Needs, Weak Incentives: Social Sector Reform, Democratization, and Globalization in Latin America*, edited by Robert R. Kaufman and Joan M. Nelson, 93–123. Baltimore: Johns Hopkins University Press.

———. 2004b. *Living Longer: Ageing, Development and Social Protection*. Zed Books.

Londoño, Juan Luis, and Miguel Székely. 1997. "Persistent Poverty and Excess Inequality: Latin America, 1970–1995." Working Paper No. 357. Washington, DC: Inter-American Development Bank.

López-Calva, Luis F., and Nora Lustig. 2009. *The Recent Decline of Inequality in Latin America: Argentina, Brazil, Mexico and Peru*. Washington, DC: Brookings Institution Press.

———, eds. 2010. *Declining Inequality in Latin America: A Decade of Progress?* Washington, DC: Brookings Institution Press.

Lora, Eduardo. 2001. "Structural Reforms in Latin America: What Has Been Reformed and How to Measure It." Working Paper No. 44. Washington, DC: Inter-American Development Bank, Research Department.

Lucas, Kevin, and David Samuels. 2010. "The Ideological 'Coherence' of the Brazilian Party System, 1990–2009." *Journal of Politics in Latin America* 3:39–69.

Luna, Juan Pablo. 2010. "The Left Turns: Why They Happened and How They Compare." In *Latin America's Left Turns: Politics, Policies and Trajectories of Change*, edited by Maxwell A. Cameron and Eric Hershberg, 23–39. Boulder, CO: Lynne Rienner.

Luna, Juan Pablo, and Elizabeth J. Zechmeister. 2005. "Political Representation in Latin America: A Study of Elite-Mass Congruence in Nine Countries." *Comparative Political Studies* 38 (4): 388–416.

Lustig, Nora. 2009. *Poverty, Inequality and the New Left in Latin America*. Democratic Governance and the "New Left." Washington, DC: Woodrow Wilson International Center for Scholars, Latin American Program.

Madrid, Raúl L. 2003. *Retiring the State: The Politics of Pension Privatization in Latin America and Beyond*. Stanford, CA: Stanford University Press.

Mahler, Vincent, and David Jesuit. 2005. "Fiscal Redistribution in Developed Countries." *Socio-Economic Review* 4 (3): 483–511.

Mahoney, James, and Dietrich Rueschemeyer, eds. 2003. *Comparative Historical Analysis in the Social Sciences*. Cambridge: Cambridge University Press.

Mainwaring, Scott. 1999. *Rethinking Party Systems in The Third Wave of Democratization: The Case of Brazil*. Stanford, CA: Stanford University Press.

Mainwaring, Scott, Daniel Brinks, and Aníbal Pérez-Liñán. 2001. "Classifying

Political Regimes in Latin." *Studies in Comparative International Development* 36 (1): 37–65.

Mainwaring, Scott, and Timothy Scully, eds. 1995a. *Building Democratic Institutions: Party Systems in Latin America*. Stanford, CA: Stanford University Press.

———. 1995b. "Introduction: Party Systems in Latin America." In *Building Democratic Institutions: Party Systems in Latin America*, edited by Scott Mainwaring and Timothy Scully, 1–36 . Stanford, CA: Stanford University Press.

———. 2003. "The Diversity of Christian Democracy in Latin America." In *Christian Democracy in Latin America*, 30–63. Stanford, CA: Stanford University Press.

———, eds. 2010a. *Democratic Governance in Latin America*. Stanford, CA: Stanford University Press.

———. 2010b. "Democratic Governance in Latin America: Eleven Lessons from Recent Experience." In *Democratic Governance in Latin America*, edited by Scott Mainwaring and Timothy R. Scully, 365–404. Stanford, CA: Stanford University Press.

Maioni, Antonia. 1998. *Parting at the Crossroads: The Emergence of Health Insurance in the United States and Canada*. Princeton, NJ: Princeton University Press.

Malloy, James M. 1979. *The Politics of Social Security in Brazil*. Pittsburgh, PA: University of Pittsburgh Press.

Mann, Michael. 1973. *Consciousness and Action among the Western Working Class*. London: Macmillan.

Maravall, José María, and Marta Fraile. 2001. "The Politics of Unemployment: The Spanish Experience in Comparative Perspective." In *Unemployment in the New Europe*, edited by Nancy Bermeo, 291–328. New York: Cambridge University Press.

Marinakis, Andrés, and Juan Jacobo Velasco. 2006. "Chile: Las lecciones de la aplicación reciente del salario mínimo." In *Para qué sirve el salario mínimo?* edited by Andrés Marinakis and Juan Jacobo Velasco, 159–208. Santiago, Chile: ILO.

Martin, Andrew. 1973. *The Politics of Economic Policy in the United States: A Tentative View from the Comparative Perspective*. Beverly Hills, CA: Sage Publications.

Martínez Franzoni, Juliana. 2007a. "Costa Rica's Pension Reform: A Decade of Negotiated Incremental Change." In *Lessons from Pension Reform in the Americas*, edited by Stephen J. Kay and Tapen Sinha, 317–39. New York: Oxford University Press.

———. 2007b. "Regimenes del bienestar en América Latina." Documento de Trabajo No. 11. Madrid: Fundación Carolina.

———. 2010. "Costa Rican Social Protection: The Accomplishments and Strains of a Showcase." Paper for the Workshop on Latin American and Southern European Welfare States, Collegio Carlo Alberto in Moncalieri (Torino), Italy, May 20.

Martínez Franzoni, Juliana, and Carmelo Mesa-Lago. 2003. *La reforma de la seguridad social en Costa Rica en pensiones y salud: Avances, problemas pendientes y recomendaciones.* San José, Costa Rica: Fundación Friedrich Ebert.

Martínez Franzoni, Juliana, Maxine Molyneux, and Diego Sánchez-Ancochea. 2009. "Latin American Capitalism: Economic and Social Policy in Transition." *Economy and Society* 38 (1): 1–16.

Matsaganis, Manos. 2005. "The Limits of Selectivity as a Recipe for Welfare Reform: The Case of Greece." *Journal of Social Policy* 34 (2): 235–53.

McCoy, Jennifer. 2010. "Venezuela under Chavez: Beyond Liberalism." In *Latin America's Left Turns: Politics, Policies, and Trajectories of Change*, edited by Maxwell A. Cameron and Eric Hershberg, 81–100. Boulder, CO: Lynne Rienner.

McGuire, James W. 2010. *Wealth, Health, and Democracy in East Asia and Latin America.* New York: Cambridge University Press.

Meltzer, Allan H., and Scott F. Richard. 1981. "A Rational Theory of the Size of Government." *Journal of Political Economy* 89 (5): 914–27.

Mendez Vives, Enrique. 1977. *Historia Uruguaya1876–1904: El Uruguay de la-modernización.* Vol. 5. 3rd ed. Montevideo: Ediciones de la Banda Oriental.

Mesa-Lago, Carmelo. 1978. *Social Security in Latin America: Pressure Groups, Stratification, and Inequality.* Pittsburgh, PA: University of Pittsburgh Press.

———. 1989. *Ascent to Bankruptcy: Financing Social Security in Latin America.* Pittsburgh, PA: University of Pittsburgh Press.

———. 1991a. "Social Security in Latin America and the Caribbean: A Comparative Assessment." In *Social Security in Developing Countries*, edited by Ahmad Ehtisham, Jean Dréze, John Hills, and Amartya Sen. Wider Studies in Development Economics. New York: Oxford University Press.

———. 1991b. "Social Security and Prospects for Equity in Latin America." World Bank Discussion Papers 140. Washington, DC: World Bank.

———. 1994. *Changing Social Security in Latin America: Toward Alleviating the Social Costs of Economic Reform.* Boulder, Colo.: Lynne Rienner.

———. 2008. *Reassembling Social Security: A Survey of Pensions and Health Care Reforms in Latin America.* New York: Oxford University Press.

Mesa-Lago, Carmelo, and Alberto Arenas de Mesa. 1998. "The Chilean Pension System: Evaluation, Lessons, and Challenges." In *Do Options Exist? The Reform of Pension and Health Care Systems in Latin America*, edited by María Amparo Cruz-Saco and Carmelo Mesa-Lago, 56–84. Pittsburgh, PA: University of Pittsburgh Press.

Midaglia, Carmen. 2009. "Las políticas sociales del gobierno de izquierda en

Uruguay: Una aproximación a sus característias y resultados." In *Consenso progresista: Las políticas sociales de los gobiernos progresistas del Cono Sur*, edited by Yesko Quiroga, Agustín Canzani, and Jaime Ensignia, 149–88. Santiago, Chile: Fundación Friedrich Ebert.

Minujin, Alberto, Jan Vandemoortele, and Enrique Delamonica. 2002. "Economic Growth, Poverty and Children." *Environment and Urbanization* 14 (2): 23–43.

Moffett, Matt. 2009. "Prudent Chile Thrives amid Downturn." *wsj.com*, May 27, sec. Economy. http://online.wsj.com/article/SB124337806443856111.html.

Molina, Carlos G., ed. 2006. *Universalismo básico: Una nueva política social para America Latina*. Washington, DC: Inter-American Development Bank.

Molina, Iván. 2007. *Anticomunismo reformista*. San José, Costa Rica: Editorial Costa Rica.

Moller, Stephanie, Evelyne Huber, John D. Stephens, David Bradley, and François Nielsen. 2003. "Determinants of Relative Poverty in Advanced Capitalist Democracies." *American Sociological Review* 68 (1): 22–51.

Morgan, Jana. 2011. *Bankrupt Representation and Party System Collapse*. University Park: Penn State University Press.

Morley, Samuel A. 2001. *The Income Distribution Problem in Latin America and the Caribbean*. Santiago, Chile: United Nations Publications.

Morley, Samuel A., Roberto Machado, and Stefano Pettinato. 1999. *Indexes of Structural Reform in Latin America*. Santiago, Chile: United Nations Press.

Mosher, James S. 2011. "Education State, Welfare State Regimes, and Politics." Paper presented at the annual meeting of the Society for the Advancement of Socio-Economics, June 23–25, Madrid, Spain.

Muller, Edward N. 1985. "Income Inequality, Regime Repressiveness, and Political Violence." *American Sociological Review* 50 (1): 47–61.

———. 1988. "Democracy, Economic Development, and Income Inequality." *American Sociological Review* 53 (1): 50–68.

———. 1989. "Democracy and Inequality." *American Sociological Review* 54 (5): 868–71.

Muñoz Gomá, Óscar. 2007. *El modelo económico de la concertación 1990–2005: ¿Reformas o cambio?* 1st ed. Santiago, Chile: Editorial Catalonia.

Murillo, María Victoria. 2001. *Labor Unions, Partisan Coalitions and Market Reforms in Latin America*. New York: Cambridge University Press.

———. 2002. "Political Bias in Policy Convergence: Privatization Choices in Latin America." *World Politics* 54 (4): 462–93.

Mustillo, Thomas J. 2009. "Modeling New Party Performance: A Conceptual and Methodological Approach for Volatile Party Systems." *Political Analysis* 17 (3): 311–32.

Neidhart, Leonard. 1970. *Plebiszit und pluralitare Demokratie*. Bern: Francke Verlag.

Nickell, Stephen. 2004. "Poverty And Worklessness in Britain." *Economic Journal* 114 (494): C1–C25.

Nickell, Stephen, and Luca Nunziata. 2001. *Labour Market Institutions Database*. London: Centre for Economic Performance, London School of Economics.

Niedzwiecki, Sara. 2010a. "Social Policy in South America: The Effect of Organized Labor and Civil Society Groups on Pension and Health Reforms in Argentina and Brazil, 1988–2008." M.A. thesis. Chapel Hill: University of North Carolina at Chapel Hill.

———. 2010b. "Social Protection in Argentina." Paper for the Workshop on Latin American and Southern European Welfare States, Collegio Carlo Alberto in Moncalieri (Torino), Italy.

Nielsen, François. 1994. "Income Inequality and Industrial Development: Dualism Revisited." *American Sociological Review* 59 (5): 654–77.

Nielsen, François, and Arthur S. Alderson. 1995. "Income Inequality, Development, and Dualism: Results from an Unbalanced Cross-National Panel." *American Sociological Review* 60 (5): 674–701.

Obinger, Herbert, Stephan Leibfried, and Francis Geoffrey Castles. 2005. *Federalism and the Welfare State: New World and European Experiences*. New York: Cambridge University Press.

OECD [Organization for Economic Co-operation and Development]. 2006. *Education at a Glance*. Paris.

OECD/HRDC [Human Resources Development Canada]. 2000. *Literacy in the Information Age: Final Report of the International Adult Literacy Survey*. Ottawa: Statistics Canada.

OIT [Oficina Internacional del Trabajo]. 2002. *Pensiones no contributivas y asistenciales*. Santiago, Chile.

———. 2004. *El futuro de la previsión social en Argentina y el mundo: Evaluación y desafíos*. Santiago, Chile.

Orloff, Ann Shola. 1993. "Gender and the Social Rights of Citizenship: The Comparative Analysis of Gender Relations and Welfare States." *American Sociological Review* 58 (3): 303–28.

Orszag, Peter, and Josep E. Stiglitz. 1999. "Rethinking Pension Reform: Ten Myths about Social Security Systems." Paper presented at the conference on New Ideas about Old Age Security, World Bank, Washington, DC, September.

Osterkatz, Sandra Chapman. 2011. "Capacity and Commitment: How Decentralization in Brazil Impacts Health Policy." Paper prepared for delivery at the meeting of the American Political Science Association, September 1–4.

Palier, Bruno, ed. 2010. *A Long Goodbye to Bismarck? The Politics of Welfare Reform in Continental Europe*. Amsterdam: Amsterdam University Press.

Palier, Bruno, and Claude Martin. 2008. *Reforming the Bismarckian Welfare System*. Oxford: Blackwell Publishing.

Palme, Joakim. 1990. *Pension Rights in Welfare Capitalism: The Development of Old-Age Pensions in 18 OECD Countries, 1930 to 1985*. Stockholm: Swedish Institute for Social Research.

Pampel, Fred, and John Williamson. 1989. *Age, Class, Politics and the Welfare State*. New York: Cambridge University Press.

Panizza, Francisco. 2005. "Unarmed Utopia Revisited: The Resurgence of Left-of-Centre Politics in Latin America." *Political Studies* 53 (4): 716–34.

Papadópulos, Jorge. 1992. *Seguridad social y política en el Uruguay*. Montevideo: CIESU.

———. 1998. "The Pension System in Uruguay: A Delayed Reform." In *Do Options Exist? The Reform of Pension and Health Care Systems in Latin America*, edited by María Amparo Cruz-Saco and Carmelo Mesa-Lago. Pittsburgh, PA: University of Pittsburgh Press.

Penfold-Becerra, Michael. 2007. "Clientelism and Social Funds: Evidence from Chávez's Misiones." *Latin American Politics and Society* 49 (4): 63–84.

Penn World Table Version 6.3. 2009. Center for International Comparisons of Production, Income and Prices. University of Pennsylvania (CICUP), August.

Perry, Guillermo, Omar S. Arias, J. Humberto López, William F. Maloney, and Luis Severén. 2006. *Poverty Reduction and Growth: Virtuous and Vicious Circles*. Washington, DC: World Bank.

Pierson, Paul. 1996. "The New Politics of the Welfare State." *World Politics* 48 (2): 143–79.

———. 2000a. "Increasing Returns, Path Dependence, and the Study of Politics." *American Political Science Review* 94 (2): 251–67.

———. 2000b. "Not Just What, but When: Timing and Sequence in Political Processes." *Studies in American Political Development* 14 (1): 72–92.

———. 2000c. "Three Worlds of Welfare State Research." *Comparative Political Studies* 33 (6–7): 791–821.

———. 2001. *The New Politics of the Welfare State*. New York: Oxford University Press.

———. 2003. "Big, Slow-Moving and . . . Invisible: Macrosocial Processes in the Study of Comparative Politics." In *Comparative Historical Analysis in the Social Sciences*, edited by James Mahoney and Dietrich Rueschemeyer, 177–207. Cambridge: Cambridge University Press.

Plümper, Thomas, Vera E. Troeger, and Philip Manow. 2005. "Panel Data Analysis in Comparative Politics: Linking Method to Theory." *European Journal of Political Research* 44: 327–54.

Pontusson, Jonas, David Rueda, and Christopher Way. 2002. "Comparative Political Economy of Wage Distribution: The Role of Partisanship and Labour Market Institutions." *British Journal of Political Science* 32 (2): 281–308.

Portes, Alejandro, and Kelly Hoffman. 2003. "Latin American Class Structures: Their Composition and Change during the Neoliberal Era." *Latin American Research Review* 38 (1): 41–82.

Prebisch, Raúl. 1950. *The Economic Development of Latin America and Its Principal Problems.* New York: United Nations, Department of Economic Affairs.

Presidencia de la República Oriental del Uruguay. 2009. "Reporte social del Uruguay 2009." Montevideo.

Pribble, Jennifer. 2006. "Women and Welfare: The Politics of Coping with New Social Risks in Chile and Uruguay." *Latin American Research Review* 41 (2): 84–111.

———. 2008. "Protecting the Poor: Welfare Politics in Latin America's Free Market Era." Ph.D. dissertation. Chapel Hill: University of North Carolina at Chapel Hill.

Pribble, Jennifer, Evelyne Huber, and John D. Stephens. 2009. "Politics, Policies, and Poverty in Latin America." *Comparative Politics* 41 (4): 387–407.

Psacharopoulos, George, Samuel A. Morley, Ariel Fiszbein, Haeduck Lee, and Bill Wood. 1997. *Poverty and Income Distribution in Latin America: The Story of the 1980s.* Washington, DC: World Bank Publications.

Raczynski, Dagmar. 1994. "Social Policies in Chile: Origin, Transformations, and Perspectives." Democracy and Social Policy Series. Working Paper No. 4. Kellogg Institute, University of Notre Dame.

Ragin, Charles C. 1987. *The Comparative Method: Moving beyond Qualitative and Quantitative Strategies.* Berkeley: University of California Press.

———. 2000. *Fuzzy-Set Social Science.* Chicago: University of Chicago Press.

———. 2008. *Redesigning Social Inquiry: Fuzzy Sets and Beyond.* Chicago: University of Chicago Press.

Reddy, Sanjay G., and Thomas W. Pogge. 2005. "How Not to Count the Poor." Paper available at www.columbia.edu/~sr793/count.pdf.

Reuveny, Rafael, and Quan Li. 2003. "Economic Openness, Democracy, and Income Inequality." *Comparative Political Studies* 36 (5): 575–601.

Roberts, Kenneth M. 1998. *Deepening Democracy? The Modern Left and Social Movements in Chile and Peru.* Stanford, CA: Stanford University Press.

———. 2002. "Social Inequalities without Class Cleavages in Latin America's Neoliberal Era." *Studies in Comparative International Development* 36 (4): 3–33.

Robinson, James A. 2010. "The Political Economy of Redistributive Policies." In *Declining Inequality in Latin America: A Decade of Progress?* edited by Luis F. López-Calva and Nora Lustig, 39–71. Baltimore: Brookings Institution Press.

Roca, Jeronimo. 2010. "Equidad fiscal en Uruguay. Cuánto y cómo modifica el estado el bienestar de los uruguayos. El impacto conjunto de los impuestos y el gasto público social en la distribución del ingreso." In *Equidad fiscal en Brasil, Chile, Paraguay y Uruguay*. Equidad Fiscal en America Latina del BID series. Washington, DC: Inter-American Development Bank.

Rodrik, Dani. 1997. *Has Globalization Gone Too Far?* Washington, D.C.: Peterson Institute.

Romer, Paul M. 1986. "Increasing Returns and Long-Run Growth." *Journal of Political Economy* 94 (5): 1002–37.

——. 1990. "Human Capital and Growth: Theory and Evidence." *Carnegie-Rochester Conference Series on Public Policy* 32: 251–86.

——. 1994. "The Origins of Endogenous Growth." *Journal of Economic Perspectives* 8 (1): 3–22.

Rosenberg, Mark B. 1979. "Social Security Policymaking in Costa Rica: A Research Report." *Latin American Research Review* 14 (1): 116–33.

——. 1981. "Social Reform in Costa Rica: Social Security and the Presidency of Rafael Angel Calderon." *Hispanic American Historical Review* 61 (2): 278–96.

Ross, Michael. 2006. "Is Democracy Good for the Poor?" *American Journal of Political Science* 50 (4): 860–74.

Rothstein, Bo, and Eric M. Uslaner. 2005. "All for One: Equality, Corruption, and Social Trust." *World Politics* 58 (1): 41–72.

Rovira Mas, Jorge. 1987. *Costa Rica en los años 80*. San José, Costa Rica: Editorial Porvenir/ICADIS/CRIES.

Royo, Sebastián. 2000. *From Social Democracy to Neoliberalism: The Consequences of Party Hegemony in Spain, 1982–1996*. New York: St. Martin's Press.

Rudra, Nita. 2004. "Openness, Welfare Spending, and Inequality in the Developing World." *International Studies Quarterly* 48 (3): 683–709.

Rueschemeyer, Dietrich. 2009. *Usable Theory: Analytic Tools for Social and Political Research*. Princeton, NJ: Princeton University Press.

Rueschemeyer, Dietrich, and John D. Stephens. 1997. "Comparing Historical Sequences: A Powerful Tool for Causal Analysis." *Comparative Social Research* 16: 55–72.

Rueschemeyer, Dietrich, Evelyne Huber Stephens, and John D. Stephens. 1992. *Capitalist Development and Democracy*. Chicago: University of Chicago Press.

Sacchi, Stefano, and Francesca Bastagli. 2005. "Italy: Striving Uphill but Stopping Halfway: The Troubled Journey of the Experimental Minimum Insertion Income." In *Welfare State Reform in Southern Europe*, edited by Maurizio Ferrera, 84–140. London: Routledge.

Salvadori Dedecca, Claudio. 2010. "Equidade fiscal no Brasil A estrutura tributaria, as transferencias publicas e a distribuiacao de renda." In *Equidad fiscal en Brasil, Chile, Paraguay y Uruguay*. Equidad Fiscal en América Latina del BID series. Washington, DC: Inter-American Development Bank.

Samuels, David, and Scott Mainwaring. 2004. "Strong Federalism, Constraints on the Central Government, and Economic Reform in Brazil." In *Federalism and Democracy in Latin America*, edited by Edward L. Gibson, 85–130. Baltimore: Johns Hopkins University Press.

Sandbrook, Richard, Marc Edelman, Patrick Heller, and Judith Teichman. 2007. *Social Democracy in the Global Periphery: Origins, Challenges, Prospects*. New York: Cambridge University Press.

Schmitter, Philippe C. 1971. *Interest Conflict and Political Change in Brazil*. Stanford, CA: Stanford University Press.

Schneider, Ben Ross. 2004. *Business Politics and the State in Twentieth-Century Latin America*. New York: Cambridge University Press.

Schneider, Ben Ross, and David Soskice. 2009. "Inequality in Developed Countries and Latin America: Coordinated, Liberal, and Hierarchical Systems." *Economy and Society* 38 (1): 17–52.

Seawright, Jason, and John Gerring. 2008. "Case Selection Techniques in Case Study Research." *Political Research Quarterly* 61 (2): 294–308.

SEDLAC [Socio-Economic Database for Latin America and the Caribbean]. 2010. Centro de Estudios Distributivos Laborales y Sociales (CEDLAS) of the University of La Plata, in partnership with the World Bank's Latin America and the Caribbean Poverty and Gender Group (LCSPP). Available at http://www.depeco.econo.unlp.edu.ar/cedlas/sedlac.

Segura-Ubiergo, Alex. 2007. *The Political Economy of the Welfare State in Latin America: Globalization, Democracy, and Development*. New York: Cambridge University Press.

Seligson, Mitchell A., and Juliana Martínez Franzoni. 2010. "Limits to Costa Rican Heterodoxy: What Has Changed in 'Paradise'?" In *Democratic Governance in Latin America*, edited by Scott Mainwaring and Timothy Scully, 307–37. Stanford, CA: Stanford University Press.

Serrano, Claudia, and Dagmar Raczynski. 2004. "Chile solidario." In *Equidad y protección social*, edited by C. Hardy. Santiago, Chile: Ediciones Chile 21.

Shalev, Michael. 1983. "The Social Democratic Model and Beyond: Two 'Generations' of Comparative Research on the Welfare State." *Comparative Social Research* 6: 315–51.

Sheahan, John. 2002. "Alternative Models of Capitalism in Latin America." In *Models of Capitalism: Lessons for Latin America*, edited by Evelyne Huber, 25–52. University Park: Penn State University Press.

Silva Lopes, José da. 2003. "The Role of the State in the Labour Market: Its Impact on Employment and Wages in Portugal as Compared with Spain." In

Spain and Portugal in the European Union, edited by Sebastian Royo and Paul Christopher Manuel, 225–40. Portland, OR: Frank Cass.

Simpson, Miles. 1990. "Political Rights and Income Inequality: A Cross-National Test." *American Sociological Review* 55 (5): 682–93.

Skidmore, Thomas E. 1967. *Politics in Brazil, 1930–1964: An Experiment in Democracy.* New York: Oxford University Press.

Skocpol, Theda. 1988. "The Limits of the New Deal System and the Roots of Contemporary Welfare Dilemmas." In *The Politics of Social Policy in the United States*, edited by Margaret Weir, Ann Shola Orloff, and Theda Skocpol, 293–312. Princeton, NJ: Princeton University Press.

Soares, Sergei. 2011. "Bolsa Família, Its Design, Its Impacts and Possibilities for the Future." Unpublished paper. Rio de Janeiro: IPEA.

Social Security Administration. 2010. *Social Security Programs throughout the World: The Americas.* Washington, DC: Office of Policy, Office of Research, Evaluation, and Statistics, Social Security Administration.

Solt, Frederick. 2008. "Economic Inequality and Democratic Political Engagement." *American Journal of Political Science* 52 (1): 48–60.

———. 2009. "Standardizing the World Income Inequality Database." *Social Science Quarterly* 90 (2): 231–42.

———. 2010. "Does Economic Inequality Depress Electoral Participation? Testing the Schattschneider Hypothesis." *Political Behavior* 32 (2): 285–301.

———. 2011. "Divisionary Nationalism: Economic Inequality and the Formation of National Pride." *Journal of Politics* 73 (3): 821–30.

Solt, Frederick, Philip Habel, and J. Tobin Grant. 2011. "Economic Inequality, Relative Power, and Religiosity." *Social Science Quarterly* 92 (2): 447–65.

Spilimbergo, Antonio, Juan Luis Londoño de la Cuesta, and Miguel Székely. 1997. *Income Distribution, Factor Endowments, and Trade Openness.* Washington, DC: Inter-American Development Bank, Office of the Chief Economist.

Steenbergen, Marco, and Gary Marks. 2007. "Evaluating Expert Judgments." *European Journal of Political Research* 46 (3): 347–66.

Stepan, Alfred C. 1988. *Rethinking Military Politics: Brazil and the Southern Cone.* Princeton, NJ: Princeton University Press.

Stephens, Evelyne Huber. 1980. *The Politics of Workers' Participation: The Peruvian Approach in Comparative Perspective.* New York: Academic Press.

Stephens, Evelyne Huber, and John D. Stephens. 1982. "The Labor Movement, Political Power, and Workers' Participation in Western Europe." *Political Power and Social Theory* 3:215–49.

———. 1986. *Democratic Socialism in Jamaica: The Political Movement and Social Transformation in Dependent Capitalism.* Princeton, NJ: Princeton University Press.

Stephens, John D. 1976. "The Consequences of Social Structural Change for the

Development of Socialism in Sweden." Ph.D. dissertation. New Haven: Yale University.

——. 1979. *The Transition from Capitalism to Socialism*. London: Macmillan.

Stiglitz, Joseph E. 2011. "The IMF's Switch in Time." *Economists' Voice* 8 (2): article 3.

Stoleroff, Alan. 2001. "Unemployment and Trade Union Strength in Portugal." In *Unemployment in the New Europe*, edited by Nancy Bermeo, 173–202. New York: Cambridge University Press.

Streeck, Wolfang, and Kathleen Thelen. 2005. "Introduction: Institutional Change in Advanced Political Economies." In *Beyond Continuity: Institutional Change in Advanced Political Economies*, edited by Wolfang Streeck and Kathleen Thelen, 1–39. New York: Oxford University Press.

Sugiyama, Natasha Borges. 2008. "Ideology and Networks: The Politics of Social Policy Diffusion in Brazil." *Latin American Research Review* 43 (3): 82–108.

Teichman, Judith A. 2001. *The Politics of Freeing Markets in Latin America: Chile, Argentina, and Mexico*. Chapel Hill: University of North Carolina Press.

Thomas, Vinod, Yan Wang, and Xibo Fan. 2001. "Measuring Education Inequality: Gini Coefficients of Education." *SSRN eLibrary*. http://papers.ssrn .com/sol3/papers.cfm?abstract_id=258182.

Titelman, Daniel. 2000. *Reformas al sistema de salud en Chile: Desafíos pendientes*. Santiago: United Nations Economic Commission for Latin America and the Caribbean.

Torche, Florencia. 2005. "Unequal but Fluid: Social Mobility in Chile in Comparative Perspective." *American Sociological Review* 70 (3): 422–50.

Trejos, Juan Diego. 2008. *Basic Social Services: Achievements and Bottlenecks since 1950. Policy Regime and Poverty Reduction: Costa Rican Case*. United Nations Research Institute for Social Development, January.

Tsai, Pan-Long. 1995. "Foreign Direct Investment and Income Inequality: Further Evidence." *World Development* 23 (3): 469–83.

UNCTAD [United Nations Conference on Trade and Development]. 2002. *Handbook of Statistics*. New York: United Nations.

UNDP [United Nations Development Program]. 2004. *La democracia en América Latina*. Santiago, Chile: Programa de las Naciones Unidas para el Desarrollo.

United Nations Centre on Transnational Corporations. 1985. *Transnational Corporations in World Development*. Cambridge: Graham and Trotman.

UNU-WIDER [United Nations University World Institute for Development Economics Research]. 2007. World Income Inequality Database. Version 2b. http://www.wider.unu.edu/research/Database/en_GB/wiid/.

——. 2008. World Income Inequality Database. Version 2c. http://www.wider .unu.edu/research/Database/en_GB/wiid.

Vartiainen, Juliana. 1999. "The Economics of Successful State Intervention in Industrial Transformation." In *The Developmental State*, edited by Meredith Woo-Cumings, 200–234. Ithaca, NY: Cornell University Press.

Vuolo, Ruben M. Lo. 2009a. "Asignación por Hijo." Ciepp: Centro Interdisciplinatio para el Estudio de Políticas Públicas, November.

———. 2009b. "Excedente fiscal, deuda financiera y deuda social." Ciepp: Centro Interdisciplinatio para el Estudio de Políticas Públicas, August.

Vuolo, Ruben M. Lo, and Fernando Seppi. 2009. "Excedente fiscal, deuda financiera y deuda social." Ciepp: Centro Interdisciplinario para el Estudio de Políticas Públicas.

Wade, Peter. 1997. *Race and Ethnicity in Latin America*. London: Pluto Press.

Wallerstein, Michael. 1999. "Wage-Setting Institutions and Pay Inequality in Advanced Industrial Societies." *American Journal of Political Science* 43 (3): 649–80.

Weber, Max. 1968. *Economy and Society: An Outline of Interpretive Sociology*. New York: Bedminster Press.

Weir, Margaret, Ann Shola Orloff, and Theda Skocpol, eds. 1988. *The Politics of Social Policy in the United States*. Princeton, NJ: Princeton University Press.

Weyland, Kurt Gerhard. 1996. *Democracy without Equity: Failures of Reform in Brazil*. Pittsburgh, PA: University of Pittsburgh Press.

———. 2004. "Neoliberalism and Democracy in Latin America: A Mixed Record." *Latin American Politics and Society* 46 (1): 135–157.

———. 2010. "The Performance of Leftist Governments in Latin America: Conceptual and Theoretical Issues." In *Leftist Governments in Latin America: Successes and Shortcomings*, edited by Kurt Weyland, Raúl L. Madrid, and Wendy Hunter, 1–27. New York: Cambridge University Press.

Weyland, Kurt Gerhard, Raúl L Madrid, and Wendy Hunter, eds. 2010. *Leftist Governments in Latin America: Successes and Shortcomings*. New York: Cambridge University Press.

Whitefield, Stephen, Milada Anna Vachudova, Marco R. Steenbergen, Robert Rohrschneider, Gary Marks, Matthew P. Loveless, and Liesbet Hooghe. 2007. "Do Expert Surveys Produce Consistent Estimates of Party Stances on European Integration? Comparing Expert Surveys in the Difficult Case of Central and Eastern Europe." *Electoral Studies* 26 (1): 50–61.

Wiarda, Howard J. 1982. *Politics and Social Change in Latin America: The Distinct Tradition*. 2nd ed. Amherst: University of Massachusetts Press.

Wibbels, Erik. 2006. "Dependency Revisited: International Markets, Business Cycles, and Social Spending in the Developing World." *International Organization* 60 (2): 433–68.

Wilensky, Harold L. 1975. *The Welfare State and Equality: Structural and Ideological Roots of Public Expenditures*. Berkeley: University of California Press.

——. 1981. "Leftism, Catholicism, and Democratic Corporatism." In *Development of Welfare States in Europe and America*, edited by Peter Flora and Arnold J. Heidenheimer, 345–82. New Brunswick, NJ: Transaction Press.

Williamson, John. 1990. *Latin American Adjustment: How Much Has Happened?* Washington, DC: Institute for International Economics.

Wilson, Bruce M. 1998. *Costa Rica: Politics, Economics, and Democracy.* Boulder, CO: Lynne Rienner.

World Bank. 1990. *World Development Report: Poverty.* Washington, DC: World Bank Press.

——. 2007. *The World Development Indicators.* Washington, DC: World Bank Press.

——. 2009. "Argentina. Income Support Policies toward the Bicentennial." Washington, DC: International Bank for Reconstruction and Development/ World Bank.

——. 2010. *Global Development Finance.* Washington, DC: World Bank Press.

Wright, Erik Olin. 1985. *Classes.* New York: Verso.

Yashar, Deborah J. 1995. "Civil War and Social Welfare: The Historical Foundations of Costa Rica's Competitive Party System." In *Building Democratic Institutions: Party Systems in Latin America*, edited by Scott Mainwaring and Timothy Scully, 72–99. Stanford, CA: Stanford University Press.

——. 1997. *Demanding Democracy: Reform and Reaction in Costa Rica and Guatemala, 1870s–1950s.* Stanford, CA.: Stanford University Press.

——. 2005. *Contesting Citizenship in Latin America: The Rise of Indigenous Movements and the Postliberal Challenge.* New York: Cambridge University Press.

Zucco, Cesar. 2011. "When Pay Outs Pay Off: Conditional Cash-Transfers, Clientelism, and Voting Behavior." Unpublished paper. Woodrow Wilson School, Princeton University.

Index